*Character Actors in Horror
and Science Fiction
Films, 1930–1960*

Character Actors in Horror and Science Fiction Films, 1930–1960

LAURENCE RAW

McFarland & Company, Inc., Publishers
Jefferson, North Carolina, and London

LIBRARY OF CONGRESS CATALOGUING-IN-PUBLICATION DATA

Raw, Laurence.
Character actors in horror and science fiction films, 1930–1960 / Laurence Raw.
  p. cm.
Includes bibliographical references and index.

ISBN 978-0-7864-4474-8
softcover : acid free paper ∞

1. Horror films—United States—History and criticism. 2. Science fiction films—United States—History and criticism. 3. Motion picture actors and actresses—United States—Biography. I. Title.
PN1995.9.H6R38 2012   791.43′6164—dc23   2012020028

BRITISH LIBRARY CATALOGUING DATA ARE AVAILABLE

© 2012 Laurence Raw. All rights reserved

No part of this book may be reproduced or transmitted in any form or by any means, electronic or mechanical, including photocopying or recording, or by any information storage and retrieval system, without permission in writing from the publisher.

Front cover image: Noble Johnson in *The Ghost Breakers*, 1940 (Photofest); cover design by David K. Landis (Shake it Loose Graphics)

Manufactured in the United States of America

McFarland & Company, Inc., Publishers
Box 611, Jefferson, North Carolina 28640
www.mcfarlandpub.com

To my parents, Margery and John Raw

Table of Contents

Preface 1
Introduction: Recognizing Repetition 3

THE ACTORS 9

Filmography 203
Bibliography 214
Index 217

Preface

In choosing to write about horror and science fiction films between 1930 and 1960, I realize that I am covering well-trodden ground. Many valuable reference books exist on the subject, which have been listed in the Bibliography. There exist several excellent studies of individual actors, such as John Carradine and Dwight Frye. What I offer here is a work devoted to both the well known and (more significantly) not so well known character actors who appeared in horror and science fiction films during the Hollywood studio period. Some of them—Harry Cording, Henry Hall and Holmes Herbert—have attracted little if any critical attention for their efforts over many years. I show how casting and performance were intrinsic to how the films ended up on screen: bit-part players were as important in this process as their more celebrated character actor colleagues.

In this book I will not cover every horror and science fiction film that an individual actor made. Instead I offer detailed analyses of performances in representative works, in an attempt to deconstruct an actor's screen *persona*. I discuss the kind of roles actors played, as well as concentrating on their idiosyncratic gestures and/or facial expressions that rendered them so popular with studio heads, directors and audiences alike. My approach has been significantly influenced by my experience of being a drama critic—first with *Theatreworld Internet Magazine* and latterly with the online site *Radio Drama Reviews* (www.radiodramareviews.com)—as well as directing student and semi-professional productions of my own.

This book underlines the inescapable fact that actors matter in any form of dramatic communication, whether live or filmed. As a specialist in adaptation studies, I also demonstrate how issues of performance and their wider relationship to industrial and/or commercial concerns assumed far greater significance than textual issues—particularly with contributions to specific film cycles. Examples of such cycles include the Universal horror films of the 1930s and mid–1940s, or Roger Corman's horror and science fiction works produced for teenage audiences in the late 1950s.

This book has been a labor of love, giving me the opportunity to indulge in the guilty pleasure of writing about actors in the kind of cult films I first encountered late at night on Britain's Channel Four, while ostensibly completing my doctoral thesis on Elizabethan and Jacobean drama.

The staffs of the British Film Institute library in London, as well as the libraries of Bilkent and Başkent Universities in Ankara, Turkey, offered assistance beyond the call of duty. I'd like to thank the various sellers in the United States, Great Britain and elsewhere for offering hitherto hard-to-obtain films for sale, as well as paying tribute to sites such as The Internet Archive (www.archive.org), which offer many of these films—now in the public domain—for free download. All photographs reproduced in this book are from the author's collection. I am grateful to the specialist outlets that helped me find them.

In the following essays, names in ALL CAPS are of persons given their own essays.

Introduction: Recognizing Repetition

The role of character actors in Hollywood films since the advent of talkies in the early 1930s has been discussed in several previous works. Alfred E. Twomey's and Arthur F. McClure's *The Versatiles* (1969) looks at the careers of more than 400 performers, those who, in the authors' words, "repeatedly personified a particular mode, sense, attitude, or emotion," while being "as important to the story as the stars[....] Many character actors spawned a wide range of emotions with the versatility of their performances[....] Dana Andrews was once quoted as saying that 'The real acting parts go to the character actors'" (Twomey and McClure 1969: 2).

The British author David Quinlan celebrates the "well-loved mannerisms and variations on a familiar performance," characteristic of character actors: "Many of them became so expert at their own game that they could steal a scene from the star at the flick of an eyelid." Occasionally character actors would try to change their screen personae by taking on unfamiliar roles, but Quinlan believes that such strategies "did not break the pattern that had been set, any more than they [such roles] met with the fans' favour" (Quinlan 1985: ii).

Danny Peary's *Cult Movie Stars* analyzes the relationship between character actors and their audiences: many actors "sparked an unusual, fiery passion in movie fans[....] The admiration and appreciation cultists felt for their favorites is different from that extended to the typical movie star — it borders on guilty pleasure[....] they [the character actors] are taken to heart, cherished, championed" (Peary 1991: 15).

Luc Sante and Melissa Holbrook Pierson suggest that character actors appear so regularly on screen that it seems "as if they are returning in our very dreams: these characters take on character." While stars are often constructed — both on and off the screen — as quasi-divine figures, character actors "become familiars [...] they are bigger than life, because they so completely embrace it in all its trademark oddities and imperfections" (Sante and Pearson 1999: xiii–xiv). They created a film's "generic color [...] as they stood out and called, perhaps, your name" (xv). They might have played identical roles in film after film, but those "ordinary Joes [and Jills]" rehearsed the struggles experienced by filmgoers of all races, classes and social backgrounds. They were not just performers; "they're us, a bigger us. They spook us, stalk us, fulfill us or fail us or fail to. Whatever it is, it's an intimate relationship" (xvi).

This volume, the first devoted specifically to character actors in horror and science fiction films during the Hollywood studio era (1930–1960), examines this relationship in more detail. It does not try to be comprehensive in its coverage (readers can consult Twomey's and McClure's or Quinlan's excellent books for this purpose), but rather comprises a series of essays (between 1,000–2,000 words in length) that concentrate on selected roles to discover how and why an individual character actor attracted such a substantial fan base. The actors surveyed range from well-known figures such as Sir Cedric Hardwicke and Claude Rains, to bit-part players who frequently did not receive screen credits. The British émigré Harry Cording spent many years as a Universal contract player in a variety of working class roles. His main claim to fame was a series of regular appearances in the Sherlock Holmes series, often as a chauffeur, menacing sailor, or cheerful

Cockney. Henry Hall had a long career, most notably in B-westerns, but also took small roles in science fiction serials such as *The Phantom Empire* (1935) and *Shadow of Chinatown* (1936). George Burr Macannan appeared in a few films either as a zombie or a heavy (*White Zombie* [1932], and *The Black Room* [1935] are two examples). While other actors— Donald Crisp, George Sanders, Lloyd Bridges, Leslie Nielsen, Raymond Burr— either established or consolidated their reputation in other genres, they made a significant impression in horror and science fiction films, which is why they have been included here.

Some of the films included, such as Arthur Lubin's *Ali Baba and the Forty Thieves* (1944) or Maria Montez extravaganzas such as *Cobra Woman* (also 1944), could be categorized as fantasies or colorful science fiction dramas. Other films such as John Cromwell's gritty drama *The Racket* (1951) could be best classified as horror *film noir*. While issues of genre have been much debated, it is obvious that they represent different things for different interest groups— producers, marketers and scholars. Bearing this notion in mind, this book adopts a liberal approach to genre by analyzing those films— including fantasy/science fiction as well as horror *film noir*— that best illustrate the "particular mode, sense, attribute or emotion" (to invoke Twomey's and McClure's phrase) of a character actor's screen *persona*.

What rendered character actors so attractive to producers, filmmakers and audiences? As the critics quoted above suggest, the main explanation was that they offered the pleasure of repetition in their performances— to such an extent that, like children, filmgoers could "remorselessly stipulate that the repetition shall be an identical one and [would] [...] correct any alterations [...] repetition, the re-experiencing of something identical, is clearly in itself a source of pleasure (Freud 1956: 35). Carolyn Jess-Cooke suggests that the success of recent film sequels stems from this Freudian idea of "the compulsion to repeat," as directors deliberately construct "remembering activities and memorialising scenarios by which spectators can access a previous text" (Jess-Cooke 2009: 130). During the Hollywood studio period, most character actors participated in similar "remembering activities." Cecil Kellaway's twinkling eyes were as significant in Joe May's Hawthorne adaptation *The House of the Seven Gables* (1940) as in René Clair's sparkling horror spoof *I Married a Witch* (1942). Gale Sondergaard made a habit of scene-stealing, as she appeared as the villain in Universal's *Sherlock Holmes and the Spider Woman* (1942), followed by a (largely unrelated) sequel, *The Spider Woman*, two years later. Although well down the cast list in the Bob Hope vehicle *The Cat and the Canary* (1939), Sondergaard manages to steal the limelight as a sinister-looking housekeeper, complete with menacing scowl. In the 1950s, Kenneth Tobey provided a rugged, reassuring presence in Cold War science fiction classics such as *The Thing from Another World* (1951) and *It Came From Beneath the Sea* (1955), while Jonathan Haze played a variety of neurotics as a member of Roger Corman's repertory company in *The Day the World Ended* (1955), *Not of this Earth* (1957) and— most famously—*Little Shop of Horrors* (1960).

Other character actors developed a repertoire of gestures and/or facial expressions that they would use in film after film. The British actor Alan Napier— who found fame in later life as Alfred the Butler in the *Batman* series on television—cast a reassuring presence by stretching out a hand of friendship, or patting a woman's forehead, or inviting people to drink tea. Even when he played an unattractive personality, such as the supercilious art critic in Jean Yarbrough's *House of Horrors* (1946), his facial expressions suggested benevolence. Thus it did not seem quite justified for the Creeper (Rondo Hatton) to kill Napier's character off so brutally by breaking his neck. Although a devout Christian off-screen, Dwight Frye possessed a pair of staring eyes; hence he was invariably cast as a psychotic in Universal classics such as *Dracula* (1931) or *Frankenstein* (also 1931). The African American actor Mantan Moreland was equally well known for his eyework (sometimes it seemed that his eyes were popping out of his face), but mostly provided comic relief — most notably as the chauffeur Birmingham Brown in the Charlie Chan cycle. Neither Jon Hall nor Tor Johnson were particularly gifted performers, but their respective physiognomies dictated the kind of parts they were given. Hall's muscular build ensured that he played handsome young heroes who inevitably had the chance to remove their shirts. Hall had only to smile to transport filmgoers to "a magical screen world which any young viewer would love to visit" (Peary 1991: 237) — even (somewhat bizarrely) in *The Invisible Man's Revenge* (1944), one of Universal's numerous remakes of *The Invisible Man* (1933). Ex-wrestler Johnson played the heavy who seldom spoke but cut a menacing presence in several low-budget Edward D. Wood, Jr., flicks (*Bride of the Monster* [1956]) and most memorably *Plan Nine from Outer Space* [1959]).

In an informative acting manual, Rosary O'Neill argues that actors, whether working in theatre, film or television, should learn how to "score" — in other words, annotate — a script, giving them the ability "to act with great expression — because it [the score] supports you with an invisible framework. You [the actor] contact your burning passion — the major objective in the scene — and then you play a hundred per cent to get it" (O'Neill 1992: 166). Hollywood character actors had little need to create this "invisible framework"; it had already been established in their previous films. Rather the script had to be reshaped to accommodate occasional dramatic set-pieces, giving actors the opportunity to show off their particular dramatic skills. Dwight Frye's death scenes are inevitably protracted, the camera focusing tightly on his facial expressions. The plot resolution of the Charlie Chan films is periodically suspended to enable Mantan Moreland to engage in comic repartee with one of Chan's numerous offspring. Lionel Atwill's and George Zucco's mad scientists are shown hard at work in their laboratories carrying out their experiments while declaring their intention to change the world. They never succeed, but filmgoers can revel in their villainy (with its roots in Victorian melodrama), as they turn directly to the camera and cackle throatily.

The repetitiveness of a character actor's performance also suited the studios, which had total control over production and exhibition in America until 1942 (when the so-called "Paramount Case" outlawed the practices of block booking and blind selling of product). They treated their contract players as virtual slaves, casting them in film after film regardless of quality. Anne Gwynne — who began her career at Universal in the 1930s and starred in numerous horror and science fiction films — recalled that "one time you got a good role, then you landed a small part in the next movie [...] I felt that you should always advance, not take two steps backward for each step forward" (Weaver 1996: 147). By contrast, Alan Napier appreciated the security of studio life, which he likened to that of a theatrical stock-company staging several plays per season with little rehearsal time in between. In this kind of environment, actors became particularly proficient at playing specific types of role: "From this necessity you get acting [...] in place of the comparatively sterile practice of behaviorism" (qtd. Twomey and McClure 1969: 3).

While most character actors enjoyed greater freedom of movement after 1942, they still found that most studios — both the majors as well as smaller outfits such as Monogram and Republic — adopted casting policies that would show off their specific "brand identity" (Christensen 2008: 171). In Monogram's case, this meant finding the kind of actors with backgrounds in horror films, who could cope with the pressures of a tight shooting schedule and primitive sets. Originality of characterization was considered less important than reliability: Universal knew what they would get when they cast Rondo Hatton as a villain in a cycle of horror films in the early 1940s, while American International Pictures (AIP) put

Tom Conway's brand of suave gentility to good use in a series of low-budget efforts a decade later. As Paul Kerr observes, in this kind of cinematic environment even the most innovative producers and directors—for example, Val Lewton, whose RKO unit produced such classics as *Cat People* (1942), and *The Leopard Man* (1943)—were obliged to standardize their casting procedures "for purposes of recognition—and reward" (Kerr 2008: 236).

Nonetheless the benefits of this casting policy were considerable, as exhibitors, journalists and filmgoers welcomed the chance to see character actors in familiar roles. Margaret Farrand Thorp reported in 1939, "From Seattle to Waterbury, Connecticut, the theatres were stormed," whenever a new Universal horror film appeared with a long list of contract players including (amongst others) Frye, Edward van Sloan, or David Manners (Thorp 1946: 22). The Rialto cinema in New York, under its charismatic manager Arthur Mayer, specialized in the "M"-product — mystery, mayhem, and murder — a bill of fare that, according to the *New York Times*, "made goose-pimples its trademark." Throughout the 1940s, both Hollywood insiders and the New York press routinely described new horror releases as "Rialto-type pictures," and judged them on the basis of their appropriateness for that venue. *The House of the Seven Gables* (1940), "a watered-down treatment of a nineteenth century classic," according to the *New York Times*, was deemed too innocuous for Mayer's "shriek-and-shiver" venue. More significantly, the Rialto was one of the birthplaces of the cult movie scene; from the early 1930s onwards audiences enjoyed the pleasures of "cult connoisseurship of horror films, and the actors who appeared in them" (Snelson and Jancovich 2011: 200).

However, the characters were not just there to entertain their audiences; they fulfilled an important ideological role in telling America about itself during a period of cataclysmic change from the Great Depression to the height of the Cold War. Michael Denning argued over two decades ago that dime novels of the late nineteenth and early twentieth centuries constructed allegories of American society; their fictional milieu were "less a representation of the real world than a microcosm [...] Individual characters are less individuals than figures for social groups." The stories of individuals and their families "became types of the citizens of the Republic, both in utopian images of its fulfillment [...] and in the stories of its betrayal" (Denning 1987: 72, 153). The same phenomenon could be observed in horror and science fiction films of the mid-twentieth century: the character actors did not portray individuals but representatives of specific interest groups. The African American actor Noble Johnson was usually cast as a tribal chief, a zombie, or (most bizarrely) a whited-up servant in *Murders in the Rue Morgue* (1932). By accepting such roles he drew attention to the major studios' institutional racism, which consigned non-white performers to secondary roles as savages or servants. The issue of gender roles in society was especially prominent both during and after the Second World War, when many women were faced with the choice between going out to work or continuing their lives as homemakers. Most horror films took a conservative line by advocating the second option: Roger Corman's *The Wasp Woman* (1959) warns filmgoers of the potential dangers of a career woman like Janice (Susan Cabot), who develops a formula for perpetual youth taken from queen wasps. She does not anticipate its harmful side-effects, and is transformed into a monster feeding off other human beings. In the wartime horror film *Weird Woman* (1944), Evelyn Ankers's Ilona Carr, another career woman, tries to break up the happy marriage between Professor Norman Reed (Lon Chaney, Jr.) and Paula (Anne Gwynne), his pretty young housewife bride from the South Seas. Riven with jealousy, Ilona considers Paul a danger to the future of American society. In truth it is Ilona herself who is the danger as she tries to wreck Norman's happy home life; as a result she has to be killed off at the end of the film, while Norman and Paula happily embrace one another. To ensure the survival of marriage as a social institution, men were also expected to fulfill their domestic responsibilities. If they neglected them, the consequences could be dire, as William Hudson's feckless husband Harry Archer discovers when he becomes one of the victims of the *Attack of the 50 Foot Woman* (1958)—the woman in this case being his abused wife Nancy (Allison Hayes).

During the late 1940s and 1950s, several character actors in science fiction films delivered homilies, designed to inform audiences about the political situation during the Cold War era, and how people should respond to it. Michael Rennie's Gort in *The Day the Earth Stood Still* (1951) exhorts the inhabitants of Earth to "join us [the aliens] and live in peace, or pursue your present course [of nuclear aggression] and face destruction." This policy could be justified, but only if America's enemies respond in similar fashion. America cannot afford to let other superpowers advance in terms of technological development, for this might affect its standing in the world. John Archer's Jim Barnes in *Destination Moon* (1950) observes: "If we [Americans] fail [in our duty], we'll take a terrible beating. So we can't fail. Not only is this [the space race] the greatest adventure awaiting mankind, but it's the greatest challenge ever hurled at American industry." More importantly, America should not pursue a policy of appeasement, like Robert Cornthwaite's scientist in *The Thing from Another World*, who advocates peaceful communication with the enemy—in this case an alien from outer space—but willfully ignores its potential capacity for destruction.

On the other hand, Americans should understand that some forms of technological and exploratory research are potentially too dangerous to pursue. Cecil Kellaway's Thurgood Elson in *The Beast from 20,000 Fathoms* (1953) believes that exploring new frontiers, whether in space or beneath the ocean, is like "leaving a world of untold tomorrows for a world of countless yesterdays." Cedric Hardwicke's Narrator in *The War of the Worlds* (1953) offers a worst-case scenario of how the American people should respond to an invasion. While they should make every effort to protect their country and its democratic traditions, they should also trust in Christianity, which teaches them to recognize the power of God's will. The Martian invaders in the film are destroyed not by human agents, but by earthly bacteria—which in Hardwicke's view can be explained by divine intervention. Through such messages, character actors offered their audiences a means of "reconciliation of the needs of the individual and the demands of living and working in a modern economy" (Stanfield 2002: 130). While witnessing their performances in horror and science fiction films, we can obtain a unique insight into the major social and political issues of mid-twentieth century America.

The working lives of most character actors during this period were not easy, as they had to contend with a cost-conscious cinematic environment that gave them little or no time for rehearsals or retakes. Faith Domergue found the experience of filming *This Island Earth* (1955) particularly traumatic: "I was never so weary in all my life. We worked six days a week. I'd go at six in the morning, and get out at six at night, so they [the producers] wouldn't go overtime with me" (qtd. Parla and Mitchell 2000: 67). The working conditions had scarcely altered since the 1930s, when B-films were shot in a week to ten days at a time. Despite such constraints, most character actors turned in the kind of performances that their audiences readily appreciated, while communicating the kind of messages that might have contravened Production Code guidelines if they had been delivered more overtly (especially if the messages related to sexual issues). In recent years, scholars have devoted more attention to the phenomena of repetition and recycling: Richard Nowell offers a flexible model for studying film cycles—including horror and science fiction — that takes into account "supply chains, target audiences, and industrial perceptions of the comparative commercial potential of other film types." Contributions to any film cycle are informed "by factors specific to the film-type in question." (Nowell 2011). Within this methodological framework the character actors assumed an important role, as their characterizations were shaped by industrial concerns as well as patterns of audience reception. While they never enjoyed as much prestige — or publicity — in the Hollywood studio period as their star counterparts, they nonetheless exerted considerable influence in determining how a horror and science fiction film would be written and shot.

The Actors

John Agar
b. January 31, 1921, Chicago;
d. April 7, 2002, Burbank, California

Born in Chicago, John Agar spent much of the Second World War working as a U.S. Army Air Force physical instructor. He shot to fame in 1945 when he married Shirley Temple, a union that lasted four years. Agar signed a long-term contract with producer David O. Selznick, but never achieved lasting stardom in "A" Pictures. However, it was a different story in the 1950s, as Agar achieved lasting popularity with his roles in low-budget science fiction films.

In Jack Arnold's *Revenge of the Creature* (1955), a sequel to *Creature from the Black Lagoon* (1954), Agar plays Professor Clete Ferguson, a marine scientist taking advantage of the fact that the creature has been captured and put on show in an aquarium in south Florida. Ferguson can conduct whatever experiments he wishes— filming the creature, examining its behavioral characteristic— in the secure knowledge that he will not be at risk. He enlists the help of attractive research student Helen Dobson (Lori Nelson). However the creature escapes from the aquarium and enacts a terrible revenge on those who tried to "civilize" it. The only way that order can be restored is through a combined operation involving the armed forces with Ferguson acting as technical advisor. They successfully hunt the creature down and kill it, allowing Ferguson and Helen to end the film in a passionate embrace. *Revenge of the Creature* shows how the desire to conduct scientific research — which led to the creature being captured in the first place — leads to social disorder. If the creature had been left to its own devices, then perhaps the crisis would not have arisen.

In the same year, Agar played Dr. Matt Hastings in Arnold's *Tarantula*. Hastings is a practicing doctor who becomes more and more disturbed by Professor Gerald Deemer's (Leo G. Carroll) experiments in giantism, which obviously interfere with the balance of nature. Hastings has due cause for alarm, as a tarantula grows to an enormous size and terrorizes the inhabitants of an isolated desert city. Although he lacks the technical know-how to neutralize the tarantula's threat, Hastings proves adept at coordinating others; we see several shots of him traveling by car down lonely desert roads in an attempt to contact the local sheriff Jack Andrews

John Agar publicity still (1955). Agar's square-jawed, rugged appearance made him an ideal leading man for many low-budget science fiction films of the 1950s, as well as westerns, as here.

(Nestor Paiva), or liaising with army chief John Nolan (Edwin Rand). Hastings refuses to pursue any course of action without taking a second opinion; this caution contrasts with Deemer's determination to pursue his experiments with little concern for their consequences. Director Arnold uses this contrast to underline the distinction between "good" and "bad" science — "good" science, in this context, is identified with the kind of experiments that guarantee rather than threaten the future of humankind.

In Virgil Vogel's *The Mole People* (1956), Agar plays another expert — the pioneering archeologist Dr. Roger Bentley. While disparaging his profession ("archeologists are underpaid agents for deceased royalty"), he leads by example, boldly entering each unexplored space with little concern for his own personal welfare. Director Vogel frequently shoots him in illuminated close-up, his face contorted with fear as he explores the mysteries of an ancient civilization. Eventually he discovers that they are located far beneath the earth's surface: Vogel's camera tracks him as he lowers himself gradually down into the abyss, sweat dripping from his forehead. As the action unfolds, it becomes clear that Bentley is a representative of the free (American) world, contrasting starkly with the despotic world of the ancient Sumerian underground. He paints rosy pictures of his civilization to the nubile young Sumerian slave Adad (Cynthia Patrick); it is a "world of light," "a heavenly world," whose heart "beats with tenderness." Although condemned to death by King Nazar (Rodd Redwing) and his evil acolyte Elinu, the High Priest (ALAN NAPIER), Bentley manages to escape and return to the world of "sunlight" — the free world of self-determination, taking Adad with him. However, she cannot adjust to his values; she makes a futile attempt to return to the Sumerian civilization, and is crushed to death by falling rock.

A year later Agar took the role of George Hastings (a distant cousin, perhaps, of Matt Hastings in *Tarantula*), the fiancé of Janet Smith (GLORIA TALBOTT) in Edgar G. Ulmer's *Daughter of Dr. Jekyll*. George does not have much to do, other than protect Janet both from herself and from the demons affecting her. He puts his arms around her, or clasps her head as she sleeps, reminding us of the importance of a woman having a suitable male protector in many 1950s horror films. George does not believe for one moment that his fiancée is the daughter of the infamous Dr. Jekyll; at one point he draws himself up to his full height and pronounces in ringing tones to Dr. Lomas (Arthur Shields): "Do you think I'm gonna let an old wives' tale affect us?" He tries in vain to make Janet forget the doctor, in the hope she will recover from her frequent bouts of hysteria, which George himself dismisses as "all nerves." Needless to say George discovers the truth about his fiancée, as he reads a book entitled *Witch, Warlock and Werewolf* and subsequently finds out that Dr. Lomas has been hypnotizing Janet into believing that she has killed several victims, when in truth it is the doctor himself who is responsible for the murders. George proves no match for the doctor in one-to-one combat, but eventually collaborates with various servants to kill him. As the film ends, George embraces the sobbing Janet and vows to protect her, exclaiming: "He [Shields] will never roam at night again."

In *Attack of the Puppet People* (1958), Agar plays much the same kind of role as Bob Westley, a clean-cut salesperson who becomes one of crazed puppet-master Franz's (John Hoyt) victims. Although the subject matter is distinctly abnormal, Westley tries to do all the "normal" things a young-ish male of the late 1950s might do, such as taking his girlfriend Sally (June Kenney) to the drive-in theatre (which is showing *The Amazing Colossal Man*, director Bert I. Gordon's previous sci-fi success from 1957), and embracing her afterwards in the back seat of his car. Such privileges are denied to Franz, which only makes him more and more jealous of Bob's good looks. Eventually the puppet-master decides to make Bob "fit the world according to his [Franz's] symphony," by making him a few inches high. Bob valiantly tries to assume the masculine role of protector, but his size prevents him; like Samson he is deprived of his strength. The only way that Bob can outwit the puppet-master is through guile; by destroying the machine that shrinks all the human beings in the first place, after having ensured that everyone is restored to their normal size. Agar's presence in the film accentuates its satiric purpose; as a tall, virile ex-physical education instructor, he is expected to be strong and protective (as in *The Mole People*, for instance). When deprived of such powers, he is reduced to nothing. Such transformations invite us to reflect on the construction of masculinity in late 1950s American society.

Agar plays a very different role in Edward L. Cahn's propaganda piece *Invisible Invaders* (1959). As Major Bruce Jay, he is entrusted with the responsibility of protecting the scientists Adam Penner (Philip Tonge) and John Lamont (Robert Hutton), who have been charged with the responsibility of destroying a race of invisible invaders. He is totally dedicated to his work ("We've got a job, and we gotta do it, now! [...] we can't afford the luxury of cracking up!"), even if it means killing people in cold blood. The experience of fighting in Korea taught him the importance of shooting first and asking questions later. Any other course of action could mean certain death. Jay is the kind of person who takes the lead in everything; when someone has to go outside the protected bunker to capture one of the invisible invaders, Jay takes on the responsibility himself, even though there are considerable risks involved. He takes on six invaders at once; although one of them shoots him in the chest, he manages to kill them all. Jay is a shining example of how any member of the American armed forces should behave; he believes that his country's future is more important than his own safety, and hence undertakes any task expected of him. More importantly, he understands the importance of teamwork; the invaders cannot be destroyed unless the armed forces work with members of the scientific community. This message is reinforced at the end of the film, where an (uncredited) narrator informs us in voiceover that the story has shown how "the nations of the world could work and fight together side by side in a common cause"—that "cause" being the extermination of the communist threat.

Evelyn Ankers
b. August 7, 1918, Valparaiso, Chile;
d. August 29, 1985, Haiku, Maul, Hawaii

Born in Chile of English parents, Evelyn Ankers began her acting career in small roles in British films such as *Fire Over England* (1937) and *Bells of St. Mary's* (also 1937). After a couple of starring roles in quota quickies like *The Claydon Treasure Mystery* (1938), she moved to the United States and signed a five-year contract with Universal Pictures in 1940.

Ankers could play heroes and villains with equal facility. One of her best early roles was that of Gwen Cunliffe in *The Wolf Man* (1941). She begins by seeming rather standoffish, as she walks away from Lawrence Talbot (Lon Chaney, Jr.) and responds to his entreaties to come out with her in an offhand tone. Her eyes, however, suggest a depth of feeling that perhaps she is reluctant to acknowledge; at least, until Talbot locks her in a passionate embrace. Gwen's devotion to Talbot seems unswerving; even when the local villagers accuse Talbot of murder, Gwen stays close to him. Director George Waggner cuts to a close-up of her face, pregnant with emotion, as she protests his innocence. But her loyalty goes unrewarded, as Talbot transforms himself into the wolf man and attacks her.

As Elsa in *The Ghost of Frankenstein* (1942), Ankers played a variation on the same role, as she remained blindly devoted to her father Dr. Frankenstein (CEDRIC HARDWICKE). Her innocence is suggested by her costume—a long white dress—as she embraces her fiancé Erik (Ralph Bellamy) in the garden, and then walks towards the camera, a big smile spread over her face. Despite her best intentions, Elsa becomes corrupted, once she finds out her father's guilty secret. In one long sequence we see her rifling through his study until she discovers the secret notes written about the creation of the monster (Lon Chaney, Jr.) Although she forgives her father, we understand how she has changed by the costumes she now wears—long black dresses gathered up at the neck—which suggest mourning for her lost innocence. Although the film ends happily, with Elsa and Erik embracing on a sunny morning, we feel that this is only transient: Elsa is doomed to a life of perpetual suffering.

Universal obviously liked Ankers in this kind of part. In *Captive Wild Woman* (1943), Ankers plays Beth Colman, another devoted woman whose efforts are rewarded this time as she releases Cheela the Ape (Ray Corrigan) from its cage. The ape kills the mad doctor Walters (JOHN CARRADINE), then runs over to the circus to rescue Fred from being mauled to death by a lion. Beth follows, and she and Fred are locked in a passionate embrace as the film ends. Ankers does not have too much to do in this film, but one of her costumes — a fur coat and headdress — invests her with a strong visual resemblance to Cheela. This is no coincidence; director Edward Dmytryk clearly suggests that Beth and Cheela (unlike Fred and the doctor) can establish authority over animals and men alike, through sheer willpower rather than violence. It is Beth who contrives Walters' demise by unlocking the door of Cheela's cage. Ankers repeats the role in the follow-up film *Jungle Woman* (1944); now she comes across as a well-dressed woman about town, dressed in expensive furs and fashionable hat, giving evidence in court about Cheela's transformation into Paula Dupree — the Ape Woman (Acquanetta).

Sometimes Ankers was forced to play passive heroines, which suggests that Universal wanted to keep her under control, so that she would not upstage her male co-stars. This is certainly the case in the lame Abbott and Costello horror spoof *Hold That Ghost* (1941) where her role as Norma Lind is confined to providing a romantic interest for Dr. Jackson (RICHARD CARLSON) and participating in one comic scene where she and Camille Brewster (Joan Davis) go upstairs in search of a ghost. At the top of the stairs we see a pair of shining eyes observing the two women; they catch sight of the eyes and scurry back down the stairs to join the men. Neither of them have sufficient courage to venture off on their own without male protection. Ankers gives vent to a full-throated scream, which became a distinguishing mark of many of her performances at Universal, and earned her the nickname "Queen of the Screamers." In *Son of Dracula* (1943), she has a minor role as the good daughter Claire Caldwell, who is deliberately contrasted with her "bad" sister Kay (Louise Allbritton). Claire wears minimal make-up and white dresses with padded shoulders — a fashionable young lady about town devoted to her father (George Irving). Kay wears black, with heavy make-up and red lips — an appropriate costume for someone fond of pursuing forbidden knowledge about the undead.

Evelyn Ankers and Lon Chaney, Jr., in *The Wolf Man* (1941). In this memorable entry from Universal's horror film cycle, Ankers plays her familiar role of a strong-willed woman who resists any attempts to suppress her.

As Isabel Lewis in *The Mad Ghoul* (1944), Ankers appears once more in a white dress. Although a talented singer, her main role in the film is to support her boyfriend Ted Allison (David Bruce), even though she would much rather marry concert pianist Eric Iversen (TURHAN BEY). Eventually the responsibility proves too great for her — despite feeling sorry for Ted (the unwilling victim of mad scientist Alfred Morris's (GEORGE ZUCCO) experiments), she follows her instincts and marries Eric. In *The Invisible Man's Revenge* (1944), Ankers wears the same costume as Julie Herrick — although dominated by her father Sir Jasper Herrick (Lester Matthews), Julie still retains sufficient self-possession to believe in her boyfriend Robert Griffin's (JON HALL) basic goodness, even though Griffin himself is a fugitive from the law. In *The Frozen Ghost* (1945), Ankers gives a similar performance as Maura Daniel, the sidekick of Alex Gregor (aka Gregor the Great) (Lon Chaney, Jr.) She remains devoted to Alex — so devoted, in fact, that she willingly allows herself to be hypnotized by him. This proves extremely useful at the end of the film, as Alex discovers that his supposed best friend George Keene (Milburn Stone) actually wants to kill him. In the climactic fight, Keene is killed and Alex at last understands Maura's depth of feeling for him.

However, there were occasions when Ankers played against type as a villain, or someone with a dubious past. In *The Voice of Terror* (1942), she plays Kitty, a good-time girl working in a seedy nightclub in London's Limehouse district. Holmes' (Basil Rathbone) determination has a profound effect on her, as she interrupts her performance to accuse the customers of collaborating with the Nazis as they refuse to tell the detective anything about the mysterious Voice of Terror. Kitty's brave stand inevitably causes her demise, as she is dragged away into a lonely house to be interrogated by Meade (Thomas Gomez), who tells her about his bloodthirsty dream to take over the world. In spite of being tortured, she refuses to tell him anything. Sadly her efforts prove in vain, as she is shot dead during the final confrontation. In a stunningly banal tribute, Holmes observes that she "merits the deepest gratitude for her efforts"— almost as if he was reluctant to say any more. To do so would be to admit that his status as a great detective has been challenged: Kitty has played a far greater part in solving the case than Holmes himself.

In another Holmes film, *The Pearl of Death* (1944), Ankers plays Naomi Drake, the villainous girlfriend of Giles Conover (MILES MANDER). Here she adopts a variety of disguises— another good-time girl with a cigarette hanging loosely from her lips; a match-seller standing outside a theatre, and a shop-worker. None of them are particularly convincing (Ankers cannot do the Cockney accent), but they give the actress the opportunity to flex her acting muscles. She appears far more convincing as Ilona Carr, the villain in *Weird Woman* (1944), the spurned ex-lover of Professor Norman Reid (Lon Chaney, Jr.). She begins by insulting the newly married couple at a celebratory drinks party, accusing the professor of being "an expert mixer"—a statement full of bitterness and resentment. Later on she confronts him in his office, moves closer to him, puts a hand on his arm and stares right into his face; Reid rejects her advances contemptuously and tells her not to be melodramatic. From then on Ilona determines to be revenged on him; she engages the young student Margaret Mercer (Lois Collier) as Reid's research assistant, knowing full well that he will be taken in by the young girl's naiveté. As Margaret begins work, director Reginald le Borg cuts to a shot of Ilona sitting behind a desk, twiddling a pencil and glowering at the professor's door. Her malignance knows no limits; she tells Margaret's boyfriend David Jennings (Phil Brown), that the professor and Margaret are having an affair, which prompts the younger man to pick a fight with the professor. This eventually leads to David's death.

As the film unfolds, Ilona's behavior becomes more and more erratic. When Evelyn Sawtelle (ELIZABETH RUSSELL) discovers the truth behind Ilona's motives and confronts her with it, Ilona screams hysterically, "Stop that! Stop that!," her head shaking from side to side as if she cannot bear to listen. On the soundtrack muffled voices can be heard, suggesting that Ilona is at last experiencing guilty feelings. She screams, grabs a bed-cover and runs into Evelyn's house crying, "I'm dying!" At last she admits her true motives, wringing her hands as she does so, before committing suicide by jumping off a balcony.

John Archer
b. May 8, 1915, Osceola, Nebraska;
d. December 3, 1999, Redmond, Washington

After graduating from the University of Southern California, Ralph Bowman drifted into acting, plating small roles in Universal and Republic serials. He won a radio contest called "Jesse Lasky's Gateway to Hollywood," where the first prize was an RKO contract made out to "John Archer." Bowman won first prize, edging out the actor Hugh Beaumont and thereby acquiring the right to adopt the pseudonym "John Archer."

Archer played in several horror and/or science fiction films between 1930 and 1960. His screen persona was that of a clean-cut young man, a symbol of normality in disordered and/or hostile environments. In Monogram's *King of the Zombies* (1941), he plays Bill Summers, the dapper sidekick of test pilot James "Mac" McCarthy (DICK PURCELL). Although physically slight, Bill has a practical outlook on life; he listens carefully to what is being said around him and takes time before coming to a decision. His basically ruminative nature is suggested by the fact that he keeps his hands in his pockets and frowns slightly whenever anyone tells him anything. This quality proves exceptionally useful; unlike McCarthy (whose impetuous nature renders him an easy victim for the evil Dr. Miklos Sangre's (Henry Victor) hypnosis, Summers remains clear-headed throughout. After having witnessed the strange events taking place on the tropical island, he comes to believe in zombies, realizing that the only way to overcome them is to employ hypnosis, and encourage them to attack the doctor. This task is successfully accomplished, and Summers can subsequently release McCarthy from his trance.

As Richard Dennison in *Bowery at Midnight* (1942), also for Monogram, Archer appears immaculately dressed in a wool suit, his black hair slicked back in the fashionable style of the day. He has a traditional worldview, in which men should go out to work, while women, such as his girlfriend Wanda McKay (Judy Malvern), should stay at home and prepare for marriage. Dennison dislikes the fact that Judy works as an assistant in a soup kitchen run by the kindly Professor Frederick Brenner (Bela Lugosi), deeming the job "inappropriate" for a woman. Brenner takes strong exception to such opinions, and gets his revenge by transforming Dennison into a zombie and imprisoning him in his cellar. The young man is only rescued right at the end of the film, when Wanda has him laid out on a bed and stares devotedly into his face. Dennison opens his eyes, and is immediately transformed back into a human being: love evidently overcomes everything. Archer has a small role as Naval Lt. Pete Merriam in *Sherlock Holmes in Washington* (1943). He appears as Nancy Partridge's (Marjorie Lord) fiancé, who ends up in Washington on a three-day pass and hopes to marry her during that time. He appears perfectly at home during an engagement party held in the young couple's honor, but is no match for the villains working for Nazi agent Heinrich Hinckel, also known as Richard Stanley (GEORGE ZUCCO). Merriam is hit over the head and thrust into a small room, while Nancy is drugged and carried off in the belief that she holds the secret as to the whereabouts of a vital microfilm. Merriam's fate underlines the risks that can befall anyone during wartime, even innocent victims.

By 1950 Archer had graduated to more middle-aged roles, such as the ever-reliable captain Jim Barnes in IRVING PICHEL's *Destination Moon*. He comes across as a no-nonsense personality, rolling up his sleeves and dedicating himself to the job in hand. When quizzed by a group of business people as to why a trip to the moon should be so necessary, Barnes offers an eloquent defense, profusely illustrated with diagrams and a cartoon film featuring Woody Woodpecker. At the end of his presentation the audience applauds his speech. Although happily involved in a relationship, Barnes dedicates himself to the job in hand; prior to take-off we witness him kissing his girlfriend goodbye and climbing into the spaceship. He shows a paternal concern for his crew's welfare, never expecting

Jane Nigh and John Archer in *Rodeo* (1952). With his pencil-thin mustache and black hair, Archer was equally adept at playing good or bad characters.

them to do anything he would not do himself. We see him hunched over the controls, piloting the ship in the best way he can, and writing down his findings in a notebook. Even if the mission proves abortive, he wants to record everything for posterity. Needless to say, things do not exactly go according to plan: Barnes responds by appealing for calm and slowly walking up and down the spaceship until he has formulated a suitable plan to ensure his crew's safe return to Earth. The trailer for the film claims that "never before has any woman sent her man on such an exploit," implying that Barnes himself had no real choice in the matter. Pichel's film shows precisely the reverse: Barnes always knows what he is doing, and what risks might be involved. It is a tribute to his skill as a scientist and a person-manager that he accomplishes the mission successfully.

Archer was also adept at playing bad guys. In Martin Gabel's horror/fantasy film *The Lost Moment* (1947), based on the Henry James novella *The Aspern Papers*, he plays Charles, who assists Louis Venable (Robert Cummings) in his quest to find the missing Aspern papers, now in the possession of aging matriarch Juliana Bordereau (Agnes Moorehead). Charles's loyalties are solely determined by financial imperatives; later on he threatens to expose Venable as a fraud, unless he receives a substantial share of the profits accruing from the papers' publication. In one sequence, Charles paces about the room, his hands behind his back, claiming sarcastically that his intentions are "noble." The character Charles does not exist in the James novella; he has been especially created for Gabel's film to underline Venable's base motives. Both men want to pry into the Bordereau family's past for personal gain.

Ten years later, Archer played rich playboy Barton Kendall in *She-Devil*. He comes across as a distinctly oleaginous personality; with his pencil mustache and heavily greased hair, he treats all women as objects to be toyed with. He describes blonde bombshell Kyra Zelas (Mari Blanchard) as "the most beautiful test tube I've ever seen." Needless to say, he makes a rapid attempt to seduce her, even though his wife Evelyn (Fay Baker) vainly tries to stop him. Kyra has no feelings towards him, but loves his wealth; having strangled Evelyn, she marries Barton with almost indecent haste. However the marriage doesn't last: Barton spends most of his time drinking champagne, a self-satisfied smile spread all over his face as he shows off his latest live acquisition. Kyra responds by telling him to leave her alone. Incensed, Barton shoots her in the shoulder, speculating as he does so on whether she is a "true" (i.e., compliant) woman or not. Kyra makes a rapid recovery (having been given a medicine by Dr. Dan Scott [Jack Kelly], that cures her instantly of any disease or wound), and takes revenge on her husband while they are out driving by pushing his car down a cliff. Barton learns to his cost how his arrogant assumptions that all women are either sex objects or servants do not apply to Kyra.

Richard Arlen

b. September 1, 1900, Charlottesville, Virginia;
d. March 28, 1976, North Hollywood, California

Born Sylvanus Richard van Mattimore, Richard Arlen served in the Royal Canadian Air Force as a pilot, but never saw active service. Once the First World War ended, he ended up winning a contract at Paramount Pictures, starting his film career in 1925. His big break came with the silent film *Wings* (1927), where he played a pilot. Other successes soon followed, including *The Man I Love* (1929) and *The Virginian* (1929), with Gary Cooper. With the advent of talking pictures, Arlen's career took something of a dip, and he became a reliable supporting actor rather than a star in a long career that encompassed television as well as films.

One such role was that of Edward Parker in Erle C. Kenton's *Island of Lost Souls* (1932), based on H. G. Wells's *The Island of Dr. Moreau*. With his clean-cut looks and white suit, he is clearly intended to provide a visual contrast to Dr. Moreau (Charles Laughton), a stocky, unattractive man with a cruel mustache and beard. Parker is appalled at Moreau's experiments in trying to transform animals into human beings: the island is peopled with half-human mutants, including the Panther Woman (Kathleen Burke), whose hands are nothing more than claws. The film is an obvious criticism of the effects of (British) colonialism, where the natives are forced to change their appearance; if they resist, they are brutally consigned to the house of pain. By contrast, Parker appears to represent freedom, as he tries vainly to rescue the Panther Woman. Despite his clean-cut appearance, Parker is as much of a colonist as Dr. Moreau, even though his methods might be different. Whereas Moreau wants to impose his authority through brute force, Parker tries to "civilize" the Panther Woman by teaching her English.

In H. Bruce Humberstone's comedy horror flick *Three Live Ghosts* (1936), Arlen plays William ("Bill") Jones, one of a trio of demobbed British soldiers returning home from the First World War, only to discover that they have been listed as missing, presumed dead by the government. They are non-persons, or ghosts, according to official records. This proves something of an advantage to Jones, who is wanted by the American government for an unspecified purpose. Despite this, he remains a fundamentally honorable person, devoted to his friends "Spoofy" Brockton (Claude Allister) and "Jimmie" Gubbins (Charles McNaughton), as well as his girlfriend Ann (Cecilia Parker). Believing that he is a wanted criminal, he tries his best not to sustain a relationship with Ann, yet at the same time remains concerned for her welfare. When she lacks the funds to pay the rent, Jones asks his friends to help out.

Although only 61 minutes in length, the film successfully dramatizes the experiences of many soldiers returning home after the end of the war. With no immediate family of his own,

Richard Arlen began his career as a matinee idol before turning to character roles. This pose from the late 1920s shows off his good looks.

Jones searches for a surrogate family. He remains devoted to his two buddies, and positively relishes the prospect of breakfasting at Gubbins's stepmother's (Beryl Mercer) house. The fact that Jones puts himself at risk by doing so (Mrs. Gubbins is keen to report him to the police and claim the £1,000 reward) is of little consequence to him. Jones' search eventually proves fruitful, as he discovers that he has inherited a considerable fortune, and can therefore marry Ann as well as provide suitable medical treatment for his shell-shocked buddy Brockton.

In Republic's *The Phantom Speaks* (1943), Arlen plays campaigning journalist Matt Fraser, whose obsession for work renders him insensitive to long-suffering girlfriend Joan Renwick (Lynne Roberts). The film is a direct remake of Universal's *Black Friday* (1940), with Stanley Ridges appearing once again as the professor, but his gangster *alter ego* played this time by Tom Powers. Initially, Fraser does not believe that Joan's father, Professor Paul Renwick, has had a brain transplant that transforms him into a Jekyll and Hyde character. Eventually, Fraser is persuaded otherwise by the weight of evidence in front of him: the murders, the newspaper articles, and the fact that Renwick seems to have no knowledge of what he has done. It transpires that his brain has been colonized by the personality of convicted gangland leader Harvey Bogardus (Powers). Fraser eventually unmasks the crime while stalling the police; like any good journalist, he is careful to protect his sources. Arlen strides through the film in a debonair manner, putting his hands in his pockets whenever he has something serious to do. However, director John English suggests that this is the right course of action; it is best for all human beings to stay true to themselves, rather than to assume other identities. This is suggested in a coda, where the camera focuses on a quotation from the Bible: "For as he thinketh in his heart, so *is* he!"

In *The Lady and the Monster* (1944), based on Curt Siodmak's novel *Donovan's Brain*, also for Republic, Arlen plays Patrick Cory, another clean-cut, hard-working type employed as an assistant to Professor Franz Mueller (Erich von Stroheim). From the outset it is clear that Cory is torn between the desire to advance his own scientific knowledge, and pursue a love affair with Mueller's other assistant Janice Farrell (Vera Hruba Ralston). The conflict becomes more intense as Cory realizes that the Professor's research into keeping alive the brain of a dead man — millionaire philanthropist Paul Donovan is technically illegal. However much Cory might protest his love for Janice, he cannot escape: his predicament is well summed up by the off-screen narrator (Frank Graham) who tells us of Cory's desire to acquire fame and reputation.

For a while it seems that Cory has managed to acquire independence of thought; director George Sherman photographs him in full close-up bathed in bright light, suggesting honesty and openness. But Cory gradually starts to acquire the personality traits associated with Donovan — self-interest bordering on narcissism, snobbishness and irascibility. His face remains perpetually in shadow, lit from below, giving him a sinister look. The once-pleasant scientist has now been transformed into a ruthless power-seeker who will stop at nothing to achieve his ends — even resorting to murder. In one powerful sequence, Cory sits with Janice in a truck waiting for a school bus to drop Mary Lou (Juanita Quigley) off near her home. Cory starts the engine, and drives at speed towards the terrified child, his eyes bulging, his face fixed in a manic stare. Janice grabs the wheel and veers the truck off into a different direction — thus sparing the child an almost certain death. Cory responds by trying to strangle Janice.

Although the scientist comes to his senses in the nick of time, he understands that he has to pay for his past misdemeanors with a prison sentence. He howls at the end of the film: "Please, please, I want to be free! I want to lead my own life!" However, we understand that he can never achieve this aim; although free of Donovan's influence, and the Professor's malignant employment, he is still subject to the narrator's control, as shown in the final frame, when the narrator, not Cory himself, informs us that "after all, there was a happy ending [to the film]."

Robert Armstrong

b. November 20, 1890, Saginaw, Michigan;
d. April 20, 1973, Santa Monica, California

Born Robert William Armstrong, he studied at the University of Washington before joining a stock company touring the United States run by the Gleason family, whose heir, James— then known as plain Jimmy — would become a Hollywood star himself. Armstrong made his film debut in the late 1920s in silent films, but his rapid-fire, world-weary mode of delivery made him a natural for talkies. In 1932, he met the director/producer combination of Ernest B. Schoedsack and Merian C. Cooper, who cast him in the first of what became a series of classic horror films, *The Most Dangerous Game* (1932). In this film, he plays Martin, a drunk who enjoys the hospitality offered him by Count Zaroff (Leslie Banks) to such an extent that he fails to understand the count's true intentions. In the end, Martin is cast out of Zaroff's house and left to roam the island as human prey for the natives. He is captured, and his head put on display in Zaroff's trophy cabinet.

In *King Kong* (1933), Armstrong plays Carl Denham, a wisecracking, pipe-smoking adventurer and filmmaker, whose excitement at the projected trip to a remote island is palpable, as he walks up and down the room, using his index finger to emphasize important points. He obviously has a high opinion of himself as a star-maker as he persuades innocent young waif Ann Darrow (Fay Wray) to join his voyage and subsequently pose in a series of melodramatic gestures in front of Denham's camera. Denham likes being the center of attention; hence his fondness for fur coats, white suits and a fedora. He searches relentlessly for King Kong in an attempt to capture him and exhibit him in New York as "The Eighth Wonder of the World." If anyone raises objections, Denham's tone of voice becomes hectoring, as if trying to browbeat them into agreeing with his wishes.

Eventually Denham succeeds in his quest, and shows off Kong to a packed theater audience. In a sequence strongly reminiscent of the opening to James Whale's *Frankenstein* (1930) — where EDWARD VAN SLOAN appears in a prologue in front of a stage curtain, warning the audiences about the forthcoming film — Denham appears on the stage in a dinner jacket and tails, lit from below (giving him a slightly sinister appearance). He brags about his adventures, and ends his speech with a crescendo, inviting the spectators to marvel at the sight of Kong struggling to break free.

Eventually Denham's plans go horribly awry, as Kong escapes and terrorizes the citizens of New York. Although the monster is eventually slain, Denham refuses to take responsibility for his actions. Rather than admitting the colonizer's folly of taking Kong from his natural habitat and transforming him into an object of derision, Denham stands over Kong's corpse and refers to how "beauty killed the beast." In his opinion it was Kong's love for Ann that led to his demise.

In *Son of Kong* (1933), the sequel to *King Kong*, Armstrong repeats his role as Carl Denham. As the film opens, we see him acknowledging the consequences of his actions; the desire to show Kong off as "The Eighth Wonder of the World" has reduced him to penury, with no money to pay the rent, let alone contest the lawsuits that loom ahead. Denham's state of mind is reflected in his body language, as he slouches round-shouldered around his grubby one-room apartment in a trench coat. Matters improve, however, once Denham encounters Captain Englehorn (Frank Reicher), as the two of them resolve to put to sea once more in search of fame and fortune. Denham exchanges his coat for a sailor's uniform and a pipe, which he smokes regularly to signify contentment with the world.

This voyage turns out to be one of self-discovery. Denham feels perpetually guilty for his treatment of King Kong; once he encounters Kong's son, he resolves to make amends. In one touching sequence, we see Denham applying first aid to one of little Kong's huge fingers, using a bandage made from Helene Peterson's (Helen Mack) undergarments. At last he understands the gorilla's true motives — rather than wanting to destroy him, little Kong wants to repay Denham's kindness towards him by offering protection. Kong fights off one monster,

Robert Armstrong (left) and James Gleason in *Oh, Yeah?* (1929). Although well-known for his roles in *King Kong* and *Son of Kong*, Armstrong lent a comic edge to his roles, as in this early comedy.

and saves Denham from certain death in an earthquake, even though Kong perishes as a result. The experience helps to humanize Denham, as he throws away the buried treasure found on Kong's island and proposes marriage to Helene instead. The film ends with the two of them embracing in the lifeboat.

In the second sequel to *King Kong, Mighty Joe Young* (1949), a much older and grayer-looking Armstrong plays wisecracking impresario Max O'Hara, a tough-looking cookie in braces and neat mustache who only wants the best acts for his shows and is prepared to go to Africa to find them. Armstrong invests the role with his familiar take-charge, off-the-back-teeth delivery; here is someone who does not like to be trifled with in pursuit of his aims. At the same time, director Schoedsack makes O'Hara seem rather absurd; despite his manner, he cannot even ride a horse properly. However, the prospect of consolidating his reputation by presenting "a gorilla [Joe Young] and a beautiful dame" Jill Young (Terry Moore) in his Hollywood nightclub proves too great. He picks himself up and dangles a contract in front of Jill, promising her untold wealth and beautiful clothes. Jill accepts, and she and Mighty Joe Young are transplanted from their African paradise into the bright lights of Hollywood.

O'Hara is here depicted as the archetypal colonizer, so preoccupied with making money that he cannot understand the mental damage he is doing both to the girl and her gorilla. As the nightclub emcee he assumes the costume of an African hunter, complete with shorts and pith helmet, but inevitably he cannot sustain the image. If Mighty Joe Young shows any sign of aggression, O'Hara's first instinct is to flee.

As one biographer remarks, however, Armstrong's screen reputation was consolidated through "good, crowd-pleasing" roles. Consequently, Schoedsack has O'Hara once again undergoing a change of heart; once the impresario realizes how unhappy Jill and Joe are, he resolves to arrange to send them back to Africa, even if it means losing money in the process. The task is not an easy one: O'Hara has to divert the police (who want to shoot Joe Young) by feigning a heart attack, and then driving a truck in the opposite direction to the truck carrying Joe and Jill. However, as O'Hara says at the end, "They [Jill and Joe] lived happily ever after." No longer the colonizer, he assumes the pose of a benevolent parent, happy that his offspring should have at last discovered contentment.

Armstrong played occasional character roles in horror films not directed by the Cooper/Schoedsack combination, such as *The Mad Ghoul* (1943). As wisecracking reporter "Scoop" McClure, Armstrong's precise movements—such as using his index finger to emphasize a point, or fixing his eyes squarely on anyone he addresses—denote someone determined to take charge of any situation. As a journalist, his responsibility consists of uncovering the truth behind any story, even if it means involving himself in risky ventures. He suspects Dr. Alfred Morris (GEORGE ZUCCO) of foul play, and thus conceives a stunt where he (McClure) pretends to be a corpse, so as to discover the truth behind the doctor's schemes. The scheme works well enough; but McClure had reckoned without the presence of Ted Allison (David Bruce), the research assistant whom the doctor has transformed into a zombie by means of poison gas. Unlike other horror films like *The Ape Man* (1943) where the reporter uncovers triumphant, McClure suffers a grisly fate as Ted strangles him to death.

Lionel Atwill

b. March 1, 1885, Croydon, England;
d. April 22, 1946, Pacific Palisades, California.

Lionel Atwill came to the United States in 1915 after an undistinguished stage career in Great Britain, and appeared on the New York stage with Lily Langtry, Nazimova, Katharine Cornell, Helen Hayes and other actresses. Atwill made silent films in New York, but only really made his name with the advent of talking pictures such as *The Vampire Bat* (1932). As Otto von Niemann, Atwill established certain elements of his screen persona — an outwardly kind doctor worrying about his patients and/or fellow citizens ("You must be more careful, Emil [Robert Frazer], very careful," he says to one of them) whose real motives are only exposed at the film's end. But the signs are already there earlier on: director Frank R. Strayer cuts to a close-up of him rubbing his hands nervously, or his jaw dropping slightly as he fears that the inspector Karl Brettenschneider (Melvyn Douglas) will discover his plans. In the end, we see von Niemann feverishly working in his laboratory, trying to discover the secret of life by creating a new being of his own. In a sequence strongly reminiscent of James Whale's *Frankenstein*, released a year earlier, von Niemann looks at Emil, his creation, and exclaims, "I have created life!" To create life, however, von Niemann must deprive another human being of their life; he captures Ruth (Fay Wray) and ties her up on a slab in preparation for taking all the blood out of her to feed his creature. Needless to say, von Niemann's plans go awry: Emil turns on him and shoots him dead, allowing Brettenschneider to rescue Ruth and hence bring about the expected happy ending. Atwill has great fun with his part, delivering his lines in a deep, throaty bass voice reminiscent of a villain in Victorian melodrama.

One of Atwill's most memorable performances came in First National's *Dr. X* (1932), directed by Michael Curtiz, where he plays Dr. Jerry Xavier, the principal of the Academy of Surgical Research, which becomes the focus of a police investigation into a series of gruesome murders in New York by the mysterious Moon Killer. Xavier comes across as a model of politeness, as he introduces his fellow scientists one by one to the investigating officers Stevens (Robert Warwick) and O'Halloran (Willard Robertson). Once the officers have left, however, Xavier reveals his true feeling about them, delivering the line "Meddling fools!" with a contemptuous scowl. It is clear that the doctor has something to hide; throughout the film he is shown fiddling with his handkerchief or his jacket buttons. He also never looks directly into the camera lens; whenever he is shown in close-up, his eyes look either to the right or the left, suggesting that he does not want to face the truth about something.

We discover that the doctor and his colleagues are engaged in a series of bizarre experiments, in which the Moon Killer murders are re-enacted using waxworks, as well as Xavier's butler Otto (George Rosener). Atwill takes a positive pleasure in giving an elaborate explanation of his work — which no one (not least the viewer) can understand — while surveying the various devices in his laboratory. While Xavier turns out not to be the murderer, director Curtiz clearly suggests that his bizarre experiments upset the balance of nature.

In *The Mystery of the Wax Museum* (1933), a rehash of *Dr. X* produced by the same company with the same director, Atwill plays Ivan Igor, the owner of a wax museum. Initially we sympathize with him, as he is apparently confined

Myrna Loy and Lionel Atwill in *Stamboul Quest* (1934). One of Hollywood's legendary bad guys, Atwill was well known for his piercing eyes, cruel mouth and clipped delivery.

to a wheelchair following a horrific fire at his museum in London. As the film unfolds, however, we soon become aware that this is an act; he comes into his underground lair and encounters Charlotte Duncan (Fay Wray) who is looking in vain for her boyfriend Jim (Frank McHugh). Igor tells her, "This is the birthplace of all my creations." He places particular stress on the word "all." Curtiz cuts to a close-up of his face staring up at Charlotte as he asks her to "help me to get back to the world." He stands up and faces her, his eyes staring unnaturally into her face, puts his arms around her and murmurs, "Marie Antoinette!" Charlotte knows what is coming to her and screams. In a later sequence, Atwill advances on Charlotte, saying in honeyed tones, "My child, why are you so pitiful and afraid? Immortality has been the dream and inspiration of mankind through the ages." He grasps her wrists, stares into her eyes and envelopes her. Terrified, Charlotte beats him in the face, and watches in horror as his mask cracks to reveal a terribly disfigured countenance below. This is what really happened to Igor in the London fire. Charlotte exclaims, "You fiend!" Igor explains, "For twelve years, twelve awful years, this terrible living dead man with his burnt hands and face has searched for this fiend [who caused the fire in the first place]. Now the account is closed!" He rushes over to a coffin, opens it, and out falls the mummified figure of Joe Worth (Edwin Maxwell), his former patron, who burned down the London museum to obtain the insurance money. The scene ends predictably, with Igor placing the prostrate Charlotte over a vat of hot wax, but eventually falling into it himself as Jim rescues her.

The entire scene shows Atwill at his vocal best; the phrase "twelve *awful* years" is delivered with a major stress on the word "awful," as he stares first at Charlotte and then at Worth's coffin. Atwill was never a naturalistic actor, but rather a master of facial expressions. This unique physiognomy enabled him to play the kind of characters who appeared outwardly pleasant, but whose polite exterior concealed evil desires. In Terry O. Morse's *Fog Island* (1945), Atwill's Alec Ritchfield partakes liberally of the hospitality offered by his host Leo Granger (GEORGE ZUCCO), drinking sherry and offering toasts where appropriate. However this is nothing more than a façade: Ritchfield eventually drugs Granger and buries him alive in a grave in the family vault. Atwill's popularity as a villain was so great with audiences, especially in the 1930s, that he rivaled Bela Lugosi and Boris Karloff for popularity.

In 1933, Atwill played another villainous role as Eric Gorman in Paramount's *Murders in the Zoo*. The familiar elements of the Atwill screen image are there: an outwardly polite personality concealing a bestial nature — at the beginning of the film he sews up Taylor's (Edward Pawley) mouth and leaves the unfortunate victim to die in the jungle. In another sequence, Gorman sidles up to his wife Evelyn (Kathleen Burke) and clasps her to his chest, as if he were a snake crushing its victim, protesting all the while that he loves her. In the climactic fight with the clean-cut hero Dr. Jack Woodford (Randolph Scott), Gorman crouches in front of his intended victim, his shadow projected on the back wall, giving him the appearance of a predatory animal. Although Gorman emerges the winner—as he injects his opponent with poison taken from a mamba snake—he subsequently meets a violent, yet particularly appropriate fate as that same snake asphyxiates him to death.

Sometimes Atwill branched out to play good characters—for example, Inspector Neumann in Tod Browning's *Mark of the Vampire* (1935) for MGM. Atwill's movements resemble those of a drill sergeant, either holding his hands down by his side or clasping them behind his back in a meditative way. It is clear that he does not believe the claims—made by many villagers—that a vampire haunts the house of Sir Karell Bolotyn (HOLMES HERBERT). Neumann becomes more and more exasperated, as his attempts to solve Bolotyn's murder seem to go nowhere. But once Professor Zelen (Lionel Barrymore) intervenes with a foolproof plan to explode the vampire myth and reveal Bolotyn's true killer, Neumann is happy to play along. He proves extremely effective at playing an outraged police officer claiming that his valuable time has been wasted.

By 1941, Atwill's star image had waned somewhat, but he was still capable of creating memorable roles, such as the mad scientist Dr. Paul Rigas in George Waggner's Universal horror flick *Man Made Monster*. Preoccupied with the idea of transforming accident victim Dan McCormick (Lon Chaney, Jr.) into an *übermensch* by injecting him with massive doses of electricity, Rigas rubs his hands together, clenches his fists and brags about the potential to "revolutionize the world" through his experiments. With his long white coat and huge goggles concealing most of his features, he appears to lack any shred of humanity—a pointed reminder to audiences of how destructive scientific research can be. Atwill thoroughly enjoys himself in the role—at one point he catches the heroine June Lawrence (Anne Nagel) rifling through his notes in an attempt to discover what has happened to McCormick. He advances towards her, his features breaking into a malicious grin as he suggests that women are far more suitable objects for experiments than men. He ties her to his operating table, and is just about to send an electric current through her when McCormick rescues her in the nick of time. Atwill used the same oleaginous grin as Professor Moriarty in *Sherlock Holmes and the Secret Weapon* (1943), particularly when he believed that he had at last outwitted Sherlock Holmes (Basil Rathbone).

Atwill repeated the role of a police inspector (this time called Arnz) in *House of Frankenstein* (1944), where he doubts that vampires like Count Dracula (JOHN CARRADINE) actually exist. Needless to say, Arnz is proved wrong, as the Count is brought to life once again by the mad scientist Professor Niemann (Boris Karloff). Atwill repeated the role for a third time in *House of Dracula* (1945), where his military bearing and gruff manners contrasts starkly with Count Dracula's (JOHN CARRADINE) more polished appearance.

Sometimes Atwill played the role of a fall guy, as in *Night Monster* (1942), where his Dr. King insists that only medical science can cure patients; anyone who believes otherwise is simply fantasizing. He emphasizes the point with frequent waves of the hand, and subsequently grasping the lapels of his suit while pausing for breath. We know that he will end up a victim of once-paralyzed killer Kurt Ingston (Ralph Morgan), who has been convinced by Hindu mystic Agor Singh (Nils Asther) that his legs will grow once more if he wills it hard enough. Our suspicions prove correct as King is brutally strangled to death in his bedroom. Atwill died two years later while playing another villainous role in the film *Genius at Work* (he was called "The Cobra"). His contribution to horror films was never particularly innovative or of great historical importance, but his stage-trained speaking voice and imposing presence added an element of legitimacy to many films which otherwise might have seemed nothing more than B-pictures.

Mischa Auer

*b. November 17, 1905, St. Petersburg, Russia;
d. March 5, 1967, Rome, Italy.*

Born Mischa Ounskowsky, the grandson of violinist Leopold Auer, whose name he took when he made his stage debut in the United States during the 1920s. Auer was born to a bourgeois family, the son of an army officer, but after the 1917 Russian Revolution he fled to Turkey with his mother. Sadly, she died not long afterwards, and Auer went to join his grandfather in New York. As an actor/musician, he made his Broadway debut in 1925, and performed with such luminaries as Walter Hampden and Eva la Gallienne.

Auer made his film debut in 1928, and soon developed a reputation for playing character roles. In the science fiction musical *Just Imagine* (1930), he plays B-36, the sidekick of servant Z-4 (Hobart Bosworth). Set in New York of 1980, director David Butler imagines a world in which numbers have replaced names, test tube babies are the norm, and all marriages are arranged by the government. As a result of a court case, J-21 (John Garrick) has been denied the right to marry his fiancée D6 (Marjorie White). He walks alone, contemplating possible suicide, when B-36 comes up to him and offers to give him (J-21) his heart's desire, in a pronounced mid–European accent. Although B-36 looks slightly sinister in his black make-up and all-black costume, J-21 agrees to the suggestion. He is eventually taken to Z-4's laboratory, where he is offered the chance of joining the crew of an expedition to Mars.

Unlike many science fiction films of similar theme that appeared in the mid–to late–1950s, *Just Imagine* offers an optimistic interpretation of space travel; as a result of this expedition, J-21 and his buddy RT-42 (Frank Albertson) will consolidate America's position as a world leader in scientific research. B-36 has been lured away from Europe in pursuit of this objective; his enthusiasm for his work is evident in the way he ensures that all the equipment operates properly prior to take-off.

Once the girlfriends of RT-42 and J-21, LN-18 (Maureen O'Sullivan) and D-6 (Marjorie

Mischa Auer publicity still (1937). Tall, handsome Russian-born actor, who could play comic and evil roles with equal ability. His highly accented English made him an ideal figure for playing "foreign" roles.

White), learn that their respective partners will return home safely, they run about the laboratory in joy, flicking switches and turning on lights, much to B-36's alarm. LN-16 jumps into B-36's arms and kisses him; B-36 just looks terrified. Although perfectly at home with scientific equipment, he is obviously unused to female company—especially the kind of women who wear their emotions on their sleeves.

In *The Monster Walks* (1932), Auer has a more sinister role as Hanns Krug, the longtime retainer at the Earlton household. His late employer, a doctor who keeps an ape for his medical studies, has left Krug and his mother Emma (Martha Mattox) very little in his will; as a result Hanns dislikes every member of the Earlton household. He delivers his lines in a slow, deliberate manner ("There's ... someone ... coming ... now"), accompanied by an expression of pure contempt. He moves silently around the room in an ape-like manner, his hands down by his side. Director Frank R. Strayer obviously finds Krug an intriguing personality, as he repeatedly cuts to close-ups of his scowling face.

The link between Krug and the ape is repeatedly stressed: the servant is shown standing beside the cage, leaning his head on the bars, while everyone around him flees in terror. Eventually we learn why Krug has become so resentful; he is actually Robert Earlton's (Sheldon Lewis) illegitimate son, who has been ordered by Robert to kill all the remaining members of the family, so that Robert can inherit the late doctor's wealth. Krug's plans go horribly wrong; instead of killing Ruth Earlton (Vera Reynolds), he accidentally kills his mother instead. Krug sinks to the floor and weeps uncontrollably; she was the sole source of stability for him in an increasingly unpleasant household. From then on, Krug is almost uncontrollable; he calls Robert "a shrunken devil!" and storms out of the room. Although he tries to kill Ruth once more, Krug no longer seems capable of the task. He carries her down to the ape's cage, but gets too close to the bars; the ape strangles him to death. In view of the sufferings he has experienced, this becomes something of a merciful release for him.

Auer has a lip-smacking role as the villain Henry in his next film, the independently made *Murder at Dawn* (1932). In his black cape, top hat and slight stoop, he cuts an imposing presence as he ties up Dr. Farington (Frank Ball) and threatens him with a grisly punishment unless the doctor writes down the formula for a new form of electricity. He corners the doctor in a small garret room, stares into his eyes and hisses, "There's a way of making you talk!" He runs downstairs, drugs the doctor's daughter, Doris (Josephine Dunn), and places her lifeless body in a chair opposite the doctor. He then wires her up so that once the dawn breaks she will be frazzled to death unless her father talks. As he works, he cackles, "All you have to do is to move your fingers ... just a little bit! [...] Surely your daughter is well worth saving ... isn't she? [...] You will write that formula, or DIE!!" Each phrase is delivered in slow, menacing tones with a deliberate crescendo at the end. Predictably Henry's plans go awry, as the doctor and his daughter are rescued in the nick of time; Henry leaves the garret room and runs across the castle parapet, looking like a large black vulture in the half-light of dawn. Eventually he loses his footing and plunges to a grisly death.

As Peter, the sidekick of mad doctor Boris Karlov (Warner Oland) in *Drums of Jeopardy* (1931), Auer casts an imposing presence, his tall, angular figure towering over the other characters. Director George B. Seitz seems fascinated by Auer's presence, as he cuts to frequent close-ups of the actor looking shiftily to the left of the camera, a spotlight shining on the lens of his small metal spectacles. Peter does not have much to say; he is a man of action rather than words, as he captures various members of the Petrov family and drags them in front of his master. Karlov wants to take revenge on the Petrovs, in the belief that they have been responsible for his daughter Anya's (Florence Lake) death. Peter's main role is to ensure that Karlov accomplishes his task: the servant clearly enjoys his work, as he is shown smiling slightly whenever Karlov interrogates one of his unfortunate victims. Eventually Peter is gunned down in a climatic confrontation with the forces of law, led by Martin Kent (Hale Hamilton).

Three years later, Auer had another notable cameo as Zan, the hunchback servant of Professor Paul Kristan (Ralph Morgan) in Frank R. Strayer's *Condemned to Life* (1935). He remains devoted to his master, even though he knows the professor's guilty secret; his mother has been attacked by a vampire while pregnant, and thus the professor himself has become a vampire. Zan decides to throw the professor's pursuers off the scent by running away, in the belief that the pursuers will chase him instead. They duly oblige; and eventually corner Zan in the depths of a dark cave. Zan crouches in fear as the people discuss various means of disposing of him, including lynching and hanging. Zan is only saved in the nick of time by the professor, who emerges from the mob, puts his arms round his servant and admits in sonorous tones that Zan "tried to save me ... from myself!" taking a long pause in between the two phrases. The professor then throws himself over a cliff, closely followed by his servant who screams "Master! Master!" as he does so.

Sometimes Auer's roles in horror/fantasy

films were overtly comic — even if they were not conceived as such. This is certainly the case in the early serial *King of the Wild* (1931), where he plays Prince Dakka, a member of one of Africa's aristocratic families. Ludicrously costumed in dark make-up and mustache, Dakka proves an eminently hissable villain as he stretches his hands out towards the all–American hero Robert Grant (Walter Miller), and tells him to return to his own country. Needless to say, Grant takes no notice, so Dakka responds by clasping his hands to his heart and proclaims that none of his people will lift a finger to help Grant in his quest to discover a fabulous diamond field. Dakka proves proficient with a sword and a knife; in one sequence he disposes of one of his enemies by stabbing him in the back, proclaiming as he does so, "You [the foreigner] have much to learn about instinct." The fact that Dakka prefers to stab in the back, rather than encounter an opponent in face-to-face combat, sums up his devilish nature.

Auer takes on a more consciously comic role as the waiter Gregory in the Abbott and Costello horror film spoof *Hold That Ghost* (1941). Immaculately dressed in dinner suit and bowtie, he observes the two protagonists with an expression of intense contempt as they repeatedly fail to carry out his instructions as to how to serve properly at the dinner table. By contrast, Gregory seems born to the role, with his aristocratic bearing and fastidious manners, carrying a menu in one hand and escorting guests to their respective tables with the other. As with all their vehicles, Abbott and Costello emerge triumphant, in spite of everything; they get their revenge on Gregory as they open a restaurant/nightclub of their own and engage him as head waiter. Despite his obvious discomfort, Auer's Gregory maintains his demeanor, bowing gracefully and exiting out of shot. The actor's aristocratic origins proved useful.

Turhan Bey
b. March 30, 1922, Vienna, Austria.

Born Turhan Gilbert Selahattin Sahultavy to a Turkish father and Czech mother. Because of his looks, he proved ideal for mysterious or villainous roles in horror films or fantasy sci-fi pictures. In *The Mummy's Tomb* (1942), he plays Mehemet Bey, the young protégé of Andoheb (GEORGE ZUCCO) who is sent to America with the mummy (Lon Chaney, Jr.) to wreak revenge on those who "violated" the Egyptians' tomb in *The Mummy's Hand* (1940), including Steve Banning (DICK FORAN) and his sidekick Babe Hanson (WALLACE FORD). Mehemet begins by delivering his lines expressionlessly, swearing devotion to his "dear one"—i.e., the mummy Kharis—and shunning any other company. He objects strongly to the presence of "occidentals"—in other words, Americans—around him, which helps to explain why he takes a job in a cemetery, once he settles in the New England town of Mapleton. With his trilby hat tilted at a rakish angle, and

Lynn Bari and Turhan Bey in *The Amazing Mr. X* (1948). Clean-cut leading man with impeccable English, Turhan Bey was actually born in Austria of Turkish and Czech parentage.

his impeccably tailored suit, he looks every inch a gentleman, but director Harold Young is also keen to orientalize him. Each night he sits by the mummy's coffin and invokes divine assistance for his quest: "The moon rises high in the sky, Kharis, There is death in the night air. Your work begins." As he speaks, he looks heavenwards; in the darkness we can hardly see anything of his face except for the whites of his eyes. This gives him a devilish air, which the film suggests is characteristic of the Egyptians.

However Mehemet's reactions begin to change, after having witnessed John Banning (John Hubbard) kissing his girlfriend Isobel Evans (Elyse Knox). Mehemet stares at the two of them embracing, and then prays to the gods to help him "resist any temptation." Unfortunately, they do not respond, and Mehemet is further stimulated when he sees the two lovers kissing once again. Director Harold Young emphasizes the erotic effect this has on the Egyptian's psyche through a series of dissolves showing Mehemet with his arms folded, and Isabel smiling direct to camera. Mehemet resolves to marry Isabel against her will; consequently he has her brought to his graveyard lair and offers her the chance "to achieve the greatest honor that can come to a woman"— to become the bride of a Priest of Karnak. The film contrasts such unscrupulousness with the impeccable behavior of the American John Hubbard, who wants to marry Isobel on the spur of the moment, prior to taking up a commission in the U.S. Army during the Second World War. According to the film's orientalist logic, Mehemet receives his just deserts— although he claims he will become immortal, once he has married Isabel, he is killed by a bullet fired from the Sheriff's (Cliff Clark) gun.

Arthur Lubin's version of *Ali Baba and the Forty Thieves* (also 1942) has Turhan playing another exotic role as Jamiel, a handsome second male lead with a cut-glass English accent who shows a slavish devotion to his mistress Amara (Maria Montez). In several sequences he is shown staring doe-eyed at her, as if bewitched by her beauty. On the other hand, Jamiel understands the importance of freedom — as the action progresses, he leaves Amara's side and joins Ali Baba (JON HALL) in the fight to liberate Bagdad from the evil Hugalu Khan (Kurt Katch). Bey proves himself expert with a sword, and eventually signals the final victory by throwing open the city gates. In the sequel *Arabian Nights* (1944), Turhan plays the Captain of the Guard, who does not have to do much other than to sit straight-backed on a horse and carry out the wishes of his evil master Nadan (Edgar Barrier). He does, however, have fun with one line, delivered through clenched teeth to the film's hero Haroun Al-Raschid (JON HALL): "We are sending you ... [where] not even Allah himself could find you!"

Sometimes Turhan challenged his screen stereotype by playing more sympathetic roles. In *The Mad Ghoul* (1943), he plays accompanist Eric Iverson who falls in love with singer Isabel Lewis (EVELYN ANKERS). With his aristocratic bearing and courtly manners, he seems an ideal marriage partner — even though hard-boiled police sergeant Macklin (Milburn Stone) suspects him of being homosexual. There is no justification for this, apart from the fact that the sergeant suspects musically-inclined people on the basis that their profession is not "masculine" enough. However, Eric gets the last laugh — despite two attempts made on his life by mad scientist Alfred Morris (GEORGE ZUCCO), the pianist eventually fulfills his romantic ambitions with Isabel. Turhan has a similar role as Franz Munzer in George Waggner's Technicolor version of *The Climax* (1944). With his pink, round face, small mustache and elegant air, Munzer certainly looks the part, as he hugs his fiancée Angela Klatt (Susanna Foster) and offers her both physical and emotional support where necessary. He plays the piano for her, gives her last-minute directions before she makes her debut as a prima donna, and sits in the orchestra pit gazing fondly into her eyes as she accomplishes the feat of performing in the operetta *The Magic Voice*, which hitherto had been cursed with the memory of the death of Marcellina (June Vincent), the soprano who ten years previously had essayed the leading role and been strangled to death by the mad doctor Friedrich Hohner (Boris Karloff).

Munzer is not, however, quite the romantic he pretends to be. He seeks to control every aspect of Angela's life — invading her dressing-room (although not formally invited), shadowing her every move, and pushing her around if she seems reluctant to implement his wishes. Although the couple frequently embraces, it is always Munzer who grabs hold of Angela, as if believing that if he did not do so, she might run away from him. Munzer's personality is also established through repeated close-ups as he watches Angela performing on stage while holding his concert program up to his face. Eventually the strain becomes too much for him, as he begins to chew pieces out of the program. While Turhan plays this sequence for laughs— especially at the end, when he spits out some half-digested paper and looks sheepishly at his fellow audience members— it nonetheless is clear that Munzer is as much of an obsessive as Hohner. As he observes later on in the film, Munzer wants his fiancée to think of nothing but her future life with him while singing in *The Magic Voice*.

In the uncredited role of the narrator at the end of *Captive Wild Woman* (1943), Turhan warns viewers of the potential threat "of a mortal who went beyond the realm of human powers and tampered with things that no one should even touch." This observation could equally well apply to Munzer — Angela should beware of remaining too long with someone with an inhuman, almost unhealthy interest in her.

Turhan enjoyed his most substantial role in a horror film in *The Amazing Mr. X* (1948), where he plays Alexis, a bogus fortune teller committed to depriving rich, gullible young women of their money. Initially he comes across as someone with a cut-glass British accent, who glides rather than moves— the epitome of a cultured person. The only indication we have that Alexis might not be what he seems is an occasional close-up of his face swathed in darkness except for a light shining directly into his eyes. This is an important aspect of his character, for it is principally through the gaze that he seeks to establish mastery over his clients, either by staring them directly in the face or observing them through one of the many secret panels scattered around his lonely house. *The Amazing Mr. X* is a fantasy of patriarchal power, as revealed through Alexis' apparent ability to predict the future.

But Alexis undergoes a change of character, due in no small part to the fact that he falls in love with Janet Burke (Cathy O'Donnell), one of his clients, and subsequently strives to save her and her sister Christine (Lynn Bari) from being killed by Christine's husband Paul (Donald Curtis). Director Bernard Vorhaus employs repeated close-ups of Turhan's face contorted in desperation, repeatedly clasping and unclasping his hands as he pursues Paul in a valiant attempt to grab his shotgun. Sadly the struggle proves futile, as Alexis is shot in the stomach and dies. In terms of the morality-scheme recommended by the Hays Office, he needs to be punished for pretending to be a medium to extort money from his victims. He does, however, have the chance to acknowledge just before his demise that the experience of loving Janet has helped him discover "a better side to his nature" that hitherto had remained dormant. The entire scene is shot in soft-focus, suggesting that Alexis has been transformed from villain into hero. The role incorporates the contradictory aspects of Turhan's screen image — he is both the smooth-talking villain with unlimited sex appeal and the elegant romantic hero. The romantic side to Turhan's image was also evident off-screen, as he was linked to Merle Oberon and Ava Gardner (amongst others).

Paul Birch

b. January 13, 1912, Atmore, Alabama;
d. May 24, 1969, St. George, Grenada.

Born Paul Smith in Atmore, Alabama, Birch entered motion pictures in small roles in westerns in the late 1940s and early 1950s. Although later making his name in television and the theatre (he was the original "Marlboro Man" in television commercials), Birch is perhaps best known for the series of roles he played in horror films during the mid–1950s.

In *The War of the Worlds* (1953), he has an

uncredited role as Alonzo Hogue, an inhabitant of a small California town, who confidently believes that the Martian invaders pose little or no threat to the security of his community. As he moves closer towards them, however, his attitude changes: Byron Haskin's camera zooms in on Hogue's panic-stricken face as he realizes just how dangerous they might be. On the soundtrack we can hear the strains of music coming from a square dance held in the barn nearby. One of his friends ironically remarks, "Welcome to California." Hogue moves closer, and is incinerated to death by a ray-gun fired by one of the invaders.

In *The Beast with a Million Eyes* (1955), he plays Allan Kelley, a rancher living in the California desert who cannot keep control of his family despite his best efforts. His wife Carol (Lorna Thayer) complains that he neglects her, while daughter Sandy (Dona Cole) feels that Carol no longer wants her. As the film unfolds, Allan understands how his domestic situation provides "the perfect place to hatch a brood of horror, or of hate [...] [a] growing twisting thing that's slowly destroying us." His entire way of life is threatened by an extra-terrestrial that seeks to control people's minds; the only way it can be repelled is for Kelley's family to overcome their various differences and work together. David Kramarsky's film suggests that the nuclear family provides the best protection against invasion, whether mental or physical: Allan observes at one point that "together we can defeat it [the creature]. If we fight it together, we'll win." Those who remain single, or who have experienced some kind of mental trauma, remain vulnerable to indoctrination: "Him" (aka Carl) (Leonard Tarver) is attacked by the creature and transformed from a mute into a ruthless killer. By contrast Allan, Carol and Sandy learn that "each of us [within the family] is bound to each other." For the family to survive, however, it is necessary that the various members understand their specific roles: Allan is the breadwinner going out each day to tend the ranch, while Carol remains the homemaker looking after the house and her children. Sandy likewise understands her future role within the family unit, once she has married boyfriend Larry Brewster (Richard Sargeant).

In Roger Corman's *The Day the World Ended* (1955), Birch plays another rancher, Jim Maddison, who takes charge of a motley band of individuals, including geologist Rick (RICHARD

Paul Birch in *Not of This Earth* (1957). With his imposing presence and cheerful, avuncular personality, Birch made a reputation playing benevolent characters in science fiction films of the 1950s. He also made a convincing bad guy.

DENNING), mobster Tony Lamont (Touch Connors), and Lamont's girlfriend Ruby (Adele Jurgens). All of them are the sole survivors of a nuclear holocaust, which has destroyed the world and its people. Maddison makes a competent leader; director Roger Corman cuts to a close-up of his face set in an expression of grim determination as he proclaims, "We might live ... we might just live." To do so, however, requires a certain degree of native cunning; in this world there is "no such thing as logic anymore." Maddison tries to lead by example, but Tony in particular will have none of it. Maddison initially responds with an indulgent smile — as if treating Tony like a small child — but his attitude soon changes; rather than delegating duties to others, he decides to undertake them himself. Maddison ventures outside the house to look for a mutant creature that threatens the mortals' future, and by doing so breathes in a fatal dose of atomic gas. No longer able to lead the group, he delegates responsibility to Rick. Maddison is a well-meaning person, whose main flaw lies in his inability to manage his subordinates effectively.

In Corman's *Not of this Earth* (1957), Birch has a completely different role as Paul Johnson, an alien from outer space who speaks tonelessly and deliberately. With his black suit, trilby hat and dark glasses, he looks like a representative of the mafia, were it not for his eyes, which are almost completely opaque. They are also extremely powerful: one glance from them can reduce everyone to a catatonic state. Throughout the film Johnson remains impassive: most of his lines are delivered in voiceover, suggesting that he is subject to the whims of an unearthly force. When he does need to impose his will, however, Johnson's features assume a steely look and his voice declines to a whisper. When Nurse Nadine Storey (BEVERLY GARLAND) comes to stay at his house, she quite naturally objects to being locked in her bedroom; Johnson looks her and replies in measured tones, "No person [in my planet] would dare ... sleep ... in insecure ... quarters." He takes slow measured pauses between the last four words for emphasis: no one who believes in self-preservation should dare oppose him. Sometimes Johnson does not even have to speak; a glance in his servant Jeremy's (JONATHAN HAZE) direction is sufficient to ensure complete obedience. Director Corman understands how a dictator's mind works: Johnson has no need to shout, but rather employs minimal gestures to reinforce his authority.

In the end, Johnson overreaches himself, as he pursues Nadine in a lengthy chase sequence, as he tells her in voiceover that any resistance to him is futile. He becomes so obsessed with catching her that he eventually dies in a car crash, thereby proving that aliens are as likely to die prematurely as human beings. The film ends with a close-up of the inscription on his headstone: "Here lies a man who was not of this earth"— a consciously ambiguous phrase paying tribute to Johnson's exceptional powers.

A year later, Birch played the owlish Professor Konrad in Allied Artists' cult classic *Queen from Outer Space*. In his brown dungarees—contrasting with the gray outfits of his fellow crew members— he stands apart as an expert, confident that his scientific knowledge will help the forthcoming expedition to space to be a success. He leans nonchalantly against a desk and draws attention to the spacecraft's most salient features. But his assurance proves misplaced, as the aircraft spins out of control and lands on Venus. The professor's expression becomes more and more perturbed, as he understands his inability to take control of a rapidly worsening situation. For the remainder of the film he takes a largely passive role, as the crew suffers at the hands of the cruel Queen Yilana (Laurie Mitchell), who hates men, and plans to destroy the Earth. The only way they can overcome her is to enlist the help of some friendly Venusians, including Talleah (Zsa Zsa Gabor) and try and outwit the Queen. Chastened by his experiences in space, the professor largely does what he is told — even though he understands that Yilana's missile (with which she hopes to destroy Earth) is not powerful enough to work successfully. The professor's judgment proves correct: the missile fails to operate, and Yilana is duly captured by the "good" Venusians. The professor is rewarded for his efforts; in the film's final sequence he is shown surrounded with three nubile young women, two of them kissing his cheeks, and the third standing behind him with a beatific smile on her face. He learns that he will not be able to return to Earth for at least a year; this news delights him (as well as his fellow crew members), as they understand that they can spend their time enjoying the pleasures offered by the Venusian women.

In Columbia's *The 27th Day* (1957), Birch has a small role as an admiral who coordinates a nuclear test designed to find out exactly what it is that the capsules (which have been given to five individuals from five different nations by an alien) contain. The test proves inconclusive; it is left to Professor Klaus Bechner (George Voskovec) to discover that only the five individuals concerned have the power to launch the capsules to whatever coordinates they choose. If they do so, then all humankind will be destroyed within a 3,000-mile radius of each capsule's location. In the end, none of the individuals actually do anything. The capsules are opened but do not cause harm, and the future of humankind is assured, so long as governments are prepared to talk to one another. Despite his authoritative presence as he coordinates the test, Birch's admiral turns out to be largely redundant in a world dominated by the threat of extinction.

Whit Bissell

b. October 25, 1909, New York City;
d. March 5, 1996, Woodland Hills, Los Angeles, California.

Born Whitner Nutting Bissell, he began his Hollywood career in the early 1940s, and for the next three decades carved out a career as a reliable character in a variety of films, particularly horror and science fiction. He specialized in playing doctors, military people, or ordinary down-to-earth personalities trying to eke out an existence under adverse circumstances. In *Brute Force* (1947), he plays Tom Lister, a "good" prisoner fond of reading books, who is unlikely to cause any trouble. However, this renders him easy prey for the sadistic Captain Munsey (Hume Cronyn), who pushes him aside in an open display of power. Lister remains terribly lonely in prison — at one point we see him staring wistfully out of the barred window while writing a letter, then turning towards the cutting of the pin-up girl on the wall. Director Jules Dassin dissolves to a shot of Lister's wife Cora (Ella Raines) living in a miserable room, sewing to pass the time. However, Lister's concern for his wife renders him ripe for exploitation: Munsey offers him privileges if he will inform on his fellow prisoners' movements; when Lister refuses, Munsey deliberately fabricates a story about Cora's infidelity. Lister stares at the warden in disbelief, buries his head in his hands and turns away. Soon afterwards he hangs himself in his cell. The implication is obvious: in the dog-eat-dog world of the penitentiary, the good guys never prosper.

Seven years later, in *Target Earth*, Bissell played intrepid scientist Tom, who remains dedicated to the task of exterminating the robots, which have reduced the city of Chicago to a ghost town. He vows to do "everything [he] can," and proves the truth of this statement by spending much of his time hunched over a console, or conducting various experiments to see

Whit Bissell in *The Time Tunnel* (1967). Although confined to playing officials, generals and other figures of authority, Bissell had a great time playing a bad guy in *I was a Teenage Frankenstein* (1958).

whether the robots have any weak spots. When General Wood (Arthur Space) asks him how things are going, Tom gives a thorough explanation accompanied by practical demonstrations; the general nods approvingly as he listens. In the same year (1954), Bissell played another scientist — Edwin Thompson — in *Creature from the Black Lagoon*. His role remains largely choric; a loyal member of the crew trying to investigate the life of the eponymous creature (Ricou Browning/Ben Chapman). Thompson finds the experience of entering "another world" of the underwater rather difficult; at first he is unwilling to believe that the creature actually exists, observing rather cynically that "for a merman he [the creature] takes a fine picture," when marine archeologist David Reed (RICHARD CARLSON) tries and fails to take a photograph of the creature. Later on he taunts Reed's colleague Mark Williams (RICHARD DENNING): "Demon, eh? No more far-fetched than your Gill-Man!" Eventually, Thompson's doubts prove unfounded, as the creature is captured and he is put on guard. He sits lazily in his chair, smoking a pipe, a gun in his hand, but eventually dozes off. Later on, he wakes up and talks to Reed's girlfriend Kay Lawrence (Julia Adams), without realizing that the creature has escaped. Thompson's negligence has disastrous results, as the creature attacks him and leaves his face horribly disfigured. Confined to bed for the rest of the voyage, Thompson is assaulted once more by the creature, whose webbed foot comes through the porthole and grabs him by the throat. The unfortunate scientist is only rescued from a grisly end by Reed's timely intervention. In an unknown or unfamiliar world, Thompson's skepticism leads to complacency, rendering both himself and his crew members liable to unexpected attack. In Jack Arnold's *Monster on the Campus* (1958), Bissell played another skeptic — Dr. Oliver Cole, a faculty member of the science department at the fictional Dunsford University, who remains perpetually suspicious of his colleague Professor Donald Blake's (ARTHUR FRANZ) research. Blake claims to have discovered how human beings can regress into an ape-like state, something "as improbable as life itself," as Blake himself observes. Cole dismisses Blake's conclusions out of hand, and advises the professor not to "encourage such nonsense." Due to professional negligence, Blake is eventually exposed to gamma rays that transform him from a mild-mannered academic into a bloodthirsty monster. Such unexpected consequences vindicate Cole's skepticism: sometimes it is best to curtail scientific research rather than uncover "the monster that dwells within [all of] us."

In 1957, Bissell played two similar villains in AIP's *I Was a Teenage Frankenstein* and *I Was a Teenage Werewolf*. As Professor Frankenstein, he initially comes across as a respectable person, immaculately tailored in a gray business suit with his hair parted at the side. But we soon understand that he is also an obsessive; he takes little notice of his fiancée, Margaret (Phyllis Coates), at dinner, and later on asks her to leave him alone in his study all night so that he can write up his research notes.

Frankenstein appears devoid of human emotion — even when cutting off the limbs of corpses, his face remains impassive, unlike his assistant, Dr. Karlton (Robert Burton), who visibly winces at the grisly sight in front of him.

Once the monster (Gary Conway) has been created, Frankenstein expects nothing less than total devotion. He expects to be called "sir," and makes the monster learn excerpts from the Old Testament about what happens to those who disobey their masters. At the same time, Frankenstein is very proud of his creation, which he described as "a wunderkind created by me, a teenage marvel!" When Margaret asks too many questions about his experiments, Frankenstein arranges for the monster to strangle her to death. This act of wanton cruelty renders his observation that he has "brought mankind one step further in the eternal battle against death" painfully ironic.

Needless to say, Frankenstein pays the ultimate price for his crimes, as the monster strangles him to death in the belief that the professor is about to cause him more pain. The film's violent ending makes it clear that teenagers can neither be created nor controlled by adults; they need to develop on their own.

In *I Was a Teenage Werewolf*, however, the

central character Tony (Michael Landon) is clearly out of control. He comes from a one-parent family, and his father works at night, which leaves Tony with no role models. He eventually is sent for treatment at Dr. Alfred Brandon's (Bissell's) psychiatric clinic. As in *I Was a Teenage Frankenstein*, Bissell initially comes across as a reassuring, rather paternal figure — until we discover that he wants to hypnotize Tony in an attempt to discover humankind's primal instincts. By doing so, Brandon believes, he will draw upon "the world of exact science" to help people "start over again." As a consequence of Brandon's experiments, Tony is transformed into a werewolf.

The director of the film, Gene D. Fowler, Jr., uses Bissell's role to make several points about teenagers and parenthood. Tony places himself in the hands of the psychiatrist, a surrogate father incapable of showing human feelings, but choosing instead to "live by facts." Brandon himself believes that he has total control over Tony's destiny; at one point he claims that he is the teenager's "only link" to the civilized world. The film also suggests that psychoanalysis is potentially dangerous to the human psyche; rather than helping his patient, Brandon treats Tony as a guinea-pig to penetrate "the deepest secrets of creation" and thereby achieve "a perfect case of regression."

As in *I Was a Teenage Frankenstein*, Bissell's character pays dearly for his experiments as Tony turns on him and strangles him to death. Tony himself also has to die, so as to ensure the future health of society. As he dies, one character observes that it is "not for man to interfere in the ways of God." If teenagers like Tony are rebellious, they should be allowed to work out their problems for themselves, rather than seeking advice from psychoanalysts.

Lloyd Bridges
b. January 15, 1913, San Leandro, California; d. March 10, 1998, Los Angeles, California.

Lloyd Vernet Bridges, Jr., first turned to acting while studying at UCLA. He made his first film in 1936, and was placed under contract to Columbia Pictures five years later. Later in the decade he became a freelance actor, working in all types of film for different studios. In Universal's serial *Secret Agent X-9* (1945), based on a comic strip of the same name, Bridges plays Phil Corrigan, aka Secret Agent X-9, charged with the responsibility of preventing a formula for synthetic fuel from falling into Nazi hands. He comes across as an all-action hero, a master of disguise who is not frightened to deal with any difficulties that come his way. He disguises himself as a Nazi agent, so that he can enter the House of Shadows, presided over by Lucky Kamber (Cy Kendall), a wheeler-dealer whose loyalty depends on how much money he can extract from his associates. For Lucky, whatever happens during wartime is viewed as a "business," an opportunity for capitalists to make money — not out of commodities but by trading secrets. Corrigan understands this well, which is why we see him conspiratorially sharing information with the bartenders in the House of Shadows. At the same time, we understand that this is purely a means to an end: Corrigan will never trade secrets if this puts the lives of American soldiers at risk. He maintains his moral and ethical principles in an amoral and corrupt world.

Corrigan uses his physical presence to great advantage; while confronting his many enemies he stands with his legs slightly astride, his face illuminated in close-up, towering above his enemies. This is the kind of person whom no one — not least America's enemies — should trifle with. While Corrigan is adept at disguise, transforming himself readily from a Nazi into a naval rating with black T-shirt and pants, he is nonetheless secure of his own identity. His loyalty cannot be bought; at one point he likens the Nazis to automata, blindly following orders without considering the consequences, while he himself, as a patriotic American, will reflect on the best course of action to take. Directors Lewis D. Collins and Ray Taylor photograph him in close-up, his face remaining impassive as he takes on and vanquishes all his enemies. *Secret Agent X-9* is predictable hokum produced at the end of the Second World War, but nonetheless makes some significant points about the importance of main-

Lloyd Bridges in *Sea Hunt* (1958). Legendary square-jawed leading man, who made his name in his early career playing in science fiction and horror *noir* films.

taining integrity in a world peopled by spies and double agents, such as the so-called "Miss Australia" (Victoria Horne), who broadcasts Japanese propaganda to Australian audiences over the airwaves.

Bridges's next film, the sci-fi noir *Strange Confession* (1945), has him playing Dave Curtis, a research scientist involved in a project with Dr. Jeff Stone (Lon Chaney, Jr.) to discover a vaccine for a deadly influenza virus. Unlike Stone, whose life is plagued by guilt at leaving his wife Mary (Brenda Joyce) at home while he goes off on a research trip to South America, Curtis remains a practical down-to-earth type, determined to finish the work at the earliest possible opportunity. When Stone at last discovers the solution to the vaccine, Curtis does a little dance of joy, exclaiming: "He'll [Roger Graham, Stone's boss] make you a medal!" His role in the film is primarily to act as a source of moral support for Stone, helping him through his work, and offering sympathy when Stone discovers the real reason for his being sent away to South America (so that Graham [J. CARROL NAISH] can make love to Stone's wife). Stone exemplifies the virtues of male bonding as protection against adversity.

Five years later, Bridges played Col. Floyd Graham in Lippert Pictures' *Rocketship X-M*. As the pilot of the mission to explore the moon, he comes across initially as a confident personality, secure in the knowledge that he is the best person for the job. We frequently see him with his back to camera operating the ship's numerous control panels. When things start to go wrong on the voyage, Graham remains calm, taking deep breaths and quoting Kipling on one occasion.

While there is much to admire in his behavior, Graham remains determinedly old-fashioned in his attitudes towards gender; he resents the presence of a female astronaut on board ship, Dr. Lisa Van Horn (Osa Massen), believing that her proper place should be in the home. When Lisa proves herself the equal, if not better than her male colleagues, Graham tries a different strategy of control, as he looks out of the spaceship's window and sees the moon close by; this inspires him to conjure up a dream of a romantic evening where he and Lisa could sit together holding hands. *Rocketship X-M* offers an interestingly complementary view of gender to *Strange Confession*; while Bridges plays the same type of role in both films, it is clear that he is much happier in exclusively male company, rather than having to deal with a woman.

Bridges also played smaller roles in several mystery/horror films during the 1940s. In Frank Borzage's *Moonrise* (1948), he plays Jerry Sykes, the wealthy son of a bank manager who delights in taunting Danny Hawkins (Dane Clark) about his poverty, as well as the fact that Danny's father, a convicted murderer, died in the electric chair. With his white tuxedo and immaculately coiffed hair, Jerry looks the image of the all–American man. Danny comes from the other side of the social tracks; incensed at Jerry's incessant taunting, he fights with him in a lonely clearing close to the local dancehall. After a struggle, Danny batters Jerry to death — a fitting end, perhaps, for a young man with so little concern for his social inferiors.

Jean Brooks

b. December 23, 1915, Houston, Texas;
d. November 25, 1963, Richmond, California.

Born Ruby M. Kelly, Jean Brooks began her career as a professional singer with Enrico Madreguera's orchestra in New York. She made her début — using the name Jeanne Kelly — as Miss Gordon in *The Crime of Dr. Crespi* (1935). The role is a small one — all she is required to do is to sit behind a desk and look official while passing on the news to one patient that his wife has just given birth to quintuplets. Brooks is involved in one comic scene as she talks to her friend on the telephone late at night, complaining all the while that there is no excitement in the hospital. As she speaks, Stephen Ross (John Bohn), who has previously been pronounced dead, but who has in reality only been drugged by the evil Dr. Crespi (Erich von Stroheim), staggers into the hospital. Miss Gordon turns round, hearing him behind her, and screams, dropping the receiver as she does so.

Brooks has a far more substantial role as the nightclub singer Kiki Walker in *The Leopard Man* (1943). She enjoys the limelight to such an extent that she is prepared to take a leashed leopard into her club as a publicity gimmick to upstage her rival, the castanets virtuoso Clo-Clo (Margo). Angered by this strategy, Clo-Clo scares the animal and it bolts; in the days that follow, several young women are mauled to death and the police comb the countryside for the creature. In an atmosphere of mounting hysteria, Kiki maintains an admirable calm; while not performing, she is seen enjoying meals surrounded by men of various ages, including her manager Jerry Manning (Dennis O'Keefe). The only indication that she might be experiencing mental strain is in the way she fiddles with her handbag while speaking. Director Jacques Tourneur contrasts her character with those of the three young women who are mauled to death — Clo-Clo, the pretty girl Consuelo Contreras (Tula Parma), and the gold-digger Teresa Delgado (Margaret Landry). All of them are Latinas — passionate and amorous — and hence more at risk of attack, especially at night. By contrast, the all–American Kiki tries her best to sustain a façade of strength, as she swings her arms vigorously and insists on the importance of doing her job, even while other young women are perpetually at risk. In the end, the strain of putting on a public face proves too great for her, as she admits to Jerry that she wants to return home and pursue a life away from her career. As she speaks, a rustling is heard in the undergrowth behind her: Kiki responds by putting on her public face once again, as she draws herself up to her full height and announces her intention to face the world with renewed vigor. The desire for a life away from the limelight is but a temporary one.

Margo and Dennis O'Keefe in *The Leopard Man* (1943), also starring Jean Brooks. Tall actress with a memorable method of delivering her lines. She made her name in Val Lewton's RKO horror cycle of the 1940s.

In the end, Kiki agrees to act as a stooge, to help confirm her suspicions that the killer is not the leopard at all, but a member of the local community with unnatural sexual desires on women. She turns out to be right; the killer is revealed to be Galbraith, the curator of the local museum (James Bell), who is himself assassinated by Raoul (Richard Martin), Consuelo's boyfriend. The last we see of Kiki is when she embraces Jerry once more, while admitting that life had taught her "not to be soft." This trait proves particularly useful: whereas the Latino men and women allow superstition to dominate their lives, Kiki realizes that she alone is responsible for her own destiny. If she stands up and faces the world, then no one can push her around. To an extent, there is a price to be paid — a career woman cannot enjoy the pleasures of home and family — but she will never allow herself to be put off by the thought that something dangerous lurks just around the corner.

In a film that deals with the ways in which women are stalked and killed, Kiki is used to foreground the theme of responsibility. Like Kiki, Jerry admits that he had been brought up to be tough, hence his apparent lack of concern over the women's deaths. While this is an admirable quality, both Jerry and Kiki undergo a therapeutic process. They become better by learning to externalize their compassion. Kiki becomes something of a heroine by putting herself in the victims' places. Sitting on a bench in the cemetery where Consuelo once sat, she presents herself to Galbraith as another potential victim. The fact that she eludes him is testament to her basic strength of character.

Brooks has another major role as Jacqueline Gibson in *The Seventh Victim* (also 1943). As a fugitive woman trying to avoid the punishment of death imposed on her by her group of devil-worshipers, Brooks' characterization is a masterpiece of suppressed emotion. She tries to look concerned for her sister Mary (Kim Hunter), but her eyes look wildly around her, as if suspecting that someone is perpetually on her tail. She willingly accepts protection from the psychiatrist Louis Judd (TOM CONWAY), but cannot stay still in one place for any length of time. She is a bundle of nervous energy. Her most intense moment comes when she is in the devil-worshipers' den, surrounded by her fellow members, including hairdresser Frances (ISABEL JEWELL) whose intense stares encourage her to drink the vial of poison placed on the chair-arm in front of her. She refuses, even though the strain is clearly visible in her face. Jacqueline eventually escapes, as one of her fellow members breaks down and drinks the poison herself. However, this proves no form of release for her, as she runs wildly through the rain-washed New York streets, convinced that someone is out to kill her. She reaches eventually her apartment, but realizes that she will never be safe. The last image we see in the film is of her apartment door being opened, showing a noose and a chair lying on the ground. She has obviously taken her own life. She therefore fulfills the film's premise of being the seventh victim.

Raymond Burr

b. May 21, 1917, New Westminster, British Columbia, Canada;
d. September 12, 1993, Sonoma, California.

Burr moved to California while still a child. His first jobs ranged from a rancher to a deputy sheriff to a night club singer. He made his film debut in 1946 after having served in the American Navy. While fondly remembered for his television roles as Perry Mason and Ironside, Burr's early film career included numerous roles in science fiction and horror films. In RKO's anti-communist science fiction parable *The Whip Hand* (1951), he plays Steve Loomis, an outwardly affable hotel-owner who welcomes magazine journalist Matt Corbin (Elliott Reid) with a slap on the back and a ready smile. But this is nothing more than an act: we discover that Loomis is actually a communist agent working for mastermind Peterson (Lewis Martin) and disaffected scientist Wilhelm Bucholtz (Otto Waldis) to instigate germ warfare in the heartland of the United States. Loomis's ruthlessness is suggested by the way his eyes glint at Corbin as the journalist walks upstairs to his room. On another occasion, the hotel owner enters Corbin's room unannounced, and put a paternal arm round his shoulder as Corbin types out an article. Corbin looks up fearfully and immediately covers up the paper in the typewriter roll, as if fearful of what might happen next. Loomis smiles and leaves the room without a word. In the end, Loomis's violent nature comes to the surface, as he prevents Corbin escaping from the hotel and its environs; he grasps the journalist in a headlock and bundles him into a truck, exclaiming ("Welcome back, Corbin!") as he does so. Although Loomis is eliminated at the end, as the hotel is stormed by U.S. government agents, his presence lingers on: in a moralizing coda to the film, Corbin warns viewers not to trust anyone, especially those strangers who appear overwelcoming in attitude.

In the independently-made *Bride of the Gorilla* (1951), Burr plays the heavy Barney Chavez, a barrel-chested hulk with scant regard for his employer Klaas van Gelder (PAUL CAVANAGH). With his smoldering eyes and tanned physique, he is almost irresistibly attracted to women; in this film he can choose between Klaas's wife Dina (Barbara Payton) and the native girl Al-long (Gisela Werbisek). Sadly Chavez makes the wrong choice, as he murders Klaas and marries Dina soon afterwards. According to the law of the jungle, Barney has committed a cardinal sin and must be punished for it, in the form of a curse placed on him by the old retainer Larina (Carol Varga). The curse has destructive effects as Barney is transformed into a gorilla; while this gives him superhuman powers (for example, identifying enemies at long distances), it also renders him liable to periods of doubt and insecurity. As the film progresses, Chavez is gradually transformed from a dominant personality into a gibbering wreck, tormented by guilt and fear as what he has become. His style of dress changes; whereas he once looked immaculate in short-sleeved shirt and pants, he wears the same sweat-soaked clothes day after day, so that he can easily tear them off while being transformed into a gorilla. The end of the film comes as a form of merciful release, as Chavez dies and the curse is correspondingly removed. As he does so, while lying prostrate on the jungle floor, his face immediately becomes youthful once again—clearly he has paid for his sins.

Three years later, Burr played in another film with a similar theme: *Gorilla at Large*. As circus owner Cy Miller, he comes across as an imposing figure in a gray suit, smoking fat cigars and imposing his authority on his employees. Anyone who dares to question his word is abruptly suppressed with a meaningful glare. His wife Laverne (Anne Bancroft) is a trapeze artist; they seem to be happily married, except for the fact that Cy keeps following her without saying anything, as if unable to trust her.

Raymond Burr in *Godzilla, King of the Monsters* (1954). Before making his name in television in *Perry Mason* and *Ironside*, Burr was a character actor of note, playing both good and bad guys.

This, however, is a film all about image—as symbolized, for instance, in one sequence in a hall of mirrors. Miller's air of authority is nothing but a façade, designed to cover up his guilt for having contributed to the death of one of his employees in the past. In one sequence, he is shown in his office drinking gin and muttering under his breath, "You've waited a long time for this, haven't you, Cupie?" (Cupie Adams is the dead man.) Miller's physical weaknesses also emerge; he is unable to open a window owing to an injury to his right hand. Miller confesses to the murder of Adams, as well as his employee Morse (John G. Kellogg), and is led away by police officers, his suit dirty and his hair sticking out in all directions—a ruined man. Eventually, it turns out that Miller was responsible for none of these crimes, but tried instead to protect the real murderer—Laverne.

Burr returns to the jungle as the poacher Vargo in the sci-fi/fantasy flick *Tarzan and the She-Devil* (1953). Dressed in white pith helmet and shorts, he looks forward to a future of wealth and prosperity, once he has successfully hunted elephants for their ivory. With his two companions, the eponymous she-devil Lyra (Monique van Vooren) and Fidel (TOM CONWAY), he toasts his anticipated success ("To ivory!") Vargo proves a cruel taskmaster; having captured a native tribe to carry the loot, the only way he can reinforce his authority over them is through the whip. He captures Tarzan (Lex Barker), and has him strung up in the hope that Tarzan will help them capture the elephants more efficiently. Needless to say, such colonialist attitudes do not go unpunished; once Tarzan learns that his faithful Jane (Joyce MacKenzie) is alive, he summons the elephants by means of his famous cry and initiates a stampede that kills off all the hunters.

In *Godzilla, King of the Monsters* (also 1954), Burr has a difficult role in an Americanized version of the Japanese original released two years earlier. All of his sequences have been inserted into the narrative; the majority of them are either close-ups or two-shots, which look as if they have been filmed on a shoestring. Burr narrates the story in a portentous tone, drawing attention to the significance of the events. As intrepid reporter Steve Martin, he stops off in Tokyo on his way to Egypt, where he witnesses Godzilla destroying the entire city. Most of the time we observe him in close-up, ostensibly listening to the official explanation of events or witnessing the ways in which the citizens of Tokyo try to deal with the crisis. He sucks meditatively on his pipe, or cocks his head on one side, suggesting that he is a reliable witness to the events taking place around him. Through repeated use of close-ups of Burr's sturdy figure, dominating the frame, the director of the American version, Terry O. Morse, makes Steve seem as important in the film as the monster. Thematically speaking, this is absolutely true: Steve bears witness to the events taking place in front of him, and he believes it is his bounden duty to recount them as objectively as possible to American audiences. His narration—delivered in slow, portentous tones—recalls that of Mark Hellinger in Jules Dassin's *The Naked City* (1948). Through such strategies, director Morse treats *Godzilla* as an anti-nuclear tract told in semi-documentary style, warning about what might happen if the American government continued to test atomic bombs. Burr has great fun informing us that "there are some forces left in the world that we don't understand," and "the menace was gone [...] the whole world could wake up and live again."

At the same time, Burr's Steve remains an outsider, a witness to events rather than someone who can directly influence them. In thematic terms, his function shows the limitations of American foreign policy; they cannot dominate the Japanese in the nuclear arms race. All they can do is to trust in journalists like Steve to report the dangers of pursuing atomic bomb tests and their potentially destructive effect on the future of humankind.

Susan Cabot

b. July 9, 1927, Boston, Massachusetts;
d. December 10, 1986, Encino, California.

Born Harriet Shapiro, Cabot began as a children's book illustrator who supplemented her income as a nightclub singer. After a bit part in Henry Hathaway's *Kiss of Death* (1947), she moved into television before signing a long-term contract with Universal. Throughout the early 1950s, she starred in a series of westerns with stars such as Audie Murphy and Tony Curtis. After having made her first film for Roger Corman, *Carnival Rock* (1957), Cabot made four other films for him, including three horror films. She always played extraordinary women who for various reasons challenge popular stereotypes of femaleness. In *War of the Satellites* (1958), she plays high-flying scientist Sybil Carrington, who is first seen in Mission Control's headquarters, witnessing yet another mysterious explosion of a satellite in space. She turns away, her head in her hands, as she learns of yet more casualties. Nonetheless, Sybil remains dedicated to her career; as she makes a speech to the United Nations, informing them of the tragedy. Director Corman photographs her in close-up, her expression remaining impassive as she listens to the debate conducted amongst delegates of various countries as to whether the space program should continue. At length a motion is passed in support of the program, and Sybil dedicates herself to her boss, Dr. Pol van Ponder (Richard Devon). Dressed in a high-necked white blouse and long black skirt, she looks every inch the executive in embryo as she presents papers for him to sign, while dedicating herself to the doctor's future research.

What Sybil does not recognize, however, is that van Ponder has been possessed by aliens who have declared war on planet Earth; whatever research he undertakes is designed to support the enemy's cause. Although initially excluded from the next satellite launch—on the grounds that she is a woman, and hence needs "protection" by staying at home—she secures a place on the craft, and straps herself in, fondly believing that she is helping van Ponder's cause by doing so. After all, he has to find out how women, as well as men, react to the ordeal of flying in space. As the flight progresses, Sybil continues to beaver away efficiently, informing fellow crew member Dave Boyer (DICK MILLER) that she is "in the middle of a computation," and hence unable to share his suspicions that van Ponder might be possessed.

In the end, Sybil's enthusiasm counts for nothing, as she discovers to her cost that van Ponder wants to destroy the Earth. He advances towards her, protesting all the while that he needs her. "Because of you, I'm human!" he says. The irony, of course, is that he is *not* human. Sybil looks at him expressionlessly, as if accepting her fate, but Dave rescues her in the nick of time. At the eleventh hour, she discovers that work is not the be-all and end-all of her life; she has to acknowledge the presence of a strong physical attraction within her for Dave. She hugs him tight, giving him encouragement for his climactic struggle with van Ponder. The film ends with Sybil and Dave strapped to their seats, returning home from their expedition, having vanquished the alien threat as well as falling in love with one another. They have taken to heart the words spoken by John Compo (Jerry Barclay), one of their fellow crew members who unfortunately died at van Ponder's hands: "I was born a human and I'll die one before I join a race [of aliens] that kills innocent people for abstract ideas!"

Corman's film suggests that while full-time

Susan Cabot publicity still (1958). Rather waif-like actress, a stalwart of Roger Corman's repertory company in the late 1950s.

female workers like Sybil need to work harder than their male counterparts in order to achieve recognition, they should acknowledge their inner feelings. To repress them is not only counterproductive, but also causes depression and (in Sybil's case) potential disillusion.

Within two years, however, Corman's liberal view of gender relationships had been superseded by a more traditional patriarchal interpretation. This is especially evident in his treatment of Cabot's role as the high-flying cosmetics company executive Janice Starlin in *The Wasp Woman* (1960). While being somewhat diminutive in size, Janice exerts considerable authority over her employees, particularly the men. Her ambitions do not stop there; she wants to transform herself into a superwoman, which encourages her to take repeated doses of a drug—derived from wasps—which gives her eternal youth. The outcome is predictable: Janice becomes so addicted that she is eventually transformed into a wasp, which can only be destroyed by the intervention of her male subordinate Bill (Fred Ersley). *The Wasp Woman* focuses on gender constructions in late 1950s America, showing how Janice will not accept the social roles imposed on her by her society—wife, mother, or subordinate. She wants to be all-powerful, not only dominating men but defying the aging process as well. Bill's reaction to her behavior is predictable; as someone who firmly believes that "when we [men] expect an answer, you [women] always come up with a question," he will never entertain the idea of gender equality. He believes that, unlike women, he has the "intuition" to understand that something is wrong with Janice's behavior, and determine the "right" course of action—in other words, restore the *status quo* with men in the ascendant and women largely confined to passive roles.

Janice's gradual transformation into a rodent is signaled by gestural changes; her gestures become wilder, her voice shriller, and she moves her head from side to side as if not entirely cognizant of the world around her. Eventually, she becomes a wasp woman — an ugly, frightening monster who strangles the innocent janitor Mr. Cooper (William Roerick) to death. As Dr. Zinthrop (Michael Mack) observes, she is not a human being any longer, but a monstrous woman, a living embodiment of male fears of female supremacy. Although destroyed in the end, she serves as a living example of what might happen if the patriarchy is dissolved, and women are given too much self-determination.

Antony Carbone
b. June 15, 1925, Calabria, Italy.

Antony Carbone was raised in Syracuse, New York. Although his range of work encompasses the stage as well as television, he is best remembered for the leading roles he played in Roger Corman's low-budget science fiction flicks in the late 1950s and early 1960s. In *A Bucket of*

Antony Carbone and Betsy Jones-Moreland in *Creature from the Haunted Sea* (1961). Imposing leading actor in several low-budget science fiction films of the late 1950s, a stalwart of Roger Corman's company.

Blood (1959), he plays pretentious diner owner Leonard de Santis who considers himself some kind of intellectual, sporting a black beret and long trench coat. He treats his staff with contempt, especially bus boy Walter Paisley (DICK MILLER), ordering him to "scrub those garbage cans," rather than listen to beatnik bard Maxwell H. Brock (Julian Burton). Director Corman shows that de Santis is nothing more than a sham: when he discovers that Paisley has been killing people and coating them in modeling clay, and passing the results off as new works of art, the diner owner cowers. While calling Paisley "a true creator" in public, de Santis wants him out of the way as soon as possible. When he sees one example of Paisley's handiwork, the unfortunate girl Alice (Judy Bamber), who has been stripped naked, strangled and coated in clay, her face in the horrible throes of death, de Santis passes out on Paisley's sofa. Unable to sustain the façade of being a great artistic patron, he proves to be nothing more than a coward.

Carbone plays another pretentious personality in *The Last Woman on Earth* (1960). As Harold Gern, a tycoon enjoying the high life of cocktail bars and illegal gambling, he likes to play the tough guy, with hands on hips or thumbs stuck inside his trouser-belt and a pipe in his mouth. On the other hand, he remains sublimely indifferent towards his wife Evelyn (Betsy Jones-Moreland); when she complains about her sterile existence, his one solution is to propose a holiday where the two of them would "take off ... and ... and ... we'll fish ... and ...." The pauses between each word suggest that he has no idea what to do with her.

Eventually, the two of them depart for the holiday, accompanied by Harold's best friend Martin Joyce (Edward Wain — the screen name for scriptwriter Robert Towne). Once they reach their island paradise, they discover that all other inhabitants have died due to an epidemic, and that they truly are the last three people left alive. Harold takes stock of the situation and proposes that the three of them should learn how to fish: "The need to work is inborn.... It's the only thing that can save our sanity." On the other hand he has no idea how to handle the emotional side of his life: "This one woman, two men situation. I don't know what to say. I guess we'll have to live with it." Inevitably, Evelyn and Martin fall in love; unlike Harold, Martin offers her emotional support. Cinematographer Jack Marquette (credited in other films as Jacques R. Marquette) photographs Martin and Evelyn locked in an embrace on the beach (recalling *From Here to Eternity*) and quoting Lewis Carroll's poem "Jabberwocky" to one another. The sequence is at once absurd yet poignant: Evelyn has been so starved of love that she now discovers it through a piece of nonsense verse. Typically, Harold lacks the emotional equipment to help her — all he can do is to repeat the phrase "You're my wife" over and over again.

Inevitably, matters come to a head as Harold asks Martin to behave decently and leave his wife alone, while admitting that all he wanted to do was establish "a system" so that the three of them could live happily on the island. The film ends with a sequence in church, where Martin dies after having been blinded. In truth, however, Harold's obsession with his businesslike image renders him blind to what is going on around him. He only acquires some kind of self-knowledge after Martin's death, as he asks Evelyn to help him find out more about himself.

Carbone's characterization makes some trenchant points about the shortcomings of the late 1950s American male, who struggles to conform to the images of strength and power constructed in the media, whether on screen or in print. The same also applies to his performance as the mobster Renzo Capetto in *The Creature from the Haunted Sea* (1961). In his efforts to transport a group of exiled Cuban nationals and a large part of the Cuban treasury out of Cuba, Capetto concocts a plan to "invent" a sea-monster, so that he can eliminate the Cubans and thus appropriate the treasure for himself. What he does not realize, however, is that there really is a sea-monster out to destroy everyone. Capetto adopts a masculine image derived from Humphrey Bogart, as he speaks his lines out of the corner of his mouth, a cigarette perpetually clamped between his lips.

Unfortunately, no one can take him seriously — especially the narrator, who observes sardonically in voiceover that he is "the most trustworthy man ever to be deported from Sicily." In keeping with the film's generally lighthearted tone, Chuck Griffith's screenplay gives Renzo some fatuous lines; when trying to explain why he has brought the Cubans on the boat, he admits that he wanted "to open up a home for aged hoodlums." Whenever he has nothing else to do, he asks his girlfriend Mary-Belle Monahan (Betsy Jones-Moreland) to sing a song; she obliges by miming to an early 1960s doo-wop tune on the soundtrack. Although the boat is assailed by the sea-monster, Capetto remains calm throughout — either he is incredibly brave or just obsessed with his masculine image. As the action unfolds, the explanation becomes clear, as he glances at his fellow passengers and then looks moodily out to sea, hoping, no doubt, that they will admire his rugged appearance. His narcissism does him no good, however, as the sea-monster devours him whole. This *dénouement* shows how men like Capetto cannot escape themselves; in spite of their desire to construct a masculine image, they are liable to be swallowed whole by potentially destructive forces (represented in this case by the monster). The only way men can deal with such forces is to confront them.

Richard Carlson
b. April 29, 1912, Albert Lea, Minnesota; d. November 24, 1977, Encino, California.

Richard Carlson's earliest ambition was to be a playwright, but his first paying job was as an English instructor at the University of Minnesota. He made his film debut in *The Young in Heart* (1938), but for most of his early career his work was confined to television, save for occasional supporting roles in spoof horror films such as the Bob Hope vehicle *The Ghost Breakers* (1940) for Paramount, where he plays Geoff Montgomery, who is evidently attracted to Mary Carter (Paulette Goddard) and will strive to protect her from evil. He is certainly a stylish person, as he appears immaculately dressed in dinner jackets or white tuxedos that contrast with the rather scruffy appearance of broadcaster Lawrence Lawrence (Bob Hope), who competes for Mary's affections. Eventually we discover that Montgomery has simply been role-playing, in an attempt to get Mary away from a haunted castle in Cubs (that rightfully belongs to her). He has found a silver mine in the castle's foundations, and wants to prevent anyone from discovering it. Montgomery's efforts prove futile, as he falls to his death through a trapdoor, leaving Lawrence and Mary free to get married. In another spoof, Universal's Abbott and Costello vehicle *Hold That Ghost* (1941), where he plays Dr. Jackson, a studious figure in thick black glasses (recalling Cary Grant in *Bringing Up Baby* [1938]) whose obsession with his work renders him incapable of understanding just how much Norma Lind (EVELYN ANKERS) loves him. He carries a suitcase full of instruments, which he brings out on any and every occasion to examine the water in the haunted house. As the film unfolds, and the events taking place in the haunted house become ever more inexplicable, Jackson takes on a more active role, leading the search for the ghost, even though he is uncomfortable with the role. Norma learns to trust in him; it is only a matter of time before she throws herself in his arms in search of both physical and emotional protection. The two of them indulge in comic exchanges ("Dear, you called me darling"/"Darling, you called me dear") and embrace, completely oblivious to the fact that someone has tried to kill them by throwing a knife in their direction. Unlike *The Ghost Breakers*, Carlson gets the girl this time, as he escapes death, removes his glasses and proposes marriage to Norma.

By the end of the 1940s, Carlson took more substantial roles: in *The Amazing Mr. X* (1948) he plays another professional — the lawyer Martin Abbott, whose character contrasts directly with that of the fake medium Alexis (TURHAN BEY). Whereas Alexis claims to trust in the power of the supernatural, Martin remains a practical man: everything has to be accomplished according to plan. Even the decision to kiss his fiancée Christine (Lynn Bari) is methodically worked out, much to her displeasure.

While visiting Alexis's house, Martin remains skeptical of the medium's motives, holding up a crystal ball and denouncing it as a fake piece of jewelry. Christine still doesn't believe him; Martin responds by telling her to "be logical" in a voice full of irritation. Although Christine eventually finds out that Martin has been telling the truth, this does not mean that the two of them will enjoy a happy life together. At the end of the film, Martin is told to give his fiancée "rest and care"—qualities that seem beyond the capabilities of a person so preoccupied with reason and logic.

In the Cold War allegory *It Came from Outer Space* (1953), Carlson plays amateur astronomer John Putnam, who observes at the beginning in voiceover that he feels "sure of the future, so very sure." His mood of serenity is soon undermined by an alien invasion from outer space. No one initially believes Carlson's claims: the scientist Dr. Snell (George Eldredge) advises him to "face the facts" and stop giving into wild imaginings. As the film unfolds, the citizens of Carlson's small town understand the consequences of the invasion, as some of them are abducted and their souls inhabited by the aliens. Complacency gives way to hysteria, as a mob of men led by Sheriff Matt (Charles Drake) take up arms and resolve to destroy the alien encampment in a disused mine. By contrast, Putnam adopts a more conciliatory tone; he understands that violence only begets violence, which will lead to the destruction of the civilized world. He keeps the mob at bay, allowing the aliens sufficient time to blast off and return to their own planet. The film ends with Putnam telling us in voiceover, "It wasn't the right time for us to meet [...] they'll be back." If and when they do return, we should try to understand their point of view rather than fight them.

In *Riders to the Stars* (1954), which he also directed, Carlson has a supporting role as scientist-turned-astronaut Jerome ("Jerry") Lockwood. Initially he comes across as rather absent-minded, as he is shown in his university shuffling through papers, and treating government agent James F. O'Herli (King Donovan) suspiciously, in the belief, perhaps, that the agent might not be what he claims. Lockwood's manner changes, however, once he leaves the cloistered world of academe for the astronaut's training camp in California. As in *The Amazing Mr. X*, Carlson plays his character as a practical person, someone keen to get on with the job in spite of his misgivings. However, Carlson's Lockwood has one fatal flaw; he occasionally allows emotion to cloud his judgment. Dr. Donald L. Stanton (Herbert Marshall) understands this, as he suspects that Lockwood is still experiencing the pain of rejection by his fiancée Susan (Dawn Addams). Lockwood's flaw eventually proves his undoing; having witnessed his colleague Walter J. Gordon (Robert Karnes) being blown up in his spaceship, Lockwood begins to shake with fear, as the memories of his wartime experiences as a pilot come flooding back. Unable to control his spaceship any more, he plunges to his death in outer space. By such means, Carlson (as director) shows the pitfalls of space exploration—it might help secure America's future as the world's leader in scien-

Richard Carlson cinema star postcard (1943). Debonair leading actor of the late 1940s and 1950s, who regularly appeared in science fiction films during the period.

tific research (demonstrating their superiority to the Soviets), but this prestige is often achieved at a price, especially for individual human beings.

In *Creature from the Black Lagoon* (1954), Carlson's character has clearly understood this lesson. As Dr. David Reed, he has carved out a brilliant career as a marine archeologist, but understands that scientific research should not be the *raison d'être* of his entire life. He shows a touching concern for his fiancée Kay Lawrence (Julia Adams), and makes sure that she comes to no harm, even if it means putting his own life at risk. At the end of the film he strikes out alone to rescue her from the Gill-Man's (i.e., the creature's) (Ricou Browning/Ben Chapman) clutches, even though he does not have much chance of winning in hand-to-hand combat. At the same time, Reed understands the importance of preserving the Gill-Man's life; he neither wants to destroy it, nor take it back to the United States, but simply study it for academic purposes. Such solicitude contrasts with the devil-may-care attitude of his boss Mark Williams (RICHARD DENNING), who wants to capture the creature and put it on display in New York, like King Kong. Needless to say, Williams meets a grisly end, as he fights the creature and is drowned, but Reed emerges unscathed; although he has to shoot the creature to rescue Kay, he allows it to return to its natural habitat. Director Jack Arnold includes several cheesecake shots of Reed's muscular physique, as he embarks on several diving expeditions dressed only in a swimming costume.

Carlson reprises the role as a supposedly heroic person affected by mental trauma as Tom Stewart in Bert I. Gordon's *Tormented* (1960). Having decided to end his long-term relationship with girlfriend Vi (Juli Reding), he confronts her at the top of a lighthouse. Vi falls backwards; the safety rail on the lighthouse breaks, and she is left clinging on by one hand, pleading with Tom to help her. Tom just looks on as her grip gradually loosens and she crashes to her death on the rocks below. The rest of the film concentrates on Tom's efforts to banish the incident from his mind, while being haunted by Vi's ghost. As in his other films, Carlson shows the practical side of the man; he continues his career as a jazz pianist, while preparing to marry his new girlfriend Meg Hubbard (Lugene Sanders). He develops a close affection for Meg's little sister Sandy (Susan Gordon); the two of them exchange secrets about Meg's feelings for him.

Director Gordon repeatedly employs point of view shots to emphasize Tom's turbulent state of mind as he is perpetually reminded of what he has done. In one sequence he is shown playing the piano: Vi's ghost enters and turns on the record player which trills out the lyrics of the film's theme song. Tom grabs the shellac disk and smashes it into smithereens in a vain attempt to banish the past. In truth this moment could be seen as symbolic of his own shattered dreams of a happy life. Although he makes valiant efforts to justify himself, both to Meg and Sandy and to the viewers (Gordon perpetually photographs him in close-up addressing his lines direct to camera), Tom eventually proves unequal to the task. Vi takes over his life, as she orders him to kill Nick the blackmailer (Joe Turkel) by stabbing him in the back. The film ends with a climactic sequence in which Tom tries to kill Sandy but ends up falling to his death. The corpses of Tom and Vi are fished out from the ocean and laid side by side; Vi's corpse rolls over, and her hand falls limply across Tom's chest. The camera zooms in to a close-up of a wedding ring on the third finger of her left hand: the two of them have been reunited in death, despite Tom's best efforts to escape.

Although described in the publicity as "a terrifying story of supernatural passion" in which "a ghost-woman owned him [Tom's] body and soul" (which might suggest that the film dramatizes male fears of being dominated by women), *Tormented* is actually a very moral film, suggesting that no one can escape punishment for their past sins. This message is reinforced by Carlson's performance, as he deliberately subverts his screen image of a safe, reliable personality to portray someone racked by guilt for what he has done.

In *The Valley of Gwangi* (1969), Carlson has a supporting role as Champ, the owner of a rodeo whose fundamental honesty contrasts with the duplicity of central character Tuck (James Franciscus). Champ's honesty is compromised by the desire for financial gain; rather like Carl Denham (ROBERT ARMSTRONG) in *King Kong*, Champ enjoys the idea of putting the monster Gwangi on show, even if it involves considerable risk. Resplendent in white suit and tie, he takes the megaphone and boasts of his great discovery to a packed audience. But his confidence proves misplaced, as Gwangi escapes and terrorizes the community, before being burned to death in a church. In the film's final sequence, director James O'Connolly's camera shows him in close-up, stroking his chin and looking down at the floor, as if unable to look the viewer in the eye out of shame for what he has done.

John Carradine
b. February 5, 1906, New York City;
d. November 27, 1988, Milan, Italy.

Richmond Reed Carradine began acting in Los Angeles in 1927, making his debut in 1930. Nicknamed "The Voice," Carradine was a natural choice for horror films of the late 1930s and 1940s. He started off in bit parts, such as playing the organist in an uncredited role in *The Black Cat* (1934). We do not see his face, but with his slicked-back hair and slim fingers, he exerts a sinister presence in Hjalmar Poelzig's (Boris Karloff) house.

Carradine's villainy was chiefly communicated through single gestures or glances. This is evident, for instance, in his performance as Dr. Sigmund Walters in Edward Dmytryk's *Captive Wild Woman* (1943). Dressed in a three-piece suit and trilby hat, he resembles a friendly professor as he walks around the circus, focusing in particular on the ways in which lions and tigers are handled by professional tamer Fred Mason (Milburn Stone). It is only when Walters is alone that his true nature is revealed. He stands by the cage containing Cheela the Ape (Ray Corrigan), gives a small smile and murmurs, "We're on the road to great things," placing particular emphasis on the word "great." Immediately we understand his desire for power. In a later sequence, we discover him working in his laboratory; having captured the ape, he has decided to transform it into an ape-woman (Acquanetta) by injecting it with hormones taken from Dorothy Coleman (Martha Vickers), one of his patients. Director Dmytryk cuts to frequent close-ups of the doctor's eyes, focusing intently on his work. When Walters has finished, he removes his surgical mask, and shouts for joy: "We've done it!" When Walters' assistant Nurse Strand (Fay Helm) accuses him of medical malpractice, the doctor moves threateningly towards her, staring into her face. The nurse retreats, and eventually falls out of the frame with a scream; we know what her fate will be. Carradine doesn't actually do much in this sequence, but the look in his face makes his intentions abundantly clear.

Walters tries the same strategy later on, when he persuades Dorothy's sister Beth (EVELYN ANKERS) to witness his experiments. He talks with palpable relish about his ability to perform the "transformation of an animal into a human being," taking a pause after the word "transformation" so as to increase the phrase's rhetorical effect. He advances threateningly towards Beth, staring right into her eyes and forces her to watch him perform his experiments. Beth proves too quick for him; she escapes his controlling gaze, runs to the side of the room and opens Cheela's cage. The ape pursues the doctor and strangles him to death.

Like many villains who appeared in horror films at this time, Carradine appears at once frightening and attractive as he relishes the prospect of achieving man's ultimate patriarchal desire to create a superwoman, entirely subservient to their will, combining the strength of an ape with the intelligence of a human being. Dmytryk seems to have been aware of this, as he inserts an epilogue delivered in sonorous tones by an off-screen narrator (TURHAN BEY) describing the exploits "of a mortal who went beyond the realm of human powers and tampered with things that no one should even touch." As Turhan speaks, an image of Walters' face is superimposed on a shot of his sanatorium.

In *House of Dracula* (1945), Carradine exploits this attractive quality as the eponymous vampire (also known as Latos). With his ramrod-straight back, top hat and black cape, he could almost pass for a Dickensian hero as he visits the house of Dr. Franz Edelmann (Onslow Stevens) in search of a cure for his nocturnal habits. His manners are impeccable; he bows and doffs his hat to every female regardless of background. However this air of urbanity proves dangerous, as it encourages Miliza Mourelle (Martha O'Driscoll) to fall for him. The Count takes a quasi-erotic pleasure in seducing her, as he sidles up behind her and paints a seductive verbal portrait of "a world without fear." Needless to say, Miliza falls for him; one night she waits open-mouthed for him to "bring [his] world closer" to her through the usual methods. She is only saved from her fate by Edelmann's timely intervention, as the doctor runs into her bedroom and scares the vampire away by means of a cross.

Carradine also specialized in playing mad scientists— as the Nazi Dr. Max Heinrich von Altermann in Monogram's low-budget *Revenge of the Zombies* (1943), he seems superficially kind, but we notice something sinister about him in the way he clasps and unclasps his left hand while talking to clean-cut detective Larry Adams (Robert Lowery). Altermann is well aware of this nervous tic; later on, he deliberately folds his arms across his chest, which only succeeds in rendering his behavior even stranger. His true nature is revealed in his exchanges with the supposed Nazi agent posing as a sheriff (Bob Steele). The two man salute one another and click their heels together in a gesture reminiscent of an SS officer. Just in case no one understands their origins, they wish each other "Auf Wiedersehen." Altermann relishes the task of creating an army of zombies, who will march across America in support of the Nazi cause. By such means the doctor believes he will be "exalted [as] one of the greatest men in history." However, his calculations do not account for the fact that the zombies might turn against him; his wife Lila (Veda Ann Borg) not only rebels against his patriarchal authority, but orders the zombies to strangle him to death. This order is readily carried out, suggesting that even zombies respond to encouragement rather than cruelty.

In *The Mummy's Ghost* (1944), Carradine gives another virtuoso performance as Yousef Bey, who has been given the responsibility of returning the bodies of ancient Egyptian princess Ananka (Ramsay Ames) and her mummy guardian Kharis (Lon Chaney, Jr.) back from America to Egypt. Needless to say, he fails in his task, as leading man Tom Hervey (Robert Lowery) takes the attention, but Carradine has great fun with the role. A tall, languid figure, reminiscent of Dr. Walters in *Captive Wild Woman* with his suit and trilby hat, he could pass for an ordinary American citizen living in New England. Once he starts praying to his gods, however, Yousef's manner completely changes; his eyes stare into space and he intones in a voice of doom that he is duty-bound to complete his quest — in other words, return the two bodies. Even though Ananka's soul has entered that of another woman, Amina Mansouri, it makes no difference; she must be brought back. Yousef seems fundamentally ruthless. He grins maniacally as Kharis kills anyone who dares to stand in his way.

John Carradine publicity still (1944). A legendary villain, whose clipped manner of delivery and tall, imposing presence gave him regular work in horror and science fiction films of the 1940s and

As the film unfolds, Yousef gradually succumbs to his emotions. As he stands at the top of a helter-skelter over Ananka/Amina's lifeless body, prior to mummifying her, he suddenly realizes that perhaps love is more important for him than duty. He communicates his thoughts in voiceover that contrasts with his formal tones as he prays out loud to Isis for guidance. His breathing becomes irregular as he leans over and defies the gods, proclaiming instead that both he and Ananka will join one another in death. However, he reckons without Kharis who, on hearing this pronouncement, immediately becomes jealous. Kharis strikes Yousef with the back of his hand; Yousef falls backwards and plunges to his death by falling out of a helter-skelter on the ground several hundred feet below.

Carradine was nothing if not versatile in his roles; in *Voodoo Man* (1944), he plays Toby, the slightly slow-witted sidekick of Dr. Richard Marlowe (Bela Lugosi). With his tattered jacket, ill-fitting trousers and wild hair hanging over his eyes, he looks the epitome of the downtrodden servant, whose only pleasure lies in talking to the hypnotized female victims of Marlowe's crazed experiments to revive his wife Evelyn (Ellen Hall), who has been dead for twenty years. Needless to say, the victims do not reply. Toby lives in perpetual fear of being beaten by his master: when Betty Benton (Wanda McKay) escapes from Marlowe's hideout, and thereby holds up the doctor's experiments, Toby scuttles of the laboratory repeating, "I'll find her, master, I'll find her, master!" in a manic tone. While Marlowe performs his experiments, to the accompaniment of Nicholas's (GEORGE ZUCCO) bizarre — and incomprehensible — prayers, Toby sits at the side, beating a drum like an automaton. This shot sums up his position in the doctor's household: he is treated like an automaton, carrying out orders without question. In *Fallen Angel* (1945), Carradine has a small role as Professor Madley, a fake medium who claims to be able to raise the "deadly deceased" in public performances. With his lank, greasy hair and grubby clothes, he looks the epitome of a small time con artist. Nonetheless, his ability to control people's minds provides a neat foretaste of one of the film's main themes, as June Mills (Alice Faye) marries Eric Stanton — even though she does not love him — as a means of escaping her dominant sister Clara (Anne Revere).

Carradine's ability to mesmerize through eyework is also evident in his cameo roles—for example, the butler Barryman in *The Hound of the Baskervilles* (1939). With his tall, statuesque gait and long flowing tailcoat, he cuts a sinister figure — someone who can instill fear into Dr. Watson (Nigel Bruce) simply by following him with his eyes. Eventually, we discover that Berryman is not actually evil at all, but rather protective of his wife (Eily Malyon) and her family. In his view, there are certain secrets involving the Baskerville household which are best kept unrevealed.

Sometimes Carradine was cast against type as a good guy — for example in Jerry Warren's *The Incredible Petrified World* (1957) — but still invested the character with a fearsome intensity. Warren comes alive when the subject of medical research comes up; in one sequence, he defends himself in the office of Dr. Matheny (George Skaff) — as he speaks, he repeatedly clasps and unclasps his hands while fixing the doctor with an unblinking stare. Here is someone who will not be prevented from continuing his work. Later on, Warren is photographed in a series of close-ups writing furiously, running his hands through his hair and planning his latest expedition. He embodies the pioneer spirit, the obsessive desire to discover new worlds in the name of America. Such qualities were especially significant at the time of the film's release, when America participated with the Soviet Union in the Space Race.

One of Carradine's most curious roles was that of Dr. John Rayburn in *Half Human* (1958) — a reedited version of the Japanese film *Jû Jin Yuki Otoko* (1955), in which the original running-time has been reduced from 99 to 63 minutes, with twenty minutes of additional footage involving Carradine and fellow actors Morris Ankrum, Russell Thorson and Robert Karnes added for American audiences. Carradine acts as the narrator, telling the story of how the abominable snowman was killed in Japan.

Sometimes his narrative commentary seems unnecessarily portentous ("Even in death his face still carried an expression of fear, shock and unadulterated terror"), but he provides a concise interpretation of the original Japanese dialogue. The film itself (directed originally by Ishirō Honda, and reedited by Kenneth G. Crane), has strong echoes of the *King Kong* trilogy (*King Kong*, *Son of Kong*, and *Mighty Joe Young*), in its characterization of the monster and his son, and in the way the monster carries one of the female protagonists in his arms into the wilds of the Himalayas.

Paul Cavanagh
b. December 8, 1888, Chislehurst, Kent, England; d. March 15, 1964, London, England.

Paul Cavenaugh (later abbreviated to Cavanagh) made a habit of playing middle or upper class roles, or slightly effete characters — often contrasted with the more "manly" leads. In *The Woman in Green* (1945), he has a supporting role as Sir George Fenwick, a member of the British aristocracy who enjoys a night out with Lydia, the eponymous woman (Hillary Brooke). The two of them are seen in the Pembroke House club enjoying themselves: when we next see Sir George, however, he wakes up disheveled in a dingy apartment, unsure about what happened the previous night. He returns home and suffers the indignity of being blackmailed by Professor Moriarty (HENRY DANIELL). Although Sir George manages to find the money — in the vain hope of protecting his reputation — he is shot through the heart.

In Fritz Lang's *Secret Beyond the Door* (1947), Cavanagh plays Rick Bennett, a financially successful member of the New York elite. With his neat three-piece suit, with handkerchief protruding from his breast pocket, he looks the perfect gentleman — someone ideally suited to looking after his younger sister Celia (Joan Bennett). However, he also suffers from heart trouble — although regularly taking medicine for it, he acknowledges that "there are no spare parts" to make it better. He does not have long to live, and when he passes away, Celia no

Paul Cavanagh cinema star postcard (1943). This British-born supporting player made his name playing effeminate characters, or members of the aristocracy.

longer has a male protector to ensure that she keeps on the straight and narrow.

In *The Strange Case of Dr. RX* (1942), Cavanagh appears as the rather effete John Crispin, brother of Dudley Crispin (Samuel S. Hinds), who turns out to be the serial killer Dr. RX. John seems perpetually frightened by the thought that his family might be implicated in any crime, and perpetually seeks to impede Jerry Church's (PATRIC KNOWLES) investigations. Such efforts prove futile, however, as Jerry manages to uncover the crime. In *Bride of the Gorilla* (1951), Cavanagh plays Klaas von Gelder, an elderly yet ineffective owner of a plantation, who cannot keep his voluptuous wife Dina (Barbara Payton) from conducting an affair with his employee Barney Chavez (RAYMOND BURR). Von Gelder tries to intervene, but physically he proves no match for the muscle-bound Chavez. The old man is knocked to the floor and poisoned by a deadly snake, while his employee looks on in triumph,

In the same year, Cavanagh played Edmund de Maletroit in *Strange Door*, an adaptation of a story by Robert Louis Stevenson. Confined to a dungeon by his brother Alain (Charles Laughton), Edmund appears to have been driven mad by his ordeal, with his hair stuck out in all directions and wild unkempt beard. He wails in blood-curdling fashion and scratches the walls like an animal, while Alain continually taunts him: "That's right, scream." Once Alain has left the dungeon, however, we discover that Edmund is merely playing at being mad; in the company of his faithful servant Voltan (Boris Karloff) he becomes quite rational once again. Edmund remains devoted to his daughter Blanche (Sally Forrest); at one point he grasps her wrists and admits candidly that he has only put on the mad act to protect her. In the end it seems as if father and daughter have been condemned to a grisly fate, as they are locked in a cell with the young hero Corbeau (William Cottrell), whose walls are gradually moving towards them. They are rescued in the nick of time by Voltan, who, although on the point of death, manages to shuffle along the ground and push the key near the door, so that Corbeau can reach through the bars and pick it up, Edmund is at last restored to his rightful position as master of the family seat; in the final sequence he is dressed in the fashionable clothes of an aristocrat, complete with goatee beard. He symbolically opens the front door to let fresh air in — the first time this has happened in many a long year.

The year 1951 proved a busy one for Cavanagh; in *Son of Dr. Jekyll*, he played nononsense police inspector Stoddard, who understands that Edward Jekyll (Louis Hayward) is being framed by devilish Dr. Lanyon (Alexander Knox), but cannot prove it conclusively. Lanyon wants to lay his hands on the Jekyll estate; to do so he tries to make it seem that Jekyll is as insane as his father. Stoddard pursues Lanyon with relentless intensity (his pensive expression seldom changes throughout the film), and eventually discovers his true motives. When Lanyon falls to his death, Stoddard permits himself a small smile in Jekyll's direction.

Two years later, Cavanagh played art critic Sidney Wallace in *House of Wax*. Neatly dressed in a three-piece suit with gloves, his appearance contrasts starkly with the wild eyes and unkempt hair of Professor Henry Jarrod (Vincent Price) — who in many ways resembles Cavanagh himself in *Strange Door*. Wallace is fascinated by Jarrod's efforts, as he moves around the exhibit his neatly rounded vowels becoming ever more pronounced. Eventually he takes a deep breath and shakes Jarrod's hand, promising — if only in principle — to finance the professor on his return from foreign climes. Three years later, the art critic returns, and admires Jarrod's work once again, even if he finds the subjects somewhat distasteful (Jarrod has by now created a new house of wax including re-enactments of recent murders). Wallace identifies Jarrod as "a man of in*teg*rity," with the emphasis placed on the second syllable of the word. This observation proves chillingly ironic: as a result of the first fire (which left him permanently disfigured), Jarrod has sacrificed his integrity to popular taste, while at the same time revenging himself on the world. His house of wax is chillingly lifelike — but then what else do we expect, when all the exhibits are actually exhumed corpses covered in wax?

Cavanagh was also seen in several cameo roles during the latter part of the 1950s, some of which were more rewarding than others. In *Francis in the Haunted House* (1956), he has a thankless task of supporting Francis the talking mule and a winsome Mickey Rooney (as David Prescott). As the gang-leader Neil Frazer, who tries and fails to lay his hands on the MacLeod family fortune, Cavanagh does not have much to do, other than assume a façade of politeness when the police come to investigate a murder. In the film's climax, he dons a suit of armor, brandishes a lance and fights a duel on horseback with Prescott, who falls to the ground, while Frazer escapes. He is seen in long shot galloping over the estate like a medieval Lone Ranger; eventually Prescott catches up with him and spears him to the ground. Frazer lies prostrate as the police pick him up and lead him away.

In *The Man Who Turned to Stone* (1957), Cavanagh has a more rewarding cameo as Cooper, a scientist whose old-fashioned style of dress (frock-coat and wing collar) contrasts starkly with his colleagues surrounding him. They are busy conducting an experiment in which a young woman is immersed in a bath of hot water and connected by wires to a tall, cavernous-featured old man Eric (Frederick Ledebur). The young woman dies as a result, while Eric is revived. Cooper dislikes what he sees, but Dr. Murdock (Victor Jory), tells him that such doubts are "unhealthy." Cooper seems strangely ill at ease throughout the film; when psychiatrist Dr. Jess Rogers (WILLIAM HUDSON) encounters him in an oak-paneled room, Cooper makes a basic mistake about the provenance of a painting hanging on the wall, claiming it is a Rembrandt painted around 1850 (Rembrandt lived between 1606 and 1689). Cooper's eyes dart wildly left to right, as if desperate to leave the room as quickly as possible.

Later on we discover exactly what ails him. He was actually born in 1733 in England, and has been kept alive for the past 220 years by the transfer of bioelectric energy from young women. If the flow of sacrificial victims dries up, then he will die. In a climactic sequence, Murdock tells Cooper that his time has come to die: Cooper's face gradually becomes more and more wrinkled, his hair whitens and his voice quivers as he slowly comes to terms with his fate. His dying words are issued as a threat: "If I die, you'll all die!" In a lengthy voiceover delivered from beyond the grave while Rogers is seen reading from Cooper's diary, Cooper explains why: all the scientists are nearly as old as he is, and have been sustained by energy vampirically extracted from female victims. Now Rogers knows the truth about their practices, and can destroy them. Cooper's long speech is delivered in sepulchral tones, resembling the voice of doom.

In *She-Devil* (1957), Cavanagh has a brief role as a rich sugar daddy who enjoys buying clothes for an attractive young woman young enough to be his granddaughter. He sits languidly on a *chaise longue*, counting out wads of money before getting up and going towards the counter to pay the check. He is such a conceited person that he fails to notice Kyra Zelas (Mari Blanchard), who comes up behind him, grabs the wallet and hits him on the head with a glass ashtray. The sugar daddy collapses to the ground while Kyra runs away with the money in her hand. In *The Four Skulls of Jonathan Drake* (1959), Cavanagh met a similarly grisly fate as Kenneth Drake, a tall, elderly man who is first observed cowering in a chair on a dark night. His fears prove justified, as a tall rangy native Indian Zutal (Paul Wexler) enters his room and cuts his neck with a stiletto. Kenneth immediately falls down dead, the victim of a family curse dictating that all male members of the Drake family will die at sixty years old, while their heads will be cut off and transformed into *tsantsas*— shrunken heads, an ancient technique of the Jivaro Indians from Northern Peru and Southern Ecuador. This is precisely what happens to the hapless Kenneth; his head is removed by witch-doctor Emil Zurich (HENRY DANIELL), placed into a steaming cauldron, and later stored in a cupboard.

Occasionally, Cavanagh enjoyed more substantial roles — such as the gangster John Kolvac in the science fiction adventure *Port Sinister* (1953). Having learned of the plan to rendezvous with the long-lost pirate island of Port Royal — which is expected to emerge from the sea for the fourth time in 200 years — Kolvac hits scientist Tony Ferris (James Warren) over the head and assumes command of the ship himself. With his unshaven face and imposing manner, reminiscent of Robert Newton's Long John Silver in the Disney version of *Treasure Island* (1950), Kolvac seems to be the ideal captain, except for the fact that he knows nothing about the seafaring life. He insists that the ship should continue its course as fast as it can, even in rough weather, with no thought for his crew's welfare. But then Kolvac is not interested in anything except the buried treasure on the island. Director Harold Daniels cuts to several close-ups of the gangster as he dreams of the "Treasure of the Spanish Main! ... Enough to make us millionaires!" There is heavy stress placed on the first syllable of the word "millionaires." Eventually, Kolvac lands on the island, and leaves most of his crew asleep while he searches for the treasure alone with his first mate Collins (William Schallert). Their persistence is rewarded: having discovered the treasure, Kolvac savors the idea of becoming "richer than we've ever DREAMED!" As he speaks, his face breaks into an evil grin. However, Kolvac's ambitions are doomed to fail: Collins is shot dead by Ferris, leaving no one to help Kolvac carry the treasure back to the ship. He is eventually drowned as the island sinks back into the sea.

Edward E. (E.E.) Clive

b. August 28, 1879, Monmouthshire, Wales;
d. June 6, 1940, North Hollywood, California.

E. E. Clive forsook a career on the London stage for the comfortable life as a Hollywood supporting player. He generally played slightly down-at-heel characters, possessing plenty of spirit but somewhat lacking in ingenuity. As the dim-witted, mustachioed Constable Jaffers in Universal's *The Invisible Man* (1933), he walks in ungainly fashion towards the inn to investigate the mysterious goings-on in Jack Griffin's (CLAUDE RAINS) room. In a futile attempt to assert his authority as a police officer (by saying "keep back, you kids there"), he enters Griffin's room and barks, "You can come along to the station with me." Griffin responds by taking off his bandages to reveal nothing underneath. Jaffers runs downstairs in fright, with sweat pouring down his face. He makes another vain attempt to arraign Griffin by hitting him with his truncheon; in exasperation, Griffin half-strangles the police officer and throws him in the corner like a rag doll. The implication is clear: Griffin has been provoked into such extreme actions by repeated unwelcome intrusions.

In *The Mystery of Edwin Drood* (1935), also for Universal, Clive thoroughly enjoys himself as the inept mayor Thomas Sapsea. With his sharp nose, impeccably tailored jacket, wing collar and top hat, he looks the very epitome of an authority figure, proclaiming in ringing tones that "no one has ever stayed missing since I was mayor." The word "mayor" is pronounced in impeccable Standard English as "mair." The only problem is that the missing person in question — Edwin Drood (DAVID MANNERS) — will never be found alive, having been murdered in cold blood by his cousin John Jasper (CLAUDE RAINS). However, no one knows the truth as yet. Sapsea has a catchphrase ("Let us proceed in order" — pronounced "aw-dah!"), which he uses in a vain attempt to impose authority over his parishioners. When the opium seller (Zeffie Tilbury) is found strangled to death, Sapsea stands over the corpse and proclaims: "Let all be done in aw-dah! Let nothing be touched! Mrs. Tope [Vera Buckland], no emotions!" No one bothers to take any notice of him: Landless (Douglass Montgomery) examines the corpse and runs out of the room, while Mrs. Tope mourns the woman's death. The best course of action open to Clive's Sapsea is to call on others to impose authority on his behalf. This he proceeds to do in the final sequences of *The Mystery of Edwin Drood*, as he calls upon his police officers to "Arrest that man! [Jasper]" and "Sound the alarm!" Sapsea is a good example of the kind of

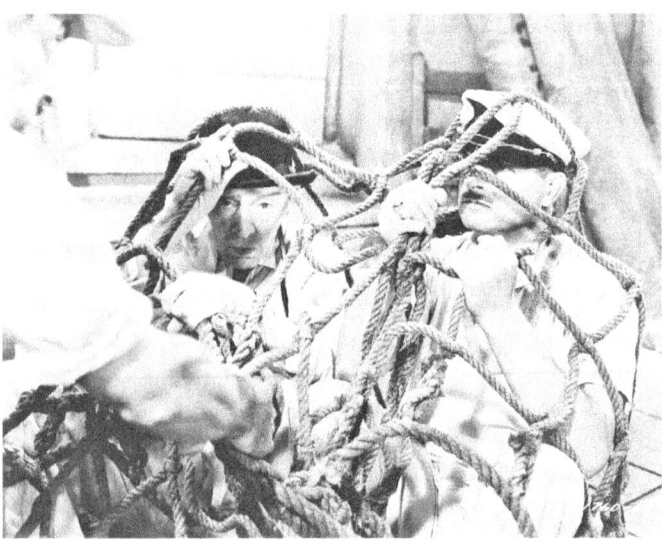

John Howard and E. E. Clive in *Arrest Bulldog Drummond* (1939). Welsh-born character actor, often playing ineffectual figures of authority such as butlers or police officers.

ineffective authority-figure that runs throughout Dickens, as well as in film adaptations of his work. In MGM's *David Copperfield* (also 1935), for instance, there is Lewis Stone's Mr. Wickfield, whose over-trusting nature renders him ripe for exploitation by Uriah Heep (Roland Young).

In Universal's *Bride of Frankenstein* (1935), directed by James Whale, Clive plays the Burgomaster, a self-important booby who tries to set an example of leadership, but eventually proves no match for the monster (Boris Karloff). The film opens with a sequence (following on from the original *Frankenstein* [1931]), showing the monster apparently being burned to death; once the fire dies down, the Burgomaster chivvies everyone back to their houses, proclaiming that "it's high time every decent man and wife was in bed." In his pith helmet and drill-stick, he looks the very image of authority, as he orders the people to chase the monster, exclaiming: "I'll show him [the monster]!" He barks out orders ("Bind him securely, feet first!"; "Take him down to the old dungeon and put him in chains!"), but actually does nothing to help. In fact, one wonders how he acquired such a position of authority, as he observes complacently that the monster is "quite harmless." While we are invited to laugh at the Burgomaster's buffoonery, we are nonetheless made aware of how inefficient the forces of authority actually are. In the original *Frankenstein*, they stood by and watched, while the people treated the monster like a victim of a lynch mob; they are quite prepared to pursue the same course of action in *The Bride of Frankenstein*. When the Burgomaster meets a sticky end (as the monster tramples him to death, having escaped from prison), we feel that he somehow deserves his fate.

Clive plays another police officer in *Dracula's Daughter* (1936). As Sergeant Wilkes, his eyes dart around in fear, as he contemplates the prospect of encountering the vampire. Slowly recovering his sang-froid, he asks for "a bit of the all right [i.e., a sip of whisky], just to keep the chill off the bones," as he takes a torch and enters the room where Dracula had been interred. Director Lambert Hillyer cuts to a close-up of his face as he discovers that the vampire has disappeared. Wilkes shines his torch around the room and tries to remonstrate with his fellow police officers, but with little effect. They have little or no power to resist the influence of the otherworldly.

Clive took small roles in the two Twentieth Century–Fox Sherlock Holmes films, *The Hound of the Baskervilles* (1939) and *The Adventures of Sherlock Holmes* (also 1939). In *The Hound*, he plays a London cab driver paying due deference to his social superiors ("Very good, sir") and bowing and scraping as he holds the door for them. He speaks in the kind of faux-cockney accent and wears the kind of uniform (neckerchief, shoddy jacket and pants with a flat cap), which Hollywood identified as characteristic of lower-class characters at that time. In *The Adventures*, Clive plays Inspector Bristol, wearing the traditional Hollywood British police inspector's garb of long coat and bowler hat. Unlike Holmes (Basil Rathbone), Bristol is not possessed of the gift of deductive reasoning; he makes conclusions based on what he sees. As a result, he consistently makes false assumptions. Inspector Bristol is clearly conceived as a prototype of Dennis Hoey's Inspector Lestrade, who appeared regularly in Universal's Sherlock Holmes series (1943–6).

Tom Conway

*b. September 15, 1904, St. Petersburg, Russia;
d. April 22, 1967, Culver City,
Los Angeles, California.*

Born Thomas Charles Sanders, the younger brother of GEORGE SANDERS, Tom Conway began his career in horror films as Dr. Judd in Jacques Tourneur's *Cat People* (1942). He plays a suave, sophisticated rogue who is so convinced of his own abilities that he has little time to listen to Irena (SIMONE SIMON). He reclines on an easy chair, playing with a silver-topped cane, attributing her condition to an excess of imagination and/or conscience. Underneath Judd's psychobabble likes an unshakeable belief in patriarchal power: women are "naturally" unreasonable, and they can only be cured if they acquire the kind of logical thought characteristic of men. Conway's carefully modulated delivery—contrasting with Simon's heavily accented vowels—emphasizes his feeling of superiority.

However, the mask of urbanity drops later on in the film, as he tries to force himself on her. As someone possessed with the ability to read her mind, he believes that it is his right and privilege to kiss her, in the hope of putting her in touch once again with her emotions. The fact that Judd himself might experience sexual pleasure from the encounter is conveniently overlooked. However, Irena's reaction is not what he anticipates; far from giving in to his advances, she expresses her independence of mind and fights back. Judd draws a sword from his cane in an attempt to stab her, but is eventually killed—a fitting demise for someone so willing to abuse his position as a medical person. Conway repeats the role in *The Seventh Victim* (1943), directed by Mark Robson. As in the earlier film, he initially comes across as a know-it-all who, although retired from full-time medical practice, can nonetheless display his knowledge to good use in books. He assumes the role of protector over Jacqueline Gibson (JEAN BROOKS)—even if it means shielding her from her sister Mary (Kim Hunter). But this is a film about knowing too much: the members of the satanic cult (who order Jacqueline to die, on account of the fact that she has talked about them in public) try to discover the unknowable, and thereby assume mastery over others. By comparison Judd's psychological know-how seems rather insignificant. In a defining moment in the film, Judd recalls the lover he once knew (i.e., Irena in *Cat People*) who now languishes in an asylum, "a horrible raving thing," as a result of his treatment. He seems genuinely regretful for what he has done — in other words, he tried to probe too deeply into the human psyche. *The Seventh Victim* ends with Judd and Jason Hoag (Hugh Beaumont) confronting the Satanists as they desperately search for Jacqueline. Hoag describes them as "lovers of evil." Judd reminds them that perhaps they might not have "taken the wrong turning" if they had only remembered the words of the Lord's Prayer: "Forgive us our trespasses, lead us not into temptation, and deliver us from evil." Such words also apply to the psychiatrist; if Judd had not been led into temptation, then perhaps he might not have destroyed Irena in *Cat People*.

In *I Walked with a Zombie* (1943), another Tourneur-directed film, Conway's Paul Holland comes across as the perfect British gentleman, a Mr. Rochester-like figure married to a catatonic wife Jessica (Christine Gordon). As in *Cat People*, all is not what it seems with Conway's character; clearly he has something to hide, as he never looks anyone in the eye — least of all the nurse Betsy Connell (Frances Dee). Even when he overcomes his inhibitions and clasps her to his chest in a gesture of affection, we feel that his reaction is a little too excessive. Eventually, we discover what the problem is; Paul is tormented by the fact that he might have driven his wife to distraction. Wesley Rand (James Ellison) has no doubt that Paul used words to his wife "like other men use their fists," and subsequently tried to avoid responsibility by cultivating an urbane exterior. The latent violence in Paul's character is revealed in one sequence, as he orders a decanter to remain on the dining table in a thunderous tone that seems totally unlike his customary way of speaking.

Tourneur does not actually blame Paul for what happened, but he does suggest that Jessica was the product of a patriarchal society that brutalizes black people and causes women to internalize their roles as massive objects that men (in this case Paul and Wesley) compete for. The film shows Paul and Betsy embracing one another, and supposedly going off to live a new life together, but we suspect that he might end up treating Betsy in the same way. Paul is imprisoned by his character—a fact emphasized by an ingenious use of filtered light that creates the effect of prison bars on the Holland plantation.

In *Bride of the Gorilla* (1951), another film with a tropical setting, Conway plays Dr. Viet — a reincarnation of Dr. Judd in *Cat People* and *The Seventh Victim*, in the sense that he claims to cure all diseases. Every patient is treated briskly yet efficiently, with instruments

Tom Conway and Martha O'Driscoll in *Criminal Court* (1946). Brother of George Sanders, Tom Conway made his name in film series such as *The Falcon*, as well as a debonair leading man in horror and science fiction films of the 1940s and 1950s.

carried round in an official-looking black bag. However, Viet remains fundamentally isolated — although in love with Dina Van Gelder (Barbara Payton), he lacks both physical presence and charisma. Moreover, he finds that medical science has no power to deal with the elemental forces of the jungle, which decree that Barney Chavez (RAYMOND BURR) must be punished for killing Dina's husband Klaas (PAUL CAVANAGH) and marrying her himself. The story assumes a quasi-biblical quality: once he has killed Klaas, Chavez sells his soul to the devil (symbolized by the presence of a snake next to Klass's corpse). While Chavez acquires undreamed-of powers—the ability to see more clearly, to deal with victims more efficiently — he is also destroyed. This is what happens at the end, as the Commissioner (Lon Chaney, Jr.) observes in a voiceover that the jungle has duly punished him for his crime. In this elemental world, Viet's medical remedies have no curative capacities whatsoever. Conway reappears with Burr once more in the sci-fi/fantasy *Tarzan and the She-Devil* (1953); this time, Conway plays Fidel, the reluctant associate of poacher Vargo (Burr). Although dreaming of "the better things in life," such as prosperity and the love of a good woman, Fidel agrees to go on an expedition to hunt elephants in the jungle. However, he meets a grisly fate, as Tarzan (Lex Barker) summons up the elephants with his famous cry and initiates a stampede that destroys all the poachers.

Voodoo Woman (1957) incorporates a wealth of intertexts from previous Conway films. Like *I Walked with a Zombie*, the action takes place in a tropical setting in which black people are consciously portrayed as savage, preoccupied with sacrificing white people to ensure the future of their race. As in *Bride of the Gorilla*, Conway plays a doctor — Dr. Roland Gerard. However Gerard, unlike Dr. Viet, has gone native; he willingly participates in tribal rituals, wearing the appropriate headgear. The reason for this soon becomes evident: Gerard wants to create a superwoman, "powerful of mind and body," by combining voodoo with the "white man's science" of administering injections to an unwilling female victim.

Conway has great fun parodying his screen image of the reserved British gentleman, as he seeks to "shatter the very foundations of science," his face breaking into an evil grin while he speaks. In *The Seventh Victim* and *I Walked with a Zombie*, he reveals a tender concern for his loved ones; this is certainly not the case in *Voodoo Woman*, as he grasps his wife Susan (Mary Ellen Kay) by the wrists and throws her to the ground, after she has implied that he might be insane. As she tries to get up he snarls: "It's too late now [for the two of them to reconcile] [...] If you try to escape, I'll kill you." Later on Gerard is discovered in his laboratory, injecting the native girl Zuranda (who lies drugged on a marble slab) with the serum that will transform her into the superwoman. He smiles and observes sotto voce that there are "no secrets that genius cannot fathom." Such sequences not only recall Conway's Dr. Judd in *Cat People* (where he establishes a similar kind of mesmeric control over Irena (SIMONE SIMON), but they also emphasize *Voodoo Woman*'s fundamentally patriarchal stance: men are 'naturally' destined to control women.

Sadly, Gerard's dream of unrestrained power evaporates rapidly. Led by the witchdoctor Chaka (Martin Wilkins), the natives decide that Gerard must be sacrificed, in addition to the other white people. Although Gerard escapes, he finds to his cost that his superwoman eventually turns on him. Director Edward L. Cahn cuts to a close-up of his petrified face as the monster places her hands round his neck and strangles him to death. The last we see of him is his corpse sinking lifelessly to the ground.

In *The She-Creature* (1956), Conway plays Timothy Chappel, another megalomaniac who finds to his cost that those whom he seeks to control refuse to recognize his authority. Chappel hopes to make a financial killing by promoting Dr. Carlo Lombardi (Chester Morris), a mysterious hypnotist; sitting behind his rolltop desk Chappel grins evilly as he talks of the millions to be made out of book promotions, personal appearances and radio spots. However, Chappel's expression abruptly changes when Lombardi decides to resist him; despite repeated requests for him to leave, the hypnotist stubbornly refuses. Chappel tries to enforce his authority but the task proves futile; he meets a violent demise as the eponymous she-creature (who has been summoned from the sea on the hypnotist's bidding) strangles him to death.

In his later career, Conway played various scientists, including Dr. Feodor Orloff, a Russian geologist — a rather appropriate piece of casting, given the actor's place of birth — in the Cold War sci-fi flick *12 to the Moon* (1960). Initially, it seems as if he is determined to prove the myth of Soviet superiority, claiming that they are "the best map-makers in the world," as well as the best inventors. He despises his colleagues from different cultures; at one point he contemptuously chides Turkish doctor Selim Hamid (Muzaffer Tema, here billed as Tema Bey) for praising Allah rather than the spaceship for helping to ensure successful take-off. Later on in the film, Orloff quite literally gets his hands burned for daring to handle a piece of moon-rock; by such means director David Bradley reminds us of how dangerous the colonizing process can be for invaders and invaded alike. Eventually, Orloff understands the value of peaceful co-existence, as he foils an attempt by a fellow member of the Iron Curtain alliance to set off a bomb that might destroy America. Orloff exclaims: "I am not only a scientist, also a human being, not an insane murderer! [...] I betray no one, particularly not myself!" He is eventually saved from death by strangulation by the intervention of American Captain John Anderson (Ken Clark). Anderson and Orloff end the sequence by shaking hands — an apt metaphor to show how international co-operation could end the Cold War.

Elisha Cook, Jr.

b. December 26, 1903, San Francisco, California; d. May 18, 1995, Big Pine, California.

Began in films by playing students and other juvenile roles, but later became more accustomed to playing intense neurotics, spineless wheeler-dealers or other low-life characters. His best-known role was that of Wilmer in John Huston's *The Maltese Falcon* (1941), the guntoting weasel to whom Humphrey Bogart spat the line, "The cheaper the crook, the gaudier the patter." Cook became so typecast in such roles that he earned the nickname of "Hollywood's Lightest Heavy."

One such role was that of Cliff in Robert Siodmak's noir horror *Phantom Lady* (1944). While playing the drums in a local jazz band, he spends most of his evenings ogling woman; the intense nature of his sexual desire is suggested in one point of view shot where the camera starts out at a girl's feet and gradually tracks upwards, pausing at her skirt. In

Nancy Kelly and Elisha Cook, Jr., in *He Married His Wife* (1940). Cook made a habit of playing lowlife characters who pretended to be strong but were usually suppressed by violent means.

another shot, Cliff is shown playing more and more intently as he stares at Carol Richman (Ella Raines); the sweat pours off his brow as the camera cuts feverishly between close-ups of Cliff and Carol, suggesting that Cliff is experiencing an orgasm. After the performance, Cliff takes Carol to his dressing room; he obviously thinks of himself as a great lover as he advances towards her and clasps her in a sweaty embrace. Carol recoils in terror, but does not leave the room, as she wants to use the occasion to find out more about what happened to her employer Scott Henderson (Alan Curtis), who has been wrongfully accused of murdering his wife. Cliff is just about to kiss Carol when the smooth-tongued killer Jack Marlow (Franchot Tone) enters; the drummer starts back in terror, and cowers in the corner as Jack comes inexorably towards him and strangles him to death, while Carol takes advantage of the confusion to run away.

Cook played some memorable roles in horror and/or science fiction films throughout his career. In *Voodoo Island* (1957), he plays Martin Schuyler, who welcomes a party of intrepid explorers led by Phillip Knight (Boris Karloff). At first reluctant to make the journey to the eponymous voodoo island, Schuyler's doubts are soon overcome by the promise of financial rewards. He looks at the camera, spreads his arms wide and smiles, observing that "we cannot live by food alone." Captain Matthew Gunn (Rhodes Reason) criticizes his spineless nature, having "sold his soul" in the hope of material gain. Schuyler is a far from ideal traveling companion: throughout the voyage to the island we see him cowering in the hold of the boat, as if fearful of what the future might bring. While exploring the island, he utters the illogical line, "These noises. Can't see 'em," suggesting that he is incapable of making sense of his new surroundings. Inevitably, Schuyler pays the price for his greed — at one point he objects strongly to the prospect of giving up his wealth to those "inferior creatures" (the natives of the island). The natives punish him by reducing him to a catatonic vegetable, plunging to his death by falling into a river off a flimsy bridge. We feel that this punishment is somehow justified for a would-be colonizer who regards people of color as second-class citizens.

Cook occasionally managed to stay alive in his horror roles. In *The House on Haunted Hill* (1959), he plays Watson Pritchard, one of the unfortunate guests invited to spend a night in a lonely mansion by eccentric millionaire Frederick Loren (Vincent Price). Pritchard's face is seen in close-up at the beginning of the film, as he recalls the experience, and how he nearly died as a result. The action then flashes back to the beginning of the evening, where Pritchard is discovered looking nervously around, shifting from foot to foot as if he clearly does not want to be there. However, he needs the money (Loren having promised his guests a $10,000 reward if they successfully spend the night in the house). Pritchard is tormented by the belief that the house is haunted: at one point, he wonders why the ghosts simply don't kill all of them off and have done with it. The only way in which he can deal with the experience is to drink; as the evening wears on, his speech becomes more and more slurred. Eventually, he slumps into a chair, making little or no attempt to involve himself in anything. Director William Castle takes great pleasure in photographing Pritchard in close-up, his wild eyes staring wildly from side to side, his voice ascending into an intense crescendo as he describes the horrors within the house. Sometimes we wonder whether he actually enjoys the experience of frightening everyone with his talk: when Frederick's wife Annabelle (Carol Ohmart) is apparently murdered, Pritchard murmurs, "They [the ghosts] haven't finished yet!" Eventually, Pritchard retires to bed, carrying a revolver. He places his armchair opposite the door, and sits in it, ready to shoot any intruders who might stray in.

We discover that the house is not haunted at all, and Annabelle — who only feigns death — has been responsible for the murders in collaboration with her lover Dr. David Trent (Alan Marshal). Both of them meet grisly fates; Trent is shot dead by Frederick, while Annabelle is drowned in a vat of acid. However, Pritchard is still convinced that ghosts haunt the house — at the end of the film he looks straight to camera and says, "There'll be more, they're coming for me now." Director Castle zooms in to a tight close-up of his face as he issues a parting shot: "Then they'll come for YOU!"

In the Laurel and Hardy spoof *A-Haunting We Will Go* (1942), Cook plays gangster Frank Lucas, a member of a gang trying to smuggle one of their own into Dayton, Ohio, using Laurel and Hardy as stoolpigeons, Cook takes on the role of "Aunt Mary," a woman ostensibly mourning the death of her son. He wears a long black dress, horn-rimmed spectacles and a wig, and dabs his eyes with a handkerchief. To complete the disguise, he knits a wooly sweater and speaks in falsetto. Needless to say, Laurel and Hardy are successfully duped, and agree to take responsibility for transporting the coffin to Dayton. Although Cook subsequently reverts to type, playing a heavy who repeatedly tries and fails to kill the two protagonists, he obviously enjoys the chance to parody his screen persona.

Harry Cording

b. April 26, 1891, Wellington, Somerset, England; d. September 4, 1954, Sun Valley, California.

Although mostly a bit part player with very few (if any) lines to speak, Harry Cording made his presence felt in several horror films of the 1930s and 1940s. This was chiefly due to his imposing physique, as well as a striking face notable for its bushy eyebrows and penetrating scowl. Such qualities are evident in his characterization of Thamal, the black-clad heavy working for Dr. Vitus Wendergast (Bela Lugosi) in *The Black Cat* (1934). While not called upon to say anything, Cording cuts an imposing presence in his black garb and finely chiseled features; clearly he is not someone to be trifled with. He stands guard over the front door of the corrupt priest Hjalmar Poelzig's (Boris Karloff) house, as Peter Alison (DAVID MANNERS) makes a vain attempt to escape, and fells Alison with one blow. Thamal subsequently picks up Alison and his wife Joan (Jacqueline Wells) as if they were rag dolls and deposits them in their respective prison-cells — an underground dungeon for Alison, a bedroom for his wife. Thamal's most spectacular moment occurs later on; with blood seeping from his mouth, he advances towards Poelzig, places his hands around his neck and attempts to strangle him. He subsequently picks the priest up, carries him down to the dungeon and strings him up by his thumbs. Now Wendergast can finally take his revenge on Poelzig by skinning him alive.

Thamal loyally stands beside his master at the end of the film, as both of them die in an explosion that rips through Poelzig's house.

Cording donned the black garb once again for his brief appearance as the First Murderer of the two young princes in *Tower of London* (1939), Rowland V. Lee's ghoulish retelling of Shakespeare's *Richard III*. The murder is first seen in close-up with his bushy mustache, beret and ruff—the very epitome of a respectable Plantagenet. However, this image is soon destroyed as he rushes towards the young King Edward (Ronald Sinclair), places his thick hands round his neck and strangles him. This sequence lasts only two or three seconds, as the camera suddenly jerks upwards, leaving the murderer to complete his work out of the viewer's gaze. All we hear is the sound of blood-curdling screams on the soundtrack. This strategy can partly be attributed to censorship restrictions (the Hays Office would never have permitted a child to be killed on screen), but it also serves a thematic purpose, suggesting that the murderer's act is so foul that no one should have to witness it. In *Strange Door* (1951), Cording has yet another cameo in a period drama as a guard of Alain de Maletroit (Charles Laughton). Whereas in *Tower of London*, he was zealously efficient in the execution of duty, in *Strange Door* he is almost too drunk to move. He rolls about the room and collapses on a slab, in a manner strongly reminiscent of Turke, the opium addict, a role Cording played in the 1935 Universal adaptation of Dickens' *The Mystery of Edwin Drood*. In *Strange Door*, Cording's guard remains oblivious to everything around him: Corbeau (William Cottrell) walks past in an attempt to escape from de Maletroit's castle. The guard's sole reaction is to look at him with bleary eyes, take another draught from his tankard and fall asleep once more, snoring loudly as he does so.

Sometimes Cording had the chance to play characters on the right side of the law—as in *Man in the Attic* (1953), a reworking of the Hitchcock film *The Lodger*, based on the Jack the Ripper case. Cording plays Detective Sergeant Bates, the reliable sidekick of Inspector Warwick (Paul Bonner); while the inspector does most of the criminal investigation, Bates offers a reassuring presence, agreeing with his superior where necessary yet asking the right questions when Warwick appears at a loss. Bates is fond of putting his hands in his pockets or playing with his watch-chain; both gestures suggest a thoughtful personality, someone keen to weigh up all the evidence presented in front of him before coming to a decision.

Harry Cording and Byron Palmer in *Man in the Attic* (1953). British-born Cording was in regular demand as a heavy, or a member of the working class. *Man in the Attic* was one of the few films where he had the chance to show his talent as a police inspector.

Cording regularly appeared in contemporary horror films, mostly for Universal. As a mine worker in *The Invisible Man Returns* (1940) he challenges his boss Willie Spears's (ALAN NAPIER) authority by laughing in his face. This act sets the mood for the rest of the film, in which Geoffrey Radcliffe (Vincent Price) becomes invisible and thereby defies the efforts of Inspector Sampson (CECIL KELLAWAY) to catch him, until such time as Geoffrey can prove his innocence of the crime of murder. Cording reprises the role of a rabble-rouser in *The Ghost of Frankenstein* (1942), who urges the villagers (who have been terrorized by the monster [Lon Chaney, Jr.]) to storm Dr. Frankenstein's (CEDRIC HARDWICKE) house and destroy everything — the monster, the scientific equipment, and preferably the inhabitants as well. With the light shining on his bowler hat and black three-piece suit, Cording cuts an intimidating figure as he rejects the entreaties of lawyer Erik (Ralph Bellamy) to stay within the confines of the law and urges the mob to follow him with an imperious wave of the hand.

Cording played yet another variation of the role as the "Rough Character in Park" in Universal's horror spoof *Abbott and Costello Meet Dr. Jekyll and Mr. Hyde* (1953). He listens with mounting impatience to the suffragette Vicky Edwards (Helen Westcott) and orders her to "go back to the kitchen where you belong!" The young hero Bruce Adams (Craig Stevens) pushes him away, exclaiming, "You can't talk to a lady like that," at which point Cording stares him in the face and laughs once again, saying as he does so, "Try and shut me up." He subsequently turns to his fellow-hecklers and tells them, "Let's get them [the women] back to the kitchen!" Cording crashes to the ground, having been hit on the head by an umbrella; later on the same fate befalls both Slim (Bud Abbott) and Tubby (Lou Costello), two inept police officers who vainly try to restore order.

Cording appeared in no less than eight of the Sherlock Holmes films for Twentieth Century–Fox and Universal. In *Sherlock Holmes and the Secret Weapon* (1943), he plays the carpenter Jack Brady, who willingly accepts a bribe in return for information, then lies back on a wooden cot, a cigarette tucked behind his ear, and laughs maniacally at the fact that has managed to fool the great Sherlock Holmes (Basil Rathbone). Brady acts as one of Professor Moriarty's (LIONEL ATWILL) heavies; he grasps Holmes by the arm, ties him up and thrusts him in a wooden cadaver. He takes the box down to the sea under the pretense of being "a simple seafaring man." Holmes is rescued in the nick of time by the timely intervention of Watson (Nigel Bruce) and Inspector Lestrade (Dennis Hoey), who chase after Brady, forcing him to drop the cadaver.

Cording plays John Simpson in *The House of Fear* (1945) — a "surly-looking chap" (according to Dr. Watson [Nigel Bruce]), who smokes a pipe and seems inherently suspicious of Holmes's presence in the house. With his tattooed chest and short, powerful forearms, Simpson cannot be trifled with, which makes his supposed death by mutilation seem all the more bizarre. Eventually, it emerges that Simpson has not been killed at all, but rather participated in an elaborate scheme to relieve Alistair (Aubrey Mather) of his insurance money. In *Dressed to Kill* (1946), Cording plays a role similar to that in *The Black Cat* of a heavy faithfully carrying out his employer's orders. The only difference this time is that Cording plays an Arab chauffeur, Hamid, working for Hilda Courtney (Patricia Morison).

Robert Cornthwaite
b. April 28, 1917, St. Helens, Oregon;
d. July 20, 2006, Woodland Hills, California.

Robert Cornthwaite made his debut on stage in 1935 at the Reed College Campus in Portland. He worked in radio in Southern California before being called up for military service during the Second World War. Returning to acting in 1945, Cornthwaite divided his time between radio, television and films, playing some notable character roles in science fiction films of the 1950s.

Perhaps his most famous part — the one that earned him entry into the Science Fiction Hall of Fame in 1993 — was that of Dr. Carrington in Christian Nyby and Howard Hawks's *The Thing From Another World* (1951). As the unofficial leader of an Arctic polar expedition, Carrington observes the crash of an unidentified alien (James Arness), and urges his military colleagues, led by Captain Patrick Hendry (KENNETH TOBEY), to investigate. Carrington's first appearance in the film takes place in his laboratory; his obsessive devotion to his work is palpable, as he does not come to welcome the captain, but expects the captain to find him. The prospect of investigating the alien excites Carrington immensely; he observes that his research could provide "the key to the stars [...] a million years of history." Henry and his colleagues remain perpetually suspicious of Carrington's motives; one of them describes the doctor as "a human clamp" who refuses to tell anyone about his discoveries, for fear that they would enhance their reputations at the doctor's expense.

In the end, Carrington's obsession with the alien's potential blinds him to its potential dangers, as he holds court in his laboratory and describes the "thinking vegetable" with "no emotions, no heart" that in his view "wants a chance to communicate" with the creatures on Earth and thereby learn the "secrets of mankind." Carrington believes that the creature "came here [to Earth] for refuge — it's wiser than we are." As he speaks, however, we understand that the sheer strain of the doctor's research has proved too much for him; he massages his head and claims that he must continue in spite of being overtired. One of his scientific colleagues concludes that Carrington is "not thinking right" in his insistence that "only science can conquer him [the creature] [...] there must be a way." This judgment proves spot-on: despite Carrington's obvious convictions, he cannot understand the alien's true intention to destroy the Earth and its inhabitants through violent means. In the film's climactic moment, Carrington advances towards the alien claiming, "I'm your friend, I want to help you [...] to use that intelligence. I'm a scientist, I'm a scientist, who's trying to tell you...." He proceeds no further as the alien knocks him to the ground with a contemptuous wave of the hand and advances threateningly on Hendry and his colleagues. In the end, the alien is electrocuted to death, leaving the crew of the spaceship to return home, and the journalist Ned "Scotty" Scott (Douglas Spencer) to send a radio report paying tribute to the American military, which went "beyond the call of duty" in its efforts to destroy the alien. Scott ends up by advising viewers to "keep looking, keep watching the stars" for future threats to the Earth's security.

The Thing from Another World emphasizes the dangers of research for its own sake — particularly if it is conducted without due concern for the future security of people on Earth. Sometimes it is better to cast aside scientists like Carrington and trust the army, whose perceived qualities of loyalty and respect for authority render it an effective fighting unit.

Cornthwaite played another scientist — Dr. Zoldeck — in another Hawks film, the science fiction spoof *Monkey Business* (1952). The film is clearly conceived as a vehicle for its stars, Cary Grant and Ginger Rogers, both of whom have the opportunity to behave like teenagers and young children. Marilyn Monroe also appears in a cameo role as a nubile secretary. Cornthwaite's Dr. Zoldeck is part of a group of doctors comprising Barnaby Fulton's (Grant)

Robert Cornthwaite, Charles Coburn and Marilyn Monroe in *Monkey Business* (1953). A studious-looking actor, Cornthwaite played scientists or other learned characters. In *Monkey Business* he acts as a comic foil to Monroe and Cary Grant.

research team; with his owlish spectacles and close-cropped hair, he appears the very epitome of respectability. When Fulton starts to behave like a teenager, Zoldeck shakes his head pityingly in the belief that this condition has been caused by overwork. On another occasion, Zolder comes into the boardroom for a meeting chaired by chemical magnate Oliver Oxley (Charles Coburn), and announces, "Fulton was not himself yesterday morning." This comment proves apposite, as Fulton comes in with his wife Edwina (Rogers) and starts to pursue her round the table. Zolder looks at their antics and observes, "It [Fulton's behavior] proves there are no landmarks to science." Zolder himself falls victim to the same condition at the end of the film (the drug that causes it had been accidentally tipped into the water carafe by a monkey); he ends up spraying a soda siphon at Oxley, and playing tug-of-war with his colleagues.

In Byron Haskin's adaptation of H. G. Wells's *War of the Worlds* (1953), Cornthwaite plays Dr. Pryor, a ginger-haired colleague of Dr. Clayton Forrester (Gene Barry) at the Pacific Institute of Science and Technology in California. He carries out most of Forrester's requests to conduct research into ways of destroying the Martian invaders, insisting as he does so that "there is a chance" that a new and more powerful bomb can be developed for that purpose. As things turn out, however, Pryor could not be more wrong, as the Martians prove impervious to anything the scientists can create. In a clear allusion to the Biblical myth of creation, the scientists are left with six days to come up with a solution or face the total destruction of the earth. We see Pryor and his colleagues beavering away, despite Forrester's rather pessimistic observation that "we now know we can't beat their [the Martians'] machines, [but] we've got to beat them." Eventually, the Martians are destroyed, but not by human intervention; instead they fall victim to what the narrator (CEDRIC HARDWICKE) identifies as divine intervention, as they fall victim to earthly viruses. Pryor's technical know-how proves useless: the film suggests that the only way to repel Earthly invaders is to trust in the Lord.

Lloyd Corrigan

b. October 16, 1900, San Francisco, California; d. November 5, 1969, Woodland Halls, California.

Lloyd Corrigan entered films as an actor in the mid–1920s and subsequently enjoyed a long career as a performer, writer and director. He was frequently seen in comic roles in horror films, or in roles where he played fundamentally weak personalities.

This second type of role is clearly evident, for instance, in Phil Rosen's *The Murder of Marie Roget* (1942), where Corrigan plays Prefect Gobelin. Made by Universal, the film shamelessly imitates the Sherlock Holmes series, with Dr. Paul Dupin (PATRIC KNOWLES) as the Holmes figure, and Gobelin as Watson. As with Nigel Bruce's Watson, Gobelin is a fundamentally decent character with

Lloyd Corrigan and Eddie Albert in *Treat 'Em Rough* (1942). With his round face and wide smile, Corrigan was a fine comic actor, playing harassed figures of authority.

a unique capacity for drawing the wrong conclusions from the evidence placed before him. In fact, he proves a hindrance to solving the murder, which explains why Dupin refuses to explain what he is doing and why. Gobelin becomes increasingly frustrated — so much so that he quite literally jumps up and down like a child deprived of their favorite toy. However, Dupin knows how to pacify him by slapping him on the back and making him feel that he is intrinsic to the solution of the case. At the end of the film, the Prefect congratulates himself on his deductive powers in bringing the murderer to justice, despite the fact that Madame Cecile Roget (MARIA OUSPENSKAYA) considers him a duffer. Corrigan plays another police officer — Detective Latham — in Universal's *She-Wolf of London* (1946). This time he has more freedom to conduct his own line of questioning, even though he pretends to show loyalty to his superior officer, Inspector Pierce (Dennis Hoey). While Latham considers himself something of a Sherlock Holmes figure, with his long overcoat and meerschaum pipe, he lacks the great detective's intelligence. One of his junior police officers (Frederic Worlock) describes him as "a barmy one." This proves an accurate assessment, as Latham ventures into a graveyard without adequate support from his officers in search of the werewolf, who sidles up behind him and strangles him to death.

Corrigan played a circus owner named Whipple in Universal's *Captive Wild Woman* (1943). He comes across as a shrewd operator with a penchant for well-cut suits and big cigars, but perhaps not quite suited for his chosen profession. Whipple is obviously scared of the circus-animals — even when they are safely behind bars, he looks at them apprehensively, clenching and unclenching his fists. When his chief tamer, Fred (Milburn Stone), enters a cage with a lion and a tiger, Whipple looks at the scene in terror, observing in an aside that "the whole scene [taking place in front of him] is unnatural." However, Whipple understands the financial benefits of allowing his tamer to perform in the cage; in the first public performance, we see him thrusting his chest out and walking round the arena looking at the packed house in supreme satisfaction. But Whipple's hopes of success are rudely curtailed: the lion and tiger resist Fred's efforts to tame them and run amok. The audience stampedes in terror, and Whipple is reduced to waving his arms ineffectually, appealing for calm. Director Edward Dmytryk views him satirically, as a greedy person lacking in moral fiber who is obviously unsuited for his chosen profession.

Corrigan's screen persona made him an ideal choice for horror spoofs such as *The Ghost Breakers* (1940), where he plays Martin, a mysterious stranger who keeps popping up in unexpected situations to greet Mary Carter (Paulette Goddard) and radio broadcaster Lawrence Lawrence (Bob Hope). He meets Mary for the first time onboard a ship bound for Cuba; as he speaks, he fingers his hat uncertainly. On the second occasion that they meet, Martin refuses to move out of Mary's way; when Lawrence challenges him, Martin runs off like a frightened rabbit. When Lawrence and Mary arrive in Cuba, they dine at a favored nightspot; once again Martin greets them and retires to his table. Corrigan has a more substantial part in the Bowery Boys vehicle *The Ghost Chasers* (1951) for Monogram, where he plays the ghost Edgar Alden Franklin Smith. In a film all about the exposure of fake mediums, Smith is an actual ghost dedicated to "put an end to all this quackery," as he puts it. Dressed in Puritan garb, completed with wide-brimmed hat, he cuts a dapper figure as he speaks in deliberately archaic English ("Thee and I shall be friends," "Thou may'st call me Edgar"). He becomes friendly with Horace Debussy "Sach" Jones (Huntz Hall), who is the only one of the Bowery Boys who can see him. The two of them play a significant part in exposing a fake medium racket: Edgar appears and disappears at will, grinning all the while at his own cleverness, as he protects Jones while making sure that his adversaries suffer as much as possible. Jones admiringly describes his ghost friend as "a bag of tricks" who "sure gets around." The film ends with Edgar turning to camera as he watches Jones being admonished by his friends (none of whom can actually see Edgar) and observing, "It's obvious, Horace, thy friends don't believe in ghosts.... Dost thou?" On the last phrase, he points his finger directly to the camera, to indicate that he is talking to the audience. If we do believe in ghosts, the film suggests, then perhaps we will also be protected from evil.

In another Bowery Boys vehicle, *The Bowery Boys Meet the Monsters* (1954), Corrigan plays mad scientist Anton Gravesend. With his small steps, fluttering arm movements and simpering tone, he resembles a little bird cowering behind his brother Derek's (John Dehner) bulky frame. The two of them form a comic double-act, with Derek playing the heavy and Anton supplying dialogue whenever Derek tries up. Anton really only comes alive in his laboratory, where he flits around like a little child building a robot which keeps losing its head, or putting together weird concoctions that transform the butler Grissom (Paul Wexler) into a gorilla. When faced with the prospect of transplanting the Bowery Boys' (Leo Gorcey, Huntz Hall) brains into his pet gorilla, Anton jumps up and down with delight, grabbing a kitchen knife and approaching them threateningly. However, he cannot cast a threatening presence, being way too short for the role. Corrigan employs the same kind of stage business that he used in *Captive Wild Woman* to denote the character's basic uncertainty as he walks up and down wringing his hands and looking heavenwards as if seeking divine inspiration. Sadly, his prayers are left unanswered as he is knocked out and his laboratory destroyed.

Sometimes Corrigan played more active roles— as in *The Ghost Goes Wild* (1947), where he takes the role of the ghost of Timothy Beecher. The film owes a clear debt to David Lean's British film *Blithe Spirit* (1945) in its use of ghosts for comic effect. In *The Ghost Goes Wild*, Corrigan is impeccably dressed in dinner suit and tie, reveling in his ability to appear and disappear at will by holding his breath and blowing out his cheeks. He takes great pleasure in passing on a secret about his wife Susan (Ruth Donnelly): we are never allowed to know what that secret it, but it is sufficient to persuade her to drop her lawsuit against cartoonist Monte Crandall (James Ellison). Timothy's other unique trait is a fondness for chewing gum; he grabs off a salver proffered by Eric the butler (Edward Everett Horton), and thrusts it into his mouth. Corrigan has great fun with this role, waving his arms around — as if conducting an imaginary orchestra — to command his interlocutors' attention, and delivering his lines with portentous glee. The word "absolutely" is spoken in four syllables ("ab-sol-ute-ly.") After an initial scare (he whimpers, "I can't get back! I can't get back," in plaintive tones), Timothy returns to the other world; his presence in the remainder of the film is confined to voiceovers—for example, sanctioning the marriage between Monte and Timothy's niece Phyllis (ANNE GWYNNE) with the comment, "We need a little red blood in this family." Whether that "red blood" belongs to Monte, Phyllis, or both of them is left deliberately obscure: what matters more is that Timothy has helped to contrive a happy ending, despite his wife's best efforts to prevent it.

Donald Crisp

b. July 27, 1882, Bow, London, England; d. May 25, 1974, Van Nuys, California.

George William Crisp began working as a stage manager as a stage manager for the renowned entertainer, composer, playwright, and director George M. Cohan. He became friends with D.W. Griffith, and went to Hollywood in 1912. From then on, Crisp pursued a career as a director, working on over seventy films until his final work *The Runaway Bride* (1930). As a character actor, Crisp became known for his versatility, appearing in everything from *The Private Lives of Elizabeth and Essex* (1939) to *Lassie Come Home* (1943). However, he did take some notable roles in horror films during the studio period. In Warner Brothers' *Svengali* (1931), he plays the Laird, one half of a comic double act with Taffy (Lumsden Hare). They participate in a farcical piece of business at the beginning, as they throw Svengali (John Barrymore) into a bath full of water. However, the eponymous hero has the last laugh as he makes off with Taffy's coat and the Laird's purse.

Donald Crisp publicity still (1944). Scottish-born Crisp's career began in the silent era and continued well into the 1950s. He made his name playing figures of authority in all walks of life.

The Laird is full of false bonhomie, one of "the three musketeers of the brush" who spend most of their time painting spurious portraits. He is unable to forge any close relationships, preferring instead to pursue vicarious pleasures — for example, painting Trilby O'Farrell (Marian Marsh). This makes him no match for Svengali who has the power to control people simply by staring into their eyes. Crisp's performance is typical of a certain type of Englishman — elderly, well-meaning yet fundamentally ineffectual — who regularly cropped up in films of the 1930s and 1940s on both sides of the Atlantic. Perhaps the best example might be Basil Radford and Naunton Wayne's Charters and Caldicott in Hitchcock's *The Lady Vanishes* (1938). The Laird cannot understand his friend Billie's (BRAMWELL FLETCHER) sufferings; he would much rather enjoy the fun of seeing "Svengali in a dress suit" or, better still, teasing Svengali about whether he is "still dodging the landladies or not."

Ten years later, Crisp had a major supporting role in Victor Fleming's remake of *Dr. Jekyll and Mr. Hyde*, as Sir Charles Emery. As a representative of so-called "polite" society, he disapproves of Dr. Jekyll's (Spencer Tracy) radical theories, suggesting that human beings have two sides, both good and evil. In one sequence, taking place at the dinner table, the camera pans the guests as Jekyll speaks, coming to rest on Emery's face. Outwardly he seems calm and relaxed, but the eyes and the furrowing brows suggest otherwise. Fleming emphasizes the difference of viewpoints between Emery and Jekyll through intercut close-ups of their faces: Jekyll becoming more and more animated as he expounds his ideas, while Emery's features remain expressionless, save for his eyes.

Yet Sir Charles is not devoid of human feeling; in another sequence, he is shown walking slowly towards a portrait of his widow, hanging above the fireplace. In the background, we see Jekyll and his fiancée Beatrix (Lana Turner) — Sir Charles's daughter — dancing to a waltz. Sir Charles turns and gazes longingly at the young couple, as if wishing that his widow could come back to life so that he too might dance. However, he is broad-minded enough to allow Jekyll and Beatrix to get married; he gives his consent in London's National Gallery, pats Jekyll on the shoulder and smiles benevolently as the lovers embrace. As he walks away, he catches sight of two (uncredited) middle-aged women gazing in horror at the unseemly sight of his daughter and son-in-law. He observes wryly that this is "just another work of art, not in the catalog." However, Sir Charles's trust proves misplaced, as Jekyll cannot control the process of transformation into Mr. Hyde. At the end of the film the old man rushes to rescue his daughter from Hyde's clutches, and is beaten to death for his pains in a particularly violent sequence.

When compared with Halliwell Hobbes's performance in the same role in the 1931 version, Crisp comes across as a sympathetic person — an old-style Englishman, obsessed with respectability, yet also well-meaning (a trait also observable in *Svengali*). But he is no match for

Mr. Hyde, whom Tracy plays—in total contrast to his customary screen image — as the embodiment of pure evil with no redeeming qualities whatsoever.

In *The Uninvited* (1944), Crisp has a major supporting role as retired Commander Beech, a white-haired, outwardly respectable pillar of the local village community, who willingly agrees to sell a house belonging to his granddaughter Stella (Gail Russell) to newcomers Roderick Fitzgerald and his sister Pamela (Ray Milland and Ruth Hussey). However, his mood of superficial affability abruptly changes, as he witnesses a developing romantic attachment between Roderick and Stella. He forbids her to visit the house, forcing Roderick to indulge in various subterfuges, such as picking Stella up from a pre-arranged location outside her house and taking her to church in his car.

Eventually, it transpires that Beech's attitude is inspired by fear for his granddaughter's safety in a house haunted by Mary's ghost. The only way he can deal with the situation is to send Stella away to a sanatorium run by Miss Holloway (Cornelia Otis Skinner), in the mistaken assumption that this will provide an effective cure. What he does not know, however, is that Miss Holloway (as Mary's one-time employee) wants to destroy Stella in the be-lief that the young girl contributed in some small way to Mary's death by falling off a cliff. While coming across as a dominant, rather overpowering personality (entering a room with such curses as "What in thunder is this?"), Beech turns out to be a fundamentally weak person trying and failing to cope with a situation "filled with malignance." Eventually he collapses to the ground, haunted by the ghosts of the past. Despite all attempts to rescue him, he passes away.

Director Lewis Allen suggests that only way to exorcize Mary's ghost is not to run away but to confront it — which is precisely what Roderick and Stella decide to do. We learn that Stella's mother was not Mary but Carmel, a gypsy woman who successfully won over Mary's father. Since that time, Mary has taken revenge by haunting Roderick's house but she no longer has influence once Stella has acknowledged her kinship with Carmel.

Henry Daniell

b. March 5, 1894, London, England:
d. October 31, 1963, Santa Monica, California.

A British actor best known for his villainous roles, Charles Henry Daniel made his stage debut in London in 1914, and pursued a long and distinguished stage career both in Britain and America. He made his film debut in 1930, and subsequently had some choice roles in classics such as *Camille* (1936) and *The Private Lives of Elizabeth and Essex* (1939).

In the next decade, Daniell played in no fewer

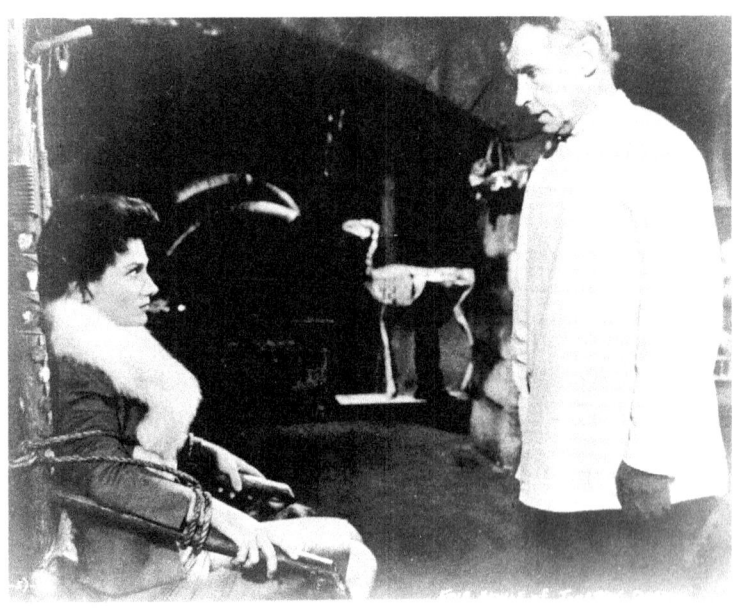

Valerie French and Henry Daniell in *The Four Skulls of Jonathan Drake* (1959). Another legendary Hollywood villain, Daniell's sharp features and husky voice rendered him eminently hissable.

than three of Universal's Sherlock Holmes series—*The Voice of Terror* (1942), *Sherlock Holmes in Washington* (1943) and *The Woman in Green* (1945). In the first of these films, he plays British government bureaucrat Sir Anthony Lloyd, who remains perpetually skeptical of Holmes's (Basil Rathbone) methods. Lloyd insists that Holmes should keep the Inner Council informed of all his activities, so as to ensure transparency. In Dr. Watson's (Nigel Bruce) view, Lloyd is "a great fellow," but he does prove something of a liability as he insists on accompanying Holmes and Watson on one of their missions. Director Roy William Neill includes several close-ups of Daniell's face, his upper lip curling slightly as he suspects Holmes of not acting in the national interest.

In *From the Earth to the Moon* (1958), based on the Jules Verne novel, Daniell plays Morgana, another pillar of the British establishment (reminiscent of Sir Anthony Lloyd in *The Woman in Green*) who funds Victor Barbicane's (Joseph Cotten) scientific experiments, even though he has no idea of how they might turn out. Daniell comes across as a forceful personality who can convince his fellows to back Barbicane, even though he might live to regret it later on. At one point, Morgana is shown in close-up shaking his head sorrowfully and murmuring that he "paid rather dearly" for his enthusiasm. Like Christopher Columbus in 1492, Barbicane seems so obsessed with his project that he is prepared to question the notion of what is possible or impossible in terms of human science. Morgana paces the room, up and down, and is only pacified once he discovers that Barbicane actually knew what he was talking about. Director Byron Haskin zooms in to a close-up of Morgana's face gazing enthusiastically skyward, as he watches Barbicane blasting off to the moon.

Daniell had the chance to play a mad scientist—Dr. Wolfe ('Toddy') Macfarlane—in Robert Wise's *The Body Snatcher* (1945), based on the Robert Louis Stevenson short story. Initially, he comes across as rather a forbidding personality—someone so committed to his research and teaching that he has no time to perform a life-saving operation on the child Georgina Marsh (Sharon Moffett). He believes that he has "a responsibility—a great responsibility" to medical science, but undercuts this impression somewhat by sitting down in a chair and reading a magazine. Perhaps there are other reasons for his reluctance. We soon find out why: in the past Macfarlane had been involved in the criminal act of stealing corpses from graves to use in medical research. One of his accomplices, the cabman John Gray (Boris Karloff), had been sent to prison, while Macfarlane escaped scot-free; now Gray has returned to hold the doctor to ransom. If Macfarlane does not agree to the cabman's demands, then the police will be informed of the truth behind the case. Macfarlane's attitude subtly changes—in place of the rather forbidding, schoolteacher-like personality of the early part of the film, he becomes almost agreeable, musing in a calm tone that "it [the operation] might be an interesting case" to undertake. We see him embracing his companion Meg Camden (Edith Atwater) who knows everything about the doctor's past, but has chosen to stand by him.

However, this affable tone is soon superseded by one of arrant terror, as he realizes just how much of a hold Gray has over him. He sits at his desk, staring wild-eyed at his papers, then storms out to the local tavern to get drunk. Despite his pleas (at one point, he looks straight into Gray's eyes and beseeches him to leave him alone), the cabman laughs and taunts him with the phrase "You'll never get rid of me." This statement proves prophetic—although Macfarlane eventually kills Gray (and celebrates his feat by announcing "There's a good riddance!" in a triumphant tone), he is perpetually tormented by the cabman's ghost. The film ends with Macfarlane driving a coach and horses through the night, his face becoming wilder and wilder as Gray's voice is heard repeating "Never get rid of me, never, never, never," over and over again. Despite his best efforts, the doctor can never escape the past. His death—caused by the carriage crashing over a precipice—comes as a merciful release from pain and suffering.

Daniell has a small role in the Maria Montez

sci-fi/fantasy vehicle *Sirens of Atlantis* (1949) as Blades, a librarian. While outwardly polite to anyone visiting Atlantis, such as the soldier Lt. André St. Avit (Jean-Pierre Aumont), Blades makes sure that they do not escape. With just a small incline of the head, he can summon Queen Antinea's (Montez's) private army, which surrounds its victims and forces them to sit down once more. To ensure that they are incapable of active resistance, Blades plies his "guests" (as he terms them) with drink, accompanied with a tight smile.

In *The Four Skulls of Jonathan Drake* (1959), Daniell has a lip-smackingly villainous role as the 180-year-old witch doctor Dr. Emil Zurich. We first discover him sitting in his lair with a smile of satisfaction spread across his face. He exudes arrogance, as he refuses to shake Inspector Rowan's (Grant Richards) hand in the belief that the police officer is his social inferior. In a later scene, he addresses Rowan without even bothering to look the police officer in the eye. Zurich enjoys the power he exerts over members of the Drake family; having obtained Kenneth Drake's (PAUL CAVANAGH) head, and boiled it in a steaming cauldron of water, he takes it out and observes that it is a "particularly ... FINE ... specimen," taking long pauses between the three words. Once the process of transforming the head into a *tsantsas* (a shrunken head characteristic of Native Indian tribes in Peru and Ecuador) has been completed, Zurich turns directly to the camera and snarls: "Next it will be Jonathan Drake [Eduard Franz] ... then the family curse will be ... FINISHED!" The last word is delivered as a shout of triumph: Zurich believes that no one will stand in his way. At first it seems as if his prediction will come true, as he tries to penetrate Jonathan's dreams. Dressed in long robes with an Indian mask covering his face, Zurich intones in a doom-laden voice: "Watch, Jonathan Drake ... WATCH ... as your skull ... joins the others!" Director Edward L. Cahn cuts to a shot of Jonathan sleeping and suddenly waking up with a start as he hears Zurich's words in his imagination. As with most villains, however, Zurich overreaches himself, as he captures Jonathan's daughter Alison (Valerie French) and takes her back to his lair, in the belief that she would enjoy the sight of her father's head being transformed into a *tsantsas*. Rowan and her father arrive in hot pursuit and drive Zurich out of his house; eventually Zurich is stabbed with the same stiletto that was used to kill Kenneth Drake. Jonathan sits astride Zurich's motionless body and cuts off the doctor's head; this is the only way to remove the family curse. Zurich's corpse immediately turns to dust.

Albert Dekker

b. December 20, 1905, Brooklyn, New York; d. May 5, 1968, Hollywood, California.

Albert van Dekker began by establishing himself as a stage actor before moving to Hollywood in 1937. He was memorable as Dr. Thorkel in Ernest B. Schoedsack's *Dr Cyclops* (1939)—an obsessive scientist who buries himself away in the Amazon jungle in his efforts to create a serum that reduces people to midgets, no more than thirteen inches high. Tall, with a slight stoop and thick-rimmed spectacles that

Albert Dekker in *Strange Cargo* (1940). A versatile actor, proficient in both comedy and drama, Dekker made a habit of playing outwardly respectable characters that turned out to be psychologically disturbed.

shine in the dim light of his laboratory, Thorkel seems a genuinely sinister figure, who will stop at nothing to be recognized as "the greatest living biologist." When he feels that Dr. Bullfinch (Charles Halton) and his fellow companions are becoming too inquisitive about his work, Thorkel transforms them into midgets, observing sarcastically as he does so that it is "strange how absorbed men have been with the size of things."

The entire film deals with the theme of sight: Thorkel might be half-blind (hence the spectacles) but by conducting his experiments he believes that he will acquire the kind of sight (i.e., scientific knowledge) that will guarantee his future reputation as a great scientist as well as ensuring domination over his fellow human beings. He towers over the midgets like a puppet master, taking a sadistic pleasure in delivering lines such as "Now I can control life absolutely." This he proceeds to do, as he picks up the midget Bullfinch in a net, puts a metal ring round his neck and asphyxiates him to death with poison wrapped in cotton wool.

The portrayal of this kind of scientist must have seemed especially sinister at a time when European dictators such as Hitler were proclaiming similar intentions both publicly and privately. Dr. Thorkel seems like a fictional representation of scientists such as Josef Mengele, otherwise known as the Angel of Death of Auschwitz, whose experiments on human beings only came to light after the end of the Second World War. As he becomes more obsessed with his work, Thorkel's mind becomes more unhinged; in one sequence, he is shown chewing on a piece of meat like an animal as he desperately seeks to record all his finds in a notebook. Later on he runs wildly round his laboratory in a desperate search for his spectacles (which the midgets have destroyed), screaming, "You would dare attack me!!" The last word is delivered in frantic crescendo. He holds his hands over his eyes and makes one last effort to see what is happening around him. In his search for scientific sight, he has become impervious to his immediate world. Thorkel plunges to his death at the end, as he falls down a large hole — originally created by himself to store the device that reduces people in size. Symbolically he is cast into Hell for his efforts.

Two years later Dekker played both twins — John and Paul Roden — in Stuart Heisler's *Among the Living*. As the successful business person John, he cuts an attractive, rugged presence — a pillar of the small town where he lives, who owns the local hotel as well as a string of successful businesses, and with an attractive young wife Elaine (Frances Farmer) in tow. His twin brother, Paul, has been institutionalized ever since he was ten years old — as a result of his father's evil machinations; since then his only company has been an African American servant Pompey (Ernest Whitman). Paul eventually escapes by strangling Pompey; and for the most part enjoys the unaccustomed experience of walking round town, renting a room, meeting the local belle Millie Pickens (Susan Hayward) and forging a friendship with her. The only indication we have as to his disturbed state of mind is a tendency for him to breathe heavily and clasp his hands to his ears at moments of extreme stress. This is a throwback to his childhood, when this provided him with the only means of protection against his sadistic father. One of these occurs in a local nightclub, where a good-time girl (Dorothy Sebastian) gives him the brush-off in the belief that Paul is not really interested in her. Paul gets up, clasps his hands to his ears and rushes out, the sound of the other punters' cruel laughter ringing in his ears. He waits in the shadows until the bar has closed, then pursues the girl into a darkened alleyway and strangles her.

These events have a predictably cataclysmic effect on the small town inhabitants, who in their desire to root out the murderer become almost as extreme in their reactions as Paul himself. The film comes to an intense climax at the Roden family house. Paul has been dragged there against his will by Millie; tormented by memories of his past, he tries to kill her. John arrives in the nick of time, accompanied by two police officers who wound Paul in the arm yet fail to prevent him from escaping. The town inhabitants arrive, and mistake John for Paul; they call for him to be hanged immediately. John sits in a corner, shivering like a caged animal, the victim of a lynch mob. However, he sees an opportunity to escape; he runs out of the house towards the family graveyard, where he finds Paul lying dead by his mother's grave. All is happily resolved, as John embraces a tearful Millie.

Dekker gives a memorable performance in this final sequence, showing how little there is to separate sanity from madness. John and Paul embody both extremes; both can be sane, but they can be abruptly transformed under extreme pressure.

In *She-Devil* (1957), Dekker has a very different role as Dr. Richard Bach, an elderly, well-meaning doctor working closely with ambitious scientist Dr. Dan Scott (Jack Scott). When Kelly discovers a serum that could provide a universal cure, Bach remains skeptical about its uses on human beings: "Charity cases are not experimental cases." However, Bach is persuaded to agree — much against his better judgment — to try the cure on TB patient Kyra Zelas (Mari Blanchard). The consequences prove disastrous: Kyra is transformed into a superwoman who can change her hair color at will, and ruthlessly disposing of anyone daring to stand in her way, including rich husband and wife Barton and Evelyn Kendall (JOHN ARCHER and Fay Baker), and an affluent (unnamed) sugar daddy (PAUL CAVANAGH). Bach rues the consequences of his actions; he is frequently shown in his consulting room rubbing his hands together and looking despairingly upwards as if seeking divine intervention to solve his predicament. Bach frequently delivers portentous statements as a way of controlling his more emotional colleague: at one point Bach emphasizes the importance of wreaking a "physical and emotional change" in Kyra, with the emphasis placed on the word "and." On another occasion, he walks up behind Scott — who is working in the laboratory — and tells the younger doctor to develop an "antidote" as soon as possible, with the stress placed on the first syllable of the word for effect.

Yet for all Bach's well-meaning exhortations, we understand that he is as much to blame as Scott for Kyra's transformation. A product of the pre-feminist era (released five years before Betty Friedan's seminal work *The Feminine Mystique*), *She-Devil* retells the Pygmalion tale in extreme form to emphasize the dangers of challenging the patriarchy; if women are given too much power, they become self-willed and destructive. Although the doctors successfully administer an antidote to Kyra in the end, Kyra passes away as a result; Bach's sole reaction is to observe that perhaps "she was meant to die [...] Did we save the life of a human being, or did we perhaps only create an in-human being?" While he regrets the consequences of his action, he still upholds the patriarchal sentiment that independent women are doomed to die for daring to challenge the existing social order.

Richard Denning

b. March 27, 1914, Poughkeepsie, New York;
d. October 11, 1998, Escondido, California.

Richard Denning (born Louis Albert Denninger, Jr.) enrolled at Woodbury Business College and majored in business and accounting. He started his acting career in little theater groups, and was encouraged to participate in a radio contest called "Do You Want to Be an Actor?" As a prize, he won a screen test at Warner Brothers; he did not secure a contract there, signing up with Paramount instead, where he changed his name. In 1942, he married EVELYN ANKERS; the two stayed together until her death in 1985.

By the mid–1950s, Denning had established himself as a reliable character actor, with several credits in horror and science fiction films. In *Creature from the Black Lagoon* (1954), he plays Mark Williams, an over-zealous marine archeologist determined to capture the Gill-Man (i.e., the creature) (Ricou Browning/Ben Chapman) and put it on display in New York like King Kong. By such means, Williams hopes to cement his reputation as a world-renowned scientist. His overweening ambition contrasts with the more modest values embraced by his colleague David Reed (RICHARD CARLSON), who wants to investigate the Gill-Man's way of life without harming it. Eventually the two men come to blows; Reed knocks Williams out, and leaves him locked up in a cabin. But Williams is too much in love with success to take a hint; he breaks the door down, and joins Reed on an another expedition to find the Gill-Man. Eventually, Williams's ambitions get the better of him; he engages the Gill-Man in underwater combat, and has his aqualung removed, leading to instant death. The last we see of him is his lifeless corpse floating in the sea. Director Jack Arnold shows how Williams's obsessive desire for scientific success blinds him to the dangers involved in trying to deal with the creature.

In *The Day the World Ended* (1955), Denning has a similar role as Rick, a geologist caught in a nuclear disaster. Not only does he have to contend with a mutated creature living in the nearby woods that threatens the future of the few remaining mortals left in the world, but he has to deal with mobster Tony Lamont (Touch Connors), who shows little or no respect for his fellow human beings. Rick's dedication to his job is suggested by his body language; with hands on hips and businesslike delivery of his lines, he comes across as someone interested in the creature for scientific purposes. As the film unfolds, however, Rick's attitude changes, as he comes to understand the importance of the survival of the human race. He mutters, "This place is cursed," as an aside, before venturing out into the wilderness to find out more information. When rancher Jim Maddison (PAUL BIRCH) becomes gravely ill, Rick assumes the role of leader; he grabs Tony by the scruff of the neck and orders him to think of other people rather than himself. In the film's final sequence, Rick jumps into the river to save his girlfriend Louise (Lori Nelson), who is in imminent danger of being destroyed by the creature. He drags her out, and the two of them sit behind a tree while watching the creature destroy itself as the rains come. Now the two of them can embark on "a new beginning," without fear of destruction. Unlike Mark Williams in *Creature from the Black Lagoon*, Denning's Rick soon comes to understand the importance of casting aside his scientific knowledge and looking after those around him.

In Sherman A. Rose's *Planet Earth* (1954), Denning's Frank Brooks is one of only a few residents left in the city of Chicago following

Richard Denning, *Picturegoer* postcard (1950). Thick-set leading man, Denning was a stalwart of second features in the 1940s and 1950s.

an invasion by giant robots. Although aware of what has happened (he is an avid reader of science fiction magazines), Brooks cannot do much to fight back; he remains an ordinary person trying to cope with an extraordinary situation. Hence he spends much of his time foraging for food and blankets in a deserted building, so as to provide temporary shelter for himself and his three companions Nora King (Kathleen Crowley)—who has recently tried to commit suicide—and sparring lovers Vicki Harris (Virginia Grey) and Jim Wilson (Richard Reeves). Brooks values the safety of others above his own, as he valiantly repels both the robots and escaped serial killer Davis (Robert Roark). Eventually, it seems that Brooks's struggles have been in vain, as the robots pursue him on the roof of a skyscraper. He is spared a grisly fate by the army's timely intervention, as they destroy the robot and guarantee the survival of humankind "till the next time." The film suggests that despite Brooks's valiant efforts, the security of ordinary Americans is continually threatened by invaders, whether from other countries or from outer space.

In Edward L. Cahn's B-flick *Creature with the Atom Brain* (1956), Denning plays reliable police doctor Chet Walker, who is thoroughly competent at his job; this is suggested by frequent close-ups of his face set in studious thought as he tries to find out how and why a small American town is being threatened by atomic-controlled zombies. He invariably smokes a pipe, which he uses as a means of emphasizing certain points to his disbelieving colleagues. Walker has the gift of persuasiveness—even when he stands at the back of a room, listening intently to members of the government and the military discussing their plans, we know that he will be the brains behind the whole operation. Cahn's tendency to illuminate his face in close-ups and long shots reinforces this belief.

At the same time Chet remains a devoted family man. There are several sequences where we see him returning home to his devoted wife Joyce (Angela Stevens) and daughter Penny (Linda Bennett). The film is redolent of the ideology of domesticity prevalent in mid–1950s America, in which women were expected to conform to their role as homemakers, leaving their spouses to pursue their business lives unencumbered by the responsibilities of family life (other than bringing in the money and occasionally playing with their offspring). However, director Cahn also suggests that Chet's family helps to protect him from indoctrination by mad European scientist Dr. Wilhelm Steigg (Gregory Gay) and his mobster sidekick Buchanan (Michael Granger), who are revealed as the brains behind the whole zombie operation. By contrast, single men such as Cpt. Dave Harris (S. John Launer) remain vulnerable to corruption; Buchanan and Steigg transform him into a zombie as a means of showing off what they can do. Through such devices, the film shows how the ideology of domesticity had political as well as social implications in Cold War America, as it helps to ensure Chet's continued well being, enabling him to destroy Buchanan and Steigg at the end.

Denning played a similar role a year later in *The Black Scorpion*. As Hank Scott, a professor of geology sent to investigate the effects of volcanic activity in Mexico, he gives an impression of reliability in his open-necked shirt and pipe, which he uses to emphasize particular points in his arguments. Unlike his Mexican hosts—many of whom are scared to venture forth into unknown territory—Hank's individualism drives him on, even when faced with the prospect of destroying giant scorpions or rescuing the inquisitive Mexican child Juanito (Mario Navarro) from certain death. Hank's daredevil streak is balanced by a love of home life; all he wants to do, once his work is done, is to marry and set up home with Teresa Alvarez (Mara Corday), even if this might involve taking her away from her Mexican homeland back to America. The ideology of domesticity helps drive Hank on to further acts of bravery; once he has destroyed the scorpions, he can contemplate the prospect of a happy home.

Edward Ludwig's film has strong links to the Western, with its shots of the rolling Mexican landscape, and horse riders competing with automobiles to see which can cover the terrain in the shortest time. This is no coincidence: Hank embodies the pioneer spirit of a century earlier, as he willingly volunteers to be lowered into a cavern to discover where the giant scorpions breed. Like a latter-day colonizer, he captures the scorpions on film before returning to his local community. In terms of the film's logic, it is almost inevitable that he should fire the shot—from an extended crossbow—that penetrates the scorpion's soft tissue and kills it. From now on all Mexicans can enjoy an insect-free life, thanks to the American colonizer's efforts.

Faith Domergue

b. June 16, 1924, New Orleans, Louisiana;
d. April 4, 1999, Santa Barbara, California.

Born in New Orleans, Faith Domergue (surname pronounced "Doh-mehre") was signed to a movie contract by Warner Brothers while still at school. Howard Hughes met her at a party while on board his yacht and bought out her contract, and tried to reinvent her as the new Jane Russell. After an undistinguished be-

Faith Domergue publicity still (1955). One of science fiction cinema's legendary screamers, Domergue made her name in low-budget epics of the 1950s.

ginning to her film career in *Vendetta* (1950) and *The Duel at Silver Creek* (1952), Domergue established herself during the 1950s in a series of classic horror and science fiction films.

In Universal's *This Island Earth* (1955) she plays Dr. Ruth Adams, a businesslike figure dedicated to her work at the research laboratory set up by the Metalunans, an alien race who have apparently come to Earth for the purposes of research. She rejects the romantic advances of her colleague Dr. Cal Meacham (Rex Reason) on the grounds of appropriateness. Eventually, the two of them are thrown together, as they understand that the Metalunans' true purpose is to colonize the Earth, and make valiant attempts to escape. Ruth proves a competent decision-maker, as well as being dedicated to the cause of freedom — at one point she exclaims: "My mind's my own and nobody can change it!" She is threatened at one point by a Metalunan monster, but it dies through lack of oxygen, giving her the chance to fall into Meacham's arms in relief. Evidently romance provides the best antidote to the stresses of space-travel.

In her next film Domergue played another scientist — Professor Lesley Joyce in *It Came From Beneath the Sea* (also 1955). Robert Gordon's film for Columbia makes an interesting statement about gender roles in mid–1950s America. Although her new boyfriend Commander Pete Mathews (KENNETH TOBEY) would dearly love to domesticate her through marriage, Joyce steadfastly refuses to conform to such roles. She is a strong woman, committed to her work as a marine biologist; director Robert Gordon repeatedly emphasizes this aspect of her character by showing her explaining to a crowd of journalists and/or fellow scientist exactly what the monster looks like and what its capabilities are. As she speaks, her eyes shine with an obvious enthusiasm for her subject. However, there is no doubt that she is attracted to Mathews; she is repeatedly shown in two-shots with him, and when he offers her the prospect of a sumptuous dish of lobster and parsley, she readily accepts. From then on it is only a matter of time before the two of them are discovered in a passionate embrace on an isolated beach, in a sequence strongly reminiscent of *From Here to Eternity* (1953). But Joyce nonetheless displays considerable strength of character in committing herself once again to her work — outlining what the possible threats the monster might pose to the people of San Francisco. Although the film follows a familiar pattern of portraying the men as active (Mathews ventures out in the submarine on the hazardous quest to destroy the monster), while the women remain passive (Joyce remains on dry land, coordinating the defense of the city), *It Came from Beneath the Sea* does suggest that women have the potential to lead lives of their own without male protection. At the end of the film the most Joyce can offer Mathews is companionship: marriage would be impractical for two career people, one of whom has to go to Cairo on academic business, while the other embarks on another naval tour of duty.

In the same year, Domergue had a leading role as the photographer Jill Rabowski in the British film *The Atomic Man* (UK title: *Timeslip*). She forms a double-act with investigative journalist Mike Delaney (Gene Nelson), as the two investigate the mysterious case of an atomic scientist Dr. Stephen Rayner (Peter Arne) who is found floating in the river with a bullet in his back and a radio-active halo around his body. Eventually Rabowski and Delaney discover that Rayner has an evil double (also played by Arne), a member of a gang carrying out a scheme masterminded by South American magnate Vasquo (Vic Perry) to destroy Rayner's experiments with tungsten. For the first part of the film, Rabowski plays a secondary role to Delaney, as she runs after him, complaining all the while about his unpunctuality and reluctance to eat anything. However, when called upon to do her job — i.e., photographing suspects and/or evidence — she proves more than qualified to assume her responsibilities. Despite all efforts to prevent her, she manages to take pictures, proving beyond doubt her strength of character. While Delaney's persistence often exasperates her — director Ken Hughes cuts to frequent close-ups of her puffing out her cheeks, or observing in an aside that she is thinking of buying a pair of roller-skates to keep up with him — it is clear that she cannot do without him: when he is shot by Vasquo's heavies, she rushes to his side and tends his wounds. In the end, she decides to go out on her own to investigate Vasquo's hideout; Hughes's camera tracks her as she lets herself into his office and riffles through his papers to find out exactly what his plans are, and how he plans to flee the country. Although this proves a foolhardy mission (as Vasquo eventually catches her in the act and ties her up), we share Delaney's admiration for Rabowski's strength of character; she will not give up until the conspirators have been successfully apprehended. Even when she is taken to Vasquo's hideout, she still has sufficient presence of mind to indicate Vasquo's whereabouts once Delaney comes to rescue her, even if this puts her at considerable personal risk.

In another 1955 film, Francis D. Lyon's *Cult of the Cobra*, Domergue plays cobra-woman Lisa Moya, whose reptilian nature is signaled by the use of close-up, in which she is seen in total darkness, with only her eyes illuminated. As the film begins, she appears to be an ideal potential mid–50s mate for ex–GI Tom Markel (MARSHALL THOMPSON), as she passively submits to his will, while gazing adoringly into his eyes. However, we understand that there is something odd about her in a sequence where she is shown walking down a deserted street, the alley cats running away from her in terror. Tom embraces her, but she seems particularly unresponsive to his advances, as she purses her lips and leans back on the couch. The only time she really comes alive is when she commits murder; she stares grimly at flirtatious young girl Julia Thompson (Kathleen Hughes) and breathes heavily. Director Lyon cuts to a close-up of Julia's petrified face, as she understands what will happen to her. At the end of the film Lisa's true nature is revealed, as she transforms herself into a cobra; as she does so, she moans: "Tom, nothing can happen to you! It just can't!" However, Tom now understands that he cannot trust Lisa's word; he grapples with the cobra-woman and throws her out of a sixth-floor apartment window. The film ends with a shot of Lisa's corpse on the sidewalk; only in death can she rid herself of the cobra's curse.

Ellen Drew

*b. November 23, 1915, Kansas City, Missouri;
d. December 3, 2003, Palm Desert, California.*

Born Esther Loretta Ray, the daughter of an Irish barber, Ellen Drew did a variety of jobs to support herself until she won a couple of beauty pageant trophies. Encouraged to try her luck in Hollywood, she was working in an ice cream parlor when the actor William Demarest noticed her, and she was signed to a contract by Paramount. Initially billed as Terry Ray, she made her debut in several programmers before having a substantial role in the Bing Crosby musical *Sing Your Sinners* (1938). Drew changed her screen name and her hair color (she became auburn), and found further substantial roles in *French Without Tears* (1940) and *Buck Benny Rides Again* (also 1940).

Although never a major star, Drew had substantial roles in some notable horror films during the 1940s. In Paramount's *The Mad Doctor* (1941), she plays Linda Boothe, a psychiatric patient trying to commit suicide by throwing herself off the top of a New York skyscraper, despite the best intentions of boyfriend Gil Sawyer (John Howard). She falls under the spell of evil analyst George Sebastian (Basil Rathbone), who marries wealthy women and murders them for their money. Linda's mental weaknesses are evident in her gestures; she wrings her hands in despair and looks heavenwards as if seeking divine guidance. When none is forthcoming, she turns towards the camera and murmurs "I might ... snap out of it [her depression]" with not a shred of conviction in her voice. When Sebastian comes into her life, she is transfixed by him, as she stares into his eyes and explains the origins of her depression — as a child, she witnessed her father being gunned down in cold blood. Sawyer contrives her to forget her mental turmoil — at least temporarily — as he takes her to Coney Island; she is seen smiling and enjoying herself at the fairground and the races, jumping up and down in excitement as her horse wins. However, once she returns home and encounters Sebastian once more, she immediately falls silent: director Tim Whelan uses frequent close-ups of her face to suggest that she has been hypnotized by him. The psychiatrist offers marriage within a week; she willingly accepts, looking into his eyes and murmuring, "Nothing wrong could happen to me ... ever!" In a later sequence on their wedding day, she places a buttonhole in the jacket of Sebastian's morning-suit and hopes that "this day ... shall never end!" taking a long pause between the words "day," and "shall."

Of course, things do go wrong, as Sebastian is discovered to be a serial killer and pursued by Sawyer and the police. Eventually, the psychiatrist takes his own life by throwing himself off a skyscraper, suggesting that he himself has adopted some of Linda's suicidal tendencies. Although the film ostensibly ends happily, with Linda resting her head on Sawyer's shoulders, her expression suggests otherwise; she has lost the only love of her life for good, and can only look forward to a life of unsatisfactory compromises.

Drew's next film for Paramount, Stuart Heisler's *The Monster and the Girl* (also 1941), has her emerging from a mist in the opening sequence dressed respectably, her arms folded. She calls herself "the bad luck penny" who "brought a million dollars' worth of trouble for everybody" by reaching "so hard for the stars" that she "forgot to look where [she] was walking." As the small-town girl Susan Webster, she always dreamed of improving herself both socially and financially; hence she marries local playboy Larry Reed (Robert Paine) on a whim, without thinking of the consequences. The next morning she wakes up in a strange hotel room, to be confronted by mobster Munn (Gerald Mohr), who denies that Larry exists, and forces Susan to pursue a career as a "hostess" in a local bar. Now she has come to court to plead on her brother Scot's (Philip Webster) behalf, as he has been accused of murder. She speaks in measured tones, looking down at the floor as she admits that she was "so sure ... so smart" in what she did. When the prosecutor J. Stanley McMasters (Onslow Stevens) asks whether as a hostess she is "unworthy of trust," Susan cannot answer; her shame is complete. Scot is convicted and sentenced to death. However his brain remains alive, as mad scientist Dr. Parry (GEORGE ZUCCO) transplants it into an ape,

Ellen Drew cinema star postcard (1943). An attractive leading lady of the 1940s, Drew's career flourished briefly in roles where she could play resourceful women.

in an attempt to prove that animals are as intelligent as human beings. The ape escapes from Parry's laboratory and embarks on a campaign of retribution against those whose testimony condemned Scot to death and ruined Susan's life. The mobsters use violent methods to force Susan to tell the truth — grabbing her wrists and smacking her face — but all to no avail. She screams hysterically: "You [the mobsters] killed Scot! Made him die a hundred times! Now you're waiting [to die]!" The ape kills all of them off before dying from gunshot wounds, leaving Susan to face an uncertain future.

In *Isle of the Dead* (1945), Drew plays Thea, a village girl dressed in a simple white cotton blouse and knitted top. As in *The Mad Doctor*, Drew's character comes across as vulnerable — someone perpetually at risk from predatory men. Initially this doesn't seem to be so: when General Nicholas Pherides (Boris Karloff) orders her to do something, she rebuffs him abruptly, claiming that she will never respect anyone responsible for killing his own people. Her refusal to submit enrages Pherides, who accuses her of being possessed by an evil force ("the enemy within") that impels her to kill others. With this thought in mind, Pherides takes it upon himself to pursue her day and night — as a result, she is transformed from a self-possessed young woman into a frightened little girl, perpetually looking over her shoulder to see if the general pursues her. Director Mark Robson frequently photographs her standing next to a barred window, with the shadow of the bars on her white blouse symbolizing her plight. In one sequence, she is shown walking up and down a confined space, wringing her hands with anxiety. The only way she can alleviate her plight is to find a male protector in the form of campaigning journalist Oliver Davis (Marc Cramer). He puts his arms around her, offering the kind of reassurance she never had in the past. Eventually, the true killer's identity is discovered: Thea can now look forward to a happy life in Davis's company. The two of them are shown climbing into a boat that will take them to freedom. Meanwhile the general lies on his bed, half-crazed with passion, claiming that he only wanted to protect Thea rather than molest her.

Douglass Dumbrille

b. October 13, 1889, Hamilton, Ontario, Canada;
d. April 2, 1974, Woodland Hills,
Los Angeles, California.

Douglass Dumbrille started off as a bank clerk. He drifted into the theatre, appearing in stock companies until his Broadway debut in *Macbeth* in 1924. Following an inauspicious debut in the silent film *The Declaration of Independence* (also 1924), Dumbrille returned to films seven years later in *His Woman* (1931). Thereafter he carved out something of a niche for himself as a villain with his stern features, beady eyes, hooked nose and pencil mustache.

Marjorie Weaver and Douglass Dumbrille in *Murder Among Friends* (1940). With his pencil mustache and perfect manners, Dumbrille came across as a perfect gentleman. But no one trusted him; he often turned out to be a villain.

In Albert S. Rogell's futuristic drama *Air Hawks* (1935), he plays Victor Arnold, whose villainous qualities are soon evident as he stands at the back of the frame wearing a trilby hat and smoking, his hands thrust deep into his pockets. He delivers his lines in memorable fashion, taking a pregnant pause in the line "I will take a little ... something for my use" to suggest his self-interest. However, he is not above trying to solicit the viewer's sympathies; on several occasions he is photographed in close-up, grinning directly into the camera lens. This is an important strategy as a way of justifying his subsequent behavior; his maltreatment of heroine Renee (Tala Birell), as he drags her into his office by the hand as if she were his plaything. He stands over her threateningly, hands behind his back, and tells her to stay away from the scientific experiments taking place outside. Arnold tries the same tactic with hero Barry Eldon (Ralph Bellamy), and receives a smack in the mouth for his pains.

Eventually, Arnold is hoist by his own petard, as he is blown up in a plane explosion detonated by the ray machine (designed to blow up aircraft) Arnold helped to perfect, as a way of eliminating Eldon's airplane company in the competition for a lucrative airmail contract. Arnold's destructiveness is contrasted with the heroic exploits of real-life flyer Wiley Post, who makes a cameo appearance in the film making a cross-country stratosphere flight.

Dumbrille has a cameo role in *Charlie Chan at Treasure Island* (1939) as Thomas Gregory, aka Stewart Salsbury, who poses as an inspector working on behalf of an insurance company investigating a blackmail case involving Paul Essex (Louis Jean Heydt). Gregory/Salsbury looks suspicious from the start: director Norman Foster cuts to frequent close-ups of him looking shiftily right to left, as if fearful that someone might discover his true identity. When Essex meets an untimely end on a flight back to San Francisco, Gregory takes his attaché case without telling anyone. Immediately Jimmy Chan (Victor Sen Yung) suspects Gregory of being the murderer, but Charlie (Sidney Toler) is not so sure. Gregory keeps reappearing unexpectedly throughout the film; while he treats Charlie with the utmost courtesy, paying homage to the detective's powers of intuition, Jimmy wonders whether this is nothing more than a charade. Likewise in Rhadini's (Cesar Romero), where a performance takes place designed to discover Essex's murderer, Gregory/Salsbury sits in the fifth row, looking nervously at the stage. However the inspector proves genuine in his quest; his apprehension is not caused by guilt, but rather by fear for his personal safety, as he investigates a case involving a psychic with the power to control human minds.

In *Jungle Woman* (1944), Dumbrille departs from his villainous role to play the District Attorney, charged with the responsibility of finding out what caused Paula the Ape-Woman's (Acquanetta) death. With his immaculately tailored suit, pencil-thin mustache, and aristocratic manner, Dumbrille looks the very epitome of an efficient lawyer — someone who will stop at nothing to win his case. He towers over the accused, diminutive doctor Carl Fletcher (J. CARROL NAISH), and sternly asks him to tell the truth. When Fletcher tells the story of Paula's origins (told in the prequel to this film *Captive Wild Woman* (1943), the attorney laughs with contempt. He gets up from his chair and tells everyone in no uncertain terms that "murder has been committed," and it is his responsibility to find out the truth. However, his skepticism proves unfounded, as he goes down to the morgue and discovers that Paula's corpse is not that of a human being but an ape. In cases such as this, the Attorney's intimidation fails to uncover the truth about what happened.

Dumbrille's finest hour as a villain came in Republic's *Catman of Paris* (1946), where he plays Sir Henry Borchard, the elegant patron of successful writer Charles Regnier (Carl Esmond). With his tailcoat, top hat and precisely trimmed mustache, Borchard comes across as a society beau, given to uttering Wildean epigrams such as, "Governments are like women ... the more you scorn them the more adventure there is." Borchard publicizes the writer's achievements in all the best Parisian mansions. He sips cognac, takes a pinch of snuff and brags about Regnier's imminent fortune (which will no doubt yield considerable income for Borchard himself in commission). However, Charles believes that he is suffering from an illness, which transforms him each night into the catman. Borchard continually consoles him by putting a paternal arm around his shoulder and taking him to several doctors, all of whom proclaim that there is nothing wrong with the writer. This diagnosis turns out to be true: despite Charles' fears for his sanity, we discover at the end of the film that the catman is none other than Borchard himself — each night he doffs his elegant costume, muddies his face and prowls the Parisian streets in search of further victims. Now he lies dying on a slab; breathing heavily he admits that he adopted the role to help further Charles' career (by giving him the raw material to write about). He has fulfilled "the cycle of his duty"; Borchard can die peacefully. Director Lesley Selander zooms in to a close-up of his face covered in hair, with a pair of protuberant fangs at each side of his mouth. Borchard was always a catman who deliberately disguised himself as an aristocrat in order to further his protégé's career. Later that year, he repeated the villainous role in the programmer *The Cat Creeps* for Universal. He plays attorney Tom McGalvey, who repeatedly deflects the finger of suspicion that he might be a murderer away from himself through repeated questioning of other suspects. Nattily dressed in a three-piece suit, a carnation in his buttonhole, McGalvey seems the last person to commit murder. He turns out to be a ruthless serial killer: once his true identity is discovered, his manner of speaking abruptly changes. In place of the measured tones of a confident attorney, he delivers his lines in a hysterical scream. Eventually apprehended by Pidge "Flash" Laurie (Noah Beery, Jr.) he scowls as he is led away.

Bramwell Fletcher

b. February 20, 1904, Bradford, Yorkshire, England; d. June 22, 1988, Westmoreland, New Hampshire.

Bramwell Fletcher made his first film in 1928, and debuted on Broadway a year later. The majority of his career was spent in American films and theatre, and from the 1940s onwards he made regular appearances on television in anthology series such as *The Philco Television Playhouse* and *Studio One*.

Fletcher made some notable appearances in horror films of the 1930s and 1940s. In Lloyd Corrigan's Fu Manchu horror film *Daughter of the Dragon* (1931), he plays Ronald Petrie, the juvenile lead enjoying the exotic prospect of falling in love with the Chinese girl Ling Moy (Anna May Wong). Petrie adopts the familiar poses of the western suitor, kneeling in front of her, clasping her wrist and gazing passionately into her eyes; but Ling Moy fails to respond. She has been entreated by her father Fu Manchu (Werner Oland) to murder Ronnie, and thereby fulfill the curse placed on the Petrie family. Fu Manchu himself disposes of Ronnie's father Sir John (HOLMES HERBERT). Despite his romantic pretensions, Ronnie is an arrant coward; following his father's demise, he runs after the police officers but cowers in the background as they investigate the scene of the crime. Later on, he is discovered sleeping in bed, the light shining on his face giving him a cherubic look: Ling Moy hovers above him, her knife at the ready to fulfill the curse; but she cannot do it. Ronnie looks almost too innocent. There is something endearing about Fletcher's performance; he plays chess with Inspector Ah Kee (Sessue Hayakawa), and jumps up and down in delight as he wins the game. When Ah Kee is kidnapped, Ronnie throws on his overcoat and rushes out after the kidnapers, speaking his lines in a high-pitched squeak of excitement. His concern is so great that he fails to notice that he is still wearing his pajamas underneath the overcoat. Eventually, Ronnie discovers the kidnapers' hideout, but cannot do much except witness the potentially gruesome prospect of seeing his fiancée Joan Marshall (Frances Dade) having acid poured over her. Ronnie screams: "It's inhuman! Anything but that!" Eventually both he and Joan are rescued in the nick of time by Sir Basil Courtney (Lawrence Grant) and his fellow police officers; he looks meaningfully at Ling Moy (as if unable to understand why such a beautiful woman should have turned to crime) before embracing Joan, a sadder, if not wiser man.

Bramwell Fletcher and Betty Lawford in *The Monkey's Paw* (1933). British-born Fletcher began his career as a slightly effeminate leading man, but graduated into character roles, often playing villains.

In Archie Mayo's *Svengali* (1931), Fletcher plays Billie, another juvenile lead who is unfortunate enough to fall in love with Trilby O'Farrell (Marian Marsh). An artist by profession, he firmly believes that things will turn out fine once she had declared her undying love for him: "You're wonderful; you're the sweetest thing I've ever known." However, the young man proves no match for Svengali (John Barrymore), who hypnotizes his victims with his eyes (rather like Karloff's Ardath Bey in *The Mummy* [1932]).

Billie is not quite the romantic hero he pretends to be. When Trilby leaves him for Svengali, Billie stares wild-eyed at the camera, and then runs into an adjoining room, ignoring his friends Taffy (Lumsden Hare) and the Laird (DONALD CRISP), who offer him their condolences. Svengali might describe Billie with contempt as "the head of the purity brigade," but in truth the young man has a wild streak drives him to pursue Svengali and Trilby all over Europe and the Middle East in the hope that Trilby will eventually return to him. Director Mayo includes frequent close-ups of his intense expression; he refuses to let Trilby go. Eventually, it appears that his persistence has paid off: Svengali dies and Billie embraces Trilby in his arms, murmuring, "I'm right here with you." However, Billie's quest is doomed to fail, as Trilby turns away from him and breathes "Svengali!!" in a final show of devotion.

In *The Mummy* (1932), Fletcher has a brief but notable cameo as Ralph Norton, the archaeologist whose curiosity gets the better of him as he removes the Scroll of Thoth from its casket and translates it. As he works, director Karl Freund's camera moves from the still form of the mummy, then back to Ralph. The camera then pans down to the scroll on the table as a hand enters the frame—a long, bony withered hand that briefly touches the scroll and then disappears. Norton turns, gives a petrified scream and backs away. Staring wild-eyed at the mummy, he begins to laugh—first in a low voice, but gradually increasing in intensity until it becomes an uncontrollable scream of madness. The action cuts to a shot of the floor, and we see the mummy's bandages trailing on the floor as Norton's insane laughter continues. The sequence only lasts three minutes, but the sheer speed of Ralph's descent into madness provides a grim warning of what can happen to those who interfere with the past. Fletcher's performance might seem over-the-top, but Freund takes advantage of the actor's capacity to communicate extreme emotion through eye-work.

Fletcher's abilities are once again put to good use in John Brahm's *The Undying Monster* (1942). He plays Dr. Jeff Colbert, who tends to Kate O'Malley (Virginia Traxler) after she has been attacked by a monster on the way home. His voice sounds reassuring as he brings out medicine from his black bag and administers them to her. However, all is not what it seems: Colbert becomes increasingly wild-eyed, particularly when Robert Curtis (James Ellison) and his sidekick Christy (Heather Thatcher) come to investigate the case. The doctor's behavior grows more and more erratic; he pretends to fall down the stairs in the crypt of the house, and falls on to the floor — thereby obscuring the monster's footprints left in the dust. In other sequences, he deliberately conceals the family history book from Curtis' gaze, and disposes of a sample of Oliver Hammond's (John Howard) blood, which Curtis has taken for analysis. Eventually, it turns out that Colbert's motives are entirely honorable, as he tries to protect the family reputation by suppressing the knowledge that the monster is actually Oliver himself. Once the secret has been revealed, and Oliver has been killed, then Colbert can return to a normal life as an eminent London surgeon. By the end of the film, Fletcher's expression has changed completely; he smiles brightly as he says goodbye to Curtis, who responds by describing the doctor as "quite a fellow."

Dick Foran

b. June 18, 1910, Flemington, New Jersey;
d. August 10, 1979, Panorama City, California.

John Nicholas Foran started as a band singer and then graduated to the radio. His initial film roles were largely confined to musical westerns interspersed with the occasion straight part. Moving from Warner Brothers to Universal in 1940, Foran played a variety of parts, including the juvenile lead of Matthew Maule in *The House of the Seven Gables* (1940), based on the novel by Nathaniel Hawthorne. He comes across as a vigorous personality, passionately committed to the Abolitionist cause, who nonetheless has a tender side: when Phoebe Pyncheon (NAN GREY) stares wide-eyed in admiration at him, Matthew instantly falls in love. Perhaps uniquely in a film about loneliness and alienation, Matthew feels at home in just about any type of company, regardless of age or class; he can engage Hepzibah Pyncheon (Margaret Lindsay) in polite chit-chat, and share a jar or two with the villagers in the local hostelry. His gregariousness contrasts starkly with his arch enemy Jaffray Pyncheon's (GEORGE SANDERS) mean-spiritedness: Jaffray always believes that people exist to be manipulated for his own ends. In the end, Matthew gets the better of Jaffray; by assuming the role of the photographer Hargrave, he worms his way into Jaffray's confidence and ultimately ruins him financially. It seems somehow appropriate that Jaffray should fall victim at the end of the film to the Pyncheon family curse, as he dies of heart failure.

As the archeologist Steve Benning in *The Mummy's Hand* (also 1940), Foran remains committed to his quest of discovering the ancient Egyptian tomb; no amount of pressure from Andoheb (GEORGE ZUCCO) can dissuade him, Banning mutters "Don't bother, professor" with cold indifference, which only serves to increase Andoheb's animosity towards him.

Foran displays the qualities expected of a leading man in Universal horror films — strength, reliability, self-reliance with a touch of humor. Although acted off the screen in one sequence set in a bar, and also involving WALLACE FORD and CECIL KELLAWAY, Foran nonetheless manages to command director Christy Cabanne's attention — even if he has to mug furiously in order to do so. His two best moments come later on in the film — the first of these is a brief sequence taking place at the entrance to his tent, while in search of the mummy's treasure, when Marta Solvani (Peggy Moran) kisses him on the cheek. He starts back momentarily, glanced briefly to camera and puts his hand to his cheek, as if surprised that she had displayed her affections so openly. The second moment takes place during the *dénouement*, as he is seen solving the hieroglyphics that will lead him to the mummy's tomb and hence rescue Marta from Andoheb's clutches. He crouches over the tablet and murmurs the translation in voice-over — as he does so, his face lights up, as he realizes that the riddle has at last been solved. The sequence celebrates American individualism and self-reliance, both of which are identified as positive virtues, especially when compared with the Egyptians' superstitious beliefs that frequently prevents them from taking direct action.

Foran repeats the role in *The Mummy's Tomb*

(1942), only this time he is thirty years older. Sitting in his living room with pipe and slippers, he looks every inch the family man as he recounts his exploits in Egypt to his son John (John Hubbard). Director Harold Young incorporates sequences from the earlier film, just to remind viewers of what happened, Steve believes that he has accomplished his task to "rid the world of an awful curse" of the mummy; but *The Mummy's Tomb* proves that this is not the case, as the mummy (Lon Chaney, Jr.) carries out Mehemet Bey's (TURHAN BEY) orders to eliminate all those involved in the "violation" of the Egyptian tomb all those years ago, Steve is strangled to death in his own bedroom.

In *Horror Island* (1941), Foran plays Bill Martin, a sea captain-cum-adventurer down on his luck. Nonetheless he retains an incurable sense of optimism — as signaled, for instance, in the way he exchanges banter with his boon companion Tobias Clump (Leo Carrillo), and throws any outstanding bills he has to pay into the hold of his ship. The prospect of future riches inspires him; he delivers the line "Fifty dollars for the treasure hunt!" with a long pause between the two syllables in the word "fif—ty." If anyone should get in his way of his financial dreams, Martin believes that fisticuffs are the best answer. While this aspect of his character does not seem especially attractive, director George Waggner ensures that we sympathize with Martin by incorporating frequent illuminated close-ups into the narrative.

Martin departs with his crew and a motley crew of customers for Morgan's Island (the horror island of the film's title) for a treasure hunt that Martin has himself organized, complete with eerie sounds and fluttering birds. However, the charade is soon forgotten as he leads the hunt for a serial killer who disposes of each customer in turn. Martin undergoes something of a personality change; now he is determined to take the lead, even if it means putting his own life at risk. The cheery smile has been replaced by an expression of grim determination, which remains constant until the killer has been apprehended. The film ends happily, with Martin receiving financial rewards for

Dick Foran in *Cherokee Strip* (1940). Rather bland leading man, Foran made his name in low-budget westerns and horror films of the late 1930s and 1940s.

his efforts—he sells the island to a speculator—and embracing his girlfriend Wendy Creighton (Peggy Moran). Foran's performance foregrounds the best aspects of his star image as a self-reliant individual perpetually concerned for the welfare of his fellow travelers, both male and female.

Later on in his career, Foran played Commander Dan Wendover in *The Atomic Submarine* (1960). He cuts an imposing presence with his high forehead and seriousness of manner, as he issues various orders to his crew, his sleeves rolled up to suggest seriousness of purpose. He commands unquestioning loyalty from his subordinates, even while they argue amongst themselves; no one dares to question his words. Whenever the submarine encounters any danger, Wendover maintains his *sang-froid*; he puts his hands on his hips, looks carefully at the screens and the controls, takes a deep breath and makes his decisions. For all his outward sophistication, the colonel embraces a down-to-earth view of life; when faced with the possibility of having to fight the Cyclops (the monster at the bottom of the sea which threatens the safety of the submarine), he observes that he will have to adopt a "bush-whacking" approach—in other words, embrace the kind of guerrilla warfare common during the American Civil War, in which small groups of people conducted a series of well-organized raids. In this case, Wendover's "bush-whacking" strategy involves sending out Lt. Cmdr. Reed Holloway (ARTHUR FRANZ) and two other officers to shoot straight into the Cyclops's single eye. The expedition proves a success; the Cyclops is destroyed; and the submarine returns to base. The film ends with a paean of praise to Wendover's efforts—although in charge of "mankind's most terrifying weapon" (as the uncredited voiceover describes it), he knows how to pilot it responsibly, so as to guarantee the future of humankind.

Wallace Ford

b. February 12, 1898, Bolton, Lancashire, England;
d. June 11, 1966, Woodland Hills,
Los Angeles, California.

Samuel Jones Grundy was sent to an orphanage in Toronto while still a child. At eleven years old he ran away and joined a vaudeville troupe called the Winnipeg Kiddies, and stayed with them till 1913. With a friend named Wallace Ford, he hitchhiked to the United States; when his friend was killed, Bolton took the name for himself. After a ten-year stint on Broadway, Ford made his debut in pictures in 1931 in *Possessed* with Joan Crawford.

Ford took a leading role in Tod Browning's *Freaks* (1932) as Phroso the clown. While enjoying the life of the circus—the camaraderie, the regular performances, and the chance to flirt with female performers such as Venus (Leila Hyams)—he is acutely aware of the discrimination against the so-called "freaks" that make up the bulk of his troupe. He treats them sympathetically, promising to buy them souvenirs and making sure that they do not suffer unnecessarily. When they gang up against Cleopatra (Olga Baclanova) and Hercules (Henry Victor), to take revenge for the suffering Cleopatra has caused Hans (Harry Earles), Phroso leaps to their aid, embracing them and saying that they are "all set now." Despite the difference in size, Phroso takes on Hercules, and prevents him from annihilating the smaller members of the troupe.

In a career lasting well over thirty years, Ford carved out a reputation as a reliable character actor in all types of film. He also had some notable roles in horror films. In Columbia's *Night of Terror* (1933), he plays wisecracking journalist Tom Hartley, who is first discovered in the back of a car, his hat rakishly pulled over one eye, and trying his best to seduce Mary Rinehart (Sally Blane). She rejects him by claiming that she is already engaged to Professor Arthur Hornsby (George Meeker), but her smile suggests that she finds Hartley very attractive. Described at one point as "a common roughneck newspaperman," Hartley is always in pursuit of an exclusive—on several occasions we see him rushing to the telephone to call his sub-editor with another account of a murder in the Rinehart household, while murmuring, "Oh, boy, what a story!" under his breath. He has little respect for Detective Bailey (Matt McHugh), telling him at one point that "compared to you [Bailey], Sherlock Holmes was a

Wallace Ford publicity still (1933). British-born Ford was particularly memorable in comic roles, playing fast-talking characters on the make.

traffic cop." Yet Hartley remains somehow endearing, despite such jokes; he chivalrously protects Mary from harm, and raises pertinent questions that help to discover the murderer's identity.

In *One Frightened Night* (1935), Ford plays Joe Luvalle who—like Tom Hartley in *Night of Terror*—has to spend a night cooped up in a rambling mansion, trying to discover a serial killer. Luvalle, or "The Great Luvalle," as he prefers to be called, is a magician who loves an audience; throughout the film he performs little tricks like pulling ping-pong balls out of people's ears or purloining Sheriff Jenks' (Fred Kelsey) badge. No one really has much time for him; he is variously described as a mountebank or a trickster. However, he shows a fatherly concern for his assistant Doris Waverly (Mary Carlisle), whom he believes to be in great danger—particularly when she learns that she is about to inherit a considerable fortune from her grandfather Jasper Whyte (Charley Grapewin). However, Luvalle has one particular shortcoming—despite his public show of bravado, he remains an arrant coward. When Tom Dean (REGIS TOOMEY) strikes him to the floor, Luvalle gets up immediately and clenches his fists, but runs away in terror when Dean makes a move to hit him once more. Later on Luvalle is seen wandering around the house late at night; someone tries to kill him with a poisoned dart, and he falls to the floor with a scream. Luvalle actually holds up Dean's efforts to find the murderer, which helps to explain why Dean keeps him out of harm's way by shutting him in a store cupboard. Once released, the magician tells Doris that "we gotta break in a new act." However, Doris has a "new act" of her own, as she embraces Dean. *The Rogues' Tavern* (1936) has much the same scenario, with Ford as detective Jimmy Kelly, supported by fellow-detective Marjorie Burns (Barbara Pepper), spending the night at the eponymous Rogues' Tavern in search of another serial killer. Jimmy comes across as a practical person full of self-belief—so much self-belief, in fact, that he often fails to take note of Marjorie's successful deductions. Despite being knocked to the floor by Bill (Jack Mulhall), one of the chief suspects, Jimmy manages to solve the crime in undemonstrative fashion, keeping his hands in his pockets for most of the time. As the killer Mrs. Jamison (Clara Kimball Young) vows to destroy everyone in the tavern, Jimmy sidles up behind her unnoticed and apprehends her. Once the crime has been solved, he asks the marriage license clerk (Robert McKenzie), to tie the marital knot as soon as possible.

In *The Mummy's Hand* (1941), Ford once again plays a comic role as Babe Hanson, the sidekick of the leading man Steve Banning (DICK FORAN). Director Christy Cabanne gives Ford numerous comic set-pieces, such as searching in his shoe in the bazaar for the $85 to buy a so-called rare Egyptian vase; or attempting to play a card trick on the magician Mr. Solvani (CECIL KELLAWAY), for a bet. The stunt goes horribly wrong, as the magician laughingly picks a card that Babe had never thought of—as a result Babe is forced to buy a drink for everyone gathered in the bar. Babe glances to the camera with a hopeless look; Solvani takes pity on him, and plays another magic trick so that Babe has enough money to settle his debt. Intrigued, Babe tries to learn the magician's art for himself; but nearly swallows a rock in the process.

Such moments are designed as comic relief, distracting us from the film's rather flimsy plot. However, Babe fulfils an important role in the action as a representative of American values; although forced to spend his time in a foreign country, he yearns to return home to Brooklyn. Such sentiments would have proved especially appealing at a time when it looked increasingly inevitable that America would be drawn into the Second World War. Compared to Steve, Babe is a coward (on at least two occasions he admits that he likes Steve around as protection against evil), but he is prepared to do his duty when necessary. Confronted with the evil Andoheb (GEORGE ZUCCO) on a precipice, Babe shoots him in the stomach—even though it might be considered dishonorable to kill an unarmed man. In a desperate situation, notions of right and wrong do not matter: the "Egyptian Mickey Finn" (as Babe describes him) has to be disposed of, so as to guarantee Steve's safety.

Babe is a fundamentally good all-American soul, even if his beliefs in women are somewhat archaic (he doubts whether Marta Solvani (Peggy Moran) will be any use to the expedition).

Ford makes a brief appearance in the same role in *The Mummy's Tomb* (1943). Now thirty years older, he is a dapper little man in a three-piece suit and monocle, visiting the New England town of Mapleton at the instigation of Steve's son John Banning (John Hubbard). Babe tries to warn the inhabitants of the impending danger of the mummy — who has come to America to wreak revenge on those who 'violated' the tomb all those years before — but no one believes him. In despair he goes to a bar, lights a cigar and tells the whole story to a visiting reporter (Vinton Hayworth). Mehemet Bey (TURHAN BEY) overhears him, and instructs the mummy (Lon Chaney, Jr.) to dispose of Babe. This order is duly carried out: Babe desperately tries to escape by climbing a fence, but the mummy pulls him down and pins him to the ground before strangling him. All we see of the unfortunate babe is his feet kicking pathetically as he puts up a futile resistance.

In *The Ape Man* (1943), Ford plays another comic role as Jeff Carter, a hard-bitten reporter with the inevitable snap-brim hat, who resents the fact that he has to work with a mere woman, Billie Mason (Louise Currie) as a photographer. While the two of them engage in light-hearted banter, we get the sense that Carter will soon discover that his patriarchal preconceptions (carried over from *The Mummy's Hand*) are about to be dispelled. And so it proves: Billie proves an admirable foil, as the two of them become involved in a quest to discover the ape-man's identity. He exclaims at one point, "Maybe you're my lucky number!"—a considerable compliment from a man who once believed that a woman's place should be in the home. Although Jeff has his regressive moments (at one point he complains that Billie will not continue the investigation for fear that "she might put a run in her stocking") he eventually takes on the responsibility of bringing the investigation to a close. He cuts the wisecracks; and instead rescues Billie from the clutches of mad scientist Dr. James Brewster (Bela Lugosi) — who transformed himself periodically into the ape-man. His hair disheveled from his efforts, Carter subsequently returns to normality — which means (unfortunately) a return to routinely sexist remarks, such as threatening to spank Billie for being cheeky.

Arthur Franz

b. February 29, 1920, Perth Amboy, New Jersey; d. June 16, 2006, Oxnard, California.

Arthur Franz developed an interest in acting while at high school. The Second World War interrupted his ambitions; he served as a navigator in the U.S. Air Force. He was shot down over Romania and spent some time in a prisoner-of-war camp. On his return to peacetime activity, Franz established a reputation in Hollywood as a reliable character actor, often playing reliable, honest men.

This is certainly the case in the comedy *Abbott and Costello Meet the Invisible Man* (1951), where Franz plays Tommy Nelson, a professional boxer wrongfully accused of murdering his manager. To escape the police, led by Detective Roberts (William Frawley), he takes an injection of serum that renders him invisible; rather like CLAUDE RAINS in James Whale's famous film eighteen years previously, Nelson cannot be seen for much of the film. When he is visible, he wears the familiar bandages and dark glasses. Director Charles Lamont uses Nelson's character to make some interesting points about masculinity. As Nelson himself observes, he now possesses "a sense of power, for good [or] for evil." For the most part, he puts this power to good use, as he enlists the help of bumbling detectives Bud Alexander and Lou Francis (Abbott and Costello) to clear his name, while taking revenge on corrupt boxer Rocky Hanlon (John Daheim) and mobster Boots Morgan (Sheldon Leonard). At one point, however, Tommy gets drunk, at which point he believes that he can assume the power of a Nietzschean *übermensch*. This mood passes quickly, as Lou accidentally knocks Tommy out in a revolving door, but we are made aware of just how powerful a human

Arthur Franz cinema star postcard (1948). With his short hair and friendly countenance, Franz often played reliable characters in science fiction films of the 1950s.

being can be, when he is liberated from the social roles imposed upon him by early 1950s American society.

Later that year, Franz played chief engineer Jim Barker in *Flight to Mars*. As in the earlier film, he comes across as a reliable personality dedicated to his work; he smokes a pipe, which he frequently uses to help emphasize particular scientific points. His only failing is a tendency to overwork and thereby neglect his close friends; this is shown in several sequences throughout the film where he is shown with his back to the camera, operating the spaceship's control panel. Bradley is particularly unaware of Carol Stafford's (Virginia Huston) feelings towards him; although they have been together for three years, it seems that the two of them have never had a proper date. As a result, Carol gravitates towards maverick journalist Steve Abbott (Cameron Mitchell). Through this plot-device, director Lesley Selander underlines the dangers of scientific research: while it might help advance the cause of human progress, it often renders individuals indifferent to their fellow human beings. Bradley eventually falls head over heels in love with Martian woman Alita (Marguerite Chapman)—a dangerous thing to do, since we are not sure whether she is supporting the space voyagers or working for the Martians (who want to destroy the voyagers and their spaceship). Eventually, Alita comes down firmly on the voyagers' side, as she tries to escape from Mars with her father Tillamar (Robert Barrat). Bradley undergoes a significant character change to aid their escape; he puts scientific research aside and unselfishly agrees to help Alita and her father. By so doing, he underlines the capacity — emphasized in many science fiction epics of the late 1940s and early 1950s— of the American male to grasp the initiative and strive for a better world.

In William Cameron Menzies's epic *Invaders from Mars* (1953), we hear Franz's voice as the narrator, describing the universe as "a vast region for growing knowledge," the object of increasing interest amongst "scientists of all ages" on earth, whether professional or non-professional. However, this interest is not dispassionate but colonialist in outlook. This mentality also characterizes the eponymous invaders from Mars, who come to earth and deprive human beings of the capacity for independent thought. Such themes are characteristic of science fiction films of this period, most notably *Invasion of the Body Snatchers* (1956). Franz's scientist Stuart Kelson resists any attempts at indoctrination; he represents a source of stability both for fellow-scientist Pat Blake (Helena Carter) and the little boy David MacLean (Jimmy Hunt), whose parents have both been transfixed. Unlike Jim Barker in *Flight to Mars*, Kelson understands that the task of ridding the world of the invaders is not an easy one, and cannot be achieved by individuals alone. It involves a team effort, with scientists collaborating with members of the U.S. armed forces, who provide the firepower and the tactical knowledge to outwit the invaders. Kelson acts as coordinator of the entire operation, while at the same time protecting Pat and David from the invaders' clutches. Franz plays much the same kind of unselfish role as Lt. Cmdr. Richard "Reef" Holloway in *The Atomic Submarine* (1960). While willingly submitting himself to Cmdr. Dan Wendover's (DICK FORAN) authority, Holloway undertakes most of the dangerous missions to destroy the Cyclops at the bottom of the sea with little concern for his personal safety. His sole objective consists of destroying the monster and ensuring the future of humankind. After several unsuccessful attempts, Holloway achieves his aim, much to the admiration of his erstwhile rival Dr. Carl Neilson, Jr. (Brett Halsey), who enthusiastically shakes Holloway's hand.

Sometimes Franz's characters were unable to intervene in situations beyond their control. In *Back from the Dead* (1957) he plays Dick Anthony, whose second wife Mandy (Peggie Castle) has been possessed by the evil spirit of his depressed first wife Felicia. As a result, she has been transformed from an attractive blonde-haired woman into a crazed killer. The plot suggests that Felicia died from depression, as she plunged to her death over a cliff, but director Charles Marquis Warren suggests that Dick's marital unfaithfulness contributed significantly towards her disturbed state of mind. Despite his protestations of love for Felicia and Mandy, he develops a strong affection for Mandy's sister Kate (Marsha Hunt). Thus it comes as no surprise to find that Felicia (who has inhabited Mandy's personality) thinks of Kate as a rival and tries to kill her. Dick seems a rather ineffective personality, frequently wringing his hands in despair, or turning away from the camera, his head bowed in shame. On other occasions he seeks to drown his sorrows in drink, even though this is nothing more than an evasion of responsibility. Although he helps to contrive a happy ending by contributing to the death of black magic practitioner Maitre Renault (Otto Reichow), and thereby expunging Felicia's ghost from Mandy, we understand that he has learned little about the effect of adultery on the female psyche. He embraces Mandy in a gesture of reconciliation, but it seems a particularly empty gesture. *Back from the Dead* teaches a moral lesson, characteristic of many 1950s horror films, about the significance of marriage as the foundation of a stable society.

By contrast, in Jack Arnold's *Monster on the Campus* (1958) Franz's character is entirely to blame for the anarchy that breaks out in the small self-enclosed world of the fictional Dunsford University. Although dedicated to his work into prehistoric animals, Blake is a careless researcher who cuts his hand on the fossil of a primitive fish, and allows several drops of the fish's serum to fall into his pipe. As a result, he is transformed into an ape-like, bloodthirsty monster that mutilates anyone unfortunate enough to stand in his way. Superficially Franz's role is strongly reminiscent of the roles he played in *Flight to Mars* and *Invaders from Mars*; but Donald Blake lacks the strength of personality that transformed Jim Barker and Stuart Kelson into role models for their respective societies. While we might sympathize with the professor's plight (despite his mistakes, he is an affable member of his department, as well as being a dedicated teacher), we are nonetheless made aware of the destructive potential of contemporary scientific research, particularly when carried out irresponsibly.

Dwight Frye

b. February 22, 1899, Salina, Kansas;
d. November 7, 1943, Hollywood, California.

Dwight Frye in *Dracula* (1931). A legendary Hollywood psychotic, Frye gave memorable performances in early Universal horror films of the 1930s. He died of a heart attack while in his prime.

Dwight Iliff Fry had a notable theatrical career in the 1920s: cast with Bela Lugosi in a 1926 production of *The Devil and the Cheese*, he ultimately appeared in at least two Lugosi films — notably *Dracula* (1931), where he played Renfield. At the beginning of the film, Renfield seems a calm, serene personality as he enters Castle Dracula carrying a raincoat, a straw boater on his head, his collar nearly buttoned up with a sober-looking tie. But appearances can be deceptive: faced with Dracula's (Bela Lugosi) threatening presence, Renfield looks wildly round the room. His style of speaking remains deliberate ("I followed your instructions ... implicitly"), but his mannerisms — a sudden look of fear passing over his hitherto impassive visage — suggest a fundamentally unstable person. Once he becomes a victim of the vampire's blood-lust, Renfield is transformed into a madman, his eyes bulging and an evil grimace spread over his features as he vows loyalty to his new master. His once beautifully styled hair now sprouts in all directions as he tells Van Helsing (EDWARD VAN SLOAN) about his bad dreams. Renfield experiences violent mood swings — a shout of agony is soon followed by an uncontrollable fit of giggling, as he warns about the potential dangers facing those who seek to exterminate the vampire. Dracula has no further use for him — despite Renfield's screams of agony, the vampire strangles him to death and contemptuously throws the corpse down the stairs. Renfield has quite literally had the life sucked out of him. Frye overacts shamelessly, but in terms of *Dracula*'s plot, his role seems plausible, showing how human beings rapidly degenerate into beasts after being bitten by the vampire.

As Fritz in James Whale's *Frankenstein* (1931), Frye plays another beast-like character, whose gait — bent shoulders and arms hanging limply in front of him — resembles that of a wolf-man. With his sweat-soaked brow and high-pitched gibber, Fritz seems deprived of all human characteristics. He seems to have found the ideal *métier* as Henry Frankenstein's (Colin Clive) servant, working in a lonely, darkened cell and fleeing in terror whenever daylight streams in. He takes a sadistic pleasure in taunting the monster (Boris Karloff) — at first with a lighted torch and subsequently with a whip (once the monster has been safely bound in chains). Predictably Fritz goes too far, and is eventually decapitated off-screen; all we hear is his high-pitched screams. No one — least of all the audience — mourns his passing.

In *The Vampire Bat* (1932), Frye plays yet another animal-like character — the bat-loving Herman Gleib. He makes a memorable first appearance on the screen, walking towards his bed-ridden mistress Martha Mueller (Rita Carlyle) as if in a trance, his hands and fingers spread wide as if he is about to strangle her. Actually, he just wants her to give him some fruit ("Martha give me apples. I like! [...] Herman get. Herman get water"). Glieb has a fondness for bats that he treats as pets, despite the fact that Martha has been attacked by a vampire bat ("They soft, like cat, they not hurt Herman.") With his hair sticking out in all directions and his monosyllabic mode of delivery, Herman is a complete social misfit; and as such becomes the prime suspect as the villagers try to find out who killed Martha. One villager sees him stroking a bat and shouts out: "You're inhuman, in league with the devil!" Gleib moves slowly towards Martha's corpse, his body quivering with emotion as he does so. He turns back the winding-sheet to reveal her dead face, whimpers slightly and then gives a full-throated scream before running off upstairs. The citizens believe — quite unjustifiably — that such reactions are characteristic of a vampire. Not so: Gleib needed Martha's protection in order to survive, and now that she is dead he has to fend for himself, a task clearly beyond him. The citizens chase him out of the village into a cave; he turns and looks at them, breathing heavily like a wild animal, and stammering, "No ... no go! Herman afraid!" Director Frank R. Strayer cuts to a close-up of his petrified face as he backs away from the citizens before falling over a precipice and plunging to his death a hundred feet below. Burgermeister Gustave Schoen (Lionel Belmore) exclaims: "That settles him!" Actually, Gleib is a man more sinned against than sinning for his mental disabilities — Karl Brettschneider (Melvyn Douglas) accurately describes him as "a poor misfit being hunted down like a dog."

Although Frye had been killed off in the original film, Whale was so impressed by his performance that he cast him once again in *The Bride of Frankenstein* (1935). This time Frye plays Karl, the sidekick to Dr. Pretorius (ERNEST THESIGER)—a sweaty, greasy figure with protuberant ears, who relishes the prospect of opening up coffins and admiring the contents inside. At one point, he exclaims "Pretty little thing, isn't she?" as he observes the corpse of a dead girl. Karl has no particular loyalties to his master; he will so long as he gets well remunerated. When Pretorius asks him to find another corpse, Karl agrees—so long as he is paid one thousand crowns. The doctor agrees, and Karl walks out of the back of the frame, placing his hands on the back of his head as he does so. However, the servant cannot be trusted to carry out the doctor's orders to the letter; he lies in wait in a dark corner, and stabs a prostitute to death. He brings the corpse back, claiming as he does so that he procured it off a local gendarme, and paid him fifty crowns for the privilege. As Pretorius and Frankenstein (Colin Clive) continue their experiments, Karl scuttles around the castle like a filthy rat, carrying out their orders to the letter (in the hope of further remuneration). However, the only reward he obtains is violent death, as the monster (Boris Karloff) throws him off the castle battlements. Frye returns again in *Frankenstein Meets the Wolf Man* (1943) as Rudi, a grave robber.

In *Dead Men Walk* (1943), Frye's performance as Zolarr, the evil servant of the vampire Elwyn Clayton (GEORGE ZUCCO) contains several intertexts referring to his earlier roles in horror films. As in *Frankenstein* he walks with his shoulders hunched forward, his arms hanging limply down by his side. Dressed from head to toe in black, he resembles a giant rat, scuttling from room to room as he carries out his master's orders. His voice assumes a screeching tone from the beginning as he faces Elwyn's brother Lloyd (also Zucco) and yells, "Your brother searched the estate for those [occult] books, and you dare destroy them!" (placing great emphasis on the alliterative phrase "dare destroy.") When the doctor tells him how relieved the local villagers are that Elwyn has passed away, Zolarr spits out his response: "Haaa, what do I care what they believe?" Just like Renfield in *Dracula*, Zolarr remains firmly under the vampire's control. The *Dracula* echoes resurface later on in the film as director Sam Newfield repeatedly cuts to close-ups of Zolarr's face, his sweat-soaked features, wild looks and bared teeth giving him a monstrous appearance. Once again Frye overacts shamelessly as he tries to hit Lloyd with a poker, and becomes involved in a life-or-death struggle. Lloyd pushes him into a cupboard, which falls forward, pinning Zolarr underneath it. The film ends with the two brothers fighting in a burning building, with Zolarr screaming "Master! Master!" his hands clasped to his face like a little child. As with Fritz in *The Bride of Frankenstein*, he experiences a gruesome death.

In *The Crime of Dr. Crespi* (1935), based on Edgar Allan Poe's "The Premature Burial," Frye departs somewhat from his familiar screen image as he plays Dr. Thomas, a put-upon junior doctor endlessly bullied by Dr. Crespi (Erich von Stroheim). At one point, Thomas quite literally cowers as Crespi roars at him: "Have the courtesy to announce yourself!" However, once Thomas soon discovers Crespi's real intention to drug Stephen Ross (John Bohn) and bury him alive, his attitude changes. His face acquires the kind of intensity associated with most of Frye's characterizations, as he stares at his superior and announces in an ominous voice that he wants to talk to him. Crespi responds by smacking him in the face and trying to strangle him. The film ends with Crespi committing suicide; as he does so Thomas lets out a piercing scream ("Don't!") reminding us of just how close he is to a nervous breakdown as the result of his ordeal.

Beverly Garland
b. October 17, 1926, Santa Cruz, California;
d. December 5, 2008, Hollywood Hills, California.

Beverly Lucy Fassenden began her career in radio and in a few nudie flicks with titles such as *Fanny with the Cheeks of Tan*. She made her name in the mid–1950s in low-budget adventure films such as *Killer Leopard* (1954), with ex–Tarzan actor Johnny Sheffield, and in horror films, several of which were either produced or directed by Roger Corman. Her first horror film, however, was *The Neanderthal Man* (1953), where she had a supporting role as server Nola Mason. In this low-budget epic, she comes across as someone fond of flirting with her (mostly male) customers—to such an extent that she agrees to accompany Buck Hastings (Eric Colmar) on an afternoon out so that he can photograph her in a white bikini. This largely irrelevant twist of the plot provides director Ewald André Dupont with the excuse for a few cheesecake shots of Garland in the forest, recalling Jane in the *Tarzan* movies. However, the sequence is abruptly curtailed with the entrance of the eponymous Neanderthal Man (actually Prof. Clifford Groves (Robert Shayne) who has been experimenting with a serum), who strangles Hastings to death and carries Nola off in his arms in spite of her hideous screams. Nola reappears later on at Groves' house in hysterics, scarcely able to recover from her experience despite being sedated by Dr. Fairchild (William Fawcett). Her experiences reveal the film's ambiguous stance concerning the female form — while the sight of Nola seminude is obviously titillating for most (male) filmgoers, the director feels that he needs to punish her for posing in public.

In *Curucu, Beast of the Amazon* (1956), Garland laid the foundations for her screen *persona*, which changed little in her subsequent horror films. As the cancer specialist Dr. Andrea Romar she comes across as a strong woman who will not take no for an answer, reveling in the fact that she seems the equal — in terms of willpower — of her male counterparts. Rock Dean (John Bromfield) refuses to take her on a journey up the Amazon, so Andrea decides to organize her own trip. Eventually, Dean gives in, but not without delivering the kind of lines characteristic of the mid–1950s American male threatened by the presence of a strong female ("Those [women] who can't get a man, choose a career," "You're a foolish little girl [for

Beverly Garland publicity still (1984). Blond-haired leading lady of science fiction films of the 1950s, Garland played women who appeared outwardly strong, yet often needed help to survive.

wanting to travel].") In spite of the obstacles placed in her way — thick undergrowth, the unexpected appearance of predatory animals — Andrea refuses to give up her quest, although Dean insists that it is "no job for a woman." She manages to establish her own space — a small makeshift hospital where she treats stricken tribesperson Tico (Wilson Viana) for an unspecified tropical disease, and eventually cures him. However, director Curt Siodmak cannot allow the idea of gender equality to prevail throughout the film: as in *Neanderthal Man*, the actress presents herself for the male spectator's delectation, as she dresses herself after taking a shower. As the jungle ordeal intensifies, so Andrea's strength of character declines: one night she wakes up and sees the eponymous Beast of the Amazon threatening her. Siodmak cuts to a close-up of her delivering a full-throated scream, as she cowers in the corner of her tent in terror. Unable to move, she is only saved from certain death by Rock's timely intervention with a shotgun. Andrea's basic weakness of character is underlined in the film's final sequence, where she looks at a *tsantas* (a shrunken head characteristic of native tribes in South America) made out of Tico's head, indicating that her knowledge of medical science has not been sufficient to save him from death in the savage atmosphere of the jungle. In spite of her education, she lacks the worldly know-how to survive in extreme conditions, and must therefore rely on Rock's strength of character to ensure her safety.

A similar conflict between strength and weakness emerges in Roger Corman's *Swamp Women* (1956), where Garland's Vera, one of a gang of four escaped female convicts, comes across as a doughty fighter fond of settling arguments with her fists. When confronted with Billie (Jil Jarmyn), a respectable girl taken as hostage by the gang, Vera reacts by hitting her in the face with the back of her hand and tearing her shirt with a flick-knife. She administers the same treatment to Billie's boyfriend Bob Matthews (Touch Connors), when he dares to make fun of her. Like several Corman films, *Swamp Women* questions the prevailing gender ideology of Cold War America, which dictated that women should become homemakers to ensure the country's future stability. Vera will have none of this; she drinks like a fish and displays a reckless attitude towards her own personal safety. One of her fellow gang-members describes her as "a neat dame."

However, Corman finds it difficult to sustain his convictions—as the action progresses, we discover that Vera actually cares for Bob, but cannot disclose her feelings for fear of seeming weak in her fellow gang-members' eyes. This eventually proves her undoing: Vera takes Bob into the Louisiana swamp, in the vain hope of establishing a new life with him. However, she is outwitted by the other three women, two of whom distract her attention while the third, the gang-leader Josie Nardo (Marie Windsor) kills Vera with a poisoned harpoon. The harpoon—clearly a phallic symbol—suggests that the (male) director has reassumed control over his female star. Vera's bid for power has evaporated into nothing, as one of the characters observes. "She always wanted to kill, kill anything, and the last thing she did was save his [Bob's] life," by shooting a rattlesnake that threatened to bite him to death.

Garland plays a similar role as Claire Anderson in Corman's *It Conquered the World* (1956). Initially, she seems perfectly content to play the doting wife to her husband Tom (Lee Van Cleef), but her fiery eyes and active body-language (she frequently throws her arms in the air in frustration) suggest a more active personality. Corman frequently photographs her in close-up as she becomes more and more worried about her husband's behavior. Once she understands the point behind his scientific researches (to mobilize an alien from Venus to take over the world), she understands that family ties no longer mean anything; it's far more important to save America from the invaders. She grabs a shotgun, jumps into her car and drives off to the cave where the monster lurks.

Yet it seems once again that Corman cannot trust his convictions, as he uses Claire's death to reinforce patriarchal values. Although outwardly an active personality, she proves no match for the monster; as she dies, Corman cuts more than once to close-ups of her face contorted with fear—a typically scopophilic move giving the (male) spectator the vicarious pleasure of experiencing female suffering firsthand. Her husband eventually destroys the monster before he perishes himself.

A year later in *Not of This Earth*, Garland plays a nurse, Nadine Storey, who stubbornly refuses to submit to the alien Paul Johnson's (PAUL BIRCH) will, despite his best attempts to intimidate her. This time Corman includes another cheesecake scene involving her changing into a swimsuit and diving into Johnson's swimming pool; later on she wanders around his house dressed only in a long sleeve shirt, showing off her legs. Despite the director's attempts to objectify here, Nadine sustains an active role in the film, as she discovers Johnson's true nature and tries to call her boyfriend Harry Sherbourne (Morgan Jones) for help. Although pursued by Johnson who proclaims all the while in voiceover that he has her in his power, Nadine emerges unscathed from her experience—a testament, perhaps, to her enduring strength of character. In *The Alligator People* (1959), Garland plays Joyce Webster, a wife who comes to a lonely retreat in a Louisiana swamp to find out precisely what has happened to her husband Paul (Richard Crane). Once again, her strength of character is put to the test, as Lavinia Hawthorne (Frieda Inescort) tries her best to persuade her to leave, and when that fails, tries to lock Joyce in her bedroom. However, Joyce will not be diverted from her task — as she observes in voiceover, she wants to find out "what secret was in this house." Eventually, she discovers that as a result of a failed medical experiment her husband has been transformed into an alligator mutant. He dies a horrible death as he sinks into a swamp.

Roy del Ruth's film invites us to reflect on whether human beings are really superior to beasts. While Paul Webster might attack all his pursuers, he seems far less of a threat than Manon (Lon Chaney, Jr.), an alligator-hating member of the household who lures her into his cabin and tries to force himself upon her. The only way to ensure the survival of the human race is to trust in one's mental strength. Joyce understands this, as she tries to overcome the psychological trauma of her experiences by dedicating herself to her work.

Peter Graves

b. March 18, 1926, Minneapolis, Minnesota;
d. March 14, 2010, Pacific Palisades, California.

Born Peter Aurness in Minneapolis, Minnesota, Peter Graves enjoyed a long career in films and television, most notably as Jim Phelps in *Mission: Impossible* (1967–1973). His early career as a Hollywood actor was spent playing regular parts in Westerns and science fiction films with an overt socio-political message. In *Red Planet Mars* (1952), he plays Chris Cronyn, a happily married scientist devoted to his work to such an extent that he has little time for his wife and two small boys. Cronyn has made a great discovery; that it is now possible to establish direct communication with citizens on Mars. This, he believes, will contribute greatly to the improvement of life on Earth. His wife Linda (Andrea King) is not so sure; she is tired of "living on the edge of a volcano"— in other words, she wants a peaceful life without the destruction that she believes will come about as a result of her husband's scientific research.

Peter Graves in *Mission, Impossible* (1966). A reassuring presence in 1950s science fiction films, Graves played reliable family men whose morals seldom deviated from the straight and narrow.

Needless to say, Cronyn ignores his wife's warnings and continues his experiments, only to discover that they threaten the fabric of the entire western world. The people on Mars are so advanced, both economically and technologically, that they have the power to colonize the Earth: whole economies are threatened, while Cronyn himself has to face the wrath of an angry crowd, protesting about their futures. He seems somewhat nonplussed by this reaction — after all, he is only a scientist, not a politician. *Red Planet Mars* rehearses familiar arguments about how the desire for progress renders individuals completely immune to the destructive potential of the space race.

However, it seems that all conflicts are successfully resolved, as the Martians communicate a message of brotherly love and submission to God's will. By such means all people on earth will learn how to co-exist with one another. The evil ex–Nazi scientist Franz Calder (Herbert Berghof) claims responsibility for the entire affair; he laid down a trail of false communications and duped the Americans (Cronyn included) into believing that such communications came from Mars. By such means, Calder hopes to take over the world. Cronyn challenges Calder's ideas, proclaiming that "God gave us free will ... it's what distinguishes us from the animals." Eventually, Cronyn proves that the Martians have indeed been communicating with the Earth, even though he destroys himself, his wife and Calder in the process. Cronyn embodies the film's Christian anticommunist stance; by sacrificing himself to ensure the future of the democratic world, he destroys Calder (the potential dictator) and reaffirms the existence of God as the ultimate authority.

In *Killers from Space* (1954), Graves plays a similar role as Doug Martin, another happily married research scientist and test pilot who, as a result of an A-bomb test that goes wrong, is possessed by aliens, who implant a cross on his left breast, symbolizing ungodliness (as all men are supposed to sit at God's right hand). Martin's behavior does not seem markedly different, except for the fact that he seems obsessed with the idea of the bomb exploding, and hence becomes a security risk. *Killers from Space* is another Cold War science fiction flick, warning filmgoers of the dangers of indoctrination. Happily married family men like Martin are transformed into neurotics, crying out, "They're here! They're here! They're going to destroy us," to anyone willing to listen. He appears to be hypnotized, bereft of the power of self-determination. However, director W. Lee Wilder is not prepared to consign his leading player to a life of perpetual slavery: through sheer willpower Martin overcomes his hypnosis and manages to destroy the aliens through sheer mental strength. The message is clear: all Americans should not only remain vigilant against possible threats to their way of life, but they must be capable of preserving their individuality, even if it means putting themselves at risk.

In Roger Corman's *It Conquered the World* (1956), Graves plays yet another happily married Euro-American man with powerful shoulders and a imposing presence, who is unwillingly sucked into a plan masterminded by disgruntled scientist Dr. Tom Anderson (Lee Van Cleef) to use aliens from Venus to take over the world. Nelson remains phlegmatic for most of the film; nothing really ruffles him, until he is faced with the stark choice of killing his wife Joan (Sally Fraser)—who has been infected by the aliens—or allowing Anderson's plan to flourish. Needless to say, he chooses the first option, but the emotional experience badly affects him, as he sits in anguish on the sofa with his head in his hands. However, he understands the importance of finishing his task: director Corman cuts to a close-up of his face set in an expression of grim determination as he leaves the family home and climbs into his open-top sports car. It is his duty to sustain the American way of life by destroying Anderson and the aliens, even at the expense of his family. In a voiceover at the end, he proclaims: "Man is a feeling creature and because of it the greatest in the universe. Men have to find their own way and make their own mistakes. There can't be any gift of perfection from outside themselves. When men seek such perfection, they find only death, fire, loss, disillusionment, the end of everything [...] There is hope, but it has to come inside from man himself."

In *The Beginning of the End* (1957), Graves plays Dr. Ed Wainwright, a scientist claiming to have led a sheltered life yet possessed of the ability to change the world. As the director of the laboratory run by the Department of Agriculture, he claims to have privileged knowledge about a bunch of locusts, which have grown to monstrous proportions and could now herald "the beginning of an era which could lead to the complete annihilation of man." Portentous words indeed, but Wainwright believes that he is the only person who can remove that threat. The army might want to intervene by destroying the locusts with an atom bomb—and blowing up the city of Chicago in the process—but Wainwright believes he can deal with it scientifically. Director Bert I. Gordon's camera tracks him pacing around the room, and then raising his right hand to hold everyone's attention as he announces that he has a solution that "just might work." Wainwright's explanation sounds somewhat technical to unscientific minds, but it does not really matter. What is more important is that he understands the importance of using science for the public good. In collaboration with the military, he coordinates the operation from a control room, his arms folded in a gesture of utter confidence. Once the operation has succeeded, Wainwright obtains his just reward, as he falls into the arms of investigative reporter Audrey Ames (Peggie Castle), who alerted people to the potential dangers of the insects in the first place.

Nan Grey

b. July 25, 1918, Houston, Texas:
d. July 25, 1993, San Diego, California.

Eschal Loleet Grey Miller worked as a contract artist at Universal throughout the 1930s and early 1940s, on such films as the Deanna Durbin vehicles *Three Smart Girls* (1936) and the sequel *Three Smart Girls Grow Up* (1939). She also played several character parts in horror films; one of her earliest was that of Nan in *Dracula's Daughter* (1936) — a lost woman picked up in the streets of London by Sandor (IRVING PICHEL) and taken back to the home of Dracula's daughter (Gloria Holden). Once she meets the vampire, Nan's expression changes; she looks uncertainly around the room and speaks in a breathy, almost hesitant tone as she agrees to take off her blouse and pose for a cheesecake photograph. Director Lambert Hillyer's camera zooms slowly towards her as she removes her clothing, culminating in a close-up of her terrified face, her saucer-like eyes almost standing out on stalks as she understands what will happen to her. She gabbles, "I think I'll go if you don't mind," and screams, but it is too late, as Dracula's daughter claps a hand round Nan's mouth and sucks the blood out of her.

In *Tower of London* (1939), Grey plays Lady Alice, a gentlewoman of noble birth devoted to her mistress Queen Elizabeth (Barbara O'Neil) yet determined to remain true to her beloved John Wyatt (John Sutton). In a film glorifying male power, as personified by the Duke of Gloucester (Basil Rathbone) — the future King Richard III — Lady Alice seems a largely passive character, whose principal responsibility seems to consist of standing in the background looking sympathetic, and offering a comforting hand where necessary to Queen Elizabeth. Lady Alice herself comments rather bitterly that she has become "inured to waiting" for Queen Elizabeth to reassume her royal authority, and for Wyatt to escape from imprisonment by Gloucester. Eventually, Alice assumes a more active role — even though she has to assume a male disguise to do so. She dons a chimney-sweep's costume and steals into the Tower of London. Through a series of daring moves, she reaches Wyatt's cell and gives him a file so that he can cut his chains and plan his escape. Although Grey has great fun with this sequence (even assuming a deep voice to make her impersonation more convincing), she also confirms the film's conservative gender construction contrasting active males with passive females.

This schema also influences Gray's role in *The Invisible Man Returns* (1940), where she plays the leading female character Helen Manson as a *femme fatale*, apparently resigned to the fact that her fiancé Geoffrey Radcliffe (Vincent Price) will be executed for a murder he did

Nan Grey cinema star postcard (1943). A Universal leading lady of the 1940s, Nan Grey frequently played insecure women in need of protection from their male costars.

not commit. Unable to mount any active challenge to his conviction, all she can do is to show unswerving devotion — as suggested through a series of close-ups as she stares directly into his eyes. Her body language — stiff back, head in the air — suggests a kind of stoicism; whatever happens to Geoffrey, she will remain at his side. When Geoffrey becomes invisible, Helen's reactions change somewhat; she screams and faints as he removes the bandages from his head to reveal nothing underneath. Nonetheless, she retains an admirable ability to recover; once she comes around, she stretches her arms out to him, even though she has no idea where he is. Geoffrey refuses the offer, in the belief that he has to clear his name before he can be restored to her. Eventually, order is restored: Geoffrey turns out to be innocent, while Richard Cobb (CEDRIC HARDWICKE) turns out to be the guilty party. The film ends with Helen standing passively over Cobb's corpse, her face fixed in an expressionless gaze. Clearly she will not be happy until Geoffrey is restored to her. Her wishes come true, as Geoffrey eventually takes the antidote to render him visible once again; in the last frame the two of them are shown embracing.

In her next film, Joe May's adaptation of the Nathaniel Hawthorne novel *The House of the Seven Gables* (also 1940), Grey plays Phoebe Pyncheon, who comes to stay with her cousin Hepzibah (Margaret Lindsay). With her white dress and curly hair, she represents a breath of fresh air in the eponymous House of the Seven Gables, which for years has been closed to all comers with Hepzibah living a hermit-like existence inside. Phoebe seems initially hesitant — particularly when faced with such a formidable-looking figure as her cousin; she admits that her coming might seem "an unforgivable intrusion." She seems equally intimidated when Jaffray Pyncheon (GEORGE SANDERS) makes occasional visits to the house, barging through the front door as if he owned the place and scarcely acknowledging Phoebe's presence. However, Phoebe's true character attitude soon emerges, as she hears that Hepzibah will open a scent-shop in her front parlor; her eyes shine and she hopes excitedly from foot to foot. Hepzibah initially does not quite know what to make of this young lady; but as time passes, she comes to understand that Phoebe represents a living reincarnation of her younger self — someone who frequently falls in love and enjoys her life to the full. Director May reinforces this link by having the younger Hepzibah and Phoebe wear the same kind of white dresses, and do much the same things, such as staring out of the window and dreaming of a happy life with their respective boyfriends: Hepzibah with Clifford Pyncheon (Vincent Price), and Phoebe with Matthew Maule, aka Mr. Hargrave (DICK FORAN). Unfortunately, circumstances conspired against Hepzibah to deny her romantic dreams: Clifford is wrongfully accused of murder by Jaffray and imprisoned for several years. Eventually, however, both women achieve their dreams; in the film's final sequence Phoebe marries Matthew, while Hepzibah and Clifford — now somewhat gray-haired, the result of years of hardship — drive away in a dog-cart, with the lawyer Philip Barton (CECIL KELLAWAY) telling them in voiceover that he would always see the two of them "as [they] were, in the very beginning."

Anne Gwynne

*b. December 10, 1918, Waco, Texas;
d. March 31, 2003, Woodland Hills,
Los Angeles, California.*

Marguerite Anne Trice first modeled Catalina swimwear and appeared in local theatre productions to gain experience. She signed a contract with Universal Pictures in 1939; her first work was in Westerns opposite minor stars such as Johnny Mack Brown, but she later graduated to supporting roles in horror pictures both for Universal and for Poverty Row studios such as Republic.

One such role was that of Jean Sovac in the Karloff/Lugosi vehicle *Black Friday* (1940) for Universal. Her father, Dr. Ernest Sovac (Karloff), a brilliant scientist working in comparative obscurity at a provincial university, conducts a brain transplant in which the injured professor George Kingsley (Stanley

Anne Gwynne in *The Enchanted Valley* (1948). Gwynne began her career as an ingénue in horror films and dramas for Universal, but graduated later to low-budget science fiction films of the late 1950s.

Ridges) is kept alive with the brain of deceased mobster Red Cannon (also played by Ridges). The operation has a disastrous Jekyll and Hyde side effect: under certain conditions Cannon's personality emerges, transforming Kingsley into a serial killer. Needless to say, Sovac is doomed to die in the electric chair for his experiments. His daughter, Jean, remains devoted to him, despite his misdemeanors; on one occasion she hugs him tightly and vows eternal support. But this does not prevent her taking the initiative on occasions; in one sequence she sits him down on a hotel bed and implores him to undo the transplant. The doctor protests that the operation is a groundbreaking one, of limitless benefit to all humankind; Jean ignores him, and starts packing his suitcases in an attempt to sprite him away before his crimes can be discovered. Her efforts prove futile: Cannon comes to the doctor's house and tries to strangle her in the belief that she will go to the police. Although Jean is saved in the nick of time, we feel that all her efforts have been in vain; her father's obsession with scientific experiment has blinded him to his familial responsibilities. Later that year, Gwynne had a small role in Universal's serial *Flash Gordon Conquers the Universe* as Queen Sonja. Dressed regally in white robes with a bejeweled tiara, Gwynne does not have much to do other than to issue orders in regal tones, confident in the knowledge that they will be carried out to the letter.

In *Weird Woman* (1944), Gwynne plays Paula Clayton Reed, a native of the South Seas who marries Professor Norman Reed (Lon Chaney, Jr.), and tries to eke out a living in the respectable surroundings of Monroe College in New York. Predictably she becomes the victim of the other wives' orientalist prejudices: Reed's ex-girlfriend Ilona Carr (EVELYN ANKERS) describes her as "a witch wife," and "a little doll who grew up in the jungle," while Evelyn Sawtelle (ELIZABETH RUSSELL) dislikes Paula's "child's face and [...] black heart." Even her husband refuses to acknowledge that Paula might possess supernatural powers, as he tells her to burn her native symbols— including a medallion hanging round her neck which Paula describes as "part of everything and for all time"— and embrace the so-called "rational" world of western academic life. In spite of her husband's superstitions, Paula believes that she must continue practicing her rituals, as a way of guaranteeing his safety; she maintains a childlike devotion to him, even when he is accused of murdering one of his students. Her belief in his basic goodness is vindicated, as Ilona is revealed as the true villain of the piece. Norman and Paula vow to "start afresh" as a happily married couple.

Gwynne's character was not so lucky in *House of Frankenstein* (1944). She plays Rita Hussmann, one of Count Dracula's (JOHN CARRADINE) victims. His hold over her is palpable as he towers over her in his black cloak and top hat, staring directly into her eyes. As she sleeps in her bed, Dracula enters her room and attacks her, transforming himself into a bat and flying out in the nick of time, as Rita's husband Karl (Peter Coe) knocks on her door. Thereafter, Rita walks around like a zombie, her face devoid of color, speaking her lines in a monotonous voice. However, this Count Dracula is not as effective as in other films: Rita is soon restored to health, as she removes a ring from her finger that Dracula had given her, and allows Karl to kiss her. The two of them quit the room in a passionate embrace — a fitting testament to the power of true love.

As befits a minor pin-up star of the Second World War, Anne Gwynne played attractive young women sometimes threatened by monsters but usually emerging triumphant in the final reel, and hence able to marry their leading men. In Republic's comedy horror flick *The Ghost Goes Wild* (1947), she plays Phyllis Beecher, a pretty young girl concerned for her Aunt Susan's (Ruth Beecher) welfare yet simultaneously head-over-heels in love with cartoonist Monte Crandall (James Ellison). Phyllis alternates between moments of uncertainty and decisiveness; when Monte kisses her for the first time, she shies away as if uncertain about whether he is serious or not. When she discovers him in the arms of married socialite Irene Winters (Stephanie Batchelor), Phyllis becomes much more decisive; she stiffens her back, puts her head in the air and pointedly ignores everything that Monte tries to say to her. In keeping with the fashions of that time, Phyllis is fond of wearing dresses with padded shoulders; this suggests a dominant nature. This might be true in public: Phyllis however reveals her insecurities in private, as her lip trembles at the thought that Monte might be dead. He isn't, of course, but only pretending to be dead so that he can escape being sued for defamation of character by Aunt Susan. Phyllis' true nature reveals itself when, having put her aunt to bed, she discovers Monte hiding in her bedroom. The two of them lock arms in a passionate kiss.

In *Teenage Monster* (1957), Gwynne has a very different role as Ruth Cannon, a single parent trying to protect her son Charles (Gil Perkins), who has been transformed into a teenage monster as a result of being exposed to rays from a meteor. Ruth tries her best to maintain a façade of normality, as she pursues a tentative love-affair with Sheriff Bob Lehman (Stuart Wade), but the responsibility proves too much for her. Deprived of the stabilizing influence of a man, she cannot keep control of her son, who repeatedly escapes from his bedroom and kills his victims, even if he does not mean to. He becomes a pawn in Kathy North's (Gloria Castillo) schemes to extort money from Ruth; if she does not pay Kathy off, then Kathy will tell the world about Charles's true identity. Eventually, Charles understands Kathy's motives and kills her; in consequence Lehman and his fellow law-enforcers hunt him down and kill him. Jacques R. Marquette's film makes some familiar points about the perils of growing up in a fatherless family — despite Ruth's best efforts, Charles lacks the stabilizing influence which might have kept him on the moral straight and narrow.

Henry Hall

b. November 5, 1876, Washington, Missouri; d. December 11, 1954, Woodland Hills, Los Angeles, California.

Born Henry Leonard Hall in Woodland Hills, California, Hall's film career began in 1926 with a small role in *The Primrose Path*. For the next decade and half, he played bit parts in a variety of films, including horror and science fiction serials such as *The Lost Jungle* (1934), which was also released as a 68-minute feature film. In this film, he plays a naval officer, a representative of authority who is contrasted with the central character Clyde (Clyde Beatty), whose sole interest in life is "lions, tigers, tigers, lions." At first, the directors Armand Schaefer and David Howard suggest that the naval officers are somehow superior; they know how to run a tight ship, and organize everyone on board. However, when they are shipwrecked on a lonely island, and face having to forage in the jungle for sustenance, the naval officer's authority breaks down; all he desires is to leave as soon as possible, even if his future might be uncertain. Instead, it is Clyde who assumes a position of responsibility, as he tames the lions and tigers and thereby ensures everyone's safety. However, *The Lost Jungle* remains slightly ambiguous in its view of Clyde's behavior — although fearless in attitude, he treats the wild animals like colonized peoples. Once they have been tamed, they can be put in cages and taken back to America as the latest attractions for Clyde's circus. This theme was to be explored once more in *Mighty Joe Young* (1949), the third in Universal's King Kong series.

In *The Phantom Empire* (1935), a twelve-part serial starring the singing cowboy Gene Autry, Hall plays a high priest, chief servant to Queen Tika (Dorothy Christy). He does not have to do much other than to nod his head in assent as the Queen implements her plans for world domination, placing her underground city Murama at the center of the universe. Hall appears in several identical sequences during the serial; this was a deliberate memorializing strategy, designed to remind viewers about what had previously happened during the twelve parts. In *The Lost City*, another twelve-part serial from 1935, Hall plays a general, who proclaims in the opening episode: "Gentlemen, I am afraid that unless we locate the source of this disturbance [a series of electrical storms], we face the destruction of the world." Director Harry Revier pans the assembled company of senior military officers and government officials in their wing collars and frock coats who all nod in assent. However, the projected crisis will be overcome by the intervention of Kane Richmond (Bruce Gordon), a communications officer who realizes he has to go to Africa to investigate the source of the storms. The camera cuts to medium close-ups of the officials' startled faces (including the general's), as they absorb this piece of information, but their attitude soon changes when they understand Richmond's seriousness of purpose. The general tells Richmond that he "will lack nothing," in his search for answers, and gratefully shakes his hand.

A year later, Hall had a small role as the warden in the fifteen-part epic detailing *The Amazing Exploits of the Clutching Hand* (aka *The Clutching Hand*). He sits behind a desk advising Joe Mitchell (Robert Walker) to follow the path of virtue. Mitchell contemptuously rejects these comments, so the warden responds with the schoolmasterly comment: "Bitterness won't get you anywhere."

Henry Hall (second from right) in *The Bride Goes Wild* (1948). A veteran character actor of many serials and westerns of the 1930s and 1940s, Hall made a habit of playing flawed figures of authority.

Hall is cast against type in the little-known haunted house horror film *Tangled Destinies* (1932). He plays a parson who gives every appearance of being ineffective but passive, as he tries to help a group of people come to terms with the experience of having to spend a night in a derelict house, as the plane carrying them has been forced to make a landing in the desert. The parson looks after the elderly members of the group, while advising others to take care of the property. In his own words, the group are "uninvited guests, you know." However his honeyed words turn out to be hollow, as he turns out to be a hired killer who murders the passengers one by one in the hope of getting his hands on a bag of diamonds. Although overpowered at the end by sheer weight of numbers, Hall's character reveals an aggression that no one—including the viewers—expects.

As the 1940s dawned, Hall gradually assumed more substantial roles. In *The Ape* (1940), a low-budget programmer from Monogram, he plays Sheriff Jeff Halliday, a practically-minded person with a talent for organization. While his fellow citizens spend much of their time debating how to deal with the twin problems of an escaped ape and the presence of a mad scientist, Dr. Bernard Adrian (Boris Karloff) within their midst, Sheriff Halliday organizes people into search parties, posts sentries where appropriate, and coordinates the search for the ape around the doctor's house, in the (justifiable) belief that Adrian knows more than he is prepared to admit. Halliday is fond of fingering his lapels as a sign of authority; no one should mess with him. Director William Nigh emphasizes this aspect of the sheriff's character by keeping him at the center of the frame; he is the fulcrum around which most of village life operates. In the end, it is the sheriff who solves the mystery by shooting the ape outside the doctor's house, and then pulling its head off, revealing Dr. Adrian in disguise. As with many monster films, the doctor's obsession with science had transformed him into a killer obtaining spinal fluid from his victims to complete the formula for his experimental serum.

In *The Ape Man* (1943), Hall plays Dr. George Randall, another pillar of the local community — a tall, statuesque doctor with an aloof manner, glowering at his subordinates through horn-rimmed spectacles. However, this proves nothing more than a façade; Randall is at heart a frightened man, who gradually understands the tragic consequences of his involvement in the experiments to transform Dr. James Brewster (Bela Lugosi) into an ape man. He lives in perpetual fear of his life — as witnessed, for instance, in one sequence where he gets up abruptly from a chair (following Brewster's unexpected entrance), thrusts some papers into his pockets and begins to walk maniacally around the room. Eventually, Brewster forces Randall to continue collaborating in the experiment; all Randall can do is to take a deep breath, grasp the lapels of his jacket and agree. But this loyalty proves misplaced: Randall meets a gruesome end as Brewster shakes him like a rag doll and strangles him to death.

A year later, Hall played the Sheriff in *Voodoo Man*. Given a rare opportunity by director William Beaudine to show off his comic talents, Hall portrays the sheriff as a world-weary cynic, announcing with a sigh that, were it not for the mysterious disappearance of several females in his town, "the sheriff's job would be a cinch." He visits the house of mad doctor Richard Marlowe (Bela Lugosi) and cracks a wry joke about the possibility of finding one of the missing girls in the doctor's living room. The sheriff inspects the dingy surroundings, commenting ironically on the "cheerful" ambience before accepting a glass of sherry.

Hall played another pillar of the community — Inspector Godfrey — in the Charlie Chan drama *The Jade Mask* (1945). Although determined to reinforce his authority — as he sits behind his desk issuing orders and waving a clenched fist in his subordinates' direction to emphasize the point — he understands that Charlie Chan (Sidney Toler) possess a far greater capacity to solve crimes than himself. When both of them visit the Harper mansion to investigate a series of murders, Godfrey willingly cedes his authority to the great detective, greeting all of his pronouncements with a benevolent smile, as if confident that the case will be successfully solved (and thereby guaranteeing Godfrey's future as a police officer). Above all, Godfrey understands how to benefit from Chan's experience.

Jon Hall

b. February 23, 1915, Fresno, California; d. December 13, 1979, North Hollywood, California.

An athletic actor who made his major film debut in *Charlie Chan in Shanghai* (1935). A year later, he had a small role as Frank Hobart, a heavy in the fifteen-part serial *The Amazing Exploits of the Clutching Hand* (aka *The Clutching Hand*), billed under his real name Charles Locher. Hobart does not have much to do, other than to look threatening; in the first episode, he appears in the Harbor Hotel in pinstripe suit and trilby hat, offering cigarettes to his fellow mobsters and carrying out orders given to him by the eponymous Clutching Hand. In subsequent episodes, Hobart is seen driving getaway cars, scrapping regularly with clean-cut detective hero Craig Kennedy (Jack Mulhall), but never losing — until the final (fifteenth) episode, that is. However, Hobart remains an all-action heavy; he is seen climbing up telegraph poles, or running up and down the fire-escapes of various buildings.

As a Universal contract player in the 1930s and 1940s, with a different screen name (he changed his name to Lloyd Crane in 1936–7, and first appeared as Jon Hall in *The Hurricane* [1937]), Jon Hall appeared in many different films, including horror flicks such as *The Invisible Agent* (1942), in which H.G. Wells's story is transposed to a World War II setting. As Frank Griffin (aka Raymond), Hall comes across as a suave, urbane figure — a source of stability in a world where no one can be trusted, who relishes the prospect of taking on the Nazi agents led by Conrad Stauffer (CEDRIC HARDWICKE). Director Edwin L. Marin gives him a long propaganda speech in praise of democracy, while pitying the Nazis when they "start appearing in bunches." Griffin shows admirable strength of character, as he resists the tortures administered to him by the evil Japanese scientist Ikito (Peter Lorre), which include angling hooks being placed near his nipples. Eventually, Griffin emerges triumphant, while being cured of his invisibility by Maria Sorenson (Ilona Massey), who spreads cold cream (i.e., the antidote) over his body.

In another sequel to Wells's story, *The Invisible Man's Revenge* (1944), Griffin plays the bad guy — Robert Griffin — a fugitive from the law who becomes invisible and takes revenge on his former friends. Like CLAUDE RAINS in the original *Invisible Man*, Robert Griffin is a basically good man transformed into a murderer through the power he has at his disposal. His whole bearing changes; his once mild-mannered tones are replaced by an evil rasp as he relishes the prospect of the "cat-and-mouse game" to recover his inheritance. Although remaining the clean-cut, all-American hero in appearance, he reveals a hitherto untapped capacity for violence, as he picks up the hapless Dr. Drury (JOHN CARRADINE) and throws him into a corner, leaving him for dead. In an ironic reversal of *The Invisible Agent*, it is Griffin

Jon Hall in *China Corsair* (1951). Hall gave his most memorable performances in Universal fantasy flicks, but provided a reassuring presence in many other dramas with exotic locations.

himself, rather than the German or the Japanese agents, who relishes the prospect of wanton sadism.

Because of his physique and his athleticism (as shown in *The Clutching Hand*), Hall frequently appeared in action-adventure or fantasy sci-films, often with an exotic setting. In *Arabian Nights* (1942), he appears as a square-jawed hero, proficient as a swordsperson and in unarmed combat. He possesses a pair of incredibly bright eyes, which flash whenever Scheherazade (Maria Montez) appears. Director John Rawlins cuts to many close ups of his bright face — aware, perhaps, of how it glistens in the film's gorgeous Technicolor palette. In the sequel *Ali Baba and the Forty Thieves* (1944), Hall plays the title role — another fundamentally good man with a pencil-thin mustache reveling in the opportunity to wear colored clothing. With his red headgear and long, flowing robes, he resembles an early version of Peter O'Toole in *Lawrence of Arabia* (1962). The part does not demand much of Hall, other than to look appropriately menacing when faced with dangerous situations — as, for instance, when he vows revenge on Hulagu

Khan (Kurt Katch) while being strung up in the public square of Bagdad. Hall becomes slightly softer in romantic situations — particularly when he fulfills the blood-pact with that he forged as a child with Amara (Maria Montez). The camera focuses on his face as he stares into her eyes; it is clear that the two of them will remain together for eternity.

Hall and Montez reappeared together later that year in Robert Siodmak's *Cobra Woman*. The director includes many close-ups of the actor's face and muscular torso, both of which glisten in glorious Technicolor as he emerges from the sea on to a remote Pacific island. Despite his physique, however, his character Ramu has little freedom to act in a despotic regime presided over by the evil Naja (Montez), the twin sister of Ramu's fiancée Tollea (also played by Montez). On at least two occasions, Rama is captured and threatened with execution; with the help of his faithful sidekick Kado (Sabu) and the mysterious Hava (Lon Chaney, Jr.) he manages to escape. *Cobra Woman* takes advantage of Jon Hall's strong-man screen image to emphasize the importance of social responsibility: at one point Ramu is presented with a choice by the exiled queen of the island (Mary Nash) — either escape to freedom without his fiancée, or stay and help to free the entire community from Naja's regime. Ramu opts to go it alone, but Naja's guards foil his bid for freedom. With Haya's help, Ramu manages to destroy Naja and kill the cobra (the symbol of the curse placed on the island). Now everyone can live in peace and tranquility, while Ramu can leave without fear of capture. Released during the last years of World War Two, *Cobra Woman* calls for all able-bodied males to set aside personal concerns — such as marriage — and fight for democracy against despotism. Ramu comes to understand this, and is duly rewarded at the end, when Tollea appears unexpectedly on his boat. Ostensibly she should have taken over as queen, following Naja's death, but she has chosen to get married instead, leaving the islanders to rule by democracy. The film ends with the lovers embracing to the sound of heavenly choirs.

Sir Cedric Hardwicke

*b. February 19, 1893, Lye, Worcestershire, England;
d. August 6, 1964, New York City.*

Cedric Hardwicke began his career in the theatre, achieving notable successes in productions such as George Bernard Shaw's *Caesar and Cleopatra* at Birmingham in 1922. He subsequently carved out a reputation as a leading actor, which resulted in a knighthood in 1934. His best-known Hollywood films include *Les Misérables* (1935), *Stanley and Livingstone* (1939), *Suspicion* (1941) and *The Ten Commandments* (1956). Hardwicke also created memorable characterizations in horror films — for example, Richard Cobb in *The Invisible Man Returns* (1940). Initially, he seems a rather sympathetic person, as he puts his arm around Helen Manson (NAN GREY) and consoles her, as she learns that Geoffrey Radcliffe (Vincent Price) is about to be executed for murdering his brother. However, we soon understand that this is nothing more than a performance: Cobb is the real murderer, who hopes to have Geoffrey convicted in the hope of securing his fortune. Geoffrey escapes conviction when he takes a drug that renders him invisible and enables him to come after Cobb. In a climactic final scene, Geoffrey — who remains invisible — confronts Cobb; Cobb gibbers in fright and then runs down the stairs in fear, his teeth chattering. Geoffrey follows him down the stairs and points a gun at Cobb's head; Cobb's face twitches nervously, and he speaks in a hoarse voice, his eyes looking wildly from side to side in the hope of discovering Geoffrey's whereabouts. The master schemer has been transformed into an arrant coward. Cobb flees for his life, and eventually plunges to his death as he falls out of a goods train as it passes over a railway bridge.

In *The Invisible Agent* (1942), Hardwicke plays another villain — the Nazi agent Stauffer. Impassive, cold and statuesque in manner, he desires at all costs to obtain the formula for becoming invisible, something that he believes is "very useful to any country ... at war." With the long pause in between the two words "country" and "at," we understand how much he relishes the prospect of battling with the Allies. Stauffer continually smokes a cigarette, blowing the smoke contemptuously into Frank Griffin's (JON HALL) face while claiming that the American is "possessed by the ideology of a decadent democracy." On another occasion, he grasps Griffin's chin before bidding him goodnight. Director Edwin L. Marin emphasizes Stauffer's sadistic nature by having him wear a pair of silver-rimmed glasses and letting the light shine into the lenses. This man has such strong eyes that he can even resist bright light. As in *The Invisible Man Returns*, Hardwicke's character meets a sticky end, as his one-time Japanese sidekick Ikito (Peter Lorre) turns on him and stabs him to death.

Vincent Price and Cedric Hardwicke in *The Invisible Man Returns* (1940). British-born character actor who made his name in the theater before turning to films, Hardwicke could play good and evil characters with equal facility.

Hardwicke was nothing if not versatile: in *The Ghost of Frankenstein* (1942), he plays Ludwig Frankenstein as a fundamentally good man endeavoring to carve out a new life as a psychiatrist. Impeccably groomed in a three-piece suit with shiny patent-leather shoes, he seems thoroughly at peace with himself; the only indication we have that something might be bothering him is in the way he continually clasps and unclasps his hands. Our suspicions prove correct — having once again encountered the monster (Lon Chaney, Jr.), Ludwig's manner totally changes. He speaks his lines hurriedly, frequently putting a hand to his forehead and murmuring, "I *must* find a way" [to cure the monster]. He dons the white coat and returns to his laboratory, where he is frequently shown pressing buttons and taking readings — the characteristic mannerisms of a mad scientist. But Ludwig remains sane throughout (unlike his colleague Dr. Bohmer (LIONEL ATWILL), who becomes crazed with the idea of creating a new superperson out of the monster). Even when he knows he is doing wrong (by replacing the monster's brain with that of his dead colleague Dr. Kettering [Barton Yarborough]), Ludwig tries to prove that his decision has been made in the monster's interests. However noble his plans might be, they end up going horribly wrong as the monster runs amok. Ludwig covers his eyes — as if not wanting to see the terrible sight before him — and falls down in a stupor. Both he and the monster perish in a fire that engulfs the family house — a suitable visual metaphor suggesting their damnation in hell.

Sometimes Hardwicke had the chance to play good guys, such as Robert Bonting in *The Lodger* (1944). Resplendent in a three-piece suit, a monocle and a cigar, he looks every inch the respectable gentleman in late nineteenth-century London. However, we learn from his wife, Ellen (Sara Allgood), that he has fallen on hard times due to poor investments, which eventually drove him to a nervous breakdown. The effects of this condition are still visible, as he walks with a slight stoop, while his hands tremble as he tries to remove his gloves. Bonting shies away from engagement with the outside world — if he has to go out (to have his top hat cleaned, for instance), he runs home as quickly as he can, scuttling along the street like a frightened rabbit. His attitude gradually alters, however, as he realizes that it is his duty as a relative to protect his niece Kitty (Merle Oberon) from the mysterious stranger Mr. Slade (Laird Cregar), who appears to take an unhealthy interest in her. Bonting's change of character is subtly signaled through gestures; he smoothes his gray hair back and strokes his beard meditatively, before striding out of the parlor and looking for Kitty. As the film unfolds, so Bonting assumes more and more of a dominant role; he escorts his niece to the theatre and makes every effort to protect her, even though the task is not an easy one. He might not cut as imposing a figure as Inspector Warwick (GEORGE SANDERS), but by the end of the film we feel that Bonting will be far more capable of looking after Kitty's welfare.

In *The War of the Worlds* (1953), Hardwicke plays the off-screen narrator, whose RP-English voice (resembling that of a BBC announcer) gives credence to the fantastic events taking place onscreen. He informs us that the Martian invaders looked around the entire solar system for a place to colonize, before deciding on "our own warm Earth": "From the blackness of outer space we were being scrutinized and studied." Once they come to Earth, they cause such havoc that "huge populations were driven from their homes." The only place to remain unaffected was Washington, D.C., which became the center of the resistance. In the end, the Martians are killed off as they fall victim to earthly viruses. The narrator attributes this to divine intervention, and invites viewers to sing His praises. The film underlines the significance of this message by having heavenly choirs singing a hymn as the final credits roll.

Rondo Hatton

b. April 22, 1894, Hagerstown, Maryland;
d. February 2, 1946, Beverly Hills,
Los Angeles, California.

Rondo Hatton joined the Florida National Guard to pursue a military career, fought in the Mexican border war and then in France in the First World War. There he was exposed to poison gas, and hospitalized with a lung injury. At some point after his exposure, Hatton developed acromegaly, a steadily progressive deforming of bones in the head, hands and feet. His grotesque appearance brought him to the attention of Henry King, who cast him in *Hell Harbor* (1930). His film career did not take off until the mid–1940s, when Universal cast him as the Hoxton Creeper in *The Pearl of Death* (1944). Hatton does not have too much to do in this film; he is mostly seen in shadow, carrying out killings on behalf of his master Giles Conover (MILES MANDER).

Hatton returned to the Creeper role in *House of Horrors* (1946), where he is seen in shadow assuming a threatening pose as the opening credits roll. Jean Yarbrough's film is about image: the sculptor Marcel De Lange (Martin Kosleck) makes a grotesque statue of the Creeper's head that he describes as his "deathless masterpiece." For journalist Joan Medford (Virginia Grey), however, the sculpture transforms the Creeper into "the perfect

Rondo Hatton in *House of Horrors* (1946). The legendary "Creeper," he made his name in Universal horror films of the mid–1940s. He died relatively young, before his career could develop.

Neanderthal man." The Creeper strangles all those critics, including F. Holmes Harmon (ALAN NAPIER), whose poisoned words have destroyed the careers of artists old and new. However, such acts of altruism, carried out on De Lange's behalf, cannot alter the Creeper's public image; to most people he is facially reminiscent of "that big gorilla down at the zoo." In the end, the Creeper comes to understand that he will always be the object of discrimination, whatever he does; hence he destroys De Lange's statue.

In *The Jungle Captive* (1945), the third in Universal's trilogy of films to feature the apewoman (the others were *Captive Wild Woman* [1943], and *Jungle Woman* [1944]), Hatton plays Moloch the brute, the sidekick of mad scientist Stendahl (Otto Kruger). He doesn't have much to do other than strangle his victims and participate in long wordless sequences where he is seen robbing a morgue, putting the apewoman's (Vicky Lane) corpse into a van and driving off to Stendahl's isolated laboratory in the country. Moloch develops a peculiar affection for Stendahl's assistant Ann Forrester (Amelita Ward), who eventually becomes one of the doctor's victims. Moloch massages the fur collar of Ann's coat, and later on insists that Stendahl should not perform any further experiments on her. Needless to say, Stendahl breaks his promise, and Moloch attacks him. The doctor has scant regard for his assistant's feelings; he considers Moloch a sub-human being, who should be attracted to the apewoman ("This is more in your line") rather than Ann.

In *The Spider Woman Strikes Back* (1946), Hatton plays Mario, the servant of Zenobia Dollard (GALE SONDERGAARD). Although unable to speak, he casts a threatening presence over the house, frequently sidling up behind Jean Kingsley (Brenda Joyce) and eyeing her, almost as if he wanted to possess her. Director Arthur Lubin frequently cuts to close-ups of his expressionless face, followed by medium shots of Jean staring fearfully at him. In one sequence, Mario comes in her bedroom while she is sleeping, sidles up to her bed and sits down on the edge of it; if he wanted to, he has her at his mercy. He picks up her limp left hand and strokes it, then puts his hands around her neck and caresses it. He is just about to pick up Jean's hand once again when Zenobia bursts in and sternly reprimands him for coming into Jean's bedroom without permission. The sequence is clearly inspired by the Beauty and the Beast myth: Mario would like to establish a relationship with Jean, but realizes that his appearance will never allow him to do so. Nonetheless, he stoically continues to look out for her welfare; on one occasion he admonishes Zenobia in the belief that Jean has been poisoned. Nothing like that has actually happened (Jean has actually just fainted), but Mario needs to be sure. This combination of stoicism and concern for others was characteristic of Hatton himself; he once explained that although he frequently wanted to do nothing more than hide himself away, "You cannot stand yourself for long, running away. It's the sympathy that gets you, most of all the self-sympathy. It's an insidious poison that gets into your soul, as this thing I've got [acromegaly] gets into your bones. In a veterans' hospital you see so many guys so much worse off than you are that—well, if there's anything left in you, you quit feeling sorry for yourself."

Although the film clearly exploits Hatton's deformity, the actor inspires sympathy rather than ridicule. As Zenobia explains, he might be an atrocious servant, but he has lived all his life in the Dollard house and would not be able to survive anywhere else. Hence all he can do is follow his mistress' orders, however much he might disagree with them. He dies trying to save her from being burned to death in a fire in her laboratory.

Hatton's last film, released after his death, was *The Brute Man* (1946), in which he repeats his role as the Creeper. Following *The Pearl of Death* and *House of Horrors*, he is first seen in shadow walking the streets of New York, a dim light focusing on his face, wearing a widebrimmed hat, ill-fitting jacket with short sleeves, and trousers too short in the leg, his shoulders hunched. He looks every inch the fearsome character that strangles his victims at will. However, director Jean Yarbrough makes some attempt to humanize him; he gives him some dialogue and invents a backstory (based partly on Hatton's own autobiography) in which the Creeper — also known as Hal Moffet — was once a successful footballer at college. Everything seemed set fair for him; he was the star player with plenty of girlfriends and a male roommate, Clifford Scott (Tom Neal), who completed all his assignments for him. However, things started to go wrong when Hal turned his attentions towards Clifford's girlfriend Virginia (Jan Wiley). Clifford responded by double-crossing Hal, with the result being that Hal was forced by his professor to stay in to finish a difficult chemical experiment. In a fit of rage, Hal smashed a test-tube, causing a major explosion that left him permanently disfigured. Now that he has grown up, he is determined to wreak revenge on all those who destroyed him — including Clifford.

At the same time, Hal retains his fundamentally gentle nature. In a retelling of the Beauty and the Beast myth, he falls for blind piano teacher Helen Paige (Jane Adams), bringing her little gifts and treating her gently, even though he refuses to allow her to touch his face. He is ashamed of his appearance; in one sequence, he looks at himself in a bathroom mirror, and is so disgusted by what he sees that he smashes the mirror with his fist. Hal/the Creeper might be a serial killer, but Yarbrough insists that he is a victim of circumstance. However, he cannot be allowed to escape scot-free (according to censorship codes laid down in the Motion Picture Production Code); he is eventually trapped by the police in a complicated set-up using Helen as bait. While *The Brute Man* remains a low-budget horror film, its plot has obviously been inspired by Hatton's own experiences of being transformed into an object of scorn as a result of disfigurement.

Jonathan Haze
b. April 1, 1929, Pittsburgh, Pennsylvania.

Jonathan Haze established his reputation as a member of Roger Corman's repertory company, appearing in a slew of low-budget productions beginning with *Monster from the Ocean Floor* (1954). A slight-framed, slightly gawky looking person, Haze specialized in playing low-life or unassuming characters. In John Parker's silent horror film *Dementia* (1955), he has a brief role as a husband; with shirt open to the waist and hair disheveled, he looks as if he has been involved in domestic violence, but he shows no resistance as two police officers lead him away. Parker's film traces the Gamine's (Adrienne Barrett) progress through the Los Angeles underworld through one night, as she encounters various low-life characters, commits a murder and tries to elude the police. In this world, the majority of the men are sexual predators or violent psychopaths, while the women are victims or whores. Violence is taken for granted, which explains why Haze's husband puts up no resistance when apprehended by the police.

As the Contaminated Man in Corman's *The Day the World Ended* (1955), Haze has a notable cameo as the victim of a nuclear holocaust. We first encounter him on a deserted landscape moaning "Kill me! Kill me," as if unable to face the future. The motley band of fellow survivors, led by rancher Jim Maddison (PAUL BIRCH), take pity on him and take him back to their house, even though they have no idea as to how and why he survived. ("[He] defied all the laws of man and god," as geologist Rick [RICHARD DENNING] observes.) However, the Contaminated Man cannot stay in one place for any length of time — he walks outside in the wilderness as if hypnotized by the power of the mutant creature threatening the house. On at least two occasions, we think he has been destroyed, but twice he manages to cheat death, even though he is gradually deprived of the power of coherent speech. Tired and exhausted, he is eventually gobbled up by the creature.

As Charlie the pickpocket in Corman's *Swamp Women* (1956), Haze confronts Bob Matthews (Touch Connors) by standing in front of him and demanding money. With his stubbly beard and half-smoked cigarette, he looks like a vagrant rather than a criminal. We soon realize this is nothing more than a performance designed to distract his victims' attention while he steals their money: as Bob

Jonathan Haze (left) in *Ghost of the China Sea* (1958). A versatile member of Roger Corman's repertory company, Haze often played cameo roles of characters experiencing mental stress.

moves out of the frame, Charlie waves the cash he has stolen aloft in triumph. Unfortunately, Charlie becomes a little too bold; in a later sequence, he encounters Bob once again and receives a smart blow to the head for his pains. Charlie is taken to the police station for questioning, where he reassumes his drunken pose in an attempt to escape a heavy fine.

A year later, Haze played the Latino soldier Private Manuel Ortiz in *It Conquered the World*, also for Corman. In a cameo role, he forms a comic double-act with Sergeant Neal (DICK MILLER), as they carry out Brigadier General James Patrick's (Russ Bender) orders without realizing that the aliens have indoctrinated their superior officer. Ortiz has one moment of slapstick comedy, as he runs back to his platoon, catches his rifle between two trees and falls over. Otherwise his role is largely confined to that of a chorus, observing at the end that "he [Dr. Anderson] acted like he knew it [the monster]." This comment restates the obvious: Dr. Anderson (Lee Van Cleef) wanted to take over the world with the help of an alien from Venus, and was only prevented from doing so by his colleague Paul Nelson (PETER GRAVES), who made Anderson understand the error of his ways.

A year later, Haze had a more substantial role as the creepy Jeremy Perrin in *Not of This Earth*. A petty crook by trade, he finds regular employment as the alien Paul Johnson's (PAUL BIRCH) batman. Clearly terrified of his employer, he walks stealthily around the house, his shoulders hunched in a posture strongly reminiscent of Dickens's Uriah Heep in *David Copperfield*. When Johnson is not around, Jeremy's attitude changes radically; he is prone to making flirtatious insinuations to Nadine Storey, and moving towards her in expectation of a kiss. When she slaps him in the face for his pain, his ardor only increases. However, Jeremy redeems himself as the film progresses, as he sets aside his romantic intentions in an attempt to unmask Johnson's true nature. He works closely with Beverly, as the two of them search through the house, even visiting the cellar (which Johnson had deemed out of bounds to both of them). Sadly, Jeremy's efforts prove fruitless, as he is killed off by a glance from Johnson's powerful eyes, which can kill anyone at any distance.

Haze was catapulted to cult film stardom as Seymour Krelboyne in *Little Shop of Horrors* (1960)—a slow-witted, accident-prone young man dressed in an ill-fitting flat cap and filthy scarf. Although happy to work in Gravis Mushnik's (MEL WELLES) flower shop, Seymour has no aptitude for the job whatsoever; when asked to put some carnations in water, he ends up pulling their heads off, before falling over a chair. Seymour lacks any redeeming features; he cringes like a frightened rabbit while talking to his pretty female colleague Audrey Fulquard

(Jackie Joseph), and remains dominated by his hypochondriac mother (Myrtle Vail), who serves him food flavored with medicine.

Seymour's character gradually changes as he discovers that the only way to satisfy his bloodthirsty plant Audrey 2 is to feed it human flesh. In one famous sequence, he visits the dentist Phoebus Farb (John Shaner) and accidentally kills him. Seymour is just about to leave when masochistic patient Wilbur Force (Jack Nicholson) approaches him in the belief that Seymour is the dentist, and urges him to pull out some teeth — preferably without gas. Seymour dons the white coat and enthusiastically obliges: the sheer effort of pulling Wilbur's tooth out makes Seymour fall on the floor. From then on, Seymour undergoes a change of character; he puts Farb's corpse into a sack and feeds it to the plant. In a later sequence, Audrey hypnotizes Seymour and sends him out to fetch more food; this time it is prostitute Leonora Clyde (Merri Welles). Seymour eventually grows so tired of working for Audrey that he offers himself as food. The film ends with Seymour's face superimposed on one of the plant-heads, wailing, "I didn't mean it!"

While *Little Shop of Horrors* should not be taken at all seriously, Haze's performance as Seymour suggests that human beings can be transformed once they overcome their inhibitions and act according to their instincts. Seymour ends up by taking revenge on those who dominated him in the past — officious medical people like Farb, and aggressive women like Leonora.

Holmes Herbert

b. July 30, 1882, Mansfield, Nottinghamshire, England; d. December 26, 1956, Hollywood, California.

Born Horace Edward Jenner, Herbert took his stage moniker from Sherlock Holmes, his favorite literary character. He was a tall, statuesque stalwart of Hollywood's English colony who began his career as a leading man in silent films, but by the coming of sound had settled down to a comfortable life as a supporting actor. Most of the time, he played run-of-the-mill English stereotypes such as Bryant the butler in *Calling Dr. Death* (1943), where he has little to do other than to keep a straight face while patiently going about his daily duties. As a good servant, Bryant says nothing, but his expression — that of wide-eyed horror — suggests an increasing concern for his employer Dr. Mark Steel's (Lon Chaney, Jr.) welfare. Herbert plays another butler, Wilkins, in Anatole Litvak's *Sorry, Wrong Number* (1948). He doesn't have much to do, other than to open the door for Henry Stevenson (Burt Lancaster) and call for James Cotterell (Ed Begley), the master of the house. However, Herbert's presence in the film sums up how far the family has traveled up the social scale since Cotterell's humble beginnings in a small town. Such knowledge only serves to increase Stevenson's sense of emasculation as he struggles to come to terms with a marriage to Cotterell's daughter Leona (Barbara Stanwyck), in which she and her father thoroughly dominate him.

There were occasions when Herbert played more substantial cameo roles. In the 1931 version of *Dr. Jekyll and Mr. Hyde*, directed by Rouben Mamoulian, he plays Dr. Lanyon, close friend of the eponymous hero (Fredric March), who upholds the values of polite society — decorum, moderation and snobbery. Although admiring his abilities as a scientist, Lanyon cannot tolerate some of Jekyll's behavioral excesses — for example, being caught *in flagrante delicto* kissing agreeable good-time girl Ivy Pearson (Miriam Hopkins), while being engaged to Muriel Carew (ROSE HOBART). Lanyon's language expresses his distaste; he calls Jekyll "disgusting" and "positively indecent.... It isn't done." For his part, Jekyll contemptuously treats Lanyon's belief in a "fair-mannered, virtuous and honorable" existence as repressive — a conscious denial of one's emotions. This is what prompts him to continue his experiments to discover an elixir that eventually transforms him into Mr. Hyde.

Lanyon's best scene comes towards the end of the film, when he discovers that Dr. Jekyll and Mr. Hyde are one and the same person. As Hyde takes the elixir that transforms him back into Jekyll, director Mamoulian cuts to a close-up of Lanyon's face contorted with fear, staring wide-eyed at what is happening in front of him while describing the transformation as an act of "supreme blasphemy." However, Lanyon soon recovers his *sang-froid* as he sits behind a desk and declares in ringing tones that Jekyll must now renounce any claim on Muriel. Lanyon understands that his friendship with Jekyll is now at an end; hence he has no qualms about telling the police about Jekyll's experiments. While we might sympathize with Lanyon's motives, we cannot help feeling that his determination to observe the conventions of polite society has harmed his social and emotional prospects. Perhaps Dr. Jekyll was right after all.

In *The Mummy's Curse* (1944), Herbert plays a variation of his role in *Dr. Jekyll and Mr. Hyde*. As Dr. Cooper, a good-hearted practitioner dressed in short white coat and possessing a kindly bedside manner, he would seem to be an ideal person to alleviate Princess Ananka's (Virginia Christine) fears of being carried off by the unearthly Kharis (Lon Chaney, Jr.). However, we soon discover that the doctor does not believe anything Ananka says to him; his sole remedy is to give her "something to quiet [her] nerves." The doctor experiences a rude awakening one night, as he comes face to face with Kharis in Ananka's caravan. He desperately tries to stop the mummy from coming near Ananka, but his resistance proves futile, as Kharis strangles him to death. Conventional medical science proves inadequate when confronting the undead.

Holmes also relished playing various types of ineffectual authority figures. As the Chief of Police in *The Invisible Man* (1933)—with a

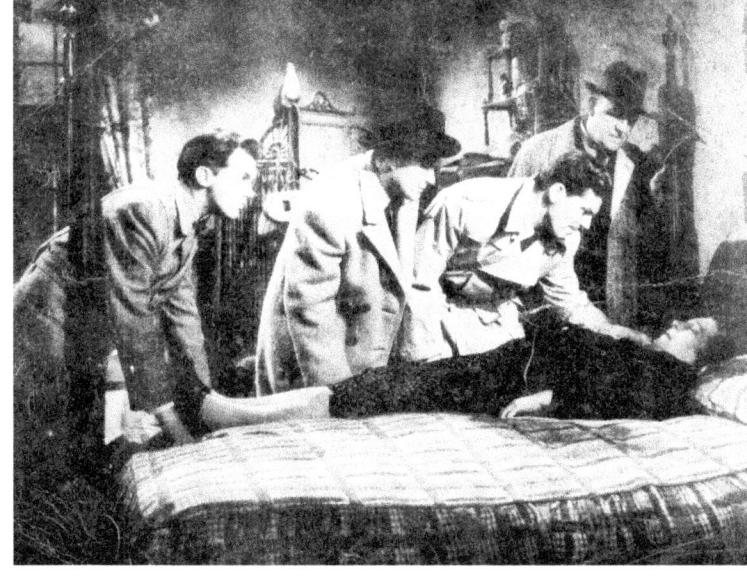

Holmes Herbert (standing, right) in *Bulldog Drummond at Bay* (1947). British-born Herbert's long career lasted over four decades, during which time he played butlers, police inspectors and other figures of authority.

businesslike manner in his long overcoat and trilby hat — he believes he has the perfect solution to catch Jack Griffin (CLAUDE RAINS). But when his best-laid plans all go wrong, and mayhem ensues (a train crashes), the Chief's demeanor radically alters. He puts his hand to his brow, and his voice becomes shriller and shriller. His mode of dress becomes more disheveled, his wing collar hanging awry as he supervises the final, coordinated movement to catch his quarry. As the chase begins, director James Whale cuts to a close-up of the Chief grasping his lapels in anxiety; this is obviously his last chance to restore law and order. The operation proves successful, but the Chief takes no pleasure in his success. On the contrary, he stares in genuine concern at Griffin's corpse, which slowly materializes in the snow after his death. Herbert played another flawed authority figure in Erle C. Kenton's *The Ghost of Frankenstein* (also 1942). As the magistrate, he proves largely incapable of sustaining order in court during the trial of the monster (Lon Chaney, Jr.) He looks fearfully to the left, then to the right, as if hoping that someone could come to his aid. Salvation arrives in the form of Dr.

Frankenstein (CEDRIC HARDWICKE), whose severe expression casts a pall of silence over the entire court. The magistrate breathes a sigh of relief and continues the trial. Herbert's cameo role in this film shows how representatives of the legal system — judges, police officers— have no means of controlling the monsters that threaten the stability of their respective societies.

Occasionally, Herbert had the chance to extend his range of parts. In *Mark of the Vampire* (1935), he plays Sir Karell Bolotyn, who has apparently been murdered by a vampire. It certainly seems that this is true: Bolotyn returns to his own house as a vampire-like figure, with an unnaturally pale face and vacant expression, walking slowly and steadily towards his daughter Irena (Elizabeth Allan), before turning around and seating himself at the organ to play a macabre tune. As the film unfolds, however, we discover that he is not really Sir Karell, but a friend of Professor Zelen (Lionel Barrymore), who has agreed to participate in a scheme designed to reveal Sir Karell's true murderer. Herbert's character changes quickly; his movements become rapid as he adapts to the demands of the situation, while his practical nature emerges as he asks Irena to treat him as her father in spite of the emotional stress involved. The criminal must be apprehended at all costs. Irena agrees; the two of them fondly embrace.

In *The Uninvited* (1944), Herbert has a brief cameo as Charlie Jessop, a country bumpkin with a floppy hat who tells Roderick (Ray Milland) that Miss Holloway (Cornelia Otis Skinner) once worked for Commander Beech (DONALD CRISP), and developed a pathological hatred for Beech's granddaughter Stella (Gail Russell). In *The Pearl of Death* (also 1944), Herbert plays the cigar-smoking sculptor James Goodram, whose passion for his work is so great that he remains completely impervious to anything else. In his view, Holmes is quite simply "mad." As Alan Cosgrave in *The House of Fear* (1945), Herbert adopts a slight Scottish accent, as he gibbers in fear as he opens an envelope and discovers to his cost that he is the next in line to be murdered by a serial killer. This is actually nothing more than an elaborate ruse; like the other supposed "victims" in this case, Cosgrave deliberately tries to kill Alastair (Aubrey Mather) in the hope of obtaining a share of Alastair's insurance policy. As Ebenezer Crabtree in *Dressed to Kill* (1946), Herbert has a juicy little cameo as an eccentric auctioneer with a monocle perpetually falling out of his right eye, who takes a positive pleasure in mispronouncing the King's English. This is chiefly done to attract buyers' attention; when not involved in an auction, Ebenezer speaks slowly and decently, answering Holmes's questions in as concise a manner as possible and making every effort to assist the detective in discovering who purchased the musical boxes that people seem so willing to kill for.

Rose Hobart

b. May 1, 1906, New York City;
d. August 29, 2000, Woodland Hills, Los Angeles, California.

Born Rose Kefer, Hobart began her career in the theatre and carved out a Broadway career before making her film debut in *Liliom* (1930).

Hobart made sporadic appearances in horror

Rose Hobart publicity still (1935). Versatile leading actress of the 1930s and 1940s, whose feisty personality made her suitable for playing both heroines and villainesses.

films of the 1930s and 1940s, playing a variety of roles. She has a major part in Rouben Mamoulian's *Dr. Jekyll and Mr. Hyde* (1931) as Jekyll's fiancée Muriel Carew. Although clearly in love, Muriel at first seems reluctant to flout the conventions of polite society; she refuses to marry Jekyll until her father, General Carew (Halliwell Hobbes), has given his consent. The prospect of continuing spinsterhood clearly depresses her, as she walks about her house with hunched shoulders, her face fixed on the ground, but she appears neither willing nor able to contradict her father's will. At the same time, we understand that she is an intense woman: Mamoulian includes several two-shots showing her staring into her fiancé's eyes, as if trying to hypnotize him. One such two-shot is followed by an intercut close-up of the lovers staring at one another; evidently nothing or no one can separate them. Jekyll's character undergoes a significant change, once he discovers how to transform himself into Hyde; he comes to rely more and more on Muriel's judgment, imploring her at one point to stay with him by falling on his knees. Such pleas give Muriel the strength to defy her father and resolve to marry Jekyll immediately rather than waiting for eight months.

But Muriel's devotion does not bring any rewards— despite her professed devotion to Jekyll (signaled in one sequence by her cradling his head in her hands and massaging him, as if he were a baby), the relationship is doomed to fail. Jekyll runs out of Muriel's house, but returns soon afterwards, having been transformed once again into Mr. Hyde. He watches Muriel for a moment, as she is slumped over the piano, crying her eyes out, then comes in and attacks her. Muriel screams, and Hyde runs out of the house pursued by her father. We feel quite sorry for Muriel — despite her efforts to throw off the shackles imposed on her by polite society, her loving relationship with Jekyll is doomed. She is something of a *femme fatale*, the unwitting victim of Jekyll's experiments.

As Anne Neville in *Tower of London* (1939), Hobart has another thankless role as wife of the Duke of Clarence (Vincent Price), who has to support her husband as he prepares to leave for battle. Although clearly concerned for his future welfare, she can do little other than to stare fearfully into the distance as he gallops away on his horse. She is merely a pawn in the film's patriarchal scheme, which dictates that "the battlefield is no place for a woman" (to use Clarence's phrase), condemning them instead to a life of servitude. Anne makes a valiant effort to escape the court disguised as a serving-wench, but the executioner Mord (Boris Karloff) recaptures her and drags her back to confront Gloucester (Basil Rathbone). Anne glances rapidly around the room, and then stares straight into Gloucester's eyes— although she lacks the physical strength to resist him, she can remain his mental equal. For most of the time she accedes to his wishes, protesting all the while her devotion to the "true and loyal" future king. But her reluctance to speak becomes an effective means of resistance: Gloucester might do what he wants with her, but he never discovers how she feels or whether she loves him or not. Following their marriage, the two of them appear on a balcony to receive the people's congratulations. While Gloucester acknowledges their welcome with an affable wave of the hand, Anne looks skywards, suggesting that she has discovered another (divine) protector who will ensure her future security.

Hobart plays a hardboiled reporter in *The Mad Ghoul* (1943), who, although responsible for "soft" news about music and the arts, is more than capable of standing up to her male counterpart "Scoop" McClure (ROBERT ARMSTRONG). With her skin-tight black two-piece suit and elegant hat, Della is the very epitome of *haute couture*, which gives her a certain social edge. This she uses to significant effect in the police station: in ordinary circumstances, a woman like Della might have been intimidated by the presence of so many male officers led by Sergeant Macklin (Milburn Stone), who surround her like a pack of wolves. However, the reporter retains her *sang-froid*, as she describes in a cool, unflustered manner the evil doctor Alfred Morris' (GEORGE ZUCCO) experiments.

In *The Brighton Strangler* (1945), Hobart's Dorothy Kent is something of a Jekyll-and-

Hyde character. She initially comes across as supremely self-confident in her fashionable knee-length dress and cigarette holder, as she pens an award-winning play for matinee idol Reginald Parker (John Loder). As the two of them part at London's Victoria Station, she stares into his eyes with a look of supreme confidence; having made him a star, she will write another piece for him, just as soon as they are married. Despite their obvious difference in height, it is clear that she dominates their relationship.

Matters do not proceed according to plan. Parker is caught in an air raid, with the result that he assumes the identity of the Brighton Strangler — the character he plays in Dorothy's play. He travels to Brighton and murders at least two innocent people — Lord Mayor Clive (IAN WOLFE) and Inspector W. R. Allison (MILES MANDER). Dorothy believes she is in some way responsible for Parker's transformation: when next we see her, she has retired from public life and changed her manner entirely. Whereas once she exuded confidence, now she looks meekly down at the floor whenever anyone speaks to her. The only way she can redeem herself is to find Parker and make him understand that he is only role-playing; this task she achieves successfully by running to a roof garden (where Parker is about to strangle another innocent victim, April Carson [June Duprez]), and applauding. Parker immediately desists, moves towards the edge of the garden and bows, as facing an imaginary theatre audience. Once again, he assumes the identity of the matinee idol.

Hobart's role in the film is an intriguing one, at once showing how women can take the lead when it comes to writing successful plays and at the same time suggesting that such literary abilities are somehow dangerous, particularly when she encounters gullible men.

Hobart has a small role in *The Cat Creeps* (1946) as legal secretary Connie Palmer. At first she comes across as self-confident, as she deals efficiently yet quickly with investigative journalist Pidge "Flash" Laurie's (Noah Beery, Jr.) questions. But this proves nothing more than a façade, as she is quite literally scared to death by the presence of a black cat that she believes has been possessed by the spirit of a dead girl.

Shemp Howard
b. March 17, 1895, Brooklyn, New York;
d. November 22, 1955, Hollywood, California.

Samuel Horwitz achieved fame as one of the Three Stooges, taking over from his brother Curly, when Curly had to leave the act because of his illness. Eventually, he made 77 short films with the group. When not working together, Shemp Howard made appearances in horror films such as *The Strange Case of Dr. RX* (1942), where he plays Detective Sergeant Sweeney, a dim-witted cop who invariably makes the wrong deductions. With his India-rubber face, large eyes and frequently hangdog expression, he exists to provide comic relief in a run-of-the-mill horror flick about a mad scientist. He forms an irresistible double-act with the African American butler Horatio B. Fitz Washington (MANTAN MORELAND); both of them delight in the misuse of English, and register several double-takes to the minute whenever they are surprised.

Two years earlier, Howard played Frankie, an inept gangster in *The Invisible Woman* (1940). From his first entrance, when he trips over a waste paper bin and falls flat on his face, it is clear that he is there to provide slapstick comedy. With his sidekick Foghorn (Donald MacBride), Frankie tries to remove the machine that renders people invisible from Professor Gibbs's (John Barrymore) laboratory, but only succeeds in dropping it on his foot. Frankie squeals in pain: "Oh, my bunion!" Once the machine has been set up again in the bad guy Blackie's (Oscar Homolka) hideout, Frankie is asked whether he wants to be the guinea-pig to test whether the machine works. He declines with the excuse: "I'm underweight." In the climactic fight sequence, where the Professor rescues the machine, aided and abetted by Kitty Carroll (Virginia Bruce), Frankie inevitably comes off second-best. He cowers behind a curtain in terror, points a gun at the wrong person, and ends up having a glass tube broken over his head and being thrown to the ground. Director

Shemp Howard in *Out West* (1947). Made his name as one of *The Three Stooges*, Howard frequently played comic cameos in other films of the 1940s and 1950s.

A. Edward Sutherland is determined to show that crime does not pay. Howard does what he can with the role, but it is clearly peripheral to the film's rather flimsy plot.

Howard specialized in cameo roles—for example, the soda jerk in the Abbott and Costello spoof *Hold That Ghost* (1941), where he indulges in comic eyework as he looks suspiciously at Dr. Jackson (RICHARD CARLSON), and subsequently turns directly to camera and raises his eyebrows, as if totally incapable of understanding the doctor's behavior. In *Arabian Nights* (1942), Howard plays Sinbad, a member of a troupe of acrobats led by Ahmad (Billy Gilbert). Howard becomes involved in one major slapstick scene, as he is part of a human pyramid that eventually collapses. Howard forms a double-act with Aladdin (John Qualen), both of whom try to find the fabled lamp to summon forth the genie to implement their every wish. Needless to say, they fail in their quest, but they have a lot of fun in the process. With his bushy black beard and rather absent-minded manner, Sinbad looks a little out of place in an Arabian fantasy—perhaps, as he says at one point—he would be happier if he could find his ship.

Shemp Howard appeared in numerous Three Stooges horror film spoofs. *Fright Night* (1947) had him playing a dim-witted boxer who accidentally knocks out the "Champ" Chopper Kane (Dick Wessel), and subsequently experiences numerous misfortunes, such as having a bucket wedged over his head, several cream-puffs thrust in his face, and being used as a human battering-ram to break a door down. At the end, Howard believes he has been hacked to death with a hatchet, but in truth he has only had a tin of red paint spilled over him. Howard's slapstick sequences in *Shivering Sherlocks* (1948) include throwing two fried eggs into the air, which land over Moe's eyes; drinking a tin of paint in the belief that it is a cup of coffee; and being pursued all over a haunted house by "Angel" (Duke York), whose appearance clearly recalls that of Lon Chaney, Jr., in *The Wolf Man* (1941). *Mummy's Dummies* (1948), a parody of James Whale's *The Mummy* (1932), gives Howard the opportunity to indulge in a comic set-piece as he plays a dentist who tries to remove King Rootentooten's (Vernon Dent) tooth with a pair of pliers. Later on, Howard impersonates a mummy, as he runs about the King's court swathed in bandages. *The Ghost Talks* (1949) returns once again to the haunted house theme by parodying the *Inner Sanctum* radio series (which spawned films such as *Weird Woman* [1944], *Strange Confession* [1945] and *The Frozen Ghost* [1945]). In this film, Howard has a hatpin thrust into his backside, tastes soot (in the belief that it is sherbet) and suffers the indignity once again of being used as a human battering-ram. *Hokus Pokus* (1949) makes fun of *Svengali* (1931) by having a hypnotist—here called Svengarlic (David Bond)—transforming the Three Stooges into various animals (Howard becomes a monkey). The three of them dance out of a sixth floor apartment on to a flagpole outside, at which point they emerge from their respective trances and discover to their horror that they cannot get back inside. More comic business ensues, as Howard hangs for dear life on to Moe's pants, which inevitably fall down to Moe's ankles.

The Three Stooges were one of Columbia Pictures' biggest moneymakers throughout the 1940s and early 1950s. Their films assume a predictable pattern of a minimal plot (often parodying box-office successes) padded out with slapstick and contemporary gags (for example, *The Frozen Ghost*, where the proverbial skeleton in the cupboard is called Red Skeleton, making fun of the comedian Red Skelton). Sometimes their humor can become tedious, but there are incidental pleasures—for example, enjoying Howard's India-rubber face which contorts itself into an infinite variety of expressions as he experiences indignity after indignity. The artist, writer and director Norman Maurer recalled that Howard was "the funniest of the three brothers [...] he was a riot. He would just open his mouth and he was funny." His expressions of fear as shown onscreen were at times genuine: the director Charles Barton recalled that Howard suffered from many phobias—on more than one occasion he "was so afraid of falling off [a precipice] [...] And he kept yelling, 'Will someone get me down from here? How much longer do I have to stay here? I'm getting sea-sick!'"

Olin Howland

b. February 10, 1886, Denver, Colorado;
d. September 20, 1959, Hollywood, California.

Olin Howland had a career in movies that stretched from the 1920s through the 1950s. After a few attempts at films in the silent era, Olin began appearing regularly in the sound pictures of the 1930s. He played small roles in mainstream Hollywood films, notably *Gone With the Wind* (1939). His roles were usually in mysteries and dramas, and he became a Western character actor in the 1940s with Republic (using the name Olin Howlin). He took a small role as Detective Dunhill in Warner Brothers' adaptation of *The Maltese Falcon*, retitled *Satan Met a Lady* (1936). He makes a striking first appearance by the grave of private detective Milton Ames (Porter Hall), as director William Dieterle's camera focuses on his feet first, and pans slowly upwards, as Dunhill tells Ames's erstwhile partner Ted Shane (Warren William) that he "must feel kinda bad losing your partner so suddenly, just when the firm was getting going." In his gray suit, black shirt and white tie, Dunhill cuts a dapper presence on screen, but he always remains one or two steps behind Shane in the quest to solve Ames's murder and find the fabled "Horn of Roland." Throughout the film, Dunhill reappears with his partner Pollock (Charles Wilson), telling Shane not to "be so stingy," and tell them precisely what he has found out. Shane takes no notice, of course, observing in an aside that to tell the cops anything would be like "contributing to the delinquency of a minor." In the end, Shane discovers that the real criminal is Valerie Purvis (Bette Davis), and travels on a train to apprehend her, while leaving a note explaining his actions for Dunhill's attention. Once Dunhill has read it, he will be "made a hero" (Shane's words) by taking the credit for solving the crime.

Howland has another small role in the Warner Brothers film *Return of Dr. X* (1939) as an undertaker. With his wing collar and neat black suit, he greets Dr. Mike Rhodes (Dennis Morgan) and campaigning journalist "Wichita" Garrett (Wayne Morris) with studied politeness. He smiles as he leads the two of them into the back of his shop to view the corpse of actress Angela Merrova (Lya Lys), on the pretext that they have been sent by Dr. Francis Flegg (John Litel)—who happens to be Rhodes's boss. As Rhodes and Garrett examine the body, looking for the synthetic blood that has kept Merrova alive (even though she was supposed to have been stabbed to death in the first five minutes of the film), the undertaker retires into the background, still smiling pleasantly. The two men leave the shop expressing the hope that they will look forward to seeing him again. The undertaker replies, "I'm sure you will," grinning at the camera as he does so. He inclines his head once again and exits. In Otto Preminger's horror noir *Fallen Angel* (1945), Howland plays Joe Ellis, an ineffectual sidekick to fake medium Professor Madley (JOHN CARRADINE), who cannot manage to drum up much publicity for Madley's public performances. Ellis certainly looks the part in his neat gray suit, black shirt and white tie, a half-smoked cigar protruding from his lips, but he lacks sufficient strength of character to persuade the citizens of the small Californian town of Walton to part with their money. In the end, Ellis cedes his role to small-time ex-publicity agent Eric Stanton (Dana Andrews), who barges into Ellis's hotel room unannounced, claiming to be Madley's bosom pal. Despite Ellis's ironic comments ("Use my toothpaste: I hope you like my brand"), Stanton spends the night in Ellis's room and subsequently takes on the responsibility of publicizing Madley's performances. Ellis melts into the background, acting as Madley's errand-boy, while praising Madley's presumed abilities as a medium ("Hit 'em [the customers] like an earthquake," Ellis observes just before one performance).

Olin Howlin and Joan Bennett in *Little Women* (1933). Howlin was mostly a bit-part actor, although he often gave memorable cameos as figures of authority — doctors, sheriffs — in Westerns and period dramas.

By the 1950s, Howland/Howlin had graduated to television in the adventure *Circus Boy* (1956–58). He also appeared in 1950s science fiction films, for example as Jensen, an inmate of a Los Angeles alcoholic clinic, in *Them!* (1954). When quizzed by Sgt. Ben Peterson (James Whitmore) and Robert Graham (James Arness) as to the whereabouts of the giant ants (who pose a real threat to the future of humankind), Jensen immediately thinks they are army officers calling him up for the draft. He offers them a deal ("Make me a sergeant and charge the booze!") and crawls under his bedclothes. Jensen is not as crazy as he pretends; he informs the two officers that he has been in the clinic for five months, during which time he has seen the ants stalking the river bed. But this moment of lucidity soon passes, and Jensen once again screams out "Make me a sergeant, gimme the booze!" while kicking the bedclothes in all directions. A tough-looking inmate leans across and silences him with a single phrase: "Please ... my nerves!" In a topsy-turvy world, the biblical prophecy that the beasts would rule the earth has come true (according to scientific expert Harold Bedford [Edmund Gwenn]), it seems fitting that the vital information as to the insects' whereabouts should be passed on by someone diagnosed as clinically insane due to alcoholism.

In *The Blob* (1958), Howlin played an old man who comes across what looks to be an inert lump of matter — somewhat rubbery in texture. He picks a piece of it up and finds to his cost that he cannot put it down. Eventually, the piece of matter begins to expand, and starts to eat him up. The old man howls in pain; in desperation, Steve Andrews (Steve McQueen) and his girlfriend Jane Martin (Aneta Corsaut) take him to the local doctor (Alden "Stephen" Chase). The doctor murmurs encouraging noises ("You'll be all right") and covers him up with a blanket in preparation for amputating the infected arm. But the matter (which turns out to be the eponymous blob) crawls up the old man's body and eventually swallows him whole; the doctor meets a similar fate, despite his valiant attempts to resist. Director Irvin S. Yeaworth, Jr., clearly intends *The Blob* as a warning to all Americans about the dangers of invasion — whether from space or (more likely, given the film's date of release) from Soviet Russia. It is part of the old man's tragedy that he falls prey to temptation; he would have been better advised to leave the blob alone. *The Blob* reinvigorates the horror genre by giving it a contemporary spin; director Yeaworth emphasizes the point by including a scene where the teenagers go to a midnight matinée at the local cinema, where the film *The Vampire and the Robot* (aka *Old Mother Riley Meets the Vampire*) is being shown. This woebegone 1952 effort features the aging Bela Lugosi sharing top billing with a British female impersonator Arthur Lucan/Old Mother Riley, and represents the nadir of the horror genre. By contrast, *The Blob* stresses that American small towns run the genuine risk of being invaded by alien forces that show no mercy to anyone — not even old men.

William Hudson

b. *January 24, 1919, Gilroy, California;*
d. *April 5, 1974, Woodland Hills,*
Los Angeles, California.

William Woodson Hudson, Jr., made his debut in 1943 in a wartime thriller *Destination Tokyo* (1943). Throughout the remainder of that decade he played bit parts in horror films such as *Weird Woman* (1943) starring EVELYN ANKERS, as well as dramas such as *Sands of Iwo Jima* (1949). Hudson spent much of the 1950s in television, appearing in *Rocky Jones: Space Ranger*, with guest spots in *Father Knows Best* and *The Roy Rogers Show*; as the decade wore on, however, he began to make a something of a name for himself as a character actor in low-budget science fiction films.

Hudson has a cameo role in *The She-Creature* (1956) as Bob, the ex-fiancé of Dorothy Chappel (Cathy Downs), who perpetually drowns his sorrows in drink. She regularly insults him by claiming that he is more interested in a whisky-bottle or "a parade of pink elephants" rather than talking to her. She is absolutely right, of course, but Bob has an important role to play in the film. Like Andrea Talbott (Marla English), the hapless assistant of mysterious hypnotist Dr. Carlo Lombardi (Chester Morris), Bob has sacrificed his capacity for self-determination to such an extent that he cannot understand the realities of the world around him. Whereas Andrea recovers this facility — as she mentally resists the hypnotist's words by the end of the film — Bob is reduced to a vegetative state, slurring his words and collapsing to the ground in a drunken stupor.

A year later, Hudson had a leading role as investigative psychiatrist Dr. Jess Rogers in *The Man Who Turned to Stone*. He stresses the character's practical side; his face remains impassive as he listens to the evidence presented before him about the nefarious activities in a ladies' penitentiary. While not appearing that interested, Rogers's hand movements — clasping and unclasping his fists — suggest otherwise; he is simply affecting disinterest. This is a good

William Hudson (right) and Larry Thor in *The Amazing Colossal Man* (1957). A thick-set leading player of the mid–1950s, Hudson could play both heroes and villains with equal facility.

move, as Dr. Murdock (Victor Jory), the principal of the penitentiary, shadows Rogers's every move, to ensure that the institution's guilty secret remains undiscovered. However, Rogers discovers what has been happening: all the staff (Murdock included) are over a hundred and fifty years old, and have been kept alive by the energy taken from sacrificial victims, such as the women in the penitentiary. Rogers takes matters into his own hands—despite overwhelming odds, he not only destroys the staff but the penitentiary as well. Throughout the film, Hudson's face remains set in an expression of grim determination; he will not cease until the evil within the penitentiary been totally eradicated.

Hudson played another professional person—the research scientist Dr. Paul Linstrom—in Bert I. Gordon's *The Amazing Colossal Man* (1957). As in *The Man Who Turned to Stone*, Hudson's character comes across as practical, the kind of man who is determined to find out at all costs why Lt. Col. Glenn Manning (GLENN LANGAN) is growing at such an alarming rate. Although sympathetic to Manning's plight (he observes that "this man's [Manning's] luck ran out long ago"), Linstrom refuses to become emotionally involved; on several occasions we see him walking in businesslike fashion through the hospital, deep in conversation with his medical colleagues. While talking to Manning's fiancée Carol (Cathy Downs), he sits on the edge of a desk, calmly and quietly describing the "regenerative power" that makes Manning grow so rapidly, but not holding out much hope for the colonel's future recovery. Linstrom eventually assumes command of a major operation, in collaboration with members of the armed forces. We see him piloting a helicopter, clearly enjoying the experience of moving out of the laboratory. The doctor has an ambiguous role in this film; on the one hand, he condemns the nuclear test that caused Manning's accident in the first place, yet on the other hand he seems more than willing to participate in the colonel's eventual destruction. It seems that the thrill of the chase overwhelms Linstrom's belief in medical ethics.

A year later, Hudson played an out-and-out bad guy in *Attack of the 50-Foot Woman* (1958). As Harry Archer, the faithless husband of Nancy (Allison Hayes), he seems completely self-absorbed, believing that "a man hasn't got a chance" to be free, particularly when saddled with a nagging wife. Thus he tries every possible means to dispose of her—putting her in a sanatorium, for instance—so that he can be with his teenage girlfriend Honey (Yvette Vickers). Although clearly too old for the role, Harry believes that he is cool, just because he sits with Honey in the local bar listening to rock 'n' roll and occasionally gyrating (so long as no one sees him). Harry's behavior inevitably demands retribution; while trying to kill Nancy with a lethal injection, he accidentally transforms her into a monster who has to be kept in chains to prevent her threatening the security of the community she inhabits. One evening she escapes, and comes to the bar where Harry and Honey (note the similarity of their names, suggesting they are partners in crime) are completely wrapped up in their own company. Nancy picks Harry up in her hand and stares at him as if he were a toy; all he can do in reply is to scream "No! No!" as he is crushed to death.

In terms of the film's logic, Nancy's transformation is the inevitable product of an age obsessed with youth and music. As one character remarks sorrowfully, she is "a case not infrequent in the supersonic age we live in." However, she is not allowed to be free—even when transformed into a fifty-foot monster. She has to die so that the (patriarchal) *status quo* might be restored—even if the patriarchy (as represented by Harry) is completely corrupt. Nonetheless, she manages to achieve her desire to wrench Harry away from his girlfriend and have him "all to herself," as one character observes. The film ends with a shot of the two of them glaring at one another in death.

Isabel Jewell
b. July 19, 1907, Shoshone, Wyoming;
d. April 5, 1972, Hollywood, California.

Isabel Jewell was signed as an MGM contract player, making her name in hits such as *A Tale of Two Cities* (1935), *Lost Horizon* (1937), and most memorably as Ruby Slattery in *Gone With the Wind* (1939).

Jewell had a major role as Marianne in *Mad Love* (1935), where she plays one of the characters involved in the performance at the Théâtre des Horreurs in Paris, in which grisly murders from the past are re-enacted. MGM decided to cut fifteen minutes from the film after its initial release, and Jewell's entire portrayal was removed. In *The Leopard Man* (1943), she plays Maria the fortune teller, a slatternly woman in long skirts and shawl, frequently seen smoking a cigarette as she walks the streets. Her head covered with a scarf — especially when at work in her booth — Maria comes across as a mysterious figure, a misanthrope believing that "men are all fools," who somewhat contradictorily believes that she should not be concerned with "putting the evil eye" on her clients. She understands the world she lives in, one whose inhabitants place too much trust in the supernatural, even while they are trying to better themselves. She criticizes Consuela Contrero (Tina Parma) for being a gold-digger, observing *sotto voce* that the young lady will come to no good in the end. And so it proves, as Consuela is mauled to death on a dark night.

At the same time, Maria remains somewhat disconcerted by the fact that, despite all her attempts to shuffle her cards — and hence predict good as well as bad fortunes — the ace of spades keeps coming up. She conceals this fact from her clients, in the belief that they have to be told something good about themselves to warrant the price of admission. Whether the reappearance of the ace is simply coincidence or part of Maria's strategy is left unexplained: what we do know, however, is that she foresees "something black" for several of her clients, especially young women such as the nightclub singer Clo Clo (Margo), who receives money from a man and subsequently meets a grisly fate. The fortune teller's stubborn determination to honor her predictions links *The Leopard Man* not just to the horror film, but to the fatalism of *film noir*. The curator of the local museum Galbraith (James Bell) — who turns out to be the eventual killer — makes this point to Jerry (Dennis O'Keefe) as he describes a ball on a jet of water in a café fountain: "We know as little about the forces that move us and move around us as that empty ball does about the water that pushes it into the air, lets it fall, and catches it again." If any of Maria's clients object to this fatalistic outlook, the fortune teller simply shrugs her shoulders and takes another pull on her cigarette; in this kind of world she is guaranteed future work.

In the end, however, both Kiki Walker (JEAN BROOKS) and her manager Jerry Manning come to realize that the only way to counteract the power of the supernatural is through self-belief; if individuals choose "not to be soft," they can determine their own destiny. Maria has an important role in the film, but only because she lives in a society whose inhabitants believe their lives are determined by a higher power.

On the other hand, Maria's power of fortune telling remains peripheral to the film's central narrative. It exerts no influence on the main events and never attracts the

Isabel Jewell (right) and Jean Brooks converse in a dramatic moment from *The Leopard Man* (1943).

scrutiny of either Kiki or Jerry. One sequence underlines this irrelevance: Maria nonchalantly passes Jerry, who ignores her as he goes into Kiki's room. Maria, Kiki and Jerry are indifferent to one another because they exist on different levels of the story. By contrasting these two levels, however, director Jacques Tourneur suggests that the division between them is unsustainable, a point that relates to the film's theme of collective responsibility. The true identity of the killer can only be discovered if people are prepared to work together *for* one another.

In *The Seventh Victim* (1943), she plays Frances Fallon, a respectable-looking hairdresser by day, but someone involved in the mysterious cult by night. She dresses demurely in white shirt and skirt, an apron around her middle, her hair in curls. At one point Mrs. Redi (Mary Newton) asks Frances what she was talking about with Mary (Kim Hunter); Frances replies that Mary "showed her a drawing." Mrs. Redi calls Frances a fool, as the hairdresser has unwittingly revealed details about the cult. Frances remains outwardly unmoved, but the repeated chords of a cello on the soundtrack sum up her tortured state of mind. In another sequence, taking place at night, Frances's true condition is revealed, as she sits opposite Jacqueline Gibson (JEAN BROOKS) and exhorts her to commit suicide, on account of Jacqueline being a murderer. Frances screams: "Drink it, Jacqueline! There's nothing else for you to do! [...] You've got to die!" Jacqueline escapes, so Frances herself takes the poison, realizing — perhaps rightly — that there is nothing else that she can do in her life. By the 1940s and 1950s, her career as a character was slightly on the wane, but she nonetheless distinguished herself in several horror films of the period. In *Man in the Attic* (1953), a remake of *The Lodger*, she has a small but colorful role as Kitty the prostitute, speaking in a stage Irish accent, who faithfully promises the two London constables (Sean McClory and Leslie Bradley) that she will refrain from wandering the streets of London and go home like a respectable woman. She flatters the constables by complimenting their "lovely manners," and smiles. We also notice that she carries a gin bottle in her hand, suggesting that she has no real home to go to. She crouches in an alleyway and waits for the constables to walk out of sight before resuming her travels round London's dimly lit streets. She subsequently encounters a stranger; at this point we do not know who he is, but discover later that it is Slade, aka Jack the Ripper. Director Hugo Fregonese cuts to a close-up of Katy's petrified face, as she screams in unadulterated terror. Her feather boa flutters to the ground as she dies.

Noble Johnson
b. April 18, 1881, Marshall, Missouri;
d. January 9, 1978, Yucalpa, California.

African American actor Noble Mark Johnson moved to Colorado Springs as a child, where he met Lon Chaney, Sr., at school. The two of them became close friends. They were reacquainted as adults in Hollywood, even though they never made any films together. Johnson

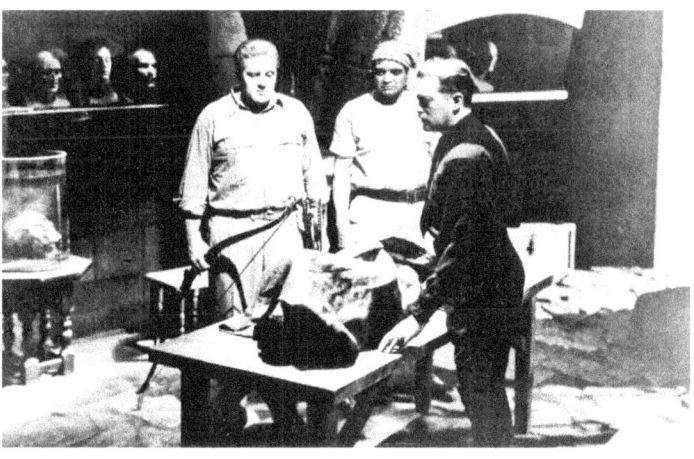

Noble Johnson (second from left), a leading African American actor of his generation, often ended up playing bit parts in horror films as zombies, tribal chiefs or other alien characters. He was a victim of the racial politics that dominated Hollywood during this period.

was much in demand during the silent and the talking picture eras as a character actor, often playing exotic characters (tribal chiefs, Middle Eastern potentates) as well as African Americans.

In *King Kong* (1933), he plays a tribal chief, who is first seen participating in a ritual designed to sacrifice a native girl to King Kong. He cuts an imposing appearance with his painted face and feathered headdress, surrounded by subjects dressed as animals. He espies the white adventurers, led by Carl Denham (ROBERT ARMSTRONG), and abruptly curtails the ceremony. In a conversation conducted entirely in an incomprehensible tongue with Captain Englehorn (Frank Reicher), the chief requests Ann Darrow (Fay Wray) in exchange for six of his tribeswomen. Needless to say Denham refuses the offer. However, the chief perseveres in his quest for Ann by invading the adventurers' ship and carrying her back to his settlement as a sacrifice for Kong. Despite his outward show of strength, the chief turns out to be a coward — particularly when compared with the adventurers. This is clearly demonstrated in one of the film's climactic moments, as the adventurers ignore received wisdom about the potential dangers involved and venture into Kong's territory in the hope of rescuing Ann. Meanwhile, the chief remains in his compound, content to rule his people.

The film rehearses traditional colonialist stereotypes: the tribal warriors are not only unable to communicate in English (and hence make themselves understood to the film's projected audience), but they are inferior to the European characters when it comes to fighting battles. Johnson does what he can with the role, but he has a thankless task.

Johnson plays another tribal chief in Joseph H. Lewis's *The Mad Doctor of Market Street* (1942). Faced with the prospect of invasion by a group of white people led by the eponymous mad doctor Ralph Benson (LIONEL ATWILL), the chief Elan observes that such invasions only bring "evil spirits" to a hitherto unspoiled world: "Every time they [the white people] come, people die." Elan's predictions look as if they will come true, as his wife Tanaa (Rosina Galli) falls ill with an unidentifiable disease. However, Benson uses some of his medicines — especially ammonia — to cure her. Elan is so grateful that he calls Benson the "god of life, we [are] your slaves." As in *King Kong*, the film suggests that nonwhites cannot survive alone, but need the colonizers' protection to guarantee their future.

In *Murders in the Rue Morgue* (1932), Johnson has a supporting role as "Janos, the Black One" (to quote the film's credits), the servant of Dr. Mirakle (Bela Lugosi). Janos cuts a threatening presence as he opens the door to any visitors unfortunate enough to visit Mirakle's laboratory. Janos himself remains impervious to what happens inside; he looks away while the doctor abducts young women and injects them with ape blood in an attempt to prove kinship between apes and human beings. Janos himself resembles an ape, clad entirely in black, his arms hanging down by his side as he walks slowly up and down the wide staircase leading up to Mirakle's front door.

Johnson has another ape-like role as the zombie in the Bob Hope comedy vehicle *The Ghost Breakers* (1940). He is first discovered lying on a bed, his eyes staring vacantly upwards. He rises up slowly, his back straight as a ramrod, and walks inexorably forward like the Monster in James Whale's *Frankenstein* (1931). Pursuing intrepid radio broadcaster Lawrence Lawrence (Hope) around the supposedly haunted castle, the zombie's head rolls from side to side, his eyes almost popping out of his head. Later on, the zombie conceals himself in a suit of armor, and tries to hit Lawrence on the head with a mace. Lawrence narrowly avoids a grisly end, and together with his faithful African American servant, Alex (Willie Best), he manages to shut the zombie up in a closet.

Perhaps Johnson's most bizarre casting came in IRVING PICHEL and Ernest B. Schoedsack's *The Most Dangerous Game* (1932), where he played Ivan, the mute servant of insane hunter Dr. Zaroff (Leslie Banks). Johnson appears in white-face with wild black hair and beard: Zaroff describes him as a Russian Cossack, "a bit of a savage," who followed Zaroff away from the Russian mainland to the tropical island where both now reside. Ivan does exactly as his master tells him; he smiles ingratiatingly to welcome

Bob Raynsford (Joel McCrea), who has been shipwrecked on the island and takes him upstairs to his room. While Ivan does not say anything, he cuts a threatening presence in several sequences as he lurks at the back of the frame, listening intently to what his master has to say. He gazes intently at the guests, as if symbolically possessing them through his looks. Should anyone try to escape, Ivan will make every effort to recapture them, using a pack of hounds to help him. The film includes several sequences where Ivan roams the island, his eyes darting left to right as he finds out whether anyone is hiding in the lush vegetation. As the film unfolds, so we understand that Zaroff intends to kill all of his guests off by offering them as prey to the native hunters. They are "the most dangerous game" of the film's title. However, Bob escapes, together with Eve (Fay Wray), in spite of Ivan's best efforts. The two of them grapple with one another in a climactic fight — despite Ivan's advantages in terms of size and build, he inevitably comes off worst, as he falls to his death.

Johnson's servile roles on screen belied his off-screen reputation. Even before he had gone to Hollywood, he had founded the Lincoln Motion Picture Company, an African American outfit dedicated to the production of films portraying African Americans in a positive light instead of racist caricatures. Johnson resigned as president in 1920. It was a sad irony that he reinforced the kind of caricatures in mainstream Hollywood horror films that he had tried to eradicate in his earlier work for Lincoln.

Arthur Batanides and Tor Johnson in *The Unearthly* (1959). Swedish-born Johnson made his name as one of Edward D. Wood, Jr.'s permanent repertory. He could hardly act, but his physical presence was sufficient.

Tor Johnson

b. October 19, 1903, Kalmar, Sweden;
d. May 12, 1971, San Fernando, California.

Like RONDO HATTON a decade earlier, Tor Johnson was one of those actors short on technique who nonetheless became a familiar presence in horror and science fiction films of the 1950s and early 1960s. Born Karl Oscar Tore Johansson, he spent most of his life as a professional wrestler, but started appearing in bit parts in Hollywood films from 1934 onwards. He graduated to roles in A-list films such as *Road to Rio* (1950) and *Abbott and Costello in the Foreign Legion* (1950). In the 1950s, Johnson worked regularly with Edward D. Wood, Jr. His first role for the director was in *Bride of the Monster* (1955), where he played the monster Lobo, sidekick of mad scientist Dr. Eric Vornoff (Bela Lugosi). Brought over to America from the wilderness of Tibet, Lobo acts as Vornoff's heavy, as he towers over his victims, his arms spread wide, and knocks them to the floor. Vornoff protests all the while that Lobo is actually as "gentle as a kitten." However, Lobo is not as tough as he might seem: Vornoff exercises a tyrannous authority over the monster, as he whips Lobo with a metal chain to ensure the monster carries out his orders. Lobo silently obeys most of the time, until he is told to pull the switch that will transform journalist Janet Lawton (Loretta King) into a superperson using atomic energy. In a clear allusion to James

Whale's *Frankenstein* (1931), Lobo has a soft spot for young women (the younger the better); he ogles Janet's lifeless form, and then turns on his master, knocking him to the floor. Lobo then turns to the operating-table, releases Janet and places Vornoff there instead. However, this is a rash move: Vornoff is transformed into a superperson with sufficient strength to rise from the table and push Lobo into the atomic energy machine. The luckless monster dies a horrible death by fire.

Johnson repeats the role of Lobo in Boris Petroff's *The Unearthly* (1957). He acts as manservant to Dr. Charles Conway (JOHN CARRADINE), while ensuring that none of Conway's patients escape from the lonely mansion where they are all incarcerated. Although employed primarily for security purposes, Lobo sympathizes with many of the patients — especially the female ones. In one sequence, he brings an evening meal to Grace Thomas (Allison Hayes), and tenderly exhorts her to "eat." Later on, he crouches over Natalie Anders's (Sally Todd) mutilated face — the unfortunate outcome of one of Conway's experiments — and looks at her with pity. However, no one has much time for Lobo: in the climactic sequence, Mark Houston (Myron Healy) and Danny Green (Arthur Batanides) treat him like the animal in a bullfight as they flourish a cloth in front of him in the hope that he will charge. He does so, and the two men put the cloth over his head and knock him out cold. At the end of the film, he is shown whimpering over Conway's corpse; with no one to look after him, Lobo has no real future in life.

Wood cast Johnson for a third time in the role for the low-budget feature *Night of the Ghouls* (1959). Lobo's master this time is the medium Criswell (appearing as himself), who treats him with contempt. With his bizarre costume — loincloth and vest — and horribly disfigured face, with a massive scar on one side reminiscent of Vincent Price's Professor Henry Jarrod in *House of Wax* (1953) — Lobo appears even more grotesque, as Criswell introduces him to the audience with the knowing phrase: "The house was not all that remained of the old scientist's quarry." Lobo has even less to do in *Night of the Ghouls* than *Bride of the Monster*; he roars periodically, raises his arms in the air in a threatening gesture, and attacks two police officers. Eventually he is repeatedly shot in the chest and falls spectacularly to the ground.

In *Plan Nine from Outer Space* (also 1959), Johnson has a brief speaking role as Inspector Daniel Clay, who is called in to investigate some strange goings-on in a graveyard. He likes to assert his authority — at one point, he tells Patrolman Kelton (Paul Marco) that he is "a big boy now," who can make decisions on his own. Director Wood has him repeatedly crossing the frame right to left, left to right, wearing a grim expression and carrying a gun. However, Clay's statement proves profoundly ironic, as he is killed by enemy aliens and buried soon afterwards. Later on, he rises from the dead as a zombie, terrorizing various human beings and carrying Paula Trent (Mona McKinnon) off to the aliens' spaceship. Johnson reverts to stereotype in these sequences as he lumbers across the screen, his mouth half-open, emitting occasional frightening roars. It seems that Wood was reluctant to let the actor do anything else for fear of alienating his cult film audience.

Anthony Cardoza was a friend of Johnson's, and cast him as "The Beast" (aka Joseph Javorsky) in his low-budget horror film *Beast of Yucca Flats* (1961). This film was shot silent, and had dubbed-in sound effects and voiceover narration: Johnson himself received only $300 as a fee. The story is a familiar one: Javorsky, a defector from Soviet Russia, has been ambushed by representatives of the KGB, who want to get their hands on a secret formula contained in a black attaché case. The case is accidentally opened, setting off a nuclear explosion which leaves Javorsky horribly disfigured as well as being reduced to a catatonic vegetable roaming aimlessly around a remote American landscape emitting occasional roars and/or guttural grunts. As he does so, the narrator reminds us of what happened — to a man who once "dedicated his life to the betterment of mankind": "Touch a button, things happen. A scientist becomes a beast [...] a once-powerful, humble man, reduced to nothing [...] Joseph Javorsky, now a fiend, a prehistoric beast in the nuclear age." Once again, Johnson has little, if nothing to do in the film apart from look menacing as he scares away two inquisitive young boys (Ronald and Alan Francis). Cornered at the end by two brave State Troopers, Javorsky puts up a brave fight but is eventually shot dead. As he lies on the ground, a rabbit comes near to him; he looks at it, smiles slightly and then passes away. This sequence suggests the character's humanity, which has been destroyed as a result of the accident.

Johnson's film career ended after this low-budget effort, although he did find subsequent work in television series and commercials during the 1960s.

Cecil Kellaway

b. August 22, 1893, Cape Town, South Africa; d. February 28, 1973, Hollywood, California.

Cecil Kellaway spent many years as a character actor in the fledgling Australian film industry, before moving to Hollywood in the mid–1930s. His first major role was as Earnshaw in William Wyler's version of *Wuthering Heights* (1939). Thereafter, he established himself as a reliable character actor, often playing doctors, police inspectors or comic Irish roles.

Cecil Kellaway publicity still (1959). A versatile actor, Kellaway was a specialist in comic roles as a leprechaun-like figure.

In *The Invisible Man Returns* (1940), he plays Inspector Sampson, a Scotland Yard inspector called in to investigate the whereabouts of Geoffrey Radcliffe (Vincent Price), who has escaped execution on a charge of murder. Kellaway appears as a symbol of reliability in his trench coat, a cigar clamped to his teeth as he interrogates Dr. Frank Griffin (John Sutton). Sampson is inclined not to believe Griffin's story about the discovery of a secret drug that renders a man invisible. However, Sampson's view soon alters, once he witnesses the sight of the invisible Geoffrey carrying objects in front of him. The inspector's cigar becomes a kind of weapon, as he realizes that the smoke will help to discover Geoffrey's whereabouts.

Sampson loses his *sang-froid* somewhat after he discovers that the murderer was not Geoffrey but Richard Cobb (CEDRIC HARDWICKE). The inspector paces up and down the room, smoking yet another cigar, as if trying to understand where his deductions went wrong. In this topsy-turvy world, where nothing is quite what it seems (especially when Geoffrey has successfully rendered himself invisible), the inspector realizes that his position as a symbol of law and order is severely threatened.

That same year, Kellaway appeared as the lawyer Philip Barton in *The House of the Seven Gables*, based on the Nathaniel Hawthorne novel. With his wide-brimmed hat and long coat, he cuts an imposing presence in court as he denounces the jury who has convicted Clifford Pyncheon (Vincent Price) of a murder he did not commit. Barton refers in ringing tones to the "travesty of justice," a product of these "barbaric times," which he believes are reminiscent of "seventeenth century witch-hunting." He perpetually looks out for Hepzibah Pyncheon's (Margaret Lindsay) interests, taking a particular pleasure in announcing that it is she, rather than her avaricious cousin Jaffray (GEORGE SANDERS), who will inherit the House of the Seven Gables on her father's death. At the end of the film, Barton presides over the marriage between Hepzibah and Clifford, who has secured his release from prison. He embraces both of them, and declares in voiceover that, despite their advancing years, he will always think of them as they were "in the beginning," in other words, when they were both young.

Kellaway played his third role in a Universal horror film in 1940 as Mr. Solvani in *The Mummy's Hand*. Another jovial character in black tail coat, vest and a buttonhole, he delights in playing tricks on unsuspecting victims such as Babe Jensen (WALLACE FORD). Having admitted that Solvani is nothing more than a pseudonym — his real name being Tim Sullivan from Brooklyn — he forms a bond with Jensen and Steve Banning (DICK FORAN). The three are almost immediately involved in a barroom brawl: while Steve fights with his fists, Solvani sits atop a rail and beats his opponents on his head with a walking stick. This not only confirms his status as a character actor (supporting the leading man) but suggests that he is always willing to lend a hand, even in situations which are alien to him. Director Christy Cabanne suggests that such traits are characteristic of Americans — as opposed to the Egyptians (as personified by Andohet [GEORGE ZUCCO]), who seek to exploit others for their own ends. At the same time, Solvani remains enduringly childlike: when questioned by his daughter Marta (Peggy Moran) about the whereabouts of his $2000 (which he has given to Steve to finance the archeological expedition), Solvani finds refuge in magic tricks such as producing a length of satin from his sleeve, and lighting a cigar with his thumb. He even tries to disappear in his own magic coffin, but finds himself hoist by his own petard as Marta locks him in and storms out of the room, leaving him to cry piteously "Let me out!" Nonetheless, his magic powers prove useful, once the expedition has begun, as they provide an invaluable diversion from the atmosphere of menace pervading the camp. Solvani might be a peripheral figure in the film, but he is imbued with a sense of community spirit that counts a lot for Americans like Steve and Babe, who are forced by circumstances to contend with an alien culture.

Kellaway thoroughly enjoys himself as mischievous spook Daniel in René Clair's *I Married a Witch* (1942). For the first half of the film we do not see him at all, but listen to his mellifluous tones in voiceover, while Clair's camera focuses on the hearth, a broomstick, or other household objects. He first appears in a long white toga reminiscent of a Roman senator: when he hears that his daughter Jennifer (Veronica Lake) has fallen in love with mortal Wallace Wooley (Fredric March), he seems rather perturbed, but soon recovers his jocular manner, even though Wooley is the descendant of the prosecutor who condemned both Daniel and Jennifer three centuries previously. Daniel assumes human form, in a tweed three-piece suit, and apparently commits suicide. When this melodramatic scene fails to break the two lovers up, Daniel tries another strategy by inhabiting the body of a drunk who falls out of the window. This proves equally ineffective, as he ends up in jail for his pains. Try as he might, he cannot disprove the old adage that love conquers everything. He eventually gives up his quest and becomes a spirit once more; as Jennifer and Wallace embrace, we hear him laughing on the soundtrack. He might not be able to break them up, but he can continue to make their lives a misery wherever possible, and thereby have revenge on the Wooley family.

Kellaway's jovial personality informs his characterization of Professor Thurgood Elson in *The Beast from 20,000 Fathoms* (1953). Although disbelieving Tom Nesbitt's (Paul Christian) story about the existence of a prehistoric monster, Elson is determined not to hurt the younger man's feelings. He smiles paternally at him, and patiently listens, while puffing away on his pipe; as in *The Invisible Man Returns*, the pipe denotes reliability. In truth, however, Elson is much more interested in his forthcoming vacation — his first for thirty years, which he anticipates with all the enthusiasm of "a schoolboy on the verge of departing for his first summer camp."

But Elson undergoes a rapid change of attitude when he hears confirmation of Nesbitt's story. His whole body animates with the prospect of re-establishing himself as America's leading authority on paleontology. Director Eugene Lourié uses several close-ups of his left profile as he explains precisely what the monster is, and where he is most likely to be found, using a wooden dowel and a blackboard to illustrate his points. Although everyone would like to see the monster destroyed, Elson wants to keep it alive. His justification for action is simple: "We're scientists. This is our job. This is a great moment for me." In spite of his reliable appearance, it is evident that the desire for academic fame has rendered him insensible to the plight of others. As with his other characterizations, however, Kellaway stresses Elson's childlike nature, as he embarks on a voyage to the bottom of the sea to look for the monster. He climbs into the divine-bell, making light of the possible risks involved and cracking weak jokes about enjoying "all the comforts of home." His shining eyes and bright smile suggest that he cannot wait to observe the monster from close quarters. Lourié cuts to several close-ups of the professor staring out of the diving-bell window like a child looking into a shop. Elson's wishes eventually come true; the monster appears, and the professor exclaims, in a high-pitched squeal, "He's tremendous! He's enormous!" However, the professor's moment of triumph turns to tragedy, as the monster crushes the diving bell and condemns its inhabitants to a watery grave. Critic Hal Erickson likened Kellaway's screen presence to that of a leprechaun with his twinkly eyes and endearing manner; he reveals such qualities to good effect in *The Beast from 20,000 Fathoms*, even if his character's desire for fame and reputation eventually gets the better of him.

Patric Knowles

b. November 11, 1911, Horsforth, Yorkshire, England;
d. December 23, 1995, Woodland Hills,
Los Angeles, California.

Born Reginald Lawrence Knowles, Patric Knowles made his debut in regional theatre before moving into films in 1932. After a notable success in Michael Powell's *Girl in the Crowd* (1935), he moved to Hollywood, supporting Errol Flynn in *The Charge of the Light Brigade* (1936) and *The Adventures of Robin Hood* (1938).

By the early 1940s, Knowles had become a

Patric Knowles, *Picturegoer* postcard taken before the actor went to Hollywood. British-born Knowles played debonair leading roles in the 1930s and 1940s, and later graduated to playing elder statespersons.

contract player at Universal, specializing in playing clean-cut leading men in horror films. In *The Wolf Man* (1941), he plays Frank Andrews, the local gamekeeper and fiancé of Gwen Cunliffe (EVELYN ANKERS). At first, Andrews seems jealous of Lawrence Talbot (Lon Chaney, Jr.), as Talbot forms a close relationship with Gwen. However, once Frank discovers that Talbot might be the wolf man, his attitude changes. Rather than sympathizing with Talbot, Frank devotes himself to his gamekeeper's pursuits— hunting and setting mantraps. Once Talbot has been killed, Frank and Gwen fall into each other's arms, but we doubt whether the relationship will continue. Frank simply does not understand the depth of Gwen's feeling. A year later Knowles starred in *The Strange Case of Dr. RX* (1942) as debonair private detective Jerry Church, who returns to New York from South America intent on giving up his career and running the family farm. Predictably, this desire remains unfulfilled as he becomes embroiled in a quest to discover the identity of a mysterious avenger, who kills five men previously acquitted of various criminal charges. Director William Nigh frames Jerry in lengthy close-ups, showing his pragmatic nature and his unique capability to master any situation. Nonetheless, he still finds time to participate in verbal sparring matches with his wife Kit (Anne Gwynne), resembling Nick and Nora Charles in *The Thin Man* (1934). The two of them seem to never agree on anything, but nonetheless appear very much in love, even though Jerry reveals the sexist assumptions of the time, criticizing Kit for not behaving "like a typical wife." At the same time, Jerry is a man of honor; if any man strikes a woman, he immediately strikes them back. Jerry becomes involved in a complicated denouement that involves the exchange of human brains with a man in a gorilla suit. He seems genuinely scared by the ordeal, but his transatlantic *sang-froid* sustains him, as he pretends to be in a trance in order to expose Dudley Crispin (Samuel S. Hinds) as the evil Dr. RX.

Knowles' next film, *The Mystery of Marie Roget* (also 1942), based on the story by Edgar Allan Poe, had him playing Dr. Paul Dupin, pathologist and master detective. There are strong echoes of Basil Rathbone's Sherlock Holmes in Knowles's performance, as he sits languidly in an armchair and listens carefully to the account of how a young woman has been found dead in the River Seine, her face horribly disfigured. When Dupin ventures out into the streets, he uses a walking cane to examine any evidence placed before him; any conclusions he draws from such evidence are carefully thought out. We understand this from director Phil Rosen's frequent close-ups on Dupin stroking his chin with his hands or looking from side to side in search of further evidence. Just like Rathbone's Holmes (who suffered Nigel Bruce's Watson invariably coming to the wrong conclusions), Dupin has Prefect Gobelin (LLOYD CORRIGAN) as his sidekick. The Prefect is more of a hindrance than a help to Dupin, which prompts the detective to conceal most of his conclusions: any false move or rash action on Gobelin's part could result in the case collapsing. Throughout the film, Gobelin is treated as a buffoon, continually blowing out his cheeks in exasperation, as he cannot understand what Dupin is doing. The two of them are completely different in terms of character: whereas Dupin conducts a slow process of deduction, Gobelin makes spontaneous (and invariably wrong) assumptions. In spite of these problems, Dupin sustains his *sang-froid* throughout, coming to the conclusion that the case was nothing more than "cold, calculated, premeditated murder." In an exciting climax to the film, Dupin reveals his athleticism as he jumps nimbly across the Paris rooftops in pursuit of the murderer Marcel Vigneaux (Edward Norris) before shooting him dead. However, the detective understands the importance of not taking the credit for solving the crime; to do so would put Gobelin's support at risk. Gobelin takes the credit for solving the crime, thrusting out his chest in self-congratulation.

In *Frankenstein Meets the Wolf Man* (1943), Knowles once again plays the clean-cut, no-nonsense hero Dr. Mannering, who at first seems convinced that Lawrence Talbot (Lon Chaney, Jr.) is stark staring mad. Eventually, Mannering comes to realize that Talbot is actually the Wolf Man, who can only be cured by a complicated scientific process involving the Monster (Bela Lugosi). Knowles has the chance to play a scene similar to that of Colin Clive in James Whale's *Frankenstein* (1931), where he performs his experiments in a dark and dingy underground laboratory. The main difference between the two actors is that whereas Clive's Henry Frankenstein is driven half-crazy by his obsessions, Dr. Mannering remains calm throughout. Even when the experiment goes wrong, and Frankenstein is left to battle it out to the bitter end with the Wolf Man, Mannering has sufficient presence of mind to quit the laboratory and retreat to a safe haven accompanied by Baroness Elsa Frankenstein (Ilona Massey).

Knowles has a cameo role as Josef Cartier in *From the Earth to the Moon* (1958), who supports Victor Barbicane (Joseph Cotten) in his experiments, even though Cartier has no idea how they might turn out. In his gray suit and white cravat, Cartier looks more like a businessperson than a scientist, but his enthusiasm for the project contrasts with Stuyvesant Nicholl's (GEORGE SANDERS) skepticism. Cartier carries out Barbicane's various requirements—secure in the knowledge that what the scientist is doing is for the benefit of all humankind. Eventually, Barbicane takes off for the moon: director Byron Haskin zooms in on Cartier's delighted expression as he watches the spacecraft blasting off. Even if Barbicane does not return, he has made a contribution to the betterment of society.

Sir Lancelot
b. March 24, 1902, Cumuto, Trinidad, West Indies; d. March 12, 2001, Anaheim, California.

He was born Lancelot Victor Edward Pinard to well-to-do Anglophile parents: oddly, though, it wasn't until schooling took him to New York City in 1940 that he discovered a love of calypso music. In a profession where successful artists commonly took names like King Radio or Lord Invader, it was natural for someone named Lancelot to choose the stage name Sir Lancelot, and with that name he wrote and performed calypso (with some acting on the side) for movies, live theater, and radio beginning in the 1940's.

Sir Lancelot played memorable character parts in some of Val Lewton's horror classics, produced during the same decade. In *I Walked with a Zombie* (1943), he is Edward, who is continually seen strumming away on a guitar, rather like a Chorus in a Greek tragedy, predicting "shame and sorrow for de family," referring specifically to the Rand family. His role in the film is to act as a mediator between the white colonizers and the African American zombies; while understanding the Rand family's predicament, he can understand why the local population should object to their presence. His calypsoes make this point explicit. Sometimes he tries to warn the Anglo characters such as Betsy (Frances Dee) of the dangers they face; but they take little heed of him, believing instead that they are somehow immune, on account of their race.

In *Ghost Ship* (also 1943), Sir Lancelot has an uncredited role as a crew member breaking occasionally into song ("I'm been here right from Trinidad.") Sometimes his songs are used as interludes to bridge certain gaps in the action — at one point, we hear him singing the shanty "Blow the man down," while we see the crazed Captain Will Stone (Richard Dix) completing his charts on the bridge. Despite all evidence to the contrary, Sir Lancelot defends the captain ("a kind man and a gentleman"), in the belief that this is the way to preserve harmony onboard ship. Unlike his fellow crew-members, he believes in maintaining the status quo— even though he is automatically treated as a second-class citizen on account of his skin color. Once again, Sir Lancelot takes on the role of a chorus figure, singing calypsos on the soundtrack while we watch Captain Stone about to commit another murder.

In *Curse of the Cat People* (1944), Sir Lancelot plays Edward, another African American willing to respect the social status quo, as he becomes the faithful butler to the Reed family. Always willing to carry out his employers' wishes, he is identified as a force for good trying to protect Amy Reed (Ann Carter) from the potentially evil influence of Barbara Farren (ELIZABETH RUSSELL). When Amy objects, Edward politely listens, takes her away from the Farren household and wags an admonishing finger at her, while saying that she certainly gave him a fight. In a dysfunctional family, where Amy's parents Oliver (KENT SMITH) and Alice (Jane Randolph) are continually at war (due in no small part to Oliver's continuing love for his dead first wife Irena (SIMONE SIMON), Edward acts as a force of stability for the little girl.

Sir Lancelot played cameo roles in other films; in the spoof horror film *Zombies on Broadway* (1945), he plays yet another calypso singer, parodying his role in *I Walked with a Zombie*. Dressed in white suit with panama hat, he conforms to western images of social respectability as he welcomes bumbling press agents Jerry Miles (Wally Brown) and Mike Strager (Alan Carney) to a tropical island with a friendly calypso. As his song continues, however, Sir Lancelot talks of the dangers lurking beneath the civilized façade; if visitors try to investigate too deeply into the island culture, they are likely to encounter evil spirits. Such lyrics warn of the perils of colonization — a message that blissfully eludes the two press agents, as they press ahead in their search for a zombie to take back and cast in a Broadway show. In *The Unknown Terror* (1957), Sir Lancelot repeats his role as a calypso singer who alludes at first to the joys of the "sunny West Indies" awaiting anyone who chooses to spend a holiday there. In another song, he describes a bottomless cave beyond the grave, deep in the jungle, where people are reborn. In this film, his function is similar to that of a Greek chorus, outlining what will follow, as Gina Matthews (Mala Powers) leads an expedition into that jungle to find her long-lost brother, only to discover the presence of a mad scientist (Patrick O'Moore) who has created a fungus monster (the "unknown terror" of the film's title) that feeds on the local inhabitants. Sir Lancelot's role in the film sums up mainstream Euro representations of the African American experience — on the one hand he portrays the Caribbean as a holiday-maker's paradise, full of sunshine, sea and limitless pleasures; on the other hand it is also a place of great danger, wherein westerners are perpetually vulnerable to attack by unknown forces. Charles Marquis Warren's film also sums up the dangers of colonialism: the unknown terror that depends for its survival on western invaders has been created by another western invader.

Sir Lancelot played yet another calypso singer with a choric role in the prison drama *Brute Force* (1947). This time his songs comment directly on the inmates' plight ("I'm here Mr. Manager, tell a lie/And I'll be right here till I die"). Despite the central character Joe Collins' (Burt Lancaster) brave attempts to break out, and overturn the despotic rule initiated by chief officer Munsey (Hume Cronyn), order is violently restored. Collins dies as a result, and Sir Lancelot comments, "They let him out, he thought he'd finished his time." The last phrase is intentionally ambiguous: Collins has actually "finished his time" on Earth, although he had once hoped to finish his time in prison.

As an African American actor, Sir Lancelot was invariably cast in subordinate roles, and was seldom portrayed as an aggressor. On the contrary, his characters seemed content to support the social status quo. However, his calypsos hinted at a darker world lurking underneath — one in which violence reigned supreme.

Elsa Lanchester

b. October 26, 1902, Lewisham, London, England; d. December 26, 1986, Woodland Hills, Los Angeles, California.

Elizabeth Lanchester Sullivan began her career at ten years old, when she enrolled at dancer Isadora Duncan's Bellevue School in Paris in 1912. Eight years later, she made her debut in music hall as an Egyptian dancer. Lanchester made her film debut in 1927; two years later she married the actor Charles Laughton. MGM offered her a contract in 1932, but her Hollywood film career faltered until she took the title role in James Whale's *The Bride of Frankenstein* (1935). She also plays Mary Shelley, who appears in the opening sequence with Percy Shelley (Douglas Walton) and Lord Byron (Gavin Gordon). The two men are heavily made up and look, talk, and act with an outlandish, caricatured femininity that has no discernible purpose except as camp comedy. The elegance of the interior, the high-pitched humor of the scene, and the relaxed, amused, adult relationship of the three present a model of what might be read as Whale's ideal family: two gay men and a sympathetic but sexually undemanding female; three intelligent, creative beings on an equal footing. It's significant that this sequence, set in the eighteenth century, suggests wholeness, pleasure, and satisfaction.

Before a roaring fire, Mary defends her Frankenstein novel by arguing that it was more than a story about a mad scientist and a monster. It was a philosophical consideration of a man who defied God's natural laws and sovereignty by daring to create life. Mary pricks herself while sewing, drawing blood and becoming squeamish at the sight. Shelley questions why Mary ended her story prematurely: "I do think it a shame, Mary, to end your story quite so suddenly." Mary contends that she has told only part of her story, and then explains that the

Elsa Lanchester in *The Bride of Frankenstein* (1935). Married to Charles Laughton, Lanchester gave a memorable performance as a grotesque monster in James Whale's film. She later played a drunken housekeeper in *The Spiral Staircase* (1945).

monster (Boris Karloff) did not perish, but survived the fire that destroyed the old windmill in the first film. Mary weaves her new tale of horror, providing a lead-in to the film's story. The camera pulls back from the trio and dissolves into the sequel: "Well then, imagine yourselves standing by the wreckage of the mill. The fire is dying down. Soon, the bare skeleton of the building will be dissolved. The gaunt rafters against the sky."

Lanchester's finest screen moment comes later on in the film, when she appears as the bride. When Dr. Pretorius (ERNEST THESIGER) removes the bandages from her eyes, two uncomprehending globes stare back. After the bandage-covered bride has her wrappings removed, indicated by a dissolve, she can be seen in her full, chilling splendor, wearing a flowing white shroud and a wild, frizzled fright wig. Streaked with white from lightning charges, her hair stands straight out behind her; stitches are visible beneath her jaw. Her angular movements are bird-like — her sharp-boned and angular head jerks and darts from one position to another. Unstable on her feet, the now-living woman wobbles and sways back and forth. The monster eagerly rushes down into the laboratory to meet and woo his new bride; she stands back warily. The ugly creature's clumsy and ludicrous overtures are rejected and repelled by the bride — she recoils and emits a piercing, ear-shattering shriek, one of the most famous screams in screen history, when he reaches out to touch her arm. The Monster is hurt and then angry, declaring with a feeling of worthlessness: "She hate me. Like others."

The fact that Lanchester takes both roles emphasizes the duality of human nature, the capacity for both good and evil. This unique character may be the ultimate female role in a horror movie, with her curious Egyptian style, as shown in a close-up when she sees the being responsible for her creation, the Frankenstein monster himself, who would be rejected in the most infernal blind date way possible. Thus, the supposed bride of Frankenstein possesses all the ingredients to be acclaimed as a Siren: mystery, beauty (in her own personal way) and alluring screen presence.

Lanchester only made one other mainstream horror film — *The Spiral Staircase* (1946) — in which she played the housekeeper Mrs. Oates. She comes across as someone devoted to her work and unnerved by the strange goings-on around her. The windows rattle; the door opens apparently of its own accord; and she crashes to the ground, tripped up by the family dog Clayton. On the other hand, she demonstrates a maternal concern for Helen Capel (Dorothy McGuire), who cannot speak — a victim of traumatic events in the past. When Helen dawdles before going to bed, Mrs. Oates tells her that she will catch her death of cold. In another shot, we see the housekeeper drying the pots, vowing to look after Helen as long as she possibly can. Mrs. Oates's concern for the young woman is once again emphasized in a dream sequence, where Helen imagines herself being married to Dr. Parry (KENT SMITH), while the housekeeper and her husband (Rhys Williams) look on with pride. However, Mrs. Oates has one major weakness — a fondness for drink. The murderer Professor Warren (George

Brent) knows this, and allows the housekeeper to steal a bottle of brandy from his cellar. This gives him the perfect pretext to murder Blanche (Rhonda Fleming) and make an attempt on Helen's life. In the film's climax, Helen throws a jug of water in Mrs. Oates's face in a desperate attempt to wake her up from her drunken stupor and raise the alarm. But all to no avail: Mrs. Oates grunts slightly and sleeps once more.

Glenn Langan
b. July 8, 1917, Denver, Colorado; d. January 26, 1991, Camarillo, California.

Thomas Glenn Langan entered films in 1939 with a series of uncredited roles in *The Bill of Rights* (1939) and *Everybody's Hobby* (also 1939). He has a very brief role in *The Return of Dr. X* (1939) as a hospital intern, who comes up behind Dr. Mike Rhodes (Dennis Morgan) and tells him to go to the operating theatre straightaway. In the next decade Langan established a reputation as a character actor: as Eddie Carstairs in Twentieth Century–Fox's *Hangover Square* (1945), he bears a strong visual and aural resemblance to Vincent Price — a tall, commanding presence with a supercilious voice, who treats George Harvey Bone (Laird Cregar) with the utmost contempt. There seems no reason why he shouldn't; for all his abilities as a classical composer and pianist, George cuts no ice with the women, especially Netta Longdon (Linda Darnell). By contrast, Eddie sweeps Netta off her feet with the promise of a singing engagement at his nightclub. In a climactic sequence, Netta informs George of her impending engagement to Eddie; George pushes past her, places his hands around Eddie's neck and forces him to the ground, almost strangling him in the process. We may be shocked by George's reactions, but there is no doubt that Eddie deserves everything he gets.

In *Dragonwyck* (1946), also for Twentieth Century–Fox, Langan co-starred once again with Price — this time as kindly doctor Jeff Turner. In his second film as a director, Joseph L. Mankiewicz establishes a strong visual contrast between the two stars: Price's Nicholas van Ryn the formal, rather remote figure, immaculately dressed in wing-collar and tails, Langan's Turner a more relaxed person, fond of wide-brimmed hats, loose neckties and a long scarf. This contrast serves a thematic purpose too: van Ryn is an old-fashioned patrician landowner, who believes that his tenants should pay him an annual "tribute" (his term) in the form of goods and money, and rejects the idea of individual freedom. In a significant line, he proclaims that he despises "the rights of man — life, liberty, the pursuit of happiness," preferring the "[aristocratic] way of life to which [he has] been born." Described as "a meddling trespasser" by van Ryn, Turner believes in individual freedom and social equality; on several occasions we see him attending meetings called by van Ryn's tenants to protest their way of life. Eventually, Turner's beliefs are vindicated: the tribute system is abolished, and the tenants have the right to farm their own land.

Mankiewicz emphasizes the contrast between the two protagonists in the way they

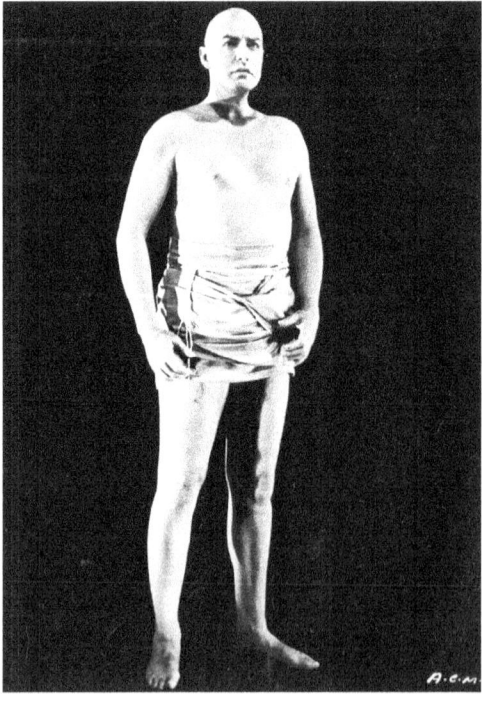

Glenn Langan in *The Amazing Colossal Man* (1957). Tall, well-built character actor, most well-known in this monstrous role, even though earlier on in his career he played smaller, more varied parts.

treat Miranda Wells (Gene Tierney). In spite of his protests of undying love, and eventual marriage to her, van Ryn never allows her to forget her social inferiority; with her modest background on a Connecticut farm, presided over by her father Ephraim (Walter Huston), she will never be fully accepted as a member of polite society. As Miranda observes at one point, she feels as if she is perpetually "visiting a different world." Van Ryn never embraces her, and rejects everything she holds most dear — her family and the love of God. By contrast, Turner treats her as his equal; he sits tenderly by her bed as she experiences the pain of childbirth, taking her hand and promising that she will recover if only she acquires self-belief. As van Ryn comes into her bedroom, Turner exits quickly (he understands that a quarrel between the two men at this point might kill Miranda), but murmurs under his breath that he will always help her. Eventually, van Ryn commits suicide — a hopeless drug-addict, he understands at last that the old patrician way of life is dead and gone in an America committed to individual freedom. Miranda leaves the van Ryn house shrouded in black; Turner bids goodbye to her, but not without indicating that he will visit her family home in Connecticut within the week. We feel that the two of them are kindred spirits who will most likely marry in the future.

Langan's best-known role in a horror film was that of the eponymous *Amazing Colossal Man* (1957), Bert I. Gordon's cult hit. He plays Lt. Col. Glenn Manning, a loyal member of the American armed forces who participates in a plutonium bomb experiment. Although devoted to his job, he remains concerned for his fellow beings; when a plane crashes in the restricted area, he rushes out to the pilot's aid, with little concern for his own safety. The bomb goes off, and Manning is horribly disfigured as a result. As a result of his exposure to radiation, his cells are affected and he begins to grow uncontrollably, reaching fifty feet tall.

Throughout much of the film, Langan appears with a shaven head and sweat-soaked brow, dressed in a loincloth that emphasizes his regression to a primitive state of existence. In one sequence, he looks up to the heavens and moans, "What sin can a man commit in as single lifetime to bring this upon himself?" He looks back on his past life, where he served with distinction during the Korean War, and found an attractive fiancée — Carol Forrest (Cathy Downs). Now all his prospects have been destroyed; the American government consider him a security risk, even though he is nothing more than an innocent victim of the arms race in the Cold War era, in which millions of dollars were spent on nuclear weapons with little concern for the human cost involved. Manning becomes increasingly bitter as the film unfolds; he sits in a corner and observes: "They call this living!" As with most monster movies (*King Kong* being the best example), Manning remains largely passive until provoked; when the army shoot at him, he turns violent and causes mayhem in the streets of Las Vegas. Eventually he falls down a ravine — apparently to his death.

Langan appears briefly in *The War of the Colossal Beast* (1958), the sequel to *The Amazing Colossal Man* with Gordon directing once again. We see a photograph of Manning as he once was before the accident happened — a handsome, loyal member of the armed forces. This is shown to the colossal man (now played by Dean Parkin rather than Langan) in a vain attempt to stimulate his conscious memory and thereby help him to rejoin the civilized world. The experiment proves a costly failure: the colossal man remains a beast, who can only communicate in a series of guttural grunts.

Rosemary La Planche
b. October 11, 1923, Los Angeles, California; d. May 6, 1979, Glendale, California.

Rosemary La Planche began her career in beauty contests, winning the Miss California title in 1940 and 1941 and the Miss America crown in 1941. Her sister Louise La Planche (born two years earlier) was also an actress, being signed to a four-year contract with Paramount. Rosemary made her debut in uncredited roles in Deanna Durbin's *One Hundred Men and a Girl* (1937) and *Mad About Music* (1938), and remained a bit-part player throughout the early 1940s.

Her first major role was that of Maria Hart in Producers' Releasing Corporation's (PRC) *Strangler of the Swamp* (1946). Director Frank Wisbar exploits her looks through close-ups of her long tresses, wide eyes and small mouth; she looks every inch the innocent in a brutal environment cursed by a ghostly presence (Nolan Leary) who seems bent on destroying all those who wrongfully condemned him to die several years previously. Unlike her grandfather Joseph (Frank Conlan), Maria refuses to be cowed by the ghost; she resolutely continues her task of ferrying people across the swamp, despite the potential dangers involved. Nor is she frightened of living alone, despite repeated warnings issued by Christian Sanders (Robert Barrat) and his son Christian, Jr. (Blake Edwards). As with many films of the post–1945 era, *Strangler of the Swamp* focuses on the social construction of gender: the majority of the male characters think that running the ferry is "no job for a woman"; she should confine herself to finding a suitable marriage partner. Maria herself actively prefers the idea of living alone; having never had a proper home before, she enjoys the experience of creating one of her own. Nonetheless, she falls passionately in love with Christian — so much so that when the ghost attacks him, it is Maria who comes to the rescue. Grimly muttering, "He [the ghost] shall *not* escape," under her breath, she offers herself as a sacrifice. ("I gave myself willingly into your hands. Take me.") Her decisiveness contrasts with Christian's fundamentally passive nature — apart from asking her to be his wife, he does little else throughout the film. Director Wisbar seems slightly uncomfortable with Maria's strength of character; hence he has her wear a top that provocatively reveals one of her bare shoulders. The message is clear — if male members don't like the idea of her assuming control of the situation, they have the chance to ogle her good looks. Nonetheless, Maria refuses to be constrained in this way; she orders the ghost to "give up the fight. Make peace with Him [God]! Make peace with him!" Amazingly, the ghost responds; he sinks down into the swamp, never to return, leaving Maria free to marry Christian, exclaiming, "He's gone, Chris! He's gone for ever," as she embraces him. Christian's name seems particularly apt here: if women and men devote themselves to God's cause, they can scare evil away. In a radical subversion of existing gender preconceptions, La Planche shows that it is permissible for a woman to dominate a man, while reaffirming the strength of the Christian religion.

Her next film for PRC, *Devil Bat's Daughter* (also 1946), reunited her with Wisbar in a *Gaslight*-like tale of Nina MacCarron, a young woman being convinced that she has a compulsion to kill by an evil psychiatrist Clifton Morris (Michael Hale). In the film's opening sequence, we understand that she is a basically passive person as she lies on a bed in a state of semi-consciousness. She wakes up, her lip trembling, her eyes staring wildly around the room, jumps up and runs into the doctor's surgery, claiming that she has seen a vampire bat, the product of a mind tormented by the memory of her late father, a scientist who experimented with such things.

In Morris's view, Nina is something of a deviant; not only does she come from a dysfunctional family (her mother died young, the victim of one of her father's vampiric experi-

Rosemary La Planche publicity still (1944). A former beauty queen, La Planche's career briefly flourished in the mid–1940s as she played pretty young women often at risk in a hostile world.

ments, while her father was more interested in his work than in caring for his daughter), but she threatens the security of Morris's own family. Hence the psychiatrist assumes sole responsibility for Nina's care, in the belief that he alone can cure her. On several occasions we hear him spouting psychobabble about Nina's "inherited criminal tendencies," and the need to eliminate them through a combination of rest, relaxation and regular medical treatments. In truth, Morris wants to exploit Nina's past for his own ends; by convincing her that she has been haunted by her father's memory, he can use her to kill off his wife Ellen Masters Morris (Molly Lamont) and subsequently elope with his secretary Myra Arnold (Monica Mars).

In this kind of environment, where she remains unloved, Nina's behavior goes from bad to worse. As a result of one of Morris's "treatments," she kills off her pet dog Joe — and is locked in her room as a result. She speaks in a hoarse, staccato whisper, as if not wanting anyone to hear what she says. Relief is at hand, as Morris's stepson Ted Masters (John James) returns home on leave and falls in love with her. She is treated sympathetically for the first time; when she buries her face in a pillow, unable to talk any more about her father's memory, Ted puts a comforting arm around her. He discovers his stepfather's true motives and calls the police: Morris is eventually shot to death as he tries to make his escape. Ted returns triumphantly to the county jail (where Nina has been imprisoned for Ellen Masters' murder) and secures Nina's release. The two of them embrace in the film's final frame, with Ted admitting that the poor girl had been "cursed by the brand of the vampire," and hence become vulnerable to exploitation by so-called medical professionals such as his stepfather.

Devil Bat's Daughter makes some trenchant points about the potential dangers of psychiatric treatment — especially when wrongfully applied. La Planche copes well with a difficult role; her eyework is especially good when she experiences her regular mental breakdowns, tormented by the memory of her father's experiments.

George Burr Macannan

b. November 30, 1887, Texas;
d. November 12, 1970, Los Angeles, California.

Stocky character actor who frequently played evil sidekicks or other miscreants in horror films of the 1930s and 1940s. In *White Zombie* (1932), he is the zombie Von Gelder, a short, balding figure staring vacantly into the distance as he walks out of the frame without speaking. Like the female victims of John Barrymore in *Svengali* (1931), Von Gelder is totally under the control of his master, the ominously named "Murder" Legendre (Bela Lugosi). The character does not speak, but shuffles around with his "empty, staring eyes." In another sequence, Van Gelder appears stripped to the waist, trying to attack the butler Silver (Brandon Hurst). The butler screams and

George Burr MacAnnan (right) in *White Zombie* (1932). MacAnnan cropped up sporadically in horror films of the 1930s and 1940s, usually playing psychotic characters or heavies.

faints—and eventually meets a sticky end rather like Clarence in Shakespeare's *Richard III*, as he is drowned in a vat of water. Van Gelder himself seems indestructible—even at the end of the film he seems impervious to any shots that might be fired at him. However, once "Murder" Legendre has been stabbed to death, Van Gelder has no means of self-determination as he throws himself off a cliff to his death. Macannan's performance emphasizes the extent to which the character is at the beck and call of a white voodoo master.

In Victor Halperin's *Supernatural* (1933), Macannan plays Max Schmitt, a glass-blower who is so wrapped up in his work, and his customers, that he fails to notice Roma Courtney (Carole Lombard)—who has been possessed by the ghost of convicted killer Ruth Rogen (Vivienne Osborne)—stealing the key to Ruth's apartment out of a pigeon-hole close to the door of Schmitt's shop. In a film about the importance of understanding, as well as seeing, Schmitt's indifference allows Roma/Rogen to pursue her path of crime as she attempts to strangle ex-lover Paul Bavian (Allan Dinehart). Macannan's shop owner comes across as well-meaning but ineffectual: when he re-enters the shop looking for Ruth, and sees Roma instead, he threatens to call the police. Later on, he is working in his shop on a glass model of a ship when Roma's boyfriend Grant Wilson (Randolph Scott) and the scientist Dr. Carl Houston (H. B. Warner) come in looking for Ruth. Houston suddenly realizes that she has been possessed by Rona; he sinks into a chair, and Schmitt runs to look after him. As he does so, the glass ship falls to the ground and smashes into smithereens—a neat visual metaphor of a world in turmoil. However, Schmitt still does not perceive the truth of the situation, as he worries more about his broken ship rather than the doctor's welfare.

In *The Black Room* (1935), Macannan has an uncredited role as one of Baron Gregor de Berghman's (Boris Karloff) retinue of servants. He is shown in various sequences—bricking up the black room (which Gregor later uses as a convenient space to dispose of his many murder victims); running around Gregor's house in a desperate attempt to repel the marauding citizens—who are looking to kill Gregor; helping Gregor prepare for his abortive wedding to Thea Hassel (Marian Marsh) by holding up a mirror so that Gregor can admire his new wig; and running after the wild dog Thor in a vain attempt to catch him. Macannan's appearance belies his social position; he lacks both the demeanor and the education to be an effective servant. However, it is clear that Gregor has no interest in his retinue—so long as they carry out his wishes to the letter, then he will employ anyone, regardless of their background.

Eight years later, Macannan had another uncredited role as Gottfried, one of the two heavies working for Professor Moriarty (LIONEL ATWILL) in *Sherlock Holmes and the Voice of Terror*. With his long coat and trilby hat, Gottfried cuts a sinister presence; at one point the back of his head faces directly to camera as he encircles Sherlock Holmes (Basil Rathbone), preventing the great detective from escaping. For most of the time, Gottfried is photographed in shadow—emphasizing his sinister nature. He grasps Holmes' left arm and pushes him into Moriarty's presence. Later on he ensures that Holmes is tied down securely on an operating table, so that Moriarty can begin his experiment to deprive Holmes of all his blood, drip by drip. However, Gottfried's efforts prove in vain, as Watson (Nigel Bruce) and Lestrade (Dennis Hoey) come to Holmes's rescue just in the nick of time; Gottfried tries to escape, but is eventually shot in the back.

Miles Mander

b. May 14, 1888, Wolverhampton, Staffordshire, England;
d. February 8, 1946, Hollywood, California.

Lionel Henry Mander served as a captain in the Royal Army Service Corps in World War I, before turning to sheep farming in New Zealand. He began his film career in British films such as *The First Born* (1928), based on his own play, and *The Private Life of Henry VIII* (1933) before moving to Hollywood in 1935. Mander subsequently carved out a career as a versatile supporting actor, whose major films

Miles Mander (second from right) in *The Brighton Strangler* (1945). British-born Mander made a habit of playing police inspectors and other figures of authority, even though he occasionally played villains (as in the Sherlock Holmes series for Universal).

included *Wuthering Heights* (1939), in which he played Mr. Lockwood, *That Hamilton Woman* (aka *Lady Hamilton*) (1941) and *To Be or Not to Be* (1942).

Mander regularly appeared in horror films in the late 1930s and 1940s; his diminutive presence and finicky, almost bird-like gestures rendered him ideal for portraying characters under stress. As the ineffectual King Henry VI in Universal's *Tower of London* (1939) he speaks in a series of staccato phrases, his left hand shaking all the while as if he has arthritis. With a paper crown on his head, he is the very epitome of a puppet monarch, ripe for exploitation by schemers such as the Duke of Gloucester (Basil Rathbone). As Gloucester outlines his plans for the future of the kingdom, Henry shifts from foot to foot, and whimpers, "My victory! My people!" with scarcely a shred of conviction in his voice. In a later sequence King Henry is shown in the midst of battle, waving his sword around ineffectually, with the visor of his helmet perpetually falling down to obscure his vision. No one attacks him, and he does not pursue anyone; he remains a peripheral figure in the overall scheme of things. He meets a predictable end, as he is seen praying to God in a small ante-room, murmuring, "O Lord, be with me." As he speaks, one of Gloucester's henchmen murders him. As someone who merely plays at being a king, without the least knowledge of the responsibilities that go with the role, he cannot expect divine assistance.

Mander had a small role a year later as Deacon Arnold Foster in Universal's adaptation of Hawthorne's novel *The House of the Seven Gables*. A member of the Abolitionist committee on his local village, Foster makes a grave error by lending some of the committee's money to Jaffray Pyncheon (GEORGE SANDERS) in the hope of obtaining quick riches. Thereafter, he makes several visits to Jaffray's house in the hope of recovering it; like Uriah Heep in *David Copperfield*, he is full of obsequious gestures and flattering words, but never manages to achieve his ends. Foster becomes increasingly desperate, as he fears that the committee will discover his crime; in his final visit to Jaffray's house he screams in terror, only to be met with another stern look and a reproving word. Foster leaves the room and shortly afterwards we hear a shot ringing out, as he commits suicide. Jaffray's brother Clifford (Vincent Price) reacts by calling Jaffray a "murderer," and thereby turns the tables on Jaffray. Earlier on in the film Jaffray had named and shamed his brother in precisely the same way, leading to Clifford's imprisonment.

As Pleydel, the ineffective photographer in Arthur Lubin's remake of *The Phantom of the Opera* (1943), Mander has little time to listen to Erique Claudin (CLAUDE RAINS). Claudin refuses to leave the studio, so Pleydel turns towards him and orders him out in a petulant tone. Claudin is just about to do so when he hears his music being played in the next room, and realizes that Pleydel is trying to steal it from him. He returns to Pleydel's studio, his face set menacingly, his hands shaking with suppressed intensity. He approaches the publisher and strangles him to death, throwing him to the ground like a rag doll when he has finished.

However, Mander could play other types of roles with equal finesse. In Columbia's *Return of the Vampire* (1944), he plays Sir Frederick Fleet, chief commissioner at Scotland Yard. He considers himself thoroughly proficient at his job, emphasizing any points he wants to make by taking his glasses off and pointing them in the direction of his interlocutor. Fleet firmly believes there are no such things as vampires or werewolves; even when his superior officers have been half-scared to death after having pursued wolf-man Andreas Obry (Matt Willis), Fleet snorts in disbelief. He firmly believes that the only way to catch criminals is through old-fashioned methods such as gathering evidence and drawing the right conclusions. Despite the protests of Lady Jane Ainsley (Frieda Inescort)—who does believe in vampires—Fleet insists that the investigation will be done his way—"or none at all!" Despite Fleet's pretensions to authority, the vampire Armand Tesla (Bela Lugosi) is finally disposed of by Andreas, who understands that "goodness is the strongest face in the world" and undergoes a change of heart. No longer a wolf-man, he turns on Armand and strangles him to death, accusing him as he does so of being deceitful. Ever mindful of his reputation, Fleet claims responsibility for bringing Armand to justice, but resolutely refuses to believe in vampires. He turns towards the camera and asks the audience directly, as if seeking support for his claims: "Do you [believe in vampires]?"

In *The Brighton Strangler* (1945), Mander plays another police officer—Chief Inspector W. R. Allison. Instead of using his glasses, he emphasizes any important points he makes with an imperious wave of his pipe. Although pleasant enough when encountering Reginald Parker (John Loder), it is clear that the inspector suspects him of being the eponymous Brighton Strangler: Allison's eyes stare directly into Parker's face, as if searching for any signs of the strangler's guilt. However, the inspector takes Parker at face value (despite Parker's abortive attempts to strangle him in the local movie theatre) and invites him home for dinner. There we discover that the inspector's true nature is not quite as respectable as we had first assumed, as he shows Parker a collection of weapons—souvenirs of the inspector's previous cases. They include guns, swords, and cords. As he shows them off, the inspector plays Beethoven on the gramophone at full volume, suggesting that he likes an accompaniment to his bizarre pastime. However, Parker shows no interest in the collection; he encircles the inspector like a lion eyeing its prey, and then strikes. Director Max Nosseck cuts to a close-up of the inspector's petrified face, the whites of his eyes showing, as he vainly tries to escape. Parker grabs him by the scruff of the neck and strangles him to death. Although the inspector is an innocent victim, we feel that in some way he has received his just desserts: anyone who glorifies violence by collecting murder weapons somehow deserves a violent end.

In the Sherlock Holmes film *The Pearl of Death* (1944), Mander displays considerable technical virtuosity as the hissable villain Giles Conover, delivering his lines with supreme self-confidence in the belief that no one will be able to penetrate his disguises and thereby prevent him from stealing the famous Borgia Pearl from London's Royal Regent Museum. According to Holmes (Basil Rathbone), Conover is so "in love with cruelty" that he will stop at nothing to achieve his ends—even if it means placing personal gain above the interests of his country. This observation is clearly designed to encourage wartime audiences on both sides of the Atlantic to fight together against the twin threats of Nazism and fascism. However, as a supremely self-interested person, Conover responds to Holmes's accusations with a contemptuous sneer. According to the restrictions placed on filmmakers by the Hays Office, Conover has to meet a sticky end—even though it seems somewhat contrived. In the light of

Mander's performance, it seems unlikely that he should run the risk of being attacked by his own henchman, the self-styled Hoxton Creeper (RONDO HATTON). However, this is what happens, as Holmes convinces the Creeper that Conover needs to be destroyed in order to save the world from dictatorship. The Creeper duly responds by breaking Conover's neck.

David Manners

b. April 30, 1901, Halifax, Nova Scotia, Canada; d. December 23, 1998, Santa Barbara, California.

Born Rauff de Ryther Daun Acklom, Manners first performed on stage as Fernando in *The Tempest*. Joining the British-born Eva La Gallienne's Civil Repertory Company, he forged enduring friendships with the legendary teacher and later with Helen Hayes when both appeared in the play *Dancing Mothers*. Manners attracted director James Whale's attention, and was duly cast in *Journey's End* (1930).

Originally groomed as a leading man, but mostly cast as a character actor, Manners plays Harker, the romantic love-interest in Tod Browning's *Dracula* (1931). Unable to contemplate the existence of a vampire, he dismisses his girlfriend Mina's (Helen Chandler) comments as the stuff of dreams. If only she could be spirited away from Dracula's (Bela Lugosi) presence, then her health might be miraculously restored. Manners speaks in a hectoring tone, either crossing the frame or walking diagonally between the front and the rear of the frame, in the mistaken belief that Dracula can be exterminated through violent means. His frustration is palpable, as he thrusts his hands into his jacket pocket or hurls a paper to the ground. Try as he might, he can never assume a dominant position in Mina's (Helen Chandler) life. Director Browning suggests this in a sequence where Harker sits with his back to the camera directly opposite Mina. The action cuts to a point-of-view shot where we look from Harker's perspective straight into Mina's eyes. She suddenly falls out of the frame and screams, as she understands just how powerful she has become; she could easily destroy Harker if she should so wish. Although Harker leans over and endeavors to console her, it's clear that he has no understanding of her state of mind.

David Manners cinema star postcard (1935). Canadian-born Manners' career flourished briefly in the 1930s as one of Universal's leading men. He did not have to do much other than to sustain his sense of debonair gentility.

In Karl Freund's *The Mummy* (1932), Manners plays a similar role as Frank Whemple, who falls in love with Helen Grosvenor (Zita Johann), but cannot understand that she is a reincarnation of an ancient Egyptian goddess and hence subject to Ardath Bey's (Boris Karloff) malign influence. Perpetually in search of romantic love, Frank climbs on top of Helen in search of a kiss; later he is just about to describe her as "the most wonderful girl in the world" when Dr. Muller (EDWARD VAN SLOAN) cuts him short. Despite all evidence to the contrary, Frank believes that "everything is going to be all right." Although restored to Helen at the end, it is only as a result of divine intervention: the goddess Isis casts a spell over Ardath and reduces him to dust. Frank embraces Helen, but Muller observes that she is still in the world of Ancient Egypt — only love can transcend the gap between past and present and bring her back again. As the film ends, we are left uncertain as to whether the young man has succeeded or not — given his past record as an ineffectual bumbler, we remain very doubtful.

Manners has a similar role as the romantic lead in Edgar G. Ulmer's *The Black Cat* (1934) as Peter Alison, a writer of mystery novels who tries to assume an authoritative pose by clasping his hands behind his back or placing his thumbs in his waistcoat pockets. In truth, this makes him look rather absurd, particularly when standing opposite the evil priest Hjalmar Poelzig (Boris Karloff) and Poelzig's deadly rival Dr. Vitus Wendergast (Bela Lugosi). Alison tries to do the right thing by accepting Poelzig's offer to stay the night, but it is clear that he is out of his depth both physically and mentally. To describe Poelzig's house as "a very tricky house" reveals a complete lack of understanding of the priest's motives. Tiring of the incessant rivalry between Poelzig and Wendergast, Alison resolves to leave the house; he walks towards the front door in a purposeful manner, while ordering his wife Joan (Jacqueline Wells) to accompany him. The outcome is inevitable: Alison is knocked to the ground by Wendergast's servant Thamal (HARRY CORDING) and thrown into a dungeon. This inevitably prompts us to reflect on his capabilities — although capable of writing fictional mysteries, he is unable to deal with the "far-fetched" events that happen to him in real life. Eventually he and his wife escape unharmed from Poelzig's house, as Wendergast skins Poelzig alive, but he perishes in an explosion.

In *The Mystery of Edwin Drood* (1935), Manners plays Drood as a good-natured man about town, lying languidly on a sofa and talking about Rosa Bud (Heather Angel). Although envying his cousin John Jasper's (CLAUDE RAINS) settled life as a choirmaster, it is also clear that Drood enjoys the experience of love — something that makes Jasper more and more jealous of him. With his statuesque walk, short fair hair and impeccable dress sense, Drood looks the epitome of an English gentleman. His behavior is not always so impeccable: when faced with a potential rival for Rosa's love, the equally tall and debonair Neville Landless (Douglass Montgomery), Drood becomes violent, both physically and verbally. He taunts Landless about his skin color (having been born and brought up in a mixed-race family, Landless is much darker than Drood), and flicks his fingers towards him in a gesture of utter contempt. Such reactions not only diminish him in our eyes (as someone with an unjustified belief in white superiority), but render him liable to exploitation by his cousin. Using the feud between Drood and Landless as a pretext, Jasper murders Drood in cold blood and tries to pin responsibility for the deed on Landless.

Manners occasionally took advantage of more active roles. In the horror-mystery *The Death Kiss* (1932), he plays screenwriter Franklyn Drew, who starts off as a romantic hero but eventually acquires self-reliance as an amateur detective always remaining one step ahead of the police. He forms a comic double-act with Officer Gulliver (Vince Barnett), who listens avidly to Franklyn's deductions and responds, "That's just what I was thinking!" Franklyn's air of self-confidence is suggested through his gait; he walks nonchalantly around the film-set, his hands in his pockets, his hat cocked at a rakish angle. Director Edwin L. Marin obviously has faith in Manners' abilities; on several occasions the actor is shown in close-up, his face set in a confident smile as he makes various deductions and follows the various leads to solve the murder-case.

Wanda McKay
b. June 22, 1915, Portland, Oregon;
d. April 11, 1996, Rancho Mirage, California.

Born Dorothy Quackenbush, Wanda McKay graduated from Fort Worth High School, Texas, and moved to New York City to become a model. She graced the covers of many magazines, and was selected as the girl to advertise Chesterfield cigarettes. Her face graced many a billboard across the United States. She won the "Miss America Aviation" title in Birmingham, Alabama, which led to her being hired as a cabin attendant for Trans-World Airlines (TWA), and later on to be given a contract with Paramount Pictures.

McKay's career began with several uncredited roles in films such as Paramount's *The Mad Doctor* (1941), where she plays a girl at a charity bazaar that takes over the running of the wheel of fortune stall from Linda Boothe (ELLEN DREW). McKay doesn't have to do much other than exclaim "What fun!" and jump up and down in joy as she reads her fortune that tells her she will take an airplane journey with her sweetheart. The girl's happiness throws Linda's suicidal tendencies into sharper focus; having tried to kill herself earlier on by throwing herself off the top of a New York skyscraper, Linda wants to leave the stall for good and run back home.

McKay established her reputation in low-budget films of the 1940s made by so-called "Poverty Row" studios such as Monogram. In *One Thrilling Night* (1942), she plays Millie Jason, newly wed wife of Horace (John Beal). Demurely dressed in long coat and beret, she looks the epitome of respectability as she prepares to spend her honeymoon night in a New York hotel. Millie believes that certain rituals have to be observed; her husband should carry her over the threshold, and she should be given the privacy to change into her wedding nightdress. However, the couple's best-laid plans are thrown into disarray, as they find themselves mixed up with gangsters, stolen money and missing bodies. Millie's initial reaction is one of horror, as her husband is successively locked in a trunk, arrested by the police and held up at gunpoint. As the plot develops, however, so Millie assumes a more active role; the only way to dispose of the gangsters is to catch them. She disarms one of them and holds him at gunpoint; and hits another over the head with a bottle. As he sinks to the ground, she climbs on top of him and beats him with her fists. Eventually, peace is restored, and she looks forward to spending the rest of the night alone with her husband. However, her hopes are dashed by the sound of the alarm; she turns towards the camera and pouts. McKay proves herself an adept comedy performer in this lighthearted romp, which William Beaudine directs with tongue firmly planted in his directorial cheek.

That same year, she took on a more serious role as Judy Malvern in *Bowery at Midnight*. Al-

Wanda McKay publicity still (1940). Publicized in her early career as a siren, McKay later graduated to leading roles in low-budget science fiction films of the 1950s.

though coming from a privileged background, she has decided to spend her life working in a soup kitchen run by Professor Frederick Brenner (Bela Lugosi). She relishes her work, which includes serving the inmates with bowls of soup and lovingly tending those who have suffered injuries. When hoodlum Frankie Mills (Tom Neal) comes into the dispensary with a cut wrist, Judy bandages it up and smiles winningly at him. As the action unfolds, she discovers that the soup kitchen acts as a front for a gang of thieves (led by the Professor) who commit a string of jewel robberies and murders. Although her aspirations have been shattered, she resolves to bring him to justice: in one scene she is shown riffling through the professor's papers, while later on she takes a considerable risk by walking unaccompanied into a darkened cellar. The professor catches her in the act and promises to bury her alive; but Judy escapes and runs upstairs to fetch the police. As in *One Thrilling Night*, McKay's character refuses to be a passive victim of a dominant male presence. She is rewarded in the final frame as her boyfriend Richard Dennison (JOHN ARCHER) embraces her.

In *The Black Raven* (1943), she plays Lee Winfield, another demure young woman at the center of a love-triangle involving boyfriend Allen Bentley (Bob Randall) and father Tim (Robert Middlemass). Initially it seems as if she is doomed to a life of disappointment, as her father yanks her away from Allen and locks her up in her hotel bedroom. However, Tim is murdered soon afterwards; not surprisingly, Allen is identified as the chief suspect. With the help of kindly hotel owner Amos Bradford (GEORGE ZUCCO), Lee contrives Allen's escape, as the real murderer's identity is subsequently discovered. In *The Monster Maker* (1944), McKay plays a similar role as Patricia Lawrence, who is devoted to her father, concert pianist Anthony (Ralph Morgan). Evil scientist Igor Markoff (J. CARROL NAISH) develops an unnatural attraction for Patricia, in the belief that she is the spitting image of his late wife, and resolves to marry her. Patricia does not reciprocate his affections, so Markoff tries to persuade her by kidnapping her father and turning him into a vegetable. Inevitably, his evil plans go awry; with the help of her boyfriend Bob Blake (Terry Frost), Patricia foils him and restores her father back to health once more. Dressed in a succession of sensible two-piece suits, her hair in ringlets, McKay looks the epitome of the girl next door; the kind of woman who believes in the importance of family as the foundation of a stable society and who will fight tooth and nail to preserve it.

In *Voodoo Man* (1944), McKay's Betty Benton comes across as a practical, no-nonsense person — dressed once again in a sensible white two-piece suit — who is genuinely concerned about the activities of mysterious doctor Richard Marlowe (Bela Lugosi). However, she becomes a victim of her own inquisitiveness, as she drives up to a mysterious garage for gas, and is captured as a result by Marlowe's sidekicks Toby (JOHN CARRADINE) and Nicholas (GEORGE ZUCCO). Betty is subsequently transformed into a zombie; in her white dress and blonde hair, she looks extremely attractive — so attractive, in fact, that Toby regularly talks to her, even though she is unable to respond. At one point, Betty escapes and returns to her family house, but cannot respond to any outside stimuli, despite her mother's (Betty Currier's) best intentions. Nicholas summons her back to the Marlowe residence by means of a voodoo ritual; as she hears it, she gets up and walks along a lonely strip of marshland, apparently hypnotized by the sound of the voodoo drums. Betty is only released from her trance once Marlowe has been shot dead; she suddenly wakes up, shakes her head, and falls gratefully into Ralph's arms. William Beaudine's film portrays its leading female actor as someone entirely subservient to men: even when she emerges from her trance, Betty immediately looks around for her fiancé.

Dick Miller

b. December 25, 1928, The Bronx, New York.

Richard Miller served in the U.S. Navy for a few years and then embarked on a career as a middleweight boxer. He settled in Los Angeles in the mid–1950s, where he was noticed by producer/director Roger Corman, who cast him in many of his low-budget films, often as unlikable characters, or people with peculiar fetishes. This was perhaps inevitable: Miller was too short to be a romantic lead (only just over 5 feet (152 cm.) tall) and his pointed nose and sharp mouth rendered him ideal for character parts. In the cameo role of Sergeant Neal in *It Conquered the World* (1956), he forms a comic double-act with Private Ortiz (JONATHAN HAZE) reminiscent of Abbott and Costello, with Neal as the authority-figure vainly trying to impose his authority. While preserving a façade of respectability, Neal doesn't have much clue about what he is doing; this is shown by the way he brandishes a loaded rifle in front of his unfortunate partner. When called into active service to save the world from the alien, Neal mutters grimly: "We're on a battlefield," and re-

Dick Miller in *A Bucket of Blood* (1959). One of Roger Corman's most loyal acolytes, Miller had his best role in this film as a crazed artist who turns out to be a killer.

treats to a safe distance, leaving his fellow soldiers to do the job for him.

Miller has a small role as the ill-fated Joe Piper, the vacuum cleaner salesperson in *Not of this Earth* (1957). He comes to Paul Johnson's (PAUL BIRCH) front door full of confidence, his collar undone, thin black tie askew, and begins his patter. Despite Johnson's repeated attempts to send him away, Piper continues his spiel, chewing his gum more and more intensely in an attempt to persuade his customer. Eventually his persistence is rewarded, as Johnson invites him down to the cellar. Piper sets up his vacuum and is just about to demonstrate its unique virtues when Johnson advances on him and pushes him into a machine that reduces him to dust. In the same year Miller played a leper in *The Undead*: dressed in a long gown with wavy hair, he pleads to the devil Quintus Ratcliff (Val Dufour) to be cured of his sickness. He speaks in plaintive tones, taking care to enunciate each word in the phrase: "they call me leper and unclean, and banish me to forest and swamp!" Quintus smiles at him and responds in magisterial tones, "Sign, leper, and be clean!" The leper duly obliges, and by doing so sacrifices his freedom of self-determination. As in *Not of this Earth*, Miller's main function in *The Undead* is to be one of the evil genius' victims.

Miller has a starring role in the space drama *War of the Satellites* (1958) as Dave Barclay, a dogged member of Dr. Pol van Ponder's (Richard Devon's) space crew who realizes that his boss has been possessed by aliens. He shows a dogged persistence as he convinces his fellow passengers (including scientist Sybil Carrington (SUSAN CABOT)) that the only way to guarantee the craft's survival is to destroy van Ponder. Although dwarfed by van Ponder in the climactic struggle, Barclay shows sufficient presence of mind to duck underneath the punches and eventually destroy the captain. In the final sequence he returns home to Earth as the pilot of the craft, holding Sybil's hand. The experience has proved beneficial for him both professionally and romantically.

Miller has another starring role in the black comedy *A Bucket of Blood* (1959) as Walter Paisley, a cringing bus boy in a local diner who by his own admission is "an obscure hobo." Although enamored of the beatnik culture that exists all around him, led by poet/raconteur Maxwell H. Brock (Julian Burton), Paisley can never be a part of it; with his hunched shoulders and nervous manner, he resembles a frightened rabbit. Once in his lonely one-room apartment, in a block presided over by Mrs. Swickert (Myrtle Damerel), Paisley vents his frustrations on a lump of modeling clay, cursing his inability to assert himself in public. However things soon change for him, as he accidentally kills Mrs. Swickert's cat, and coats it in modeling clay, passing it off as a work of art. His reputation instantly improved amongst the beatniks: diner-owner Leonard de Santis (ANTONY CARBONE) commissions more models, and Paisley responds by killing other people, including local police-officer Lou Raby (Bert Convy) and good-time girl Alice (Judy Bamber), and coating them once again in clay. As he works, Paisley murmurs "It's crazy, it's crazy, I didn't know you had it in you!"—in the belief, perhaps, that his new-found recognition as an artist will lead to a change of character. However, Paisley's hopes prove as false as the models he pretends to create; he asks local girl Judy (Barboura Morris) to marry him, and when she turns him down, he pursues her round the streets in a vain attempt to kill her and coat her in clay. When this fails, Paisley realizes the futility of his life, and hangs himself in his own apartment. Miller's eyework is quite outstanding — especially at the end when his eyes bulge with fear, as he understands how his life as a pseudo-artist has destroyed him. The film offers some penetrating comments on the basic superficiality of beatnik culture — despite its pseudo-radical discourse, railing against the perceived inequalities of American society, it is as false as the models that Paisley creates.

In *Little Shop of Horrors* (1960), he appears as Burson Fouch, an apparently ordinary customer in sports jacket and open necked shirt making purchases at Gravis Mushnik's (MEL WELLES) flower shop, He recommends, quite logically, that Mushnik's trade might improve if a star attraction can be introduced; Welles' employee Seymour Krelboin (JONATHAN HAZE) obliges by bringing in the man-easting plant Audrey 2. However, Fouch has one particular peculiarity; rather than putting his flowers in water, he nonchalantly eats them one by one, as if it was the most normal thing in the world. Such occurrences are commonplace in a film where distinctions between "normal" and 'abnormal' behavior are gleefully subverted, as director Roger Corman allows his characters to indulge themselves — sometimes as a means of self-exploration (as in Seymour's case), and sometimes out of sheer fun (as in Fouch's case).

Clayton Moore as the Lone Ranger. Before he made his name with this role, Moore had regular work as a villainous sidekick in Republic's serials of the 1940s.

Clayton Moore

b. *September 14, 1914 [possibly 1908], Chicago, Illinois; d. December 28, 1999, Los Angeles, California.*

Born Jack Carlton Moore, Clayton Moore was a handsome leading man, best known for his television role as the Lone Ranger, but who starred in several B horror films and fantasy serials during the early 1940s. He began life as a circus acrobat, but eventually pursued a career as a male model, making his Hollywood debut in 1938. Four years later, he played Dick Martin, the clean-cut FBI agent in *Black Dragons*. With his snap-brimmed hat and long overcoat, he looks the very model of efficiency — that is, until he falls in love with Alice Saunders (Joan Barclay). Martin's fresh-faced looks are contrasted with the haggard countenance of the mad scientist Dr. Melcher (Bela Lugosi), who has been employed by the Nazis to concoct a dastardly scheme with the Japanese, by which six Japanese agents impersonate prominent Americans and cause mayhem to American industrial plants. Eventually Martin works out Melcher's plan and lays a trap for him, pausing only to embrace Alice and observe in a jocular tone that "I don't know what this is all about, but I like it." Martin proves himself a good American by standing up to the doctor and killing him "in the interests of this country." Director William Nigh emphasizes the point by dissolving to a shot of the Stars and Stripes as the film ends.

In the same year, Moore had another heroic role as Dr. Larry Grayson in the adventure/fantasy serial *Perils of Nyoka* (aka *Nyoka and the Lost Secrets of Hippocrates*) (1942). Although ostensibly set in the hills of Libya, William Witney's plot has strong links to the western; the characters gallop across the dusty landscape on horseback shooting one another with pistols. Instead of Native Americans, the enemies here are the Arabs, who all wear flowing white robes and headdresses (thus disguising the fact that most of them are played by Anglo actors). They prove worthy opponents for Grayson, the intrepid Nyoka (Kay Aldridge) and their followers, as both sides try to find the golden tablets of Hippocrates. When the characters are not shooting at one another, they indulge in frequent sword-fights: *Perils of Nyoka* shamelessly alludes to classic swashbucklers such as *The Adventures of Robin Hood* (1938) in the way it stages such sequences with the characters jumping nimbly across a split-level set to the accompaniment of stirring background music by Arnold Schwarzwald. Moore does not have much to do in this serial other than to display his skills at riding and sword fighting, and administer miracle cures to his wounded fellow-explorers. *Perils of Nyoka* provides an early opportunity for him to display the kind of technical skills that made him such a successful Lone Ranger from 1949 onwards.

Sometimes Moore played the part of the villain in his pre–Lone Ranger career — as, for example, in Fred C. Brannon and William Witney's Republic serial *The Crimson Ghost* (1946). As Ashe, he cuts a dapper figure in his blue pinstripe suit and snap-brim hat, but in this case appearances flatter to deceive: anyone unfortunate enough to get in his way is ruthlessly dealt with. Ashe has no respect for anyone — especially women: on at least two occasions during the twelve-part serial he grabs the heroine Diana Farnsworth (Linda Stirling) by the wrist and throws her to the ground. The only person capable of resisting him is Professor Duncan Richards (Charles Quigley), who spends the entire serial trying to discover the identity of the Crimson Ghost. Ashe and Richards scrap on numerous occasions; Richards generally emerges victorious, but Ashe escapes in the nick of time to fight another day.

Despite his physical strength, Ashe has little capacity to think for himself. He is regularly shown in two-shots standing to the Crimson Ghost's right, nodding his head in agreement. Such blind loyalty contrasts with Richards's capacity to make the quick decisions that help him emerge unscathed from the various misfortunes that befall him — car crashes, explosions or cars falling into the sea. The contrast between hero and villain was typical of Republic serials (most of which were shot very quickly on shoestring budgets), but Brannon and Witney give it a topical spin in *The Crimson Ghost*, as we discover that the Ghost works for a foreign (most likely European) dictator Count Fator (Stanley Price), who wants to indoctrinate the world with his beliefs. Although not identified as such, Fator, the Ghost and Ashe are obviously Communists — the enemies of the free world as represented by Richards and Diana Farnsworth.

Moore plays a similar role as the heavy Graber in Brannon's serial *Radar Men from the Moon* (1952). He works for evil mastermind Krog (Peter Brocco), who himself works for Retik, the ruler of the moon (Roy Barcroft). Graber faithfully carries out any orders he is given without question; to do so would be to challenge Retik's absolute power. Smartly dressed in suit and snap-brim hat, he proves himself to be highly proficient with a shotgun, as he kills various police officers, as well as anyone else foolhardy enough to stand in his way. As with Ashe in *The Crimson Ghost*, Graber shows no mercy to anyone — particularly women, as he grabs Commander Cody's (George Wallace) girlfriend Joan Gilbert (Aline Towne), takes her up in a plane, and leaves her to die as the plane loses its steering wheel and he parachutes to safety. Joan only escapes a grisly end through Cody's timely intervention, as he uses his jet-propelled boots to soar into the air and catch her before the plane crashes into the mountains.

Nonetheless, Moore's Graber does possess some attractive qualities, which help to explain why the actor was subsequently cast as the Lone Ranger. He is a clean-cut, presentable personality who proves highly skilled as a driver and a pilot: Graber regularly eludes the police in a black sedan, and pilots the aircraft with one hand, while shooting at his enemies with the other. If he has not chosen to work for Retik, he would be an ideal candidate for a heroic role. Cody is the only person who can successfully stand up to him.

Mantan Moreland
b. September 3, 1902, Monroe, Louisiana; d. September 28, 1973, Hollywood, California.

Moreland began running away from home at the age of 12 to join circuses and medicine shows, only to be brought back time and again. During these times he sharpened his comic skills and developed routines and acts that eventually became popular on the vaudeville stage, or what was then called the "chitlin' circuit." Mantan's focus gradually shifted his trade toward film, where he initially appeared in secondary roles. However, his talent for making people laugh soon gave him the chance to play more substantial roles, even if he did reinforce the negative stereotype of the African American as both servile and a figure of fun.

In *King of the Zombies* (1941) and *Revenge of the Zombies* (1943), Moreland plays Jeff, a comic chauffeur. In both films he is deliberately separated, both in terms of costume and delivery, from the other white actors; he speaks in a curious argot, in which the endings of individual words often get lost, and wears a loud suede jacket with a white handkerchief protruding from the breast pocket. He obviously considers himself well dressed, but in terms of white mainstream society, he is just loud. However director Steve Sekely gives him full opportunity to show off his comic talents. In several sequences, he encounters one of the zombies, either in person or (more frequently) by seeing one of their arms protruding from the ground, or from the trunk of his car. Jeff's reaction is predictable; his whole body trembles, his voice declines to a stammer, and he runs away as fast as possible. When a convenient escape route does not seem feasible, Jeff reacts by pulling the trilby hat off his head and fingering it nervously, as if hoping that it would provide him with some protection. Jeff employs a range of facial expressions to signify alarm; his favorite being to purse his lips and stare wide-eyed at what happens in front of him before running away.

He is also not averse to making a fool of himself; in one sequence, he is shown in the kitchen dressed in a white pinafore, helping with the washing-up. While such activities confirm Jeff's status as an African American—and hence second-class—citizen (according to the ideology of the time), he overcomes such negative stereotypes by running out of the kitchen into Dr. Altermann's (JOHN CARRADINE) laboratory freeing clean-cut white detective Larry Adams (Robert Lowery) from captivity. If this was not enough, Jeff is shown taking matters into his own hands by breaking the laboratory door down with an axe, thereby preventing Altermann from continuing his experiments. He fully deserves his status as one of the film's principal attractions.

Moreland had another cameo as a waiter in the Laurel and Hardy horror spoof *A-Haunting We Will Go* (1942). He breaks into peals of laughter when the boys attempt to pay for an evening meal with false money, but suddenly becomes serious when they threaten to leave without settling the check. His eyes stand out on stalks as he runs out of the right of the frame to fetch the manager, leaving Laurel and Hardy looking at one another in astonishment, as if unable to believe what has just happened. In Monogram's *Phantom Killer* (also 1942), Moreland plays Nicodemus, a witness called in the case brought by lawyer Ed Clark (DICK PURCELL) against rich philanthropist John G. Harrison (John Hamilton). In his gray suit and white hat, Nicodemus looks every inch the man about town; that is, until he takes the stand and answers the questions put to him by Clark and District Attorney John W. Rogers (Gayne Whitman). Moreland employs his usual repertory of gestures and vocal inflections to suggest the character's insecurities; his hands shake, his eyes look wildly from side to side and he stammers out his replies, none of which are very helpful to Clark's cause. The performance confirms existing racist stereotypes by por-

Mantan Moreland (right) as Birmingham Brown and Keye Luke in *The Sky Dragon* (1949). Although reinforcing the stereotype of the comic African American, Moreland made the best of his limited comic opportunities in many Chan films of the 1940s.

traying the African American as a figure of fun incapable of dealing with incisive questions posed by a white lawyer. The gales of laughter emanating from the packed courthouse only serve to reinforce this stereotype.

Moreland appeared in several Charlie Chan films from 1944 to 1949 as the chauffeur Birmingham Brown, opposite Sidney Toler and Roland Winters as Chan. In *Black Magic* (1944), he takes a brief vacation from working for Chan (Toler) to act as servant to a group of spiritualists and occultists. With the help of a book entitled *How to Disappear*, Birmingham repeatedly tries to vanish into thin air by clicking his fingers and murmuring "Abracadabra." Needless to say, nothing happens. However, he becomes more and more disturbed by what happens around him; at one point he observes that he would spend "an elegant time in a cemetery," rather than working in this kind of environment, where there appears to be "trouble, trouble and more trouble." Needless to say, Chan brings about a happy ending: Birmingham celebrates by taking vitamin pills, only to discover that they are actually Mexican jumping beans. He ends up by bobbing up and down like a pogo stick.

In *The Jade Mask* (1945), Birmingham forms a comic double act with Chan's number four son Eddie (Edwin Luke). The two of them provide a choric commentary on Chan's detective work, and occasionally try to intervene themselves—even though they are more of a hindrance than a help. Birmingham's eye-work is very evident in this film, as he glances quickly at Chan, then at Eddie, in the hope that they can find a solution to the crime and hence get away as soon as possible from the Harper mansion. At one point, Birmingham has a gun pointed in his face, he gibbers slightly and looks resignedly at the camera in the vain hope that the audience might help him out. Needless to say, he escapes unscathed, observing later on that he is far keener on "fast running" than "fast questioning." The film ends comically with Sheriff Mack (Alan Bridge) driving away from the house, with Birmingham striving to keep up on foot; now that the case has been solved, the chauffeur has the freedom to escape as fast as he can.

In *The Feathered Serpent* (1949), the penultimate film in the Monogram series, Birmingham travels with Chan (Roland Winters) and numbers one and two sons (Keye Luke, Victor Sen Yung) to Mexico, where they become involved in uncovering a plot to kidnap a professor (Robert Livingston) who can read the ancient Aztec script providing the key to the location of some buried treasure. Birmingham observes, "Uh-oh, here we go again!" as the plot becomes more and more complicated, and he is forced to travel into the remote Mexican mountains at Chan's side. In one sequence, Birmingham is asked to stand guard at the mouth of a cave; director William Beaudine cuts to a close-up of his face, asking the audience directly, "What am I doin' here by myself?"

His fears are perfectly justified, as the villains bundle him up in a tarpaulin and take him into their hideout. However, all ends happily, as Chan and his sons overpower the villains, and subsequently continue their vacation in Mexico, much to Birmingham's relief.

Jeff Morrow

b. January 13, 1907, New York City;
d. December 26, 1993, Canoga Park, California.

Born Leslie Irving Morrow, Jeff Morrow began his stage career in Pennsylvania in the late 1920s, using the stage name Irving Morrow, and later graduated to Broadway, acting with luminaries such as Katharine Hepburn, Luise Rainier and Maurice Evans. He began his film career in 1953 with a supporting role in *The Robe*. Throughout the 1950s, he played leading roles in a variety of science fiction films.

In Universal International's *This Island Earth* (1955), he plays the friendly alien Exeter; with his shock of white hair and white eyebrows, he provides a striking visual contrast to the handsome, brown-haired American scientist Dr. Cal Meacham (Rex Reason). In a familiar scenario for science fiction films of this period, Exeter comes to the planet Earth to do research that will help to save his dying planet Metaluna, and asks Meacham and his colleague Dr. Ruth Adams (FAITH DOMERGUE) to help him. However, Meacham discovers that the Metalunans want to take over the Earth; he tries to escape, but is eventually kidnapped (along with Dr. Adams) and taken to Metaluna where they are accused of blowing up the Metalunan Earth laboratory during their escape. Needless to say, they escape with Exeter's help and return to Earth, while Metaluna self-destructs.

As a representative of a civilization seeking to colonize the Earth, Exeter is chillingly urbane, speaking in calm, measured tones throughout. His face is everywhere; it frequently appears on television screens to talk to Meacham, claiming quite falsely that the Metalunans' research will save the Earth from itself. Exeter represents the most dangerous threat to the (Western) democratic way of life, as he ingratiates himself with Meacham in an attempt to convince him about the justness of the Metalunans' cause. In the end, however, Exeter undergoes a conversion, as he secures Meacham's and Dr. Adams's escape, even though he destroys himself in the process. In director Joseph M. Newman's view, Exeter's action represents a heroic sacrifice, as he embraces the democratic cause rather than committing himself to totalitarianism.

In *The Creature Walks Among Us* (1956), the third in a sequence of films featuring the Gill-Man (the others were *Creature from the Black Lagoon* and *Revenge of the Creature*), Morrow plays Dr. William Barton, a scientist who firmly believes that the creature can be transformed into an air-breather and hence be used as the means to "create new forms of life." Although the leader of an expedition to find the creature, Barton remains a passive figure, leaving much of the responsibility for capturing it to his colleague Dr. Thomas Morgan (Rex Reason). Bar-

Jeff Morrow (left), Rex Reason and Faith Domergue in *This Island Earth* (1955). A short yet imposing leading man, Morrow had his best role in this film as an alien with an ability to communicate with visitors from earth.

ton also engages in continual arguments with his wife Marcia (Leigh Snowden), whom he suspects of having an affair with Morgan. John Sherwood's film suggests that Barton lacks those masculine qualities (strength of character; concern for his wife) that make a good leader; he is too obsessed with his scientific reputation, which will be greatly enhanced through his experiments with the Gill-Man. In the end, Barton's self-interest proves his undoing as the Gill-Man attacks him and throws him off the balcony to his death.

In Kurt Neumann's *Kronos* (1957), Morrow plays Dr. Leslie Gaskell, a scientist so preoccupied with his work that he has little time for his fellow scientist and girlfriend Vera Hunter (Barbara Lawrence). Even when the two of them are out for a late evening drive, Gaskell believes that he should be back at the laboratory to check on the progress of a meteorite that has crashed into the ocean near Mexico. In this case, Gaskell is proved right; his colleague Dr. Hubbell Eliot (John Emery) has been possessed by an alien force, and is now controlling the actions of a 100-foot-tall robot (the Kronos) of the title that rises from the ocean and threatens to take over the United States. Gaskell himself likens it to "a wounded animal rushing at its tormentor"—the tormentor in this case being those people who try to destroy it.

Kronos offers another Armageddon-like vision of the consequences of nuclear war, with Kronos as the enemy sucking the life-blood out of the American people, thereby increasing its destructive potential. The only person with the scientific know-how to thwart it is Gaskell, who eventually comes up with the idea that Kronos can be destroyed with its own energy. He writes down the scientific theorem on a blackboard, and subsequently programs the computer (nicknamed Susie) to suit his purposes. Finally, he acts as a coordinator for the American armed forces who implement his suggestions. The operation proves successful. Kronos is burned alive, and Gaskell now has the chance — at last — to go to the movies with Vera.

Gaskell remains impassive throughout the ordeal, realizing — quite rightly — that he has to keep calm to guarantee the operation's success. He emphasizes the importance of a non-violent response to Kronos's threat; it is no use trying to destroy the monster with nuclear bombs, because that will simply increase its destructive potential. The only way to succeed is to turn the monster on itself. The film ends with Gaskell grimly proclaiming that, should there be any future threats to America's security, "We'll be ready for 'em."

In *The Giant Claw* (also 1957), Morrow plays a similar role as Mitchell "Mitch" McAfee, a research scientist and radar expert passionately committed to his work. Once again the Earth's future is threatened, this time by a giant dinosaur-like bird which prowls the globe destroying buildings and consuming human beings in its wake. Like King Kong in the famous 1933 film, it attacks New York, destroying the Empire State Building and the United Nations headquarters (a potent symbol of world peace). Initially dismissed as a crank by the American military — as he warns them about the bird's presence — McAfee eventually works closely with them to find a way of eliminating it. We see him hard at work in his laboratory, assisted by fellow-scientist Sally Caldwell (Mara Corday), working on what he identifies as a series of "cock-eyed concepts." He comes up eventually with a suitable weapon and kills the bird off. By doing so, he vindicates the ideas set forth in the film's opening frames by the narrator (played by the film's director Fred F. Sears): "Free men [like McAfee] struggle with the elements to create some measure of defense to protect that selfsame freedom [of the Earth]." As in *Kronos*, Morrow delivers long speeches of techno-speak that do not mean much, other than to show his enduring commitment to the cause of science, which he believes is the only way to guarantee the Earth's freedom.

J. Carrol Naish

b. January 21, 1896, New York City;
d. January 24, 1973, La Jolla, California.

Joseph Patrick Carrol Naish made his screen debut in 1930. He established a reputation for playing a variety of lowlife characters, including Chinese people, hoodlums and sidekicks. One

J. Carrol Naish autograph star postcard (1945). Naish was one of Hollywood's most versatile character actors, playing villains and good guys with equal facility. His bushy eyebrows made him ideal casting for foreign roles.

of his earliest roles was that of the gangster Ramon Salvatore in *The World Gone Mad* (1933). With his double-breasted suit, thick Italian accent and gelled hair, he looks like the typical heavy. However, this image is challenged somewhat by his fondness for reading *The Life and Loves of Casanova*— even though he himself shows no aptitude for attracting members of the opposite sex. Naish cuts a sinister figure in his limited time on the screen, placing his hands in his pockets and muttering through his teeth, "I did not keel [kill] Anderson!" or "I no lika do these [this]," as he shoots one of his enemies through the heart. Salvatore meets a predictable fate as he himself is shot dead by the good guy Lionel Houston (Neil Hamilton).

Naish had a particular talent to suggest obsession through eyework. In Sam Newfield's *The Monster Maker* (1944), for instance, Naish plays Igor Markoff, who is first seen amongst the audience for a recital given by pianist Anthony Lawrence (Ralph Morgan). Markoff espies Anthony's daughter Patricia (WANDA MCKAY) sitting in the adjacent box, and stares at her in a scopophilic way, as if he were trying to possess her. This is precisely what Markoff desires: Patricia bears a striking resemblance to his late wife, and he resolves to marry her whether she likes it or not. To this end, he injects Anthony with a serum that reduces him to a gibbering wreck; unless the pianist gives his consent, Markoff will not cure him.

With his slight German accent and impeccable manners, Naish gives a chilling performance in a film designed to alert wartime American audiences to the threat of the enemy within. Dressed in his smoking-jacket, an ever-present cigarette in his right hand, Markoff cultivates a façade of respectability. While at work, he assumes a sympathetic bedside manner — especially when trying to explain to Patricia that her father is very sick and must remain in hospital for further treatment. Nonetheless, we are repeatedly reminded of his sadistic tendencies; at one point he grasps his assistant Maxine's (Tala Birell) wrist and tells her to carry out his requests or face the consequences. On other occasions, a mere glance — where we see the whites of his eyes flashing — is sufficient to quell her. Although the Nazi atrocities at Auschwitz were not revealed until the camp was liberated in 1946, Markoff bears a strong resemblance to Dr. Josef Mengele, the notorious SS Officer who was publicly feted for saving the lives of German soldiers, while performing human experiments on Auschwitz inmates. Like the monster maker Markoff, Mengele had a nickname ("The Angel of Death").

In *Strange Confession* (1945), Naish plays another villain — Roger Graham, who like Markoff is prepared to go to any lengths to ensnare the woman of his dreams. This time the object of his affections is Mary Carter (Brenda Joyce), the pretty young spouse of research scientist Jeff Carter (Lon Chaney, Jr.). Once again Graham appears outwardly respectable with his neat business suit and perfect manners. However, Naish once again uses eyework to suggest his character's true motives; the whites of his eyes shine with almost unnatural intensity. In one sequence, Jeff comes into Graham's office to ask for a raise; Graham politely refuses, but once

Jeff has left the room, Graham's manner radically changes, as he instructs his sidekick Stevens (Milburn Stone) to ensure that Jeff will never be able to find alternative employment in this town. Later on, Graham invites Jeff and his wife to a dinner party at his house — despite the fact that Graham makes every effort to make his guests feel welcome, we cannot help but notice that he holds his cigarette holder like a magic wand, taking pleasure in his Prospero-like abilities to rule other people's lives. Graham eventually achieves his aim, as he persuades Jeff's wife to come alone to his house, plies her with champagne and embraces her, murmuring all the while that he is crazy about her. Just at that precise moment, Jeff enters, grabs a scimitar off the wall and hacks his employer to death, in the belief that Graham had stolen everything from him — his research, his brain and (most importantly) his wife.

Naish was also adept at playing eccentrics as well as villains. In Twentieth Century–Fox's *Dr. Renault's Secret* (1942), he plays Noel, the servant of eminent scientist Dr. Robert Renault (GEORGE ZUCCO). Noel's behavior seems somewhat strange from the outset; he does not respond immediately to what people say to him and refuses to look them in the eye. When he does he speak, he does so slowly and deliberately, as if experiencing learning difficulties. He is devoted to Renault's niece Madelon (Lynne Roberts), and attacks anyone who dares to cast aspersions on her reputation. As the film unfolds, we discover the reason why Noel behaves as he does; he is actually an ape, plucked from the Javanese jungle and transformed into a human being through glandular injections and given intensive language training. Dr. Renault is proud of his work, but treats Noel like a slave, beating him with a horsewhip and locking him up in a cage if the ape-man dares to question his word. Noel eventually eludes his tormentor: he escapes from the cage and pursues the doctor and Madelon to the local fair. After having strangled two local shopkeepers who have insulted him, including Marcel the barber (Charles La Torre), Noel confronts the doctor and strangles him too. In the film's climax, Noel throws Rogell (Mike Mazurki), a convict who has kidnapped Madelon, into a water wheel before plunging to his death. Naish makes a great effort to convince us that, like many animals before him (for example, King Kong), Noel is a victim of overweening ambition; the obsessive desire for fame that renders human beings totally insensitive to the feelings of others.

Naish made a habit of playing sympathetic villains—characters who find themselves victims of their own insatiable ambitions. This is clearly true of his Carl Fletcher in *Jungle Woman* (1944). He shows a touching concern for Paula the Ape-Woman's (Acquanetta) welfare, making sure she has the best of care and keeping unwanted strangers away from her. But at the same time he wants to find out everything he can about her. We see him furtively looking around her bedroom, rifling through her drawers and her personal effects, looking for evidence of how she transforms herself from pretty girl into an ape. As he searches, his eyes dart around the room, fearing discovery. Director Reginald LeBorg rarely shoots Fletcher in direct close-up; when he does, Fletcher's eyes are inevitably looking to the right or left of the frame, as if frightened that someone might discover what he is doing. The struggle of pursuing scientific research while seemingly looking after Paula proves too great for the doctor, as he is forced to kill her in self-defense. In the ensuing court case, he looks perpetually down at the ground, speaking in hushed tones, his hands clasped on his lap, as he regrets what he has done.

Naish takes on a completely different role as the dogged Inspector Gregg in *Calling Dr. Death* (1943). Here he acts as the voice of conscience, trying to persuade Dr. Mark Steel (Lon Chaney, Jr.) to admit to murder. Gregg's disheveled appearance (rumpled suit with tie slightly awry) contrasts with his eyework; the actor's eyes glint as he observes, "You [Steel] robbed her [his wife] of her life," while pacing slowly about the room, his thumbs in his waistcoat pockets. Gregg never actually sits in a chair; he perches on the edge of a desk in a calm, relaxed manner, giving the impression that he is thoroughly in control of what he is doing. In one sequence, director Reginald Le Borg's camera tracks Gregg as he enters unexpectedly and deliberately knocks over a standard lamp: Steel responds by turning around in terror. Gregg apologizes, explaining that it must have been Steel's nerves which caused him to react so violently. Gregg also suspects Stella Madden (Patricia Morison) of foul play — as the action develops, the inspector observes that her somewhat erratic behavior "makes the chase interesting." As with all good detectives, Gregg solves the mystery by putting two and two together: Steel offers Gregg a book of matches, Gregg looks at it and his face lights up, as he understands that this is the vital link in the chain, revealing Stella's guilt. The film ends with the inspector assuming his characteristic pose — sitting on the edge of Steel's desk — lighting another cigarette and observing somewhat cynically that his job always "start[s] with death [...] I look for life and then look at how it has been destroyed." This contrasts with Steel, who as a psychiatrist is always looking to discover his patients' inner secrets. Le Borg cuts to a shot of a wall plaque displaying a quote from Hippocrates: "To share my substance with Him with purity and holiness/I pass my life and practice my art." This ostensibly refers to Steel, but it could equally well apply to the inspector, who "practice[s] his art" with equal dedication. Naish plays another police inspector in *The Beast with Five Fingers* (1946), a partial remake of *Mad Love* (1935) with the same star (Peter Lorre). Naish has a wonderful time playing the Italian commissioner Ovidio Castanio, full of expressive gestures and a tendency to emphasize any point he wants to make with an imperious wave of his cigar. Despite all evidence to the contrary, Castanio resolutely refuses to believe in the presence of the supernatural — any unearthly happenings that take place in the estate of a recently deceased pianist can be rationally explained. To an extent, the commissioner is absolutely right, as we learn how Hilary Cummins (Lorre) has murdered several people while absolving himself of responsibility, putting the blame instead on the ghostly presence of the pianist's severed hand. At the end of the film, Castanio turns to the camera and asks the audience whether they believe in the supernatural — as he speaks, he smiles, but his eyes betray his real feelings, as they look fearfully from left to right. Perhaps there *is* something spooky about the estate that Castanio does not want to disclose to anyone.

Alan Napier

b. January 7, 1903, Birmingham, England;
d. August 8, 1988, Santa Monica, California.

Alan Napier-Clavering began his career in British films but, like many of his contemporaries in the 1930s, he made the move to Hollywood in search of more secure employment. Napier found regular work in horror and science fiction films throughout the 1940s and 1950s. In *The Uninvited* (1944), he plays kindly Dr. Scott, who initially believes that Stella Meredith's (Gail Russell) hallucinations are nothing more than the products of a diseased mind. As he spends more time in her house, however, he realizes that it is haunted by Mary, the ghost of Stella's dead mother. He willingly participates in a séance, but when that fails, he collaborates with Stella's boyfriend Roderick Fitzgerald (Ray Milland) in trying to find out

Alan Napier as Alfred in *Batman* (1966). British-born Napier entered Hollywood in the 1930s, and played police inspectors, critics and other figures of authority before achieving stardom late in life with *Batman*.

why Mary should continue to ruin Stella's life from beyond the grave. In *Dark Waters* (1944), Napier repeats the role of a kindly doctor looking after Leslie Calvin (Merle Oberon). But director André de Toth suggests there is something sinister about him; he occupies almost the entire frame as he stands over Leslie and tells her to relax. In the next sequence, we see him taking notes; his hands and the notebook dominate the center of the frame, while Leslie is seen in the background. This suggests that the doctor quite literally "speaks" for Leslie; she lacks the personality to stand up for herself. The doctor reinforces his dominance by smiling at her in a paternal manner as she receives a letter, ostensibly from her aunt, inviting her to convalesce in New Orleans.

In *House of Horrors* (1946), Napier has a brief role as supercilious art critic F. Holmes Harmon. Elegantly attired and with a military-style bearing, he looks down his nose as he describes Marcel De Lange's (Martin Kosleck) latest artistic creation as "tripe, with an overtone of sheer lunacy." Later on, we see him typing his latest review in his office; he pauses for a moment and tells his colleague Joan Bedford (Virginia Grey) that his job as critic requires him to "deflate [...] the egos of artistic pretenders," such as Jill's artist boyfriend, Steve Morrow, who possesses a "moronic viewpoint." Harmon deserves to suffer for his prejudices; he is eventually strangled to death by the Creeper (RONDO HATTON). Napier's role as an opinionated art critic anticipates fellow Briton PAUL CAVANAGH's portrayal of a similar role in *House of Wax* (1953).

In the Bowery Boys' horror spoof *Master Minds* (1949), Napier plays the mad Dr. Druzik, who believes that he can transform a monster into a human being. With his immaculately tailored suit, trilby hat and aristocratic manner, Druzik appears outwardly respectable, but his folded arms and unnatural stare at Atlas the Monster's (GLENN STRANGE) muscular frame suggests otherwise. As Sach (Huntz Hall) is put in a trance and rendered the unwilling victim of Druzik's experiments, the doctor rubs his hands in gleeful anticipation and claims that he will become the greatest scientist in history, as he makes Atlas and Druzik exchange personalities. This provides the pretext for some rather labored comedy, as Sach pretends to be a monster while Atlas assumes an ostentatiously effeminate manner. Meanwhile, Druzik ensures that no one prevents his experiments from succeeding; at one point he threatens to transform his assistant Nancy Marlowe (Jane Adams) into the monster. As in *Dark Waters*, Napier cultivates a gentlemanly image, but beneath this lurks a megalomaniac desire to dominate those physically weaker than himself—particularly women. His plans are doomed to fail, as Atlas the monster turns on him and forces him to cower in a corner until apprehended by the police.

In *Hangover Square* (1945), Napier has a supporting role as the conductor/impresario Sir Henry Chapman, father of Barbara Chapman (Faye Marlowe). Immaculately dressed in a dinner suit, white scarf and monocle, he seems the very epitome of a bourgeois gentleman, a regular habitué of London's salons and concert halls. He represents the kind of person that pianist George Harvey Bone (Laird Cregar) would like to become, were it not for the fact that Bone's life has been poisoned by his love affair with music hall dancer Netta Longdon (Linda Darnell). Director John Brahm ensures that Sir Henry occupies the center of the frame, whether conducting the orchestra or simply introducing George to London's musical cognoscenti. This is the kind of role Napier seems born to play: the aristocrat effortlessly demonstrating social grace and poise (a role he later honed to perfection as Alfred the butler in the 1960s television series *Batman*). In *Strange Door* (1951), he plays Count Grassin, one of the supposed best friends of evil Alain de Maletroit (Charles Laughton). He pretends to be the life and the soul of the party, making weak jokes and stuffing food into his mouth to hide his embarrassment when no one laughs at them. He apologizes weakly for his outspokenness, on the grounds that age has robbed his tongue of diplomacy. But this is nothing more than an act: when Corbeau confidentially explains that he is being held in de Maletroit's house against his will, Grassin volunteers to help him. Fixing his eyes on Corbeau like a school teacher and sipping from a small glass of wine, Grassin promises to have a coach ready at two o'clock that morning. The escape will not be easy; this is evident from Grassin's expression, as we see the whites of his eyes. This prediction proves tragically correct: de Maletroit finds out about it, and has Grassin stabbed to death with a knife and his corpse placed in the coach, just to remind Corbeau about the futility of trying to escape. Napier's characters are often condemned to die violently; in *Isle of the Dead* (1945), he plays St. Aubyn, the British consul, who falls victim to the plague. He is seen writhing in agony on a bed, and then lying stock-still, his eyes staring glassily up at the ceiling.

In *The Mole People* (1956), Napier does a fair imitation of Boris Karloff (without the lisp) as Elinu, the High Priest. Clad in long robes, with a tall headdress and wispy beard, he speaks his lines in dulcet tones ("In my hand I hold [...] the sacred weapon of Ishtar, the golden rod, the secret of death") to the sound of a drum in the background. When the team of archeologists, led by Dr. Roger Bentley (JOHN AGAR) invades his world, Elinu immediately plots to have them put to death, proclaiming that ("You will die [...] in the fire of Ishtar"). The line is delivered as a crescendo, with the final word turned into two lingering syllables ("Ish ... TAR!"). Elinu is talked out of his decision by King Nazar (Rodd Redwing), who believes that the archeologists are servants of Ishtar: Elinu's reaction is to scowl at the camera in frustration. He believes in Ishtar's power. At one point, he proclaims, in another crescendo, "Does not she not see us [...] with her all-pervading eyes?" with the stress placed on the word "all-pervading.") But he mistrusts the archeologists. Elinu presides over a world where cruelty is commonplace: human beings are ritually whipped for the tiniest transgression, while their slaves—the beasts—are kept in perpetual starvation. This, it appears, is what the ancient Sumerian civilization understands by good government. Elinu metes out his various punishments in cold, unemotional tones, emphasizing as he does so that "the king's will is the law!" He takes a malicious pleasure in presiding over a death ceremony, where three young nubile women are forced to walk into dazzling bright lights. The great double doors of the royal chamber are closed behind them; soon afterwards their charred bodies are brought out by servants. This ritual, in Elinu's opinion, celebrates "the g-l-ory of death," as well as recognizing Ishtar's ultimate authority.

The only thing he has to fear is the archeologists' torch, which brings unaccustomed bright lights into the underworld of darkness. He instructs his soldiers to steal it in ringing tones ("Bring ... me ... that ... CYLINDER!"). However, he does not understand that the torch battery has a limited life; once he has purloined it, he tries to shine it in the beasts' face — and thereby destroy them for good, just as the three unfortunate women were destroyed during the sacrificial ritual. But the torch fails to ignite and Elinu is hacked to death, the victim of a bestial world he helped to create.

In Twentieth Century–Fox's Cinemascope epic *Journey to the Center of the Earth* (1958), Napier at last manages to survive the entire film. He plays the Dean of the faculty at Edinburgh University, who ostensibly determines the research agenda of brilliant scientist Sir Oliver (James Mason), but in reality allows Sir Oliver a free hand to do what he wants. The Dean's role is largely symbolic; he gives Sir Oliver an encouraging pat on the shoulder at the beginning of the film, and stands in the background (dressed in full academic regalia) at the end while Sir Oliver recounts the details of his perilous journey to an assembled audience of students. Once the speech has concluded, the Dean shakes Sir Oliver by the hand.

Leslie Nielsen

b. February 11, 1926, Regina, Saskatchewan, Canada; d. November 28, 2010, Fort Lauderdale, Florida.

Leslie William Nielsen studied at the Academy of Radio Arts in Toronto before moving on to New York's Neighborhood Playhouse. He started his acting career at an early age, after being forced to lie to his father, who was a strict disciplinarian.

Best known for his comic roles in 1980s spoof films such as *Airplane*! (1977), Nielsen spent

Leslie Nielsen in *Return to the Forbidden Planet* (1956). Before *The Naked Gun* films made him a superstar, Nielsen gave memorable performances as a clean-cut commander or scientist — as in this famous film, based on Shakespeare's play *The Tempest*.

much of his early career in films and television as a juvenile lead. He played roles in a variety of genres, including several roles in the ABC science fiction anthology series *Tales of Tomorrow* (1951–3). In "Appointment on Mars," first broadcast on June 27, 1952, Nielsen plays Robbie, the captain of a three-person spaceship, which has just landed on Mars. The crew begins their explorations as the best of friends, laughing and joking with one another. This soon turns to ecstasy as they discover the presence of uranium on the planet. Robbie exclaims, "Let's start getting this stuff mapped out!" They want to do it as soon as possible, so that they can become millionaires. Like true colonists, the astronauts will deprive Mars of its natural resources in pursuit of financial gain.

As the drama unfolds, however, the crew's attitudes begin to change. Robbie's co-astronaut Bart (William Redfield) feels that someone is watching them, while Jack (Brian Keith) becomes strangely short of breath, despite claiming that he had never had a day's illness before. Robbie tries to keep their spirits up with a display of false bonhomie, rubbing his chin and telling them to "forget about everything" before they go to sleep. But no one heeds Robbie's advice: Bart wakes up and threatens Jack with a gun. Robbie intervenes, but accidentally shoots Bart. Jack accuses Robbie of murder; and then two of them fight quite literally to the death. Director Don Medford's playlet ends with two voiceovers—the inhabitants of Mars—pitying the human beings for their "simple minds," which led them to suspect one another's motives and hence destroy themselves.

In "Another Chance," broadcast on February 13, 1953, Nielsen plays Harold Mason, a thief racked with guilt for his crime. He paces about his one-room apartment, unable to sit still, with sweat pouring off his brow. His wife Carlotta (Virginia Vincent) criticizes him for his lack of guts, which only serves to make him more nervous. The only solution he can find is to visit a mysterious doctor, John Borrow (Robert Middleton), who offers him the chance to rewrite history by going back seven years in time. Mason sleeps, waking up with a new identity; he is now known as Jack Marshall, while his wife (once again played by Vincent) is called Regina rather than Carlotta. However, we soon understand that the past cannot be changed. Like Mason, Marshall turns out to be a petty thief who cannot live with the thought of what he has done. His spouse Regina — also played by Vincent — calls him "a ninny," while Dr. Borrow tells him that his past resembles "a broken record." Marshall returns to his seedy apartment in a paroxysm of despair and strangles Regina/Carlotta to death; outside, the wail of the police siren can be heard, reminding him of his inevitable fate.

Nielsen has ample opportunities to display his acting technique as he clasps and unclasps his hands, runs his hands through his hair and clasps his forehead to emphasize Mason/Marshall's emotional turmoil. At the end of the film, he loses his reason completely as he throws his wife's corpse on the bed before looking wild-eyed direct to camera. In "Ghost Writer" (broadcast March 27, 1953), Nielsen plays Bert Tyler, a struggling writer experiencing similar agonies. Despite the fact that he promises his wife Joan (Gaby Rodgers) to go it alone, Tyler accepts an offer to collaborate with Lee Morton (Murray Matheson), an enigmatic crime writer, who pays him $1,000 to complete two murder stories. Things start to go wrong when the murder stories come true: innocent people die in precisely the same fashion that Tyler wrote. One such victim is Joan, who perishes in a car crash. In the film's final scene, Morton visits the news agent's where Joan worked and observes sagely to the manager, "If you want anything badly enough, you pay the price." Nielsen communicates Tyler's increasing anxiety through a series of gestures—gnawing his lip, looking furtively from side to side in fear of discovery, or throwing his coat on to chair and rapidly picking it up once again.

Three years later, Nielsen played a very different kind of role as Commander J. J. Adams in Fred M. Wilcox's *Forbidden Planet* (1956). Adams likes to play by the rules; any course of action he wants to pursue on the planet Altair 4 has to be sanctioned by the American government. This attitude contrasts starkly with that of Dr. Edward Morbius (Walter Pidgeon), who has lived on the planet for the past twenty years, spending most of time researching into the lives of the Krell (a now-defunct race). Morbius believes that individuals, not institutions, should possess the ultimate power of authority. Nonetheless, there is much to admire about Adams' view of the world; he shows a paternal concern for his fellow crew members, mourning the death of his chief engineer Quinn (Richard Anderson)—a victim of the monster that passes unharmed through the security fence surrounding Adams' spaceship. On the other hand, Adams runs a tight ship, disciplining the cook (Earl Holliman) for breaking ranks and spending the night drinking bourbon with Robby the robot.

Adams never asks his crew to do anything he would not do himself; hence he undertakes the responsibility of finding out just who or what the monster actually is. He discovers to his horror that Morbius created it subconsciously; it is a monster from the id, embodying Morbius' suppressed desires, which came into being two decades previously when Morbius' crew voted to return to Earth rather than stay on Altair 4. Morbius had demurred and the monster had ended up killing the crew. Morbius at last accepts this truth, and is mortally injured while trying to renounce the monster. As he does so, he instructs Adams to press a lever that sets the entire complex to self-destruct, including the monster. Throughout this sequence, Adams reveals a terrier-like desire to discover the truth at all costs, forcing Morbius to contemplate the consequences of his action. The film ends with Adams and his crew, plus Robby and Morbius' daughter Altaira (Anne Francis) taking off to return to Earth, with Adams uttering the homiletic phrase: "We are after all, not God." In the interests of world peace, it is advisable to follow Adams' precepts of loyalty to the government, rather than uphold Morbius' philosophy of unrestricted individualism.

However, Adams possesses a softer side, revealed in the difficulties he experiences in talking to Altaira. She is just *too* innocent; she cannot be treated with the same genial brusqueness that characterizes Adams' relationship with his crew. In one sequence, she is shown bathing naked in a clearing; Adams comes across her and immediately turns his back, exclaiming, "Oh, murder!" Altaira laughs at Adams' embarrassment, for her nakedness is something perfectly natural. We observe once again Nielsen's abilities to communicate emotional turmoil through gesture as he fiddles with a leaf, his back turned away from Altaira, while the girl hides behind a bush and dons her new white dress. He guiltily realizes that "something new has been added" to the planetary world through his guilty reactions. Like Adam and Eve after the Fall, Altaira covers herself in an attempt to compensate for Adams' (and the audience's) shame at seeing her in a state of *déshabillé*.

Maria Ouspenskaya

b. July 29, 1876, Tula, Russia;
d. December 3, 1949, Los Angeles, California.

The daughter of a lawyer, Maria Ouspenskaya came to America with the Moscow Art Theatre in 1922 and stayed to forge a successful career on Broadway. In 1929, she founded the School of Dramatic Art in New York; many of her film roles were intended to provide the financial means to keep it going. She made her debut in *Dodsworth* (1936) and followed this with a major role in *Love Affair* (1939), with Irene Dunne and Charles Boyer.

With her pronounced accent and fondness for astrology (which often drove her fellow film workers to distraction), Ouspenskaya was frequently cast in exotic roles. In *The Wolf Man* (1941), she plays Maleva the gypsy — a small, white-haired woman with piercing black eyes and long brass earrings, who appears to know the Wolf Man's (Lon Chaney, Jr.) guilty secret. As the action unfolds, she assumes a maternal role, first by suggesting that they should take him home, and then praying to God that his "suffering is over, my son, now you will find peace." By comparison, her treatment of Sir John (CLAUDE RAINS) remains standoffish, almost as if she somehow blames him for Talbot's corruption. She sits stony-faced in the driving seat of a horse and cart, and advises Sir John that the only way to kill the Wolf Man is to beat him to death with a silver-topped cane. By contrast, Maleva's role in the film's final sequence is extremely touching, as she leans over him and observes, "Tears run to a pre-destined end, now you [Talbot] will find peace for eternity." In the follow-up *Frankenstein Meets the Wolf Man* (1943), Ouspenskaya repeats the role. She pronounces, "I shall ... watch over him [Talbot]," and looks up with maternal affection into his tortured face. Maleva becomes his permanent traveling companion, but her foreignness eventually puts her at risk from the outraged villagers living near Frankenstein's castle, who believe she is a witch — and thereby partly responsible for letting the Monster (Bela Lugosi) run wild. One villager, Vazec (Rex Evans), proves particularly sadistic, as he glares at her and accuses her of being part of a "gang of murderers." To her credit, Maleva remains completely unmoved by the accusation, preferring instead to remain silent. Anything she knows about the Wolf Man or the Monster will remain a secret.

Maria Ouspenskaya in *The Wolf Man* (1941). Russian-born character actor Ouspenskaya often played witches, gypsies or other figures of menace. Her sallow features helped her greatly in such roles.

In *The Mystery of Marie Roget* (1942), based on the Edgar Allan Poe short story, Ouspenskaya plays Madame Cecile Roget, grandmother of Marie and Camille Roget (Maria Montez, Nell O'Day). Cecile sits regally in her chair in her sitting room, fingering a silk handkerchief and delivering her lines in ringing tones: "Where — have — you — been?" She silences the Prefect Gobelin (LLOYD CORRIGAN) with a hard stare, pronouncing as she does so that "there's — no — more — need — for — the police — MonSIEUR," with the stress on the final word emphasizing her contempt. Dr. Paul Dupin (PATRIC KNOWLES), who has been assigned to solve the case of Marie's murder, understands the importance of treating Cecile with respect. Whenever she speaks, he stands to attention and inclines his head respectfully — a gesture that meets with Cecile's tacit, if somewhat grudging approval (she nods her head slightly). Although Cecile is severely disabled — she walks unsteadily on two sticks around her boudoir before collapsing into a comfortable chair — she commands authority through words alone. As M. Henri Beauvais (John Litel) observes at one point, "She commands, she doesn't ask." Director Phil

Rosen gives her some choice insults, primarily directed at the unfortunate Gobelin—at one point she advises him to "go have [himself] STUFFED!" The emphasis is placed on the final word in the phrase.

Despite her rather threatening presence, it is clear that Cecile represents a source of stability in the Roget family. Unlike her granddaughter Marie—whom Dupin reveals to be a habitual criminal—Cecile does not dissemble; she sits at the center of her room, and refuses to be ruffled by anything happening around her. Even when Dupin forces her to tell the truth about her family, she speaks in slow, measured tones, as if determined to retain the initiative. At the end, when Marie's murderer has been revealed, she grudgingly thanks Dupin for his efforts, but cannot resist another sly dig at Gobelin, calling him "dumb," as he takes the credit for solving the crime.

Scott Peters
b. July 12, 1930, Canada;
d. January 15, 1994, Monterey Park, California.

Peters (real name Peter Sikorski) was a stalwart supporting actor in several low-budget sci-fi flicks of the late 1950s. In *Invasion of the Saucer Men* (1957), he plays an unnamed U.S. Air Force sergeant charged with protecting an American small town from invasion. He comes across as efficient, loyal and willing to carry out his superior's orders without question. He is a model service person, in fact. However, it is his unthinking devotion to duty that renders him insensible to what happens around him; like his fellow recruits, he remains totally oblivious to the presence of little green men on Earth, who have come to the small town with bad intentions. The town is only saved from destruction by the timely intervention of teenage couple Johnny Carter (Steve Terrell) and Joan Hayden (Gloria Castillo) and their friends, who surround the little green men and shine their car headlights full in the aliens' faces, causing them to vanish in a puff of smoke. Edward L. Cahn's film, while tongue-in-cheek in tone, makes a case for the late 1950s teenager as a fundamentally responsible person, even though their appearance and behavior might suggest otherwise. By contrast, the representatives of officialdom, as personified by the sergeant, are identified as ineffective and self-interested.

Peters repeats the role in *The Amazing Colossal Man* (1957); this time he plays Sgt. Lee Carter, who worked in a unit commanded by Lt. Col. Glenn Manning (GLENN LANGAN) participating in a plutonium bomb experiment. Carter is quite clearly petrified; he is seen cowering in close-up wearing dark glasses, waiting for the bomb to go off. When an unidentified plane lands in the restricted area set aside for the blast, Carter remains at his post. While concerned for the pilot's future, he has learned to respect his superiors' orders. His behavior contrasts starkly with that of his superior officer: Manning leaps out from the bunker to the pilot's aid, and receives the full force of the bomb blast as a result. While Carter only has a small role in the film, he is identified as a representative of those institutional forces—the

Attack of the Puppet People (1958). Rear, left to right: Laurie Mitchell, Scott Peters, Susan Gordon and Ken Miller. June Kenney and John Agar at front. Clean-cut character actor Peters made a habit of playing teenagers or other young people at a loss in a disordered world in science fiction films of the late 1950s.

army, the medical profession, as well as the American government—whose obsession with procedures (orders, rules, statutes) renders them indifferent to human suffering.

Peters plays another member of the armed forces in *Attack of the Puppet People* (1958). As Mac, a former U.S. Army soldier, he dedicates himself to a life of pleasure—chiefly alcohol and listening to rock 'n' roll. In terms of the film's morality, he is seen to be neglecting his responsibilities to society as a whole. Thus he deserves to be transformed into a plaything by evil puppet master Franz (John Hoyt). As with many films of the time designed for the drive-in market, *Attack of the Puppet People* has a theme song, delivered in rock 'n' roll rhythms by Laurie (Marlene Willis). The lyrics ("You're a dolly, you're so cute ... you're so precious, you're so darling") sum up Mac's fundamentally passive nature; having spent the early part of his life fighting for his country, he allows himself to become a mad scientist's victim. Unlike Bob Westley (JOHN AGAR), who tries to recover something of his lost masculinity by outwitting Franz, Mac does not do much, save for encouraging Bob's girlfriend Sally (June Kenney) to pick up the telephone receiver—which seems enormous—and try to call the police. On another occasion, Mac tries to write a help note that the characters hope to lift up and poke out of an upper window in Franz's laboratory. But the letter falls down to the floor, leaving them helpless.

Mac's position expresses the dilemma experienced by American men in a changing, post–Kinsey world, where constructions of masculinity and femininity were continually subject to revaluation. On the one hand, McCarthyism and Cold War rhetoric demanded adherence to traditional concepts of nationalist virility. On the other hand, it was also considered acceptable to adopt other forms of masculinity such as nonconformity, unrestrained sexuality and even homosexuality (witness the films of Marlon Brando during this period, for instance). Peters's Mac remains determinedly nonconformist, even if this means transforming himself into someone else's plaything.

In Phil Tucker's *The Cape Canaveral Monsters* (1960), Peters plays mathematical genius Tom Wright who, together with sweetheart Sally Markham (Linda Connell), has to face up to the fact that some human beings have been inhabited by extra-terrestrial beings. Despite his intellectual gifts, Wright is initially not taken very seriously: his mentor Professor van Hoften (Billy Greene) regards him as a typical American teenager with "more freedom" to misbehave compared to teenagers in Europe. But Tom shows resourcefulness beyond his tender years; while driving one evening in his open top sports car, he discovers that the rock 'n' roll music on his transistor radio is being intercepted by messages from the extraterrestrials. Tom and Sally investigate, despite the risks involved, and are eventually captured and imprisoned in the extraterrestrials' spaceship. Director Tucker includes frequent close-ups of Tom's face deep in thought, as he searches for a means to escape — at first he offers to bargain with the extraterrestrials, promising to keep silent if he and Sally are released ("Our freedom for our knowledge"). When this proves fruitless, Tom takes matters into his own hands and engineers an escape; his scientific knowledge proves superior to that of his captors.

While the film celebrates the resourcefulness of young American males, it also suggests that they need to learn a lot about the opposite sex. Tom proposes to Sally while the two of them are trying to escape; needless to say, Sally chides him for the inappropriateness of the request. She admires him for his loyalty ("I knew you wouldn't have left me without a good reason"), but emphasizes at the same time that personal issues should be set aside until the extraterrestrials have been destroyed. Both she and Tom return to the Professor's laboratory to rescue the Professor from captivity; then they subsequently blow the spaceship into smithereens. With the Professor looking admiringly at them in the background, Tom and Sally move towards the camera and silently embrace. They then climb into a police car and drive away, with the sound of further explosions still echoing in the background. Now that the threat to the human world has been removed, the two lovers can get married.

Irving Pichel

b. June 24, 1891, Pittsburgh, Pennsylvania;
d. July 13, 1954, Hollywood, California.

Irving Pichel began his career in musical theatre. He first achieved fame as the title character in the Pasadena Playhouse production of Eugene O'Neill's *Lazarus Laughed* (1927). He began his Hollywood career as an actor, but later carved out a career as a director.

Pichel's acting career in horror films contained some notable highlights. In Edward Sloman's *Murder by the Clock* (1931), he plays Philip Endicott, who at first seems to be the dutiful son, carrying flowers and walking behind his mother, murmuring: "Look. I am strong. Look." With his pudding-basin haircut and vacant expression, he appears somewhat slow-witted—due, perhaps, to his mother Julia (Blanche Friderici) and the housekeeper Miss Roberts (Martha Mattox) being rather overprotective towards him. Miss Roberts guides him up the stairs as if he were a baby. Philip wants to be a soldier, making use of "no guns, knives, but my hands!" His greatest strength—his hands—is also his basic weakness; if he is left alone with anyone, his mother and his housekeeper fear that he will strangle someone. Thus, when Laura meets a grisly end, Philip is automatically viewed as the prime suspect. The next time we see him, he is in jail, moving about the cell like a wild animal, threatening to break the cell door down at any moment. He escapes and runs about like a wild animal, killing Miss Roberts in the process. None of this is actually Philip's fault; he has been transformed from a dutiful son into a beast by the combined efforts of Laura and Herbert Endicott (Lilyan Tashman and Walter McGrail), who want to use him as their hired killer, so that they can escape with the family fortune. Based on a little-known play and cheaply filmed, *Murder by the Clock* foreshadows *King Kong* (1933) in the way it treats Pichel as a noble savage falling victim to a corrupt society.

As Sandor, the evil servant of Dracula's daughter (Gloria Holden) in Lambert Hillyer's film of the same name (1936), Pichel plays Sandor, an out-and-out villain with slicked back hair, long coat and turned-up collar. Speaking in dulcet tones while apparently staring into space, he speculates about "what tomorrow will bring," before informing us that Dracula's daughter casts "evil shadows," while causing wolves to bark in terror. He is particularly fond of the word "death"—repeating it in a sonorous tone, almost as if he expects everyone to fall victim to his mistress' influence. Sandor also possesses a particular way of moving around the frame; he seems to glide around silently, while turning up in the most unlikely places. At the same time, he is someone to be feared—as the young girl Lili (NAN GREY) discovers when she encounters him one dark night. Unable to escape from his staring eyes, she allows herself to be persuaded to come back to Dracula's daughter's house, and thence to meet her inevitable fate.

Eventually, Sandor's devotion to his mistress counts for nothing, as he gradually becomes aware of the fact that she has fallen for the psychiatrist Jeffrey Garth (Otto Kruger). In a climactic confrontation, he tries to shoot the doctor with a bow and arrow, exclaiming all the while, "You won't wait long!" However, it is Sandor himself who doesn't have to wait long for death, as the doctor kills him before driving a stake through Dracula's daughter's heart.

Pichel had a rare starring role in Victor Halperin's B-flick *Torture Ship* (1939) as the mad doctor Hubert Stander, who charters a vessel filled with criminals, who function as guinea-pigs for his experiments in trying to transform them into law-abiding citizens. Pichel cuts an imposing figure, his bulk filling the frame to such an extent that his two "nurses" Ezra Matthews and Steve Murano (Leander de Cordova and Dmitri Alexis) are hardly noticeable. He is perhaps most dangerous when he claims that his researches are conducted for the public good, to "make better men and women" out of habitual law-breakers. This line is delivered calmly, contrasting starkly with his next line, where he refers to the various methods used to punish criminals—"the electric chair, hangman's noose, or G-Men's bullets." Superficially it seems that he is a liberal-minded reformer working to reduce the crime rate; it is only when the torture ship has left New York that we

Irving Pichel and Gloria Holden in *Dracula's Daughter* (1936). Pichel had great fun in this film as a pathetic yet sinister figure. While occasionally playing villainous roles, he later became a successful director (***Destination Moon*** [1950]).

discover his true motives — to play God with people's lives. He forces his nephew Lt. Bob Bennett (LYLE TALBOT) to act as a human sacrifice. Stander deals with his affairs in a calm, businesslike manner — putting and taking off his surgical gloves, and putting his hands in his waistcoat pocket to emphasize a particular point. Any violence that needs to be committed — such as knocking out one of the criminals, or tying Bennett down so as to "prepare" him for the experiments — is left to the nurses. Stander eventually gets his comeuppance, as he is wounded in a vain attempt to protect his laboratory from destruction. The last we see of him is on his deathbed, bathed in bright light, his face screwed up in pain as he protests that what he had tried to do was fundamentally good. The proof, in his view, was in the way Poison Mary Slavish (Sheila Bromley) had undergone a change of character; whereas once she was a desperate fugitive from justice, now she displays genuine human feeling as she puts her arm around her secretary Joan Martel (Jacqueline Wells/Julie Bishop). However, we understand that this is completely untrue: Mary has only changed because it seems advantageous for her to do so. It is this ability to persuade people — both viewers and characters within the film —

that makes Stander such a dangerous person. Even when he dies, he does so with a beatific smile on his face, as if convinced of his own rightness.

Don Porter

b. September 24, 1912, Miami, Oklahoma; d. February 11, 1997, Beverly Hills, Los Angeles, California.

Don Porter began his career in theatre before being signed as a contract player by Universal in 1939. He made his name in the early 1940s, playing straight roles in numerous films, including horror flicks such as *Night Monster* (1942). As pulp fiction writer Dick Baldwin, he comes across as a clean-cut, respectable character in trenchcoat and trilby hat, using his pipe to make particular points. Although a close friend of rich recluse Kurt Ingston (Ralph Morgan), Baldwin understands that Ingston has an unnatural power over all of his guests — something increased by the sinister presence of mystic Agor Singh. Baldwin's initial response is to protect psychiatrist Dr. Lynn Harper (Irene Hervey) from possible harm; on several occasions, he comes into a room in the nick of time to save her from possible molestation by lecherous chauffeur Laurie (Leif Erickson). Eventually, Baldwin decides to take the mystic's words seriously; he puts his hands in the pockets of his suit and listens intently, then sits down and observes wryly that this is unlike anything that would appear in one of his whodunits.

As the film unfolds, however, Baldwin understands that he must take direct action to find out what is happening. When the three doctors invited to Ingston's house are brutally strangled in turn, Baldwin is the first person to witness the scene of the crime, telling Dr. Harper to stay out of the room, as the sight of the doctors' brutally twisted bodies might prove too traumatic for her. He soon realizes that the only way to protect Dr. Harper is for both of them to escape from the house as quickly as possible; they run into the garden on a foggy night, closely pursue the killer (who turns out to be

Ingston himself). Baldwin and Ingston grapple with one another on a bridge, and Baldwin is thrown to the ground. Ingston is about to kill Dr. Harper when he is shot dead by Constable Beggs (Robert Homans), who has followed them into the garden. Baldwin gets up and dusts himself down, observing wryly that he turned out to be a fine hero in the end. While favoring direct action (in terms of investigating the crimes), he does not possess sufficient physical strength to carry it through.

In *She-Wolf of London* (1946) Porter moves up the social scale to play Barry Lanfield, a respectable-looking lawyer fond of riding horses. He cannot quite believe that Phyllis Allenby (June Lockhart) has actually witnessed a werewolf at large in the local park; like a true patriarch, he ascribes her hallucinations to her disturbed state of mind. As the film unfolds, so Barry's views begin to change (rather like Baldwin's views in *Night Monster*)—particularly when the Mrs. Danvers-like housekeeper, Martha Winthrop (Sara Haden), prevents him from seeing Phyllis. The only way for Barry to wear Martha down is to stare straight into her eyes and insist quite firmly that he will not go until she relents. Once Barry is restored to Phyllis, he tries every method he knows—freely quoting Plato, Pythagoras and Shakespeare—to make her understand that she is suffering from a mental disorder. As things turn out, however, Phyllis is proved right: Barry leaves the house and resolves to find out exactly what has happened in the park. Director Jean Yarbrough invites us to share his quest as he photographs him in close-up, his eyes glinting in the darkness as he tries to penetrate the London fog and discover the true explanation for the crimes. We learn that Martha is the murderer; Barry returns to the house in the nick of time to rescue Phyllis from certain death. The film ends with her staring gratefully, if somewhat hazily into his eyes (as she has been drugged), while Barry embraces her. Here Porter is seen in a more positive light—as compared to *Night Monster*—since his character's direct action leads to the heroine being saved.

That same year, Porter played a brilliant scientist—Professor Claude Ruppert—in Universal's *Danger Woman*. He comes across as a conscientious worker, sitting at his desk with a pipe in his mouth, dictating notes to his devoted secretary June Spenser (Brenda Joyce). Unlike Dick Baldwin in *Night Monster*, Porter's Claude Ruppert is a man of science rather than action; he would rather retire to his study than publicize his groundbreaking theory of how to adapt atomic power for business purposes, in the belief that the theory could be destructive to society if it fell into the wrong hands. Ruppert shies away from emotional engagement; whenever June, or his wife Eve (Patricia Morison), come close to him, he turns away from them in embarrassment. Emotions, he believes, are "vague" and "unscientific" and should therefore be suppressed. Yet director Lewis D. Collins shows Ruppert undergoing a significant transformation, as he uncovers a plot to steal his theory led by Gerald King (Milburn Stone). Ruppert proves beyond doubt that King murdered his wife (despite King's protestations of innocence), and subsequently mourns his wife's passing. He understands—too late—that his emotional immaturity helped transform her into the "danger woman" of the film's title. The

Don Porter in *Gidget* (1966). Debonair leading man Porter began his career at Universal playing trustworthy, reliable middle-class men. He later graduated to playing dubious bureaucrats.

film ends with Ruppert vowing to change the world (described earlier on by King as "the age of opportunity" in which "every man [works] for himself") and embracing community values as he leaves his house arm-in-arm with June.

In his later career, Porter shied away from horror films, although he did have a powerful cameo as the racketeer R. G. Connolly in John Cromwell's horror noir *The Racket* (1951). Sat behind a desk in the front office of "the old man"—i.e., the (unseen) boss of a national crime syndicate, operating in this town under the front of the "Acme Real Estate Company"— Connolly looks the epitome of the efficient executive. He speaks quietly in measured tones, without resorting to the kind of violence characteristic of local crime boss Nick Scanlon (Robert Ryan). However, Connolly can prove equally intimidating, as he sidles up to his victims and towers over them, looking down his sharp nose as he observes quietly that "the old man won't like that." Eventually, the syndicate's plans to elect crooked prosecutor Welsh (Ray Collins) as a judge are foiled by honest cop Thomas McQuigg (Robert Mitchum) and loyal patrolman Bob Johnson (William Talman). However, Connolly's position remains unaffected; he will continue to operate as the acceptable front for the syndicate in the future.

Dick Purcell
b. August 6, 1908, Greenwich, Connecticut;
d. April 10, 1944, Hollywood, California.

Dick Purcell, a thick-set leading player, began his career as a contract player for Warner Bros., but eventually moved into Poverty Row studios such as Monogram and Republic. He made several horror films, including *King of the Zombies* (1941), where he played James "Mac" McCarthy, a test pilot whose plan crashes into a remote island somewhere close to the United States. Together with his clean-cut companion Bill Summers (JOHN ARCHER) and their African American servant Jefferson ("Jeff") Jackson (MANTAN MORELAND), he falls into the clutches of evil scientist Dr. Miklos Songre (Henry Victor), who transforms people into zombies after having extracted vital military secrets from them and passed the information on to the Germans. "Mac" McCarthy cuts an aggressively masculine figure, with his open combat jacket and square jaw. Despite being slightly portly, he appears to be able to take care of himself—that is, until he is hypnotized by Dr. Songre. Director Jean Yarbrough obviously implies that no one is safe in a wartime environment; even the strongest people are at risk. McCarthy contributes to his own downfall, as he resolutely (and, some might say, rashly) trusts in his physical strength to resist the doctor's mind games. Although he recovers his wits by the film's end, he plays no part in the doctor's downfall. It is left to the more practical Bill Summers to do the job on his own.

A year later Purcell played hotshot lawyer Edward ("Ed") A. Clark in *Phantom Killer*. His body language provides a reliable guide to his emotions: when in control of the situation he sits languidly in his chair, his thumbs on the desk, his head inclined slightly forward as he speaks. If circumstances go against him, his voice becomes shrill, and he starts throwing papers around in frustration. The sole stabilizing force in his life is his girlfriend Barbara "Babs" Mason (Joan Woodbury), who buoys him up in adverse situations as well as providing a pleasurable alternative to work. Described as "cocky" by his fellow advocates, Clark offers a convincing performance in court as he tries to bring rich philanthropist John G. Harrison (John Hamilton) to justice, on suspicion of being the mastermind behind a series of unsolved murders. Despite his undoubted vocal talents, as he paces the courtroom with an authoritative air, his head held high, Clark loses the case. As the film unfolds, Clark begins to understand that success does not always depend on sheer force of personality; it is sometimes better to remain silent and wait for the suspects to reveal themselves. When he visits Harrison's mansion, he confines himself to the background, allowing Sergeant Pete Corrigan (Warren Hymer) to do much of the talking. Clark notices something suspicious about Harrison's piano; and after playing a few chords he discovers that one of the keys opens a secret door leading to Harrison's hideout. From then on it

Dick Purcell publicity still (1941). Purcell died tragically young of a heart attack, just as his career was beginning to develop. However, he did have the chance to play good leading roles in a variety of second features in the early 1940s.

is simply a matter of time before Clark gets his man; keeping his hands behind his back, he lets the police capture him before turning towards Barbara and embracing her. Despite his imposing physical presence on screen, Purcell refrains from acting the heavy, giving a nuanced performance that rises above the film's predictable plot.

In his brief career, which was cut short by his untimely death from a heart attack in 1944, Purcell had the distinction of being the first actor to play Captain America in the Republic serial of the same name (1944), directed by John English and Elmer Clifton. In his daytime incarnation of District Attorney Grant Gardner, Purcell strides purposefully through the film in a gray suit and trilby hat. As in *Phantom Killer*, Purcell remains in control of most situations without having to resort to physical violence, as suggested through clearly defined gestures such as pointing a finger to emphasize a point, or swinging his arms to and fro as he enters or exits from a building. With his barrel chest and square jaw, Grant Gardiner can certainly take care of himself in a fight; no one manages to get the better of him. He is also a crack shot and an agile gymnast, who manages to avoid death on at least two occasions by jumping out of his car, just before it goes crashing over a precipice. Gardiner proves a master of the quick change; a convenient store cupboard is all he requires to transform himself into Captain America. On at least two occasions, Gardiner manages to don his disguise while chasing his enemies in a black sedan, hastily pulling on his mask with one hand, and gripping the steering-wheel with the other. Needless to say, Captain America remains an honorable man who only uses violence when absolutely necessary in his quest to expose the identity of the evil Scarab (LIONEL ATWILL). The serial ends predictably, with Gardiner triumphant (even though everyone now knows that he is also Captain America) and listening to the chimes of the clock striking twelve — the appointed time for the Scarab's death in the electric chair. On the last chime, Gardiner remarks that it is "the time of doom"— as he speaks, the directors cut to a stock close-up of Big Ben in London. The image might seem incongruous (for a serial set in an unnamed Californian city) but does suggest that order has been restored.

Purcell does not have too much to do in the role of Captain America, but his tongue-in-cheek characterization emphasizes the actor's screen image as a man of strength and honor, who uses violence only as a last resort.

Claude Rains

b. *November 10, 1889, Camberwell, London;*
d. *May 30, 1967, Laconia, New Hampshire.*

William Claude Rains made his debut at the age of eleven and subsequently trained in the London theatre. He came to the United States in 1913. With the outbreak of the First World War a year later, he returned to Britain and served in Europe. Once the war had ended, he continued his career in the London theatre, serving as a member of Beerbohm Tree's acting company and later becoming a teacher of drama at London's Royal Academy of Dramatic Art (RADA). He made his American film debut in 1933 as Jack Griffin in Universal's version of H. G. Wells's *The Invisible Man*, taking over from Boris Karloff. Rains exerts a commanding presence onscreen; his personality is made evident very early on, when the landlady Jenny Hall (Una O'Connor) comes back into his hotel room to bring him the mustard. Director Whale cuts to a reaction shot of her horrified face as she sees him; Rains' Griffin instinctively puts a handkerchief to his mouth and warns her in a voice that will brook no argument. "I told you not to disturb me," he says, with a heavy stress placed on the word "not." Although dedicated to scientific research, Griffin has also realized how much power he might enjoy as a result of his invisibility.

The topicality of such subjects to 1933 audiences is made painfully evident. When Constable Jaffers (E. E. CLIVE) threatens to lock him up, Griffin responds, "All right you fools. You've brought it on yourselves. Everything would have come right if you'd left me alone. You've driven me near madness [...] and now you'll suffer for it!!!" He then plucks off his false nose and unwraps his bandages to reveal nothing underneath. Griffin uses gestures during this speech instantly recognizable from newsreel footage of European dictators, waving his hands in the air like Adolf Hitler and holding up his hands in a Nazi-like salute. In a later speech, Griffin talks to his fiancée Flora Cranley (Gloria Stuart) and describes the power he might enjoy: "Power to go into the gold vaults of the nation, into the secrets of kings, into the holy of holies!

Claude Rains cinema star postcard (1934). British-born Rains made his name in *The Invisible Man* (1933), and later went on to become one of Hollywood's most reliable and enduring character actors.

Power to make multitudes run squealing in terror at the touch of my little invisible finger! Even the moon's frightened of me, frightened to death!" *The Invisible Man* attacks the visions of aspiring dictators, those who seek to control by force and have little or concern for human feeling. Many sequences are quite shockingly violent: Griffin later shown riding a bicycle down a village street and willfully knocking a woman's pram to the ground with the baby still inside. He skips down a lane wearing a pair of trousers, singing, "Here we go gathering nuts in May," but he later batters a policeman to death with a stool. At one point he exclaims that "an invisible man can rule the world [...] We'll begin with a reign of terror, a few murders here and there. We might even wreck a train or two." He fulfills his promise by taking over a signal-box and changing the points, so that a crowded express train falls down a mountain, killing over one hundred people.

In one scene, his colleague Dr. Kemp

(William Harrigan) is shown sitting in his living room listening to a radio report about the mayhem caused by the invisible man in the village. Suddenly the radio appears to switch off automatically, and we hear Griffin's voice on the soundtrack continuing the report: "And everyone deserves the fate that's coming to them. Panic, death, things worse than death. Don't be afraid, Kemp. It's me." Once his existence has been publicly confirmed, Griffin causes mass panic—as shown in a later sequence when a dance is interrupted by a newsflash, telling people to be on their guard against him. Whale's camera tracks through the crowd to a close-up of the radio speaker telling how Griffin has "attacked and killed a police inspector, and is now at large."

At heart, *The Invisible Man* is about an outsider whose alienation from the rest of the world prompts him to take revenge on it.

Rains gives another bravura performance as John Jasper in Universal's adaptation of Charles Dickens's *Mystery of Edwin Drood* (1935). We first encounter him in an opium den, breathing heavily in close-up as he finishes his latest fix. Director Stuart Walker dissolves to a shot of Jasper in a white cassock, presiding over the choir at a church service and singing his heart out. These two sequences suggest that Jasper is a person of extremes—apparently devoted to God, but unable to cope with depression without the help of opium. This impression is reinforced by the way he stares obsessively at Rosa Bud (Heather Angel) to ensure that she plays the right notes in her public performances. Rosa is clearly frightened of him; she observes at one point that Jasper haunts her "like a dreadful ghost." The explanation for such behavior is obvious: Jasper has always been in love with Rosa, despite the considerable age gap between them, and wants to remove anyone he identifies as a competitor for her love. This drives him to murder his cousin Edwin Drood (DAVID MANNERS), and attempt to pin the blame for the crime on Neville Landless (Douglass Montgomery), another rival for Rosa's love. Jasper puts on a great act of public grief, as he looks straight into Landless's eyes and says, "What—have—you—done—with—Ned!" He takes long pauses between each word for dramatic effect. However, the strain of sustaining this façade proves too much for him, and he returns once more in the opium den. He lies on a concrete slab under the influence of the drug and murmurs over and over again: "I've done it! ... It was pleasant to do ... It was done so soon ... so soon! ... Ned! ... Oh, my boy! ... Rosa!" Rains plays this scene with utter conviction, suggesting that Jasper's mind is beginning to turn with the knowledge of what he has done. He places his hands round the opium seller's (Zeffie Tilbury) neck and tries to strangle her in the belief that she has been in some way responsible for Edwin's death.

From then on, it is only a matter of time before Jasper resolves to kill himself. After having tried to kill Landless, in a vain attempt to silence him, Jasper climbs up the church spire, once more screaming, "Ned! Ned! What have I done?!" He reaches the top, looks down at the crowd below and shouts, "Rosa! The journey's made," before plunging to his death. Although a multiple murderer, we feel sorry for Jasper at the end, as we understand how he has failed to deal with his obsession.

Rains had a leading role as Erique Claudin in Arthur Lubin's Technicolor remake of *The Phantom of the Opera*. At the beginning of the film, he seems like an insignificant member of the orchestra of the Paris Opera; a violinist who, although talented, will never receive recognition for his efforts. He trudges back to his apartment, after having been pensioned off, and sits moodily at a piano while his landlady Madame Lorenzi (Nicki André) berates him for not paying his monthly dues. Once he starts to play a florid tune on the piano however we understand that underneath that urbane exterior lurks a passionate man, whose nature strongly recalls that of John Jasper in *The Mystery of Edwin Drood*. This becomes more and more evident as the action progresses: he goes to the office of music publisher Pleyel (MILES MANDER) full of confidence in the hope that his concerto will be made available to a wider audience, but discovers to his cost that the publisher has stolen the piece, while pretending to have lost it. Director Lubin cuts to a close-up of Rains clasping his hat, his cheekbones shaking with pent-up emotion. He screams out, "Thief! You've stolen my music!" and strangles the publisher to death. In desperation, Pleyel's maid Georgette (Renee Carson) tries to break up the fight by throwing a tray of acid in Claudin's face; he howls like a dog and runs out of the shop clutching one side of his face.

Claudin is a changed personality from then on. No longer the meek and mild violinist, he takes revenge on all those who stand in his way — police officers, members of the opera company, and even members of the audience. His face covered with a mask, his black cloak and hat giving him an unearthly look, Rains's method of delivering the lines closely resembles that of Frank Griffin in *The Invisible Man*— words are rolled out on the tip of the tongue, accompanied by wild eye-movements and gestures. The film climaxes with Claudin taking his protégée Christine Dubois (Susanna Foster) down to the Paris sewers, and forcing her to sing while he plays the piece that forms the heart of his concerto. She duly obliges; her face contorted with fright; but as she hears Claudin playing, she gradually understands his true identity beneath the mask. Claudin meets a predictable end, being crushed to death beneath falling masonry as the roof of the sewer collapses on top of him; but director Lubin zooms in to a close-up of his violin and mask — a poignant reminder of what Claudin was like both before and after his unfortunate mishap.

In *The Lost World* (1960), Rains plays Professor George Edward Challenger, a maverick scientist who stands out from the crowd with his bushy ginger hair and beard. With his silver topped cane and cigar, he clearly enjoys the limelight, thrusting his chest out self-importantly and silencing anyone who dares to contradict him with a steely glance and an aggressive wave of the cane. His journey to the lost world of the Amazon is not only scientifically successful (as he proves beyond doubt that the dinosaurs actually exist), but turns out to be a voyage of self-discovery, as the professor learns to acknowledge the feelings of his fellow crew members. This is especially evident following one hair-raising sequence, where Lord John Roxton (MICHAEL RENNIE) and Ed Malone (David Hedison) rescue the professor in the nick of time, as he accidentally falls off a ledge and very nearly tumbles into a river of molten lava several feet below him. From then on, the professor tries his best to ensure that everyone escapes safely from the lost world.

Michael Rennie

b. August 25, 1909, Bradford, Yorkshire, England; d. June 10, 1971, Harrogate, Yorkshire, England.

Eric Alexander Rennie worked as a car salesperson and factory manager before turning to acting. After an early career in British films with successes such as *I'll Be Your Sweetheart* (1945), Rennie signed a contract with Twentieth Century–Fox in 1951. He essayed a variety of roles; some of his best were in science fiction films such as *The Day the Earth Stood Still* (1951), where he plays Klaatu, the visitor from another planet who comes to warn the people of Earth about their impending doom, should they decide to pursue a policy of nuclear aggression. Sallow-faced, with a slightly sorrowful look,

Michael Rennie publicity still (1951). After a nondescript career in British films, Rennie crossed the Atlantic to become a handsome leading man, with one of his most memorable roles being in *The Day the Earth Stood Still* (1951).

Klaatu at once sympathizes yet despairs of the human race, as they view his presence amongst them with a mixture of fear and suspicion. Rennie employs a series of minimalist gestures—a small smile, a raised eyebrow, a slight shrug of the shoulders—to convey the character's feelings. If the people on Earth do not listen to him, then "the planet would have to be ... eliminated." Rennie takes a long pause between the last two words to emphasize his point. He uses the same technique when informing Professor Barnhardt (Sam Jaffe) that "something dramatic ... but not destructive" might have to be done, so as to convince the people of Klaatu's intentions; in this phrase, the pause comes between the words "dramatic" and "destructive." This "dramatic" act involves cutting the world's electricity supply for half an hour; Klaatu is clearly a force to be reckoned with.

Outwardly Klaatu seems "a very nice man," as one character describes him, as he dons a suit and assumes human form. His manners are exemplary, his gestures neat and unostentatious. However he is almost *too* perfect—which helps to explain why people are so suspicious of him. The only person to understand him is young single mother Mrs. Bailey (Patricia Neal), who undertakes to help him escape from the U.S. Army, once his true identity had been discovered. At this point in the film, Rennie's manner changes; whereas once he concealed his feelings under a veneer of *sang-froid*, now he looks desperately from side to side, as if fearing for his future safety. It seems as if his attempts to elude his captors have been futile, as a soldier shoots him down in cold blood.

But Klaatu is no ordinary mortal; with the help of his robot Gort and the intervention of "the Almighty Spirit," he is resurrected, and emerges from his spaceship with Mrs. Bailey at his side, to deliver a climactic speech on the importance of maintaining peace. In other planets, wars no longer exist; robots are employed as police officers, programmed to suppress any potential uprising. If the Earth does not put its house in order, then these robots will return to destroy it. Klaatu speaks these lines in measured tones, allowing for each phrase to be clearly understood; this warning is directed both to the people of Washington D. C., and the audience watching the film. Director Robert Wise's camera slowly zooms in on Rennie's face, as he finishes his speech and turns slowly back towards the spaceship before blasting off to home once more. Klaatu's words must be heeded, if a nuclear catastrophe is to be avoided.

In *I'll Never Forget You* (1951), Rennie has a supporting role as Roger Forsyth, atomic scientist and close working colleague of Peter Standish (Tyrone Power). As in *The Day the Earth Stood Still*, Rennie plays a slightly reserved, rather standoffish personality; only this time this is identified as something negative, compared to the emotional Standish. In this film, national stereotypes matter—as an American Standish is identified with progress, development and prosperity, while the British characters (including Forsyth) are equated with tradition and/or precedent. Forsyth tries his best to dissuade Standish from pursuing research into time travel, in the belief that it might be potentially dangerous. The fact that it might also lead to greater historical understanding is conveniently ignored. Being British, Forsyth does not actually say this *directly* to Standish, but invents a series of mealy-mouthed excuses: Standish needs a holiday, he seems overtired from too much research, he needs a good rest, and so on. What the film suggests, however, is that characters should be true both to themselves and to others: Standish finds love in the past, and although he eventually has to return to the present, leaving his beloved Helen Pettigrew (Ann Blyth) behind, he can take her words to heart. Love overcomes everything, even time and space. However, it is only the Americans (Standish and Helen) who have the mental agility to appreciate this fact.

In *The Lost World* (1960), Rennie reprises the role of a fine old British gentleman as Lord John Roxton, dressed in gray suit and blue blazer, and speaking his lines in a cut-glass New England accent. Possessed of an old-fashioned outlook on life (he firmly believes, for instance, that "woman's place is in the home"), Roxton likes to think of himself as a big-game hunter—someone accustomed to the rigors of an expedition who can readily survive on his own as well as leading his fellow travelers. In his green combat suit and rifle, he looks admirably suited for the part. As the film progresses, however, we understand that Roxton has feet of clay; he apparently visited the lost world three years previously, during which time he managed not only to lose his fellow travelers, but also showed little concern for their whereabouts. Roxton admits his guilt in a pivotal sequence, where he is shown first with hands on hips, then thrusting them firmly into his pockets. No longer the big-game hunter, he rather resembles a naughty schoolboy unwillingly forced to admit that he has done wrong. From then on, it is the Professor (CLAUDE RAINS), aided (or possibly abetted) by the juvenile lead, journalist Ed Malone (David Hedison) who assume responsibility for the expedition. Roxton still shows off his bravery — most obviously when he helps prevent the professor falling off a tiny ledge into a river of molten lava — but he now assumes a secondary role.

Angelo Rossitto

*b. February 18, 1908, Omaha, Nebraska;
d. September 21, 1991, Los Angeles, California.*

Small in stature at only 2 feet 11 inches (88.9 cm), Angelo Salvatore Rossitto was nonetheless much in demand as a supporting actor. He first appeared alongside Lon Chaney and John Barrymore in silent pictures before making major talking picture debut in Tod Browning's *Freaks* (1931) as Angeleno. He speaks very few lines, but the camera focuses on his face as he looks at those members of the circus troupe who are taller than himself, in perpetual fear that they might attack him. At one point, he exclaims: "We're just filthy things!" In another sequence, he is shown enjoying himself at the dinner table, looking at Cleopatra (Olga Baclanova) with scorn as she takes advantage of Hans (Harry Earles). Although vastly different in height, Cleopatra treats Hans as if he were her lover: in common with his friends, Angeleno understands that she is merely toying with Hans's affections. She is offered a loving cup; far from accepting it willingly, she jumps up from the table and screams, "Freaks! Freaks! Freaks! Get out of here!" Hans, ashamed of his diminutive size, looks down at the ground, and it is left to Angeleno and his friends to shepherd him back to his caravan. In the end, Hans's friends decide to mount a campaign against Cleopatra: Browning's camera focuses on Angeleno as he listens to the plans being concocted, and nodding in assent when he is given his orders. At one point he listens to Hans, who grimly murmurs: "we'll be ready [to attack Cleopatra]." She might have caused suffering to those people she derogatorily described as "freaks," but this will not happen again. In the end, she is reduced to a catatonic vegetable, an object of the circus patrons' gaze, unable to speak or communicate properly. Angeleno remains a sympathetic character, who puts on a happy face even in the most adverse of circumstances, while displaying an unswerving loyalty towards his fellow performers. He might be a "freak" to Cleopatra, but he possesses the kind of stability and consistency of purpose that sets him apart from those larger than himself.

Throughout the remainder of his career Rossitto was almost invariably typecast as a dwarf in horror and/or fantasy films, especially those with an exotic setting such as *Ali Baba and the Forty Thieves* (1944). In *Spooks Run Wild* (1941), a comic horror flick starring the East Side Kids, he appears as Luigi, sidekick to Nardo (Bela Lugosi), a mysterious-looking figure who takes over the deserted Billings Estate. In his black cloak and trilby hat, Luigi cuts a fine figure as he escorts the Kids into the house, a candle held in front of him like a trophy. Luigi has a non speaking role, but his features speak volumes: at one point Nardo bids the Kids good night, and director Phil Rosen cuts to a close-up of Luigi staring meaningfully at them as they leave the room. No wonder one of them describes Luigi as "a little termite" to Nardo's vulture. In the end, the Kids manage to capture Luigi and thrust him in a cupboard, while they try to find out what has happened to Peewee (David Gorcey), whom they suspect has been transformed into a zombie. Their suspicions prove unfounded: Nardo and Luigi are actually practicing magicians looking for a place

Angelo Rossitto on the set of *Samson and Delilah* (1949). Although given limited choices of roles, Rossitto cut an imposing presence on screen, often as a villainous sidekick.

to perfect their latest illusions. Once the real criminal Von Grosch (Dennis Moore) has been apprehended, Nardo gives a performance; Luigi stands at his side, encouraging the audience to applaud in the proper places. Although resembling an imp in his black attire, his smile suggests benevolence rather than evil.

Rossitto and Lugosi are cast together once more in *The Corpse Vanishes* (1942) as Dr. Lorenz and his evil sidekick Toby; while Toby remains a victim of casual cruelty, he is determined to sustain a cheerful façade. As Patricia Hunter (Luana Walters) enters Lorenz's house, Toby hopes that she will "sleep good ... maybe," with a long pause taken between the last two words, followed by a peal of laughter. However, Toby meets a sticky end as the doctor kills him for knowing too much about the evil activities going on in the house — specifically the ways in which Lorenz steals the corpses of young virgins and extracts gland fluid in an attempt to keep his ancient wife (ELIZABETH RUSSELL) perpetually young.

In *Scared to Death* (1947), Rossitto once again appears as Lugosi's evil sidekick Indigo. This time he can neither hear nor speak, but understands what people say through lip-reading. Director Christy Cabanne treats him like a little cartoon dog running after his master to the accompaniment of a saxophone on the soundtrack.

Despite such treatment, Rossitto became a well-known figure during the early 1940s. He had a brief cameo in William Nigh's Mr. Wong mystery/horror flick *Doomed to Die* (1940) for Monogram, as a newspaper seller proclaim-ing a recent disaster at sea. He shouts to the camera, "Extra! Extra! Read all about it! Four hundred persons dead!" Hiappearance ends with him jumping off his box with a big smile. Rossitto's presence added to the bizarre, threatening nature of many horror films and he became as well known to fans of these low-budget movies as Lugosi, GEORGE ZUCCO or any of the other credited stars. He has a small role in *Mesa of Lost Women* (1953) as a lab assistant, working for mad physician Dr, Aranya (Jackie Coogan) crouching over smoking test-tubes and grinning evilly at his potential victims Dr. Tucker (Robert Knapp) and Doreen Culbertson (Mary Hill). Rossitto exerts a powerful influence over the lost women, not by saying anything, but rather staring at them intently until they carry out his orders. Despite his size, he tries to possess them. Directors Ron Ormond and Herbert Tevos emphasize the assistant's evil nature through repeated close-ups of his face, grinning at the camera. Rossitto is obviously very at home with this kind of role, having played it (albeit with some dialogue as well) in *The Corpse Vanishes*.

Elizabeth Russell

b. August 2, 1916, Philadelphia, Pennsylvania; d. May 4, 2002, Los Angeles, California.

Elizabeth Russell had minor roles in several B-flicks before coming to prominence as the cat woman in *Cat People* (1942). Dressed entirely in black, she walks past Irena (SIMONE SIMON) and her husband Oliver (KENT SMITH) and greets them with a malicious-sounding purr. Director Jacques Tourneur's camera tracks her as she moves past their table towards the door and exits silently. Although only uttering one word, the Cat Woman has the potential to transfix everyone into a state of nervous panic; she reveals the kind of latent power within women, which Irena has not yet acknowledged but will do so by the end of the film. They do not have to be violent, but can protect themselves should the occasion arise.

Russell assumes a far more substantial role as Barbara Farren in *Curse of the Cat People* (1944). She is the classic example of a neglected child whose mother Julia (Julia Dean) denies her very existence (referring to her as "that woman"), in the belief that her real daughter passed away when young. Barbara resents little Amy Reed's (Ann Carter) presence in their house — particularly when the girl strikes up a relationship with the old woman. Yet Barbara cannot express her resentment openly — all we see of her is her silhouette walking slowly down the stairs, followed by a quick medium close-up of her face bathed in a lurid light, staring at the little girl. Hence it comes as no surprise to find Barbara wanting to kill Amy at the end of the film. The little girl stands at the top of the stairs, with Barbara at the bottom in her trademark black dress, a light again shining on her face. She accuses Amy of having stolen her mother from her. Directors Robert Wise and Gunther von Fritsch cut to a point of view shot from Amy's perspective; she does not see Barbara in front of her, but Irena instead. Murmuring "my friend" in a low voice, Amy walks into Barbara's arms; for a few moments, we believe that the girl's vivid imagination has caused her destruction. The action cuts to a close-up of Barbara's arms snaking around Amy's head; but she lets go abruptly just at the moment when Oliver and his wife Alice (Jane Randolph) burst into the house to rescue their daughter. Russell's features do not change much in this sequence, except for the look in her eyes, which alters from pure hate to delight as the child willingly accepts her embrace. This is a classic example of how small gestures can have an immediate effect on the spectator.

In another Val Lewton-produced film, *Bedlam* (1946), Russell plays Mistress Kitty Sims, the rapacious sister of prison governor George

Elizabeth Russell and Julia Dean in *Curse of the Cat People* (1944). Tall and sinister, Russell made her name in Val Lewton's cycle of horror films for RKO in the mid–1940s.

Sims (Boris Karloff). With her tall, erect manner and fashionable outfits— tall hat, frilly skirt and tight-fitting bodice — she likes to appear a woman-about-town, the ideal potential mistress for Lord Mortimer (Billy House). Unfortunately, Kitty is too old and not sufficiently attractive for the peer, who pursues attractive campaigner Nell Bowen (Anna Lee) instead. Kitty responds by persuading her brother to deal with Nell, proclaiming nastily that "the girl has a high enough price!" George responds by inventing a trumped-up charge to consign Nell to Bedlam. In truth, Kitty is hardly the kind of person that Mortimer would desire as a companion; she drinks far too much gin, and takes a sadistic pleasure in hearing about other people's sufferings. When George proposes to apprehend Nell, and take away her pet parrot, Kitty whoops with delight: "Arrest a parrot! I'll drink to that!" Director Mark Robson suggests that Kitty's fondness for alcohol is chiefly due to insecurity; she realizes she is losing her looks (as she covers her face with conspicuous beauty-spots), and does not relish the taste of "piety"— in other words, opting for a pious life rather than finding new male paramours.

In *Weird Woman* (also 1944), Russell has another meaty role as Evelyn Sawtelle, the sour-faced, expressionless wife of Professor Millard Sawtelle (Ralph Morgan), who resents the fact that Professor Norman Reed (Lon Chaney, Jr.) achieved academic success at her husband's expense. Unable to cope with his public humiliation, as well as his wife's criticism, Millard commits suicide; Evelyn responds by screaming "Murderer! Murderer!" in Reed's face. She then strides up to Reed's wife, Paula (ANNE GWYNNE), and calls her a witch before chasing her around the room. Reed enters and tries to restrain Evelyn; she responds by squaring up to him and shouting, "Let go of me, you murderer!" The ordeal of her husband's death has clearly driven her into hysterics.

Evelyn's manner alters abruptly, however, once she discovers that Ilona Carr (EVELYN ANKERS) drove Millard to commit suicide. Director Reginald le Borg cuts to a close-up of Evelyn's face, one hand clamped to her ear as she learns what happened. She immediately concocts a scheme to persuade Ilona that a curse has been placed on her (nothing of the sort has happened, but Evelyn believes that this is the best way to make Ilona tell the truth). Even if she has lost her husband, Evelyn has sufficient presence of mind to recognize that Ilona must be prevented from destroying anyone else. The ruse proves successful: Evelyn takes charge of the situation by grabbing Ilona's arm and literally wrenching the truth out of her.

George Sanders
b. July 3, 1906, St. Petersburg, Russia;
d. April 25, 1972. Castelldefels, Barcelona, Spain.

Born in St. Petersburg of English parents, George Sanders entered the theatre as a chorus boy, later graduating to cabaret and radio. He made his film debut in 1936 in *Find the Lady*; his Hollywood debut came later that year in *Lloyds of London*. Sanders took numerous major roles in horror films, especially those based on classic novels. In Joe May's version of Nathaniel Hawthorne's *The House of the Seven Gables* (1940), Sanders plays Jaffray Pyncheon, an upstart judge who will stop at nothing to achieve his ambition of absolute power — even to the extent of denouncing his brother Clifford (Vincent Price) for a crime Clifford did not commit. In one sequence, a crowd of townspeople, photographed from an open window, gather to watch Judge Pyncheon (Charles Trowbridge) and Clifford quarrel. The judge has a seizure and dies on the spot; Jaffray enters and proclaims Clifford guilty for having caused the tragedy. Enraged by the accusation, Clifford grasps Jaffray by the neck and threatens to throttle him if he should make such an accusation again. This only enrages the crowd of citizens witnessing the whole event. The point here is obvious: Jaffray forces everyone to accept without question everything he says, even if it means denying the evidence of their own eyes. Sanders speaks his lines with a supercilious sneer, looking disdainfully down his nose at his brother and then up at the crowd as if defying them to challenge the truth of what he is saying.

George Sanders publicity still (1951). Russian-born Sanders enjoyed a long career as a suave, sophisticated actor, adept at playing villains as well as heroes. The brother of Tom Conway.

But Jaffray's arrogance leads to his destruction. In a newly written ending, we discover that he has funded the slave trade and cannot repay his debts. His creditors turn up at the front door to demand money; unable to pay them, Jaffray dies of apoplexy. He clasps his hand to his heart, then to his throat and collapses to the ground, suggesting that he has quite literally been cursed. In visual terms, Sanders' thick-set features and rounded vowels contrast starkly with the young Price, who plays a rare romantic role using a soft, almost effeminate tone. We have little difficulty separating the hero from the villain in this film.

In Albert Lewin's rendering of Oscar Wilde's *The Picture of Dorian Gray* (1945), Sanders plays another supercilious character—Lord Henry Wotton, who is much given to pronouncing Wildean epigrams. Although a guest in painter Basil Hallward's (Lowell Gillmore) house, Wotton treats it as his own, as he relaxes in an easy chair, takes his top hat off and cradles it in his hands. In a later sequence, he walks around the living room wearing his hat and thrusting his hands deep into his pockets; not only does this show contempt for social conventions (a guest in a Victorian house would never dream of such familiarity), it also reveals Henry's sublime arrogance. Such traits were characteristic of Sanders's screen persona, particularly when playing villainous roles.

Henry's body language plays an important part in our interpretation of his speeches. Although offering Dorian (Hurd Hatfield) some sound advice ("Let nothing be lost upon you, be afraid of nothing"), we wonder whether Henry actually means what he says, or whether he is playing another verbal game. Despite all his accomplishments, it is clear that Henry cannot escape from his existence; this is indicated by a quick shot of a bird fluttering around in a golden cage, following one of his epigrams. In another context, Henry might be allowed to express his affection for Dorian; however in the rarefied world of Victorian London he repressed it, preferring instead to remain a cynic, unwilling to make any emotional commitment. Others describe him admiringly as "an unmitigated cad," but this reputation has been acquired at the expense of his soul. When Sybil Vane (Angela Lansbury) commits suicide, Henry informs Dorian in a matter-of-fact tone, while refusing to look the younger man in the eye. Instead he idly picks up an object lying on the mantelpiece and looks at it through a magnifying glass.

All of Henry's posturing—his epigrams, his consciously antisocial behavior, his world-weary cynicism—is an act designed to cover up his emotional inadequacies in a society that declares homosexuality illegal. He resembles Wilde himself in his inability to voice his feelings directly.

While the remainder of the film focuses on Dorian's demise, as he stabs himself and transforms himself into an old man (leaving the picture exactly as Basil had painted it), Lewin allows Henry one moment of pathos, as he looks wistfully at the picture and arranges for Dorian's girlfriend Gladys (Donna Reed) to be taken home. Henry can only express his emotions for a fleeing moment: society condemns him to leading a half-life.

Sometimes Sanders could play the good guy — as in John Brahm's remake of *The Lodger* (1944) for Twentieth Century–Fox, based on the novel by Marie Belloc Lowndes. As Inspector Warwick, he cuts an imposing figure — someone dedicated to his job yet with a soft spot for Kitty Langley (Merle Oberon). In one sequence he takes Kitty to the Black Museum, a room set aside in the police station for displaying objects used in violent crimes. While Kitty picks up each object and asks about it, the inspector pursues her around the room, determined to persuade her to come out on a date with him. Once she agrees, the inspector's normally impassive face breaks into a smile, as he realizes that his quest has been successful. However, this is one of the few occasions where he assumes mastery of the situation; most of the time, he ends up being hopelessly outwitted by Mr. Slade (Laird Cregar), who is clearly based on Jack the Ripper. The inspector's manner changes, as he becomes more and more obsessed with catching the criminal. This is summed up in a telling moment, where he is shown looking at a piece of evidence through a magnifying glass; his eye is artificially enlarged, giving him a monstrous appearance. In the end Slade eludes him as he jumps to his death from an upper-floor window into the River Thames. The inspector's response ("A river sweeps the city clean") demonstrates his powerlessness; the police can no longer cleanse London of its criminals, but have to rely on the river to do their work for them.

Following his brother TOM CONWAY, who essayed a similar role in Jacques Tourneur's *Cat People* (1942), Sanders plays the police psychiatrist Allan Middleton in *Hangover Square* (1945), Twentieth Century–Fox's follow-up to *The Lodger* based on the novel by Patrick Hamilton. A tall, authoritative presence, he seems to understand precisely George Harvey Bone's (Laird Cregar) schizophrenic nature, which combines romanticism with frequent mental blackouts, during which time Bone commits murder. Middleton waits outside Bone's house, his hands meditatively thrust in his overcoat pockets; once the police officers have left, Middleton returns and confronts Bone with what he has done. In a masterly sequence of *film noir*, director John Brahm photographs Middleton from behind — a dark, shadowy figure whose face remains unseen — as he walks up towards Bone. The action cuts to a close-up of Middleton's face, half of which is illuminated by bright light, the other half remaining in total darkness, suggesting that the psychiatrist, like his patient, has two sides to his nature. All we can hear on the soundtrack is Middleton's clear, well-modulated tones, as he explains how Bone strangled Netta Longdon (Linda Darnell), and burnt her corpse at the top of a bonfire celebrating Guy Fawkes Day (November 5). Brahm cuts to a close-up of Middleton's face, which is in darkness, save for a steely light shining on his eyes. Although sympathetic to Bone's plight, it is clear that Middleton will not let him go free. In the end, however, Bone escapes, and dies — like Netta — in a fire. Meanwhile, Middleton walks up to Bone's fiancée Barbara Chapman (Faye Marlowe) and observes quietly that "it's better this way" — i.e., it is better for Bone to commit suicide rather than spend the rest of his life in an asylum.

In his later career, Sanders had at least two good roles in horror and science fiction features. In Byron Haskin's *From the Earth to the Moon* (1958), based on the Jules Verne novel, he plays Stuyvesant Nicholl, who acts as a voice of skepticism pouring scorn on Victor Barbicane's (Joseph Cotten) invention of a new source of power called Power X. Sanders plays the role with a perpetually curled lip, as if contemptuous of Barbicane's efforts; later on, however, we learn that Nicholl is actually frightened of Power X's potential. Nicholl might be a scientist, but he likes to keep within "acceptable" limits — i.e., those limits that do not pose a danger to the future of his social position. In Wolf Rilla's *Village of the Damned* (1960), made for MGM in Great Britain, with a screenplay based on the John Wyndham novel *The Midwich Cuckoos*, Sanders plays Professor Gordon Zellaby, in a role originally slated for Ronald Colman. He initially comes across as a happy family man with a young wife Anthea (Barbara

Shelley) and son David (Martin Stephens). Zellaby makes every effort to be a good parent, extolling the fact that David seems to exhibit the kind of maturity that belies his tender years. The professor's opinions only change once he attends a meeting of British Intelligence in London, and learns that his son (like many other children in his village) are mutants, without conscience or emotion, who have the power to force people to do things against their will. One sequence shows a man running his car into a wall; his brother later commits suicide by shooting himself.

In the face of this threat, Zellaby resembles a mad scientist who consciously vetoes any attempt to destroy the children, as he hopes to find out more about them. This he believes can be accomplished only through painstaking research and analysis, despite the threat that they pose to the village's security. Zellaby's role here recalls that of other scientists in 1950s and early 1960s science fiction films (for example, Robert Cornthwaite in *The Thing from Another World* [1951]), whose obsession with their work blinds them to what is happening around them. Sanders suggests this preoccupation by delivering his lines in an earnest, plaintive tone, as if sincerely believing that scientific research cannot be halted, even if it costs human lives.

Zellaby's opinions only change in the film's concluding sequence, as he characterizes his attempts to understand the children as analogous to reasoning with a brick wall. If he wants to protect himself, he has to use this metaphor. However, things do not go according to plan: David scans Zellaby's mind and solemnly tells his father, "You're not thinking of atomic energy, you're thinking of ... a brick wall!" The professor's eyes shine in obvious terror; David rejects paternal authority and actively seeks to control his father's mind. In such circumstances, the professor's academic credentials count for nothing. In a finale of mounting tension, intercutting between the professor's terrified face and the children staring impassively at him, they gradually break down Zellaby's mental wall; at the point of discovery, Zellaby sets off a time-bomb, destroying himself and the children in the process. *Village of the Damned* offers Sanders the chance to show off his technical skill as a fundamentally good man, whose academic complacency and naïve belief in the strength of his family are both destroyed by alien forces. In this kind of world, scientific research counts for nothing: self-preservation assumes far greater importance.

Simone Simon
b. April 23, 1910, Marseille, France;
d. February 22, 2005, Paris, France.

Simone Thérèse Fernande Simon made her screen debut in *Le Chanteur Inconnu/The Unknown Singer* (1931). After seeing her in *Lac aux Dames/Ladies' Lake* (1934), Darryl F. Zanuck brought her to Hollywood. After several undistinguished years, Simon returned to France and then returned to Hollywood as a contract player for RKO Radio Pictures.

Director William Dieterle exploited her French identity in his horror-cum-morality tale *The Devil and Daniel Webster* (1941). She plays

Simone Simon cinema star postcard (1944). French-born Simon enjoyed her finest hour in *Cat People* and *Curse of the Cat People* playing an outwardly attractive woman with feline tendencies.

Belle Dit (literally translated as "beautifully spoken"), shortened to Belle, who is sent by the devil Mr. Scratch (Walter Huston) to tempt poor farmer Jabez Stone (James Craig). The task isn't very difficult — although happily married to Mary (Anne Shirley) with a little son, Jabez soon falls victim to Belle's charms. Her role as temptress is readily suggested by her heavy make-up — even in the mornings she wears lipstick and rouge — and her décolleté dresses contrasting vividly with Mary's homespun attire. Belle never looks directly into the camera; she either glances from left to right, as if tempting viewers (as well as Jabez) to guess her motives. They are clear enough; in one sequence Belle pours liquor and helps Jabez win at cards. In keeping with her diabolic origins, she resorts to euphemism rather than direct statement, as she repeatedly tells Jabez that she has come to see him from "over the mountain." In keeping with the film's propagandist purpose, Daniel Webster (Edward Arnold) tells Jabez that the only means of driving Belle away is to acknowledge his sins and embrace the American — rather than the French — way of life, as true American citizens "cannot be forced into the service of a foreign prince [or princess]." Jabez successfully accomplishes this task, and learns the importance of not letting his country — America — "go to the Devil." The fact that France and America were allies during World War II is conveniently overlooked — as a non–American Simon is automatically identified as the devil's worker.

Simon was best known for her central performances in Val Lewton's *Cat People* (1942) and the sequel *Curse of the Cat People* (1944). Lewton liked her on account of her little kitten-face; cute and soft and cuddly, and seemingly not at all dangerous. Simon's performance as Irena contains numerous memorable moments of peripheral distraction, bemusement and fretfulness; this is evident, for instance, in the moment where she happily watches her pet canary playing in the cage. She puts her hand in to pick it up, only to witness it dying of fright. Her expression abruptly changes to one of horror as she understands the presence of evil within her, however hard she might try to suppress it. Irena's subsequent decision to throw the dead bird to the caged panther might be considered sadistic, but it is entirely coherent with her beast-like instincts.

On the other hand, Irena can be childlike; in one sequence, she takes a bath and cries all the while. On the soundtrack, the psychiatrist Judd's (TOM CONWAY) banal diagnoses can be heard over and over again. This moment illustrates just how much of a social outcast Irena is; no one (least of all, her husband Oliver [KENT SMITH]) actually takes her feelings into account, and even when they do, they make no attempt to understand her psychology. American society treats people like her as deviants or children. Lewton's casting of Simon, a French national, is especially effective here; her accented mode of delivery as well as her feline gestures contrasting starkly with her husband's American pragmatism (revealing itself in the desire to reduce complex phenomena to a series of trite phrases).

In the counseling sessions involving Irena and the psychiatrist Judd, he towers above her, as he lights a cigarette and points it at her as if accusing her of wrongdoing. Irena breathes quickly and remains calm; on the surface it seems as if she will endure such humiliation for her husband's sake. However, we understand the latent violence within her nature in a later sequence, as she is shown scratching the back of a sofa, her fingers shaped like cat's claws. Irena might be misunderstood, but she is perfectly capable of striking back, if pushed too far. On this view, *Cat People* might be seen as a film about racism and sexism: women like Irena need to be contained within mainstream society, even if it means committing them (in order words, penning them up like the panther in the zoo). However, Irena is not prepared to endure such treatment: when Judd tries to force himself on her, all that violence which we saw in her scene with the canary comes to the surface, as she kills him and escapes with a wound to her shoulder. She runs to the zoo, opens the panther's cage and climbs in, as if expecting to be killed; the panther duly obliges. While this moment helps to create a happy ending (Oliver has been released from an unhappy marriage and can now go off with his lover Alice [Jane

Randolph]), it also shows Irena successfully resisting patriarchal abuse.

In *Curse of the Cat People* (1944), Simon's Irena is a very different person, as she is summoned back from the dead to act as a companion/friend to Amy (Janet Smith), the daughter of Oliver and Amy — a little girl ostracized at school because she thinks differently, and misunderstood by her parents, who expect her to conform to strict behavioral standards. In one disturbing sequence, Oliver takes Amy upstairs to bear her; like Judd in *Cat People* he believes that he can do as he pleases in a patriarchal society. Resembling the Virgin Mary in her long white dress and flowing black locks, Irena shows the little girl that alternative role models do exist for those who search for them.

The film once again stresses the contrast between Irena, Oliver and Alice. At Christmastime, for instance, the parents indulge in carol-singing and putting presents around the tree, but Amy is drawn towards Irena, who stands alone outside the house, humming carols in French and showing the kind of maternal care and affection the girl so badly yearns for. Irena might be a representative of the other (both physically and in terms of national identity), but she understands how to look after children.

The only way Oliver and Alice can come to terms with their daughter is to acknowledge how the past continues to influence the present. Irena might be dead, but she exerts a spellbinding presence over all of their lives. Simon's performance is very different in *Curse of the Cat People*; whereas the earlier film showed her as childlike as she tried to come to terms with her innermost feelings, the sequel proves she is at peace with herself and the world around her. She delivers her lines in soft, melodious tones that contrast with Oliver's strained, apprehensive voice.

At the end of the film, Irena disappears from view, as Oliver at last acknowledges her presence in his life. Now, it seems, that the family can be at peace, having come to terms with their feelings of guilt, while Irena can return to the grace, secure in the knowledge that she helped Amy to overcome her psychological difficulties. Although this ending might seem a little too contrived (we have yet to be convinced that Oliver will change for the better), Simon points the way for any woman seeking to come to terms with their identity. Sometimes our inner lives are overtaken by strange ideas and unlikely beliefs. But no matter how unscientific or irrational they seem to others, these shadowy undercurrents affect us in undeniable ways. They might threaten our existence, but alternatively they might make us whole.

Kent Smith

b. March 19, 1907, New York City;
d. April 23, 1985, Woodland Hills,
Los Angeles, California.

Frank Kent Smith who came to films after a distinguished Broadway career in the 1930s, in which he appeared with leading ladies such as Lillian Gish, Katharine Cornell and Ethel Barrymore. He made his film debut in *The Garden Murder Case* (1936). His stage work brought him to the attention of producer Val Lewton, who cast Smith as Oliver Reed in *Cat People* (1942) and its sequel *Curse of the Cat People* (1944). Smith exudes good looks and healthy appeal — the ideal marriage partner. But this is nothing more than a façade: Oliver conceals deep-seated prejudices beneath a caring veneer. In *Cat People* he talks blithely of being "reasonable" by helping to "cure" his wife Irena's (SIMONE SIMON) condition by taking her to a psychiatrist. In the few moments of intimacy that the two of them share, Oliver's face remains impassive, delivering his lines in a flat, toneless voice; he possesses neither the physical nor the emotional equipment to understand Irena.

The reason for this is self-evident: Oliver believes it is his responsibility to conform to prevailing norms of 1940s American masculinity by finding a suitable marriage partner and working hard to create a life for both of them. His wife meanwhile should stay at home and look after the children (once they arrive on the scene). His Americanness manifests itself in a variety of ways; in Sally Lund's restaurant near his office, he eats nothing else but apple pie. It is hardly surprising that he should fall for Alice

Kent Smith publicity still (1953). Square-jawed Smith made a habit of playing reliable, trustworthy leading men both in the cinema and later on television.

(Jane Randolph), the archetypal blonde-haired, blue-eyed beauty.

Director Jacques Tourneur stresses Oliver's cruelty, even while attempting to be kind; he chooses to have Irena committed to a mental institution "for her own good," even though this is nothing more than a ruse, designed to bring him closer to Alice. Irena has her revenge, as she stalks Alice and nearly frightens her to death; Oliver responds by holding up a cross in his wife's direction, in the mistaken belief that she can be repelled like Dracula. Although *Cat People* ends happily for him as Irena dies, we understand that he has learned nothing about himself or his shortcomings; he still firmly believes in the patriarchy as the core of a stable society.

Returning to the role of Oliver two years later in *Curse of the Cat People*, Smith shows that the character has hardly changed at all. His childlike side emerges on numerous occasions, as we see him preoccupied with a tiddlywinks game set out for his daughter Amy's (Ann Carter) birthday party, building model shops and playing cards with Alice. He is so wrapped up in himself that he does not take the trouble to apologize for his daughter's oversight in forgetting to distribute the invitations to her birthday party. This only causes Amy further stress, as her friends accuse her of ignoring them. Such moments underline a fundamental if unrecognized similarity between children and grown-ups, while they also foster a feeling of just how much the fantasizing impulse lingers, almost unnoticed, in human activities. Smith's performance also highlights his paternal shortcomings, as he tells her to be "rational" rather than giving rein to her imagination. Once Amy ignores this advice, Oliver's sole reaction is to beat her, thereby revealing the brutal side to his supposedly wholesome nature. The film ends with father and daughter supposedly reconciled to one another, as Oliver admits his faults and promises to participate in Amy's fantasies, even if he cannot see her imaginary "friend" (Irena) for himself. However, Smith's emotionless method of delivery suggests that he doesn't actually believe in what he says. We are left wondering whether he is just trying to appease his family for the sake of future happiness.

In Robert Siodmak's *The Spiral Staircase* (1945), Smith plays another outwardly wholesome character, Dr. Parry—a respected member of the community possessing both the humanity and the knowledge that his colleague Dr. Harvey (Erville Alderson) apparently lacks. He not only cares for old Mrs. Warren (Ethel Barrymore), but develops a passionate concern for Helen Capel (Dorothy McGuire), who has been rendered speechless by the traumatic experience of witnessing her parents burning to death in a fire in her childhood. We initially consider him a stable, levelheaded kind of person, as he strides purposefully through the Warren family house, walking in straight lines from room to room as if completely acquainted with the interior. However, once again this proves nothing more than an illusion; as with Oliver Reed in the two *Cat People* films, Dr. Parry has a cruel streak that emerges when he tries to communicate with Helen. He picks her up by the wrists and shakes her like a rag doll in a desperate attempt to make her speak, but only succeeds in driving her further into her cocoon of silence. Steve Warren's (Gordon Oliver) observation is pertinent here—despite his good looks and pleasant nature, Parry is little more than "a country hick doctor," with little understanding of how trauma can affect a person. Director Siodmak removes him from the action soon afterwards: Parry is not involved in the film's thrilling climax, as Helen rediscovers the power of speech on her own, telephoning for the police after Mrs. Warren has shot the murderous Professor Warren (George Brent), only to die of a heart attack herself immediately afterwards.

Frequently dismissed as a statuesque actor, lacking the kind of "charisma or sex appeal for audiences to latch on to," Kent Smith nonetheless deserves to be remembered as someone whose performances highlighted the shortcomings of the all–American stereotype of masculinity in 1940s horror films.

Gale Sondergaard

b. February 15, 1899, Litchfield, Minnesota; d. August 14, 1985, Woodland Hills, Los Angeles, California.

Edith Holm Sondergaard was one of the main inspirations for the Wicked Witch in Disney's *Snow White and the Seven Dwarfs* (1937), and was also considered for the evil witch in *The Wizard of Oz*. However, she rejected the latter role and played opposite Paul Muni in *The Life of Emile Zola* (1937) instead.

Sondergaard made her reputation playing sinister roles. As Miss Lu the housekeeper in Paramount's *The Cat and the Canary* (1939), she is first seen through a barred window, suspiciously watching the lawyer Crosby (GEORGE ZUCCO) arriving for the reading of her late employer's will. As soon as she opens the front door to him, she says in a faraway voice that she has friends from the other world who support her solitary life in the house, and that Crosby's presence there is clearly unwanted. To emphasize her point, she stares at the lawyer down her nose with an expression of utter contempt. When the rest of the family arrives, Miss Lu's peace of mind is further disturbed, so she resolves to make their stay as unpleasant as possible. In one sequence, as they are all seated around the dining table, she suddenly clasps her hands, looks towards the ceiling and calls to her employer: "Tell me ... tell me the name [of the person who inherits the Norman fortune] ... Master!" On another occasion, she rushes up to Wally Campbell (Bob Hope) and claims that he has the power: "There are spirits all around you!" None of this is actually true of course, but all part of the housekeeper's plan to evict the entire family, whom she perceives as intruders. This theme of intrusion, of people prying into other people's business, is reinforced throughout the film through point of view shots, as well as shots of Miss Lu peeping behind doors. When the lawyer Crosby is strangled under mysterious circumstances, she claims that "the demon in the house has got him" and warns Joyce Norman (the named heir to the Norman fortune) that she might be the next victim. This immediately leads us to suspect that Miss Lu and the demon could be one and the same person — particularly when we see the housekeeper looking at Joyce undressing through a mirror, while slyly emptying a revolver of its bullets and placing it in Joyce's bedroom drawer. If anyone attacks Joyce, she will

Gale Sondergaard in *The Climax* (1944). Sondergaard's memorable voice, which enunciated dialogue very precisely and carefully, made her an ideal villain.

be unable to defend herself. Miss Lu contributes to the atmosphere of tension through her observations, intoned in a doleful voice, frequently with her arms folded ("The warning has come again ... nothing can stop it!")

It turns out that the housekeeper is not the murderer at all (it is actually Charles Wilder (Douglass Montgomery), who tries to take revenge on those whom he believed denied him his rightful fortune. Miss Lu has the pleasure of shooting him dead with a shotgun as he tries to kill Joyce. The film ends happily for her; having understood that the Norman fortune puts her in great danger, Joyce gives up her claim to it, and it devolves on Miss Lu instead. The entire family quits the house, leaving the housekeeper in charge once more. By a combination of luck and judgment, she has achieved her aim of evicting all her unwanted guests and returning to a life of solitude. It is thus hardly surprising that we see her smiling for the first time right at the end of the film, as she bids Joyce and Wally goodbye, waving a handkerchief as she does so.

Sondergaard plays almost exactly the same role as Abigail the housekeeper in Universal's comedy-horror spoof *The Black Cat* (1941). Although supposedly based on Poe's story, the film is obviously modeled on *The Cat and the Canary*. She keeps a deadpan face, even while listening to some of Mr. Penny's (Hugh Herbert) endless jokes. Clearly suspicious of all the family members, who have come to the house of elderly matriarch Henrietta Winslow (Cecilia Loftus) to listen to the reading of her will, Abigail is seen listening behind doors to all of their conversations. Sondergaard clearly enjoys herself delivering lines such as, "Whom a black cat follows.... Dies!" or "Pack and ... leave!" She stresses the final words of each phrase. Eventually, it is Abigail herself who becomes a victim of crazed murderer Myrna Hartley (Gladys Cooper), who needs to dispose of Henrietta and her servants in order to secure Henrietta's fortune for herself. In one scene, Abigail is hit over the head and shut in a trunk, only to be rescued in the nick of time by snooping salesperson Gil Smith (Broderick Crawford). However, Myrna makes no mistake the second time, as she chokes Abigail to death by stringing her up behind a door by her neck.

Cast as the eponymous Spider Woman Adrea Spedding in the Sherlock Holmes film of the same name (1944), Sondergaard comes across as equally manipulative. Whether sprawled seductively across a sofa or moving in a feline, almost nonchalant manner, she appears to be every man's dream woman. Once she has them in her power her attitude changes, as she stares into their eyes and in a soft voice murmurs lines like "I think it will cut up rather large" (i.e., the victim). Her costumes have an orientalist feel to them — she wears a black headscarf that only served to highlight her pale face. This suggests exoticism — the kind that can attract any man but will prove fatal in the end. Adrea proves more than a match for Holmes (Basil Rathbone) with her capacity for concocting elaborate deceptions and indulging in verbal sparring. Although she is outwitted in the end, we sense that this is chiefly due to director Roy William Neill's desire to tie up the film's loose ends and bring about a happy ending.

Sondergaard reappears in *The Spider Woman Strikes Back* (1946) which, although bearing a similar title to the earlier film, has absolutely nothing to do with it. This time she plays Zenobia Dollard, who—like Miss Lu in *The Cat and the Canary*—lives in an isolated house with only her manservant Mario (RONDO HATTON) for company. Initially, it seems as if Zenobia deserves our sympathy, as she apparently suffers from blindness as well as loneliness. She appears to have need for a full-time companion like Jean Kingsley (Brenda Joyce), who will read to her as well as offering mental and physical support. However, we should remember from *Sherlock Holmes and the Spider Woman* that Sondergaard's characters are proficient at role-playing in pursuit of their evil aims. Zenobia puts on a blind act to lure innocent young women to her house, and subsequently extracts blood from them to feed her poisonous plants. There is no doubt, however, that Zenobia is a convincing performer; with her bright smile, long black dress and maternal manner, she can easily fool young innocents like Jean. The only indication we have of Zenobia's true nature is her tendency to overemphasize certain phrases—for example, "We hope she [Jean] sleeps better tomorrow," where her stress on the word "better" suggests that she actually wants to put Jean permanently to sleep.

Zenobia grows so tired of maintaining the pretense of blindness that she drags Jean down to her laboratory and explains her intentions in detail. She grasps Jean's hand and tells her, "Those stupid farmers are leaving [their land] because their cattle are dying." This is something that Zenobia has deliberately engineered; she has created a poison out of her plants, which has subsequently been administered to the cattle. Once the farmers have left, Zenobia wants to buy their land and thereby recover social prosperity. Jean is simply a pawn in this scheme: Zenobia's face breaks into an evil grin as she informs her that "she [Jean] is going to die [...] but you'll live on in this beautiful plant!" By contrast, no one will suspect Zenobia of anything, "not dear ... blind ... Zenobia!" Sondergaard delivers the line in a staccato voice, making it seem as if her position is virtually impregnable.

As in *Sherlock Holmes and the Spider Woman*, *The Spider Woman Strikes Back* poses a problem for director Arthur Lubin: Sondergaard's performance transcends the film's rather hackneyed plot. The only way he can contrive a happy ending is to have Zenobia accidentally burning herself to death as a result of her experiments. This seems particularly implausible, in view of the care with which she conducts them — at one point, she is shown stroking one of her plants and describing it as "a beautiful creature! You love Zenobia, don't you?"

Even in supporting roles, Sondergaard understood the importance of small gestures as a means of characterization, As Lady Herrick in *The Invisible Man Returns* (1944), Sondergaard cuts an authoritative figure, with her short hair and prim and particular manners. Although apparently solicitous towards Robert Griffin (JON HALL), it soon emerges that she suspects him of being a murderer. She mutters the line "You'll get what's coming to you" through her teeth as she drugs his drink, forcing him to collapse to the floor. Director Ford Beebe cuts to a close-up of her face, her small mean mouth fixed in a tight smile — anticipating Zenobia in *The Spider Woman Strikes Back*— as she crouches over Griffin's body and calls him a madman.

In *The Climax* (1944), Sondergaard's role as the servant Luise is superficially reminiscent of Miss Lu in *The Cat and the Canary*— a housekeeper devoted to the memory of her late employer, the soprano Marcellina (June Vincent). Now Luise works for the mad doctor Friedrich Hohner (Boris Karloff), and jealously guards his privacy. When the young would-be soprano Angela Klatt (Susanna Foster) comes to the doctor's house, Luise scowls at her; later on she contemptuously informs Angela's fiancé Franz Munzer (TURHAN BEY) that the doctor is not at home. This film also reveals another side to Sondergaard's screen persona, as she shows a softer side to her nature. When the doctor tries to prevent Angela from singing the lead role in the operetta *The Magic Voice*, Luise takes pity on her and sprites her away from his house. She subsequently confronts the doctor and accuses him of murdering Marcellina; Hohner tries to strangle her, but she fixes him with a threatening stare and announces that she is not afraid. The last we see of Luise is her standing backstage, looking on happily as Angela performs her role to a standing ovation from a packed theatre audience.

Glenn Strange

b. August 16, 1899, Weed, New Mexico;
d. September 20, 1973, Los Angeles, California.

George Glenn Strange grew up as a real-life cowboy in Texas before joining a radio singing group, the Arizona Wranglers" that toured America throughout the 1920s. He made his film debut in 1930; and went on to play the bad guy in hundreds of B Westerns, as well as serials such as *Flash Gordon* (1936).

By the early 1940s, Strange had expanded his range into horror films, where he played monsters, heavies and comic sidekicks. In *The Mad Monster* (1942), he plays the simple-minded handyman Petro, who is transformed into a werewolf by the mad scientist Dr. Lorenzo Cameron (GEORGE ZUCCO). Strange plays

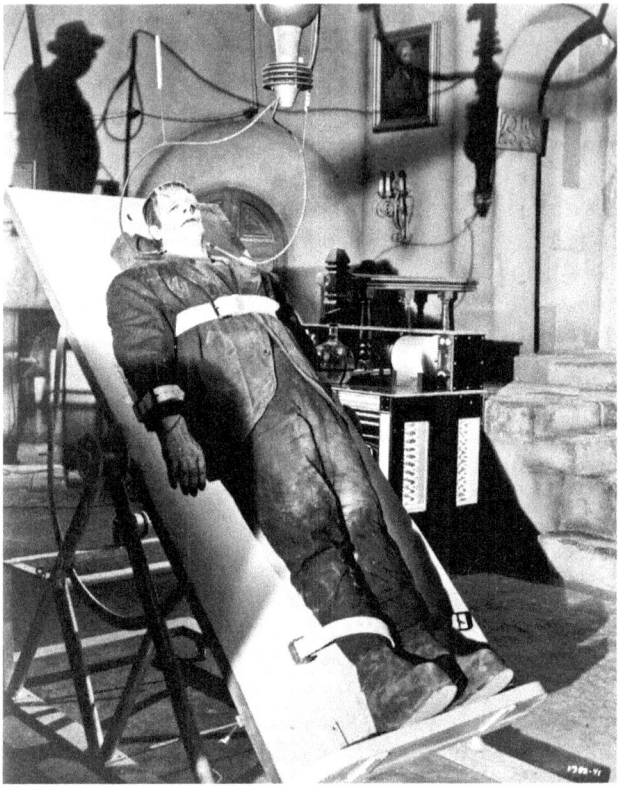

Glenn Strange in *The House of Frankenstein* (1944). A thick-set character actor, his lumbering presence made him an ideal choice to play the monster. He did not have too much dialogue, but he towered over the other characters.

this role for sympathy, as someone totally unaware of the fact that he is roaming the countryside and killing Cameron's fellow scientists. He perceives himself as a country boy, describing in slow, deliberate tones the fact that his "pop made [him] promise to say nuttin'" about his family, while tending the garden. As the film progresses, however, Petro gradually comes to realize that something has happened to him; he screws his face up in shame as he understands how he has become a wolf-man. The only form of retribution he knows is to take revenge on his master — which is precisely what happens at the end, as he sets Cameron's laboratory on fire and throws the doctor into it. By such means Petro hopes to symbolically cleanse himself of his guilt.

In *The Black Raven* (1943), Strange once again appears as an ingenuous, yet rather foolish character — Andy, the empty-headed employee of Amos Bradford (aka The Black Raven) (GEORGE ZUCCO). Dressed in a long overcoat and solar toupee, Andy's reactions are slow-witted, to say the least; every statement addressed to him is greeted with a broad smile (showing a set of beautiful white teeth) but little understanding. Andy seems singularly unfortunate, either falling down stairs or discovering people in mysterious places — an experience that sends him scurrying back to Amos in terror. He tries to be brave — shown in several sequences as he grasps the lapels of his overcoat, draws himself up to his full height (6 feet 5 inches or 1.96 m.) and takes a deep breath. But this is nothing more than an act of false bravado.

In *The Monster Maker* (1944), Strange puts his strength to good effect as Steve, Igor Markoff's (J. CARROL NAISH) sidekick. Steve sits quietly outside Markoff's laboratory door, apparently minding his own business, but springs to his feet and glares at anyone daring to come too close. Steve also proves a useful ally in helping Markoff carry out his evil experiment to inject concert pianist Anthony Lawrence (Ralph Morgan) with the acromegaly virus. Lawrence makes several attempts to escape, but Steve always brings him back, either by holding Lawrence in a headlock or yanking him by the scruff of the neck. By such means director Sam Newfield suggests to his wartime audiences how America's enemies (personified by Markoff) impose their will on others through violence. Steve's final appearance comes late on in the film, where he struggles to prevent Markoff's assistant Maxine (Tala Birell) from making the experiments public. The fact that Steve is shown hitting her and tying her up attests to the brutality of Markoff's world.

Strange's build also made him an ideal candidate to play the monster in Universal's Frankenstein sequels. In *House of Frankenstein* (1944), he moves with slow, deliberate movements as he strangles Daniel (J. CARROL NAISH) and carries Professor Niemann (Boris Karloff) away, in the vain hope that the professor will be able to rescue him from Frankenstein's burning castle. The two of them meet an equally slow death as they gradually sink into quicksand.

Director Erle C. Kenton makes effective use of Strange's screen image to create a monster who is at once trusting yet readily exploited by those cleverer than himself (as in *The Mad Monster*, for instance). Perhaps this was not an image at all — but actually part of Strange's character. The actor recalled that on one occasion Lon Chaney, Jr. (playing the Wolf Man) got him extremely drunk. In the climactic scene, Strange had to be stuck for hours in quicksand (actually cold mud), waiting for the cameras to roll. Taking advantage of Strange's ingenuous nature, Chaney recommended that alcohol would keep Strange warm as he wore the make-up. Strange reprised the monster's role in Universal's *House of Dracula* (1945); he is brought to life at the end of the film by mad scientist Dr. Franz Edelmann (Onslow Stevens). Strange does not have much to do, other than to walk threateningly round the laboratory, throw the Inspector Holtz (LIONEL ATWILL) into a machine (which electrocutes the hapless police officer to death), and pursue Lawrence Talbot (aka The Wolf Man) (Lon Chaney, Jr.) Talbot escapes in the nick of time, while the monster is burned to death — yet again — in a fire.

Strange repeats the role for a third time in Universal's spoof *Abbott and Costello Meet Frankenstein* (1948). For the most part, he is either shown lying supine on a slab, waiting for Count Dracula (Bela Lugosi) to energize him by giving him Wilbur Grey's (Lou Costello's brain), or walking slowly and deliberately behind Wilbur in a deliberate attempt to frighten him. Unlike Karloff's Frankenstein — who eventually learns to talk — Strange's monster is limited to a few phrases, such as "Yes, master." He no longer cuts a threatening presence — except, perhaps, for Wilbur — and at one point is addressed as "Frankie." In an ending stolen from James Whale's 1931 film, the monster is eventually burned to death in a fire caused by lighted gas fumes. A year later Strange appeared as a monster in another horror spoof — Jean Yarbrough's *Master Minds* (1949), starring the Bowery Boys. He begins the film in familiar mode, grunting occasionally and pursuing Dr. Druzik (ALAN NAPIER) in a threatening manner. When Sach (Huntz Hall) is unlucky enough to stand in his way, Atlas chases him off in the belief that Sach represents some kind of competition for the doctor's attention. As a result of Druzik's experiments, Atlas and Sach exchange personalities; Atlas becomes consciously effeminate in his manner, his wrists hanging limply in front of him, while Sach becomes the monster. Strange looks rather uncomfortable in his new role, and with some justification; it seems rather bizarre for such a physically imposing person to act like this. Atlas recovers his natural personality, and thoroughly enjoys himself chasing Druzik round the laboratory before penning the unfortunate doctor in a corner. Although the police eventually apprehend the monster, we know that he will not suffer any significant punishment.

Lyle Talbot

b. February 8, 1902, Pittsburgh, Pennsylvania;
d. March 2, 1996, San Francisco, California.

Lyle Talbot (born Lysle Henderson) came from a theatrical family; both of his parents were riverboat performers. His mother died when he was still a child, so an aunt (Mary Hollywood Talbot) raised him. He adopted her surname when he became an actor. Talbot began his career in stock companies, and even formed one of his own in Memphis, Tennessee, but gravitated towards Hollywood as the talkies were maturing. He enjoyed a lengthy career in films and television, making his first film in 1931 (*The Clyde Mystery*) and his last in 1986 (*George Carlin, Playin' with Your Head*).

Although Talbot appeared in just about every kind of film, he gave some versatile performances in horror and science fiction films. One of his early films was *A Shriek in the Night*

(1933), where he starred opposite Ginger Rogers (playing Pat Morgan) as Ted Kord, a wisecracking journalist with a heart of gold. He begins the film by competing with her to see who can get the story first. As the action unfolds, the two of them become partners in trying to solve a series of murders committed in an apartment building. As they do so, they indulge in a series of witty exchanges — as, for example, when Ted comes to Pat's apartment with a toothbrush, a revolver and a blackjack, so as to protect himself against any possible intruders. Pat sighs in exasperation; Ted responds by putting his hands in his jacket pockets and smiling, as if hugely enjoying himself. At the same time, Ted envisages a future with Pat in which "a woman's place is in the home." Pat doesn't object; after her experiences in the apartment, she relishes the opportunity for a quiet life. Despite his conventional approach to gender roles, Ted remains a fundamentally decent person — someone who can be trusted, even while pursuing a good newspaper story.

Lyle Talbot (center) in *Murder Among Friends* (1941). A versatile character actor for several decades, who began his career as a leading man and ended as a member of Edward D. Wood, Jr.'s repertory company.

Talbot had a rare starring role as Lt. Bob Bennett in the horror flick *Torture Ship* (1939). He initially appears as a typical officer, well versed in running a ship, yet unprepared for what his uncle Dr. Hubert Stander (IRVING PICHEL) wants him to do—command a vessel that doubles up as a laboratory for Stander's experiments on human beings, to find out whether criminals can be transformed into law-abiding citizens through endocrinology. Talbot shows his surprise through eyework — staring wildly at the rogues' gallery of criminals gathered around the dining table, as if uncertain what he has let himself in for. After a while, he realizes that it is duty as an honorable man to protect the innocent Joan Martel (Jacqueline Wells/Julie Bishop) from her unscrupulous employer Poison Mary Slavish (Sheila Bromley). However, Bennett is not prepared for the shock that awaits him: Stander ignores all family ties and decides to perform his experiments on his nephew. Bennett undergoes a dramatic change of character, as he tries to strangle Joan. Later on, he is strapped into a chair and prepared for more operations; the camera zooms into him as he moans: "Why don't you just do away with me, get it over with?" This mood of despair passes quickly, however, as Bennett remains completely in control of his mental faculties, even while pretending to be drugged. Through a combination of mental strength and physical toughness, he emerges triumphant, by killing off most of the criminals or knocking them out — so that they can be transported back to the American mainland. The film ends with a familiar scene where Bennett embraces Joan; they deserve a few moments of quiet together, after the ordeal they have endured.

In the comedy-thriller *One Body Too Many* (1944), designed as a vehicle for the vaudeville actor Jack Haley, Talbot plays another decent personality — who begins by telling Albert Tuttle (Haley) to "cut out the shenanigans" and get on with his work. Eventually Davis' manner softens, as he understands that Tuttle is trying to sell the family insurance, not protect them (as people had first assumed). Tuttle was "just the wrong guy" for the job. On the other hand,

Davis proves as susceptible as anyone else to the idea that if Rutherford's instructions are ignored, then the family will somehow inherit more of his fortune. We frequently witness Davis in shadow, as he removes Rutherford's corpse and buries it outside the house — in strict defiance of the instructions set down in the millionaire's last will and testament. Despite his indiscretions, director Frank McDonald forgives Davis for his indiscretions, as he joins the hunt for the real murderer and eventually helps bring him to trial.

Talbot had the dubious experience of being involved in one of Edward D. Wood, Jr.'s low-budget efforts, *Glen or Glenda* (1953). As Inspector Warren, he comes across initially as the typical hard-boiled cop, with slicked-back hair and large cigar. As the film unfolds, however, so his attitude changes; he listens intently to what Dr. Alton (Timothy Farrell) has to tell him about the discrimination experienced by transvestites in contemporary American society. His face melts into a smile as he hears about the importance of the "other self" for certain people. Alton asks Warren to speculate on why men choose to wear women's clothes: Wood cuts to a close-up of the inspector shifting uncomfortably in his chair, as if reluctant to answer such a question. Once he has listened to the story of Glen/Glenda, however, Warren's face melts once again into a smile, as he nods his head in assent while Alton delivers the film's final line: "The end is only the beginning." Wood begins the film with another epigram: "You are society ... judge ye not." The inspector ends up by subscribing to this view: even if he does not approve of transvestites, he has sufficient magnanimity to allow them to pursue their own lifestyles. Four years later, Talbot appeared in Wood's *Plan Nine from Outer Space* as a general based in Washington, D.C. He sits behind a desk in a business-like manner and admits to Colonel Edwards (Tom Keene) that flying saucers do exist, in spite of official denials to the contrary. The government had set up an installation whereby they could talk to the aliens and ascertain their demands. The general clasps his hands and leans over the desk towards the colonel, emphasizing the importance of what he has to say. He rises from his chair, paces the room and orders the colonel to "see what in hell it is they want" by traveling down to the graveyard in downtown Hollywood where they have been discovered. The general might be a passive character, but his authority is palpable.

In *Tobor the Great* (1954), Talbot has an uncredited role as another member of the armed services—an admiral who visits the house of Professor Arnold Nordstrom (Taylor Holmes) to assess the robot Tobor's suitability for the American space program. He finds himself being drawn into a plan initiated by scientist Dr. Ralph Harrison (Charles Drake) to rescue the professor from foreign spies. While Tobor is programmed to find the spies' hideaway and destroy it, the human characters follow close behind and look after any casualties. The admiral plays a major part in the success of this scheme, as he stops the spies from escaping—proving beyond doubt that the best American service personnel are those who act in the national interest, in this case, ensuring that Tobor does not fall into the enemy's hands. Talbot had a lip-smacking role as the Narrator in the low-budget sci-fi flick *Mesa of Lost Women* (1953). Although never seen on screen, he has ample opportunity to show off his vocal skill as he sets the scene for what is to follow: "An American oil surveyor has chosen to explore this particular terrible corner of the earth [...] a desert of death [...] one thing is certain, miracle or not, they [human beings] will not be living things for long, The desert will soon convert them into dead things." These lines are delivered with pauses in between the words "particular," "terrible," and "corner" and "soon," "convert them," and "dead things," coupled with particular emphasis on the alliterative phrase "desert of death." Such sentiments set the tone for what is to follow, in a manner similar to the narrator's role in *The Indestructible Man* (1956).

Terrell's narrator thoroughly relishes the task of describing the scene; later on he mocks the human beings' vain efforts to make sense of the eponymous lost women: "[The women behave] in a way so fantastic and horrible as to make a man of science doubt his senses." This phrase is delivered as a crescendo, with a long pause taken between the words "science," and "doubt," clearly suggesting that the aliens' presence defies scientific investigation. The narrator returns at the end of the film, when order has been restored and the aliens destroyed, and describes the scene as perfectly normal: "Not a thing different about it ... or is it?" The rhetorical question once again invites us to question the power of science: can it actually explain all the unexplainable phenomena in the universe?

Gloria Talbott

b. February 7, 1931, Glendale, California;
d. September 19, 2000, Glendale, California.

Gloria Maude Talbott grew up in the shadows of the Hollywood studios and made her debut as a child star in small parts in films such as *Maytime* (1937) and *A Tree Grows in Brooklyn* (1945). After leaving school, Talbott started her own drama group, playing in various venues, but then left the acting world altogether to get married. Following her divorce in 1953, she resumed her career, working as a leading player in many cult horror films during the 1950s.

One such film was Bert I. Gordon's *The Cyclops* (1956), in which she plays Susan Winter, the leader of an expedition to Mexico in search of her fiancé Bruce, who disappeared three years previously. The three men in her party, scientist Russ Bradford (James Craig), prospector Marty Melville (Lon Chaney, Jr.), and pilot Lee Brand (Tom Drake) all try to assert their masculine authority over her, but Susan remains strong throughout. She understands the significance of silence; by not responding to her male companions' manifold requests—to go home, or not to continue the quest to find her fiancé—she imposes her will over them, despite the potential dangers involved. Her expression remains fixed in a look of determination, something emphasized through frequent close-ups. However, director Gordon seems not to have the courage of his convictions: when Susan encounters the Cyclops (Duncan Parkin), she stares at the camera in terror, and embarks on a screaming fit reminiscent of Fay Wray in *King Kong* (1933). Once a strong woman, she now relies for protection on her two surviving companions, Lee and Russ. She nonetheless summons up sufficient courage to talk to the Cyclops, and understand to her horror that it is actually her fiancé, who has become a victim of the high uranium levels in the region. Like all living things, he has grown to an enormous size—and will continue growing—while his face has been mutilated beyond recognition. When Susan understands what has happened to Bruce, she bursts into tears. The film ends with her escaping the region in a plane, and allowing Russ to caress her face. The two fall into one another's arms: in spite of her strength of character, Susan welcomes another male protector to replace Bruce in her affections.

A year later in *Daughter of Dr. Jekyll*, Talbott took a more passive role as Janet Smith. Director Edgar G. Ulmer includes one sequence where she is photographed in her underwear dressing for dinner, reminding us of just how sexy she could be. It is this sexiness that attracts scheming Dr. Lomas (Arthur Shields), who convinces her into believing that she has

Gloria Talbott publicity still (1958). A rather slight figure with a memorable voice, Talbott became a popular leading lady in 1950s science fiction films.

roamed the landscape at night and mutilated various victims. The real murderer is the doctor himself, a descendant of the notorious Dr. Jekyll. Janet spends much of the film in a state of near-hysteria, as she wakes up to discover that her hands are covered in blood. Convinced that she is guilty, she throws herself at her fiancé George Hastings's (JOHN AGAR) feet and begs him to kill her. In the climactic fight, between Hastings and Shields, she remains a passive spectator, screaming throughout, reminding us of how vulnerable women in most 1950s horror films actually were. She has to find a suitable male protector, who will not only guard her from assault by other men but also sustain her mental stability. George vows to undertake his role, as he caresses her head at the end of the film while informing her that the doctor has now died.

In Gene Fowler, Jr.'s *I Married a Monster from Outer Space* (1958), Talbott plays Marge Bradley Farrell. Continuing the theme of relationships raised in *The Cyclops*, it seems as if Marge has achieved her childhood dream of finding a suitable husband — the tall, handsome Bill (Tom Tryon). However, she soon discovers that Bill is not the man she fell in love with; he seems totally uninterested in her, preferring to go out on his own late at night rather than share the marriage bed. There is a simple explanation for this; his body has been taken over by an alien from outer space. The plot bears strong resemblances to *Invasion of the Body Snatchers* (1956), as the masculine population — Bill, his friend Harry (Robert Ivers), the friendly police captain H. B. Collins (John Eldredge) and his colleague Officer Hank Swanson (Peter Baldwin) — all lose their capacity for individual self-determination as they are possessed by the alien force. It is left to Marge to rescue them by escaping from her family home, jumping into her car and alerting the National Guard. They mount an attack that initially fails, as the aliens prove immune to their bullets; but the police dogs eventually savage the aliens to death. The National Guard troops force open the aliens' spaceship door, and see the luckless men hanging from meat hooks like carcasses waiting for slaughter. When they are released, they re-inhabit their bodies once more, allowing Bill and Marge to continue their happy marriage.

Through its fantastic plot, *I Married a Monster from Outer Space* questions established constructions of gender. The male characters no longer dominate; it is left to women such as Marge to bring about a happy ending. Initially, she seems unable to fulfill such responsibilities; she has been brought up to believe that men should do all the decision-making, while she looks after home and family. Rather than trying to rescue her husband, she simply bursts into tears. However, Marge soon understands the importance of her task; she eludes Bill by pretending to be asleep one night, and steals out in her car. While the police try every means possible to prevent her escaping from the village or communicating with the outside world — for example, inventing fake detours or tearing up her cablegrams — she ultimately outwits them, proving beyond doubt that women are equal to, if not better than men when it comes to decision-making. Although Marge falls with a sigh of relief into Bill's arms at the end of the film, we doubt whether she will be happy to assume a subordinate role in the future.

In Columbia's *The Leech Woman* (1960), Talbott returns to a more passive role as Sally, devoted assistant of research scientist Dr. Paul Talbot (Philip Terry), and fiancée of lawyer Neil Foster (Grant Williams). Edward Dein's film focuses on the consequences of marital frustration, as Talbot travels with his wife June (Coleen Gray) to the African heartland in search of a drug that will restore youth to aging women. They discover it, but also find out that it will only take effect if a male is sacrificed beforehand. June eagerly accepts the drug, and uses her husband as a sacrifice — in her view this is a fitting revenge for years of neglect. However, she can only sustain her youth if she sacrifices more men; as a result, she becomes a serial killer. By contrast, Sally leads a "normal" existence, as she looks forward to marrying Neil and giving up her career. However, her future security is threatened by June, who makes advances towards Neil. Sally confronts June, and is strangled — her corpse then is thrown in a store-cupboard. While June should take responsibility for her actions, *The Leech Woman* suggests that her husband is ultimately to blame for transforming her into a monster. If he had devoted more time to his marriage, instead of pursuing the unattainable secret of eternal youth, he might have saved her.

Ken Terrell

b. April 29, 1904, Georgia;
d. March 8, 1966, Sherman Oaks, California.

Ken Terrell followed a path trodden by many actors during the late 1940s and early 1950s of taking television roles interspersed with supporting parts in all kinds of films, from *The Conqueror* (1956) to *The Ten Commandments* (also 1956) and *Elmer Gantry* (1960). One such role was the second heckler in *Abbott and Costello Meet Dr. Jekyll and Mr. Hyde* (1953). In his flat cap and mustache, he enjoys sitting on a park bench listening to Vicky Edwards (Helen Westcott) giving a speech preaching votes for women. He turns towards her and tells her to "go home and fight your old man!"—a somewhat impractical request given Vicky's extreme youth. It is clear he has not come to listen to the speech; what interests him more is the way the ladies show their legs as they dance to attract an audience. Director Charles Lamont cuts to a shot from the heckler's point of view as he watches the ladies' legs clad in black stockings and garters.

Terrell specialized in parts in horror and science fiction films, often playing hoodlums, buffoons or characters under pressure. In the Republic serial *The Crimson Ghost* (1946) he takes an uncredited role—in chapters ten and eleven (of twelve)—of a heavy who fights the clean-cut hero Duncan Richards (Charles Quigley) in a warehouse. While the scrap contains plenty of physical activity, the outcome is predictable, as Richards duly emerges victorious. In another Republic serial—*The Perils of Nyoka* (aka *Nyoka and the Lost Secrets of Hippocrates*) (1942)—Terrell is virtually unrecognizable beneath his flowing white robes and elegant white headdress as Ahmed, a diminutive heavy employed by villain Vultura (Lorna Gray). In the 1953 science fiction feature *Port Sinister*, Terrell

Ken Terrell (left) and Audie Murphy in *Drums Across the River* (1954). Terrell's character acting career lasted nearly three decades, where he played everything from villains to Indians to officials.

has a supporting role as Hollis, who forms part of the crew of gangsters led by Kolvac (PAUL CAVANAGH) which commandeers a ship bound for Port Royal, a mythical seventeenth century Caribbean port lost beneath the sea that resurfaces only once every 200 years. Hollis has a mostly choric role, commenting on the appearance of the island ("There she comes! Look at her!"), the smell of sulfur that scares off potential invaders ("I don't like it!") and the eventual discovery of the treasure lying at the heart of the island ("Hey, look at this!") Having been abandoned by Kolvac and his first mate, Collins (William Schallert), Hollis and his fellow crew members make a desperate bid to escape from the island as it sinks back into the sea. Hollis is eventually swallowed up by quicksand.

Three years later in *The Indestructible Man*, Terrell plays another gangster—Joe Marcelli, one-time associate of jailed mobster Charles "Butcher" Benton (Lon Chaney, Jr.), who gives evidence to the police to put Benton away in jail for life. Now Benton has been sentenced to death in the electric chair, Marcelli feels that he is safe; he can spend Benton's money without fear of reprisal. Marcelli is seen sitting complacently at a bar in black shirt and trilby hat, carelessly smoking a cigarette.

What Marcelli does not realize, however, is that mad scientist Professor Bradshaw (Robert Shayne) has revived Benton by means of an elixir that transforms him according to the narrator into "a vicious brutal animal with an almost inconceivable amount of strength." Benton determines to take revenge on all of his supposed friends who helped to convict him — Marcelli includes. In a documentary-style chase sequence set in downtown Los Angeles (using locations that no longer exist), we see Marcelli desperately trying to escape on crutches, pursued by Benton. The two of them reach a deserted warehouse; Marcelli climbs the stairs as fast as he can, but his efforts prove to be in vain. Benton catches Marcelli up, hits the cripple with his crutches, puts one hand underneath his chin and throws him down the stairs to his death.

In *Attack of the 50-Foot Woman* (1958), Terrell plays Charlie, a weasel-like character wearing a cowboy hat, who frequents the local bar. He truly believes that he is the life and soul of any social gathering, exchanging banter with Sheriff Dubbitt (George Douglas), and pursuing anything in skirts. Charlie dances outrageously in a vain attempt to please Honey Parker (Yvette Vickers), but understands the futility of his quest when he sees her cuddling up close to Harry Archer (WILLIAM HUDSON). Despite his shortcomings, Charlie remains a fundamentally good-hearted person, who wants to participate in anything. The only snag is that no one — neither Harry nor the Sheriff — takes him seriously. Charlie is restricted to providing occasional comic relief, speaking his lines breathlessly and opening his eyes wide in astonishment as he hears about Harry's wife Nancy (Allison Hayes) being transformed into a monster. Charlie's catchphrase is deliberately memorable, redolent of comic strips ("Holy Toledo!")

Terrell has an uncredited role in *Daughter of Dr. Jekyll* (1957) as an unspecified monster, who is photographed in close-up at the beginning and end of the film. He intones in sonorous tones that "Dr. Jekyll is dead" and then turns his head towards the camera, pauses for one or two beats and exclaims: "Are you sure?" Director Ulmer continues the action by fading to black, with the sound of Terrell's cackling laugh ringing on the soundtrack. This neat little visual conceit provides the justification for the story — as well as any subsequent versions of *Dr. Jekyll and Mr. Hyde* that directors choose to make. Dr. Jekyll never dies, even though we see him dying at the end of every film version of the story.

Ernest Thesiger
b. January 15, 1879, London, England;
d. January 14, 1961, London, England.

Born in London, Ernest Thesiger made his stage debut in 1909 and established his reputation as an actor in musical comedy as well as in classic dramas. In 1925, he appeared in Noël Coward's *On With the Dance*, portraying an elderly woman sharing a bed in a boarding house and undressing in bed in a sketch of prudish embarrassment. Such roles helped establish Thesiger's reputation as a character actor, at home both in comedies and classical roles (he played the Dauphin in George Bernard Shaw's *Saint Joan* later on in the 1920s).

Noted director James Whale cast Thesiger in *The Old Dark House* (1932), a film that offered the actor the opportunity to display his vocal and technical skills. Living in a cold, isolated house with his sister Rebecca (Eva Moore), Femm treats his unwanted guests Philip and Margaret Waverton (Raymond Massey and Gloria Stuart) and Roger Penderel (Melvyn Douglas) with the utmost disdain. Dressed in a suit with tight wing-collar, he looks down his nose as he tells them that it is their misfortune to be staying the night. Nonetheless, we get the sense that this might be nothing more than a performance; in truth Femm is a frightened

Colin Clive and Ernest Thesiger (right) in *The Bride of Frankenstein* (1935).

man, worried about being shut up perpetually in the house. This is signaled by Thesiger's gestures, as he wrings his fingers while talking.

Nonetheless, Femm continues to put on an act, as he asks his guests to join him in a drink: "It's only gin, you know. I like gin." He holds the glass delicately between thumb and forefinger and takes small sips; he obviously thinks of himself as a paragon of effeminate gentility. In a comic sequence, Femm becomes master of the dinner table, as he asks all the assembled guests to take a potato from the dish, and holds the dish in front of them until they do so. Even if they don't actually want to eat potatoes, they are browbeaten into doing so.

Nonetheless, Whale always photographs him in close-up looking sideways or downwards, never directly to camera — suggesting once again that Femm has some inner fear that he does not want to reveal. Eventually, we discover what that fear actually is: Femm's brother Saul (Brember Wills) has been incarcerated in a room on one of the house's upper stories. If anyone were to release him (and the butler Morgan [Boris Karloff] is perpetually liable to do this), then Femm and his sister's lives would be put at risk, as Saul wants to set the whole house on fire. When Rebecca asks Femm to fetch a lamp from upstairs, Femm looks from side to side in genuine terror. Although accompanied by Penderel, it is clear that Femm is looking for the earliest possible opportunity to escape.

Femm reappears in the film's final sequences, once Saul has been killed and thereby rendering the house a safe place to live. He looks sympathetically on his guests (all of whom have endured a terrible night), and wishes them good health. As they depart, Whale photographs him from the outside stand-ing at the front door, waving goodbye to them, a pleasant smile spread across his face. He grins at Rebecca standing at the window; she turns away from him in disgust, as if realizing that she will never redeem him, despite her protestations that he is a fundamentally simple man.

In *The Bride of Frankenstein* (1935), Thesiger plays the archetypal mad scientist — a gaunt, white-faced figure with wild gray hair protruding in all directions moving stealthily in all directions. He desires to work in collaboration with Henry Frankenstein (Colin Clive) so as to "reach a goal undreamed of" by other human beings. If Frankenstein has created the perfect monster, Pretorius has created much smaller versions of human beings, which he puts on display in glass bottles. This clearly gives him great pleasure; as he observes to Frankenstein, he has "created life — as we say — in God's own image." The word "God" is heavily stressed, emphasizing the fact that Pretorius considers himself godlike in his potential power. Once Frankenstein has been persuaded to collaborate, the doctor celebrates by pouring himself a drink of gin and toasting "a new world of gods and monsters!" Thesiger makes great play with these lines, taking a long pause between "world" and "of," and emphasizing the consonants in "gods" and "monsters." He then makes a grand exit, his black cloak flowing in all directions.

In a later scene, Pretorius is discovered alone in the depths of his house, celebrating the potential success of his work by having another drink of gin, while the monster (Boris Karloff) moves ominously towards him. Completely unfazed by the monster's presence, Pretorius observes in a nonchalant tone: "I thought I was alone. Good evening." No one has treated the monster with such politeness; he stops short and smiles. Pretorius offers him a cigar, claiming as he does so that the monster "can be very useful" in the doctor's future researches. Director Whale's handling of this sequence not only reveals an underlying humor (Pretorius' rather camp voice stands in stark contrast to the monster's aggressively masculine tones), but also shows that the monster is not frightening at all, if people treat him with respect. Pretorius might be a mad scientist, but is he nonetheless humane.

However, this side of the doctor's character is rapidly concealed, as he becomes more and more obsessed with his experiments. Whale shoots the climatic sequence (where he and Frankenstein end up creating the Bride [Elsa Lanchester]) in a series of tilted close-ups, suggesting that the whole scheme is an affront both to God and the "natural" order of things. As the monster rises from her bed, Pretorius clasps his hands in anticipation, then stretches them out in triumph, exclaiming as he does so that he has at last managed to create "the Brrrrride of Frrrrrr-ankenstein!!" His moment of triumph is short-lived, however, as he is burned to death in the laboratory, together with the Bride. Only Frankenstein escapes in the nick of time, accompanied by his wife Elizabeth (Valerie Hobson).

Thesiger also distinguished himself in the British-made *The Ghoul* (1935), where he played the servant Laing, who steals a gem from Professor Moriant's (Karloff) body, only to find the professor returning from the dead to seek his revenge.

Marshall Thompson

b. November 27, 1925, Peoria, Illinois;
d. May 18, 1992, Royal Oak, Michigan.

James Marshall Thompson appeared in several local drama productions and eventually enrolled at Occidental Liberal Arts College in Los Angeles. He was spotted by a Hollywood talent scout while performing with the college drama group in 1944, and signed to a Universal contract. After filming *Reckless Age* (1944), he was brought over to MGM, where he made a minor name for himself in nice guy roles. By the mid–1950s Thompson had lost his MGM contract, but established himself as a clean-cut leading actor in several horror and science fiction films on both sides of the Atlantic.

In *Cult of the Cobra* (1955), he plays GI Tom Markel, who tours an unspecified Asian city with his friends. They visit a local attraction, where it is claimed that human beings can be transformed into animals; although skeptical, they pay the entrance fee, and are told in no uncertain terms not to take photographs of what they see. One of the service personnel disregards the advice and takes a photo — as a result Morkel and his friends are cursed. Needless to say, they treat the entire episode as a

Marshall Thompson cinema star postcard (1957). A reassuring presence as a leading man in science fiction films of the 1950s, Thompson later found stardom in the television series ***Daktari.***

joke — except for Markel, who understands just what a *faux pas* they have committed. He provides the voice of reason in a group of GIs who really have no idea how to behave in different cultures.

Unfortunately, Markel is not so successful in his relationships with the opposite sex; he tries and fails to woo Julia Thompson (Kathleen Hughes), and eventually ends up falling in love with cobra-woman Lisa Moya (FAITH DOMERGUE). True to his gender upbringing, Markel tries to take the lead in the relationship, but finds himself continually frustrated by Lisa's apparent indifference. She keeps running away: Markel interprets this as an example of needless flirting, rather than understanding Lisa's true nature. She cannot entertain close relationships with any man, being the human embodiment of the curse placed on all the GIs. Once Markel discovers this, his attitude changes; he admits to being frightened of her, and director Francis D. Lyon's camera closes in on his petrified face. In the end, he has to destroy her to guarantee his own safety; he grabs the cobra woman and throws her out of the window. This gives him no pleasure — in destroying Lisa, he has also destroyed the love of his life.

In the British-made (but American-financed) *Fiend without a Face* (1958), Thompson's Major Cummings is dedicated to his job in the U.S. Air Force, which operates a base in Canada including a nuclear power plant, where scientists are developing a missile control system. Needless to say, the local townspeople fear what is going on there, especially when four of them perish in mysterious circumstances. It is the Major's job to smooth over relations between the military and the civilian populations: while insisting that "we're all human here," he resolves to continue the scientific experiments. Director Arthur Crabtree emphasizes Cummings' fundamental seriousness of purpose by cutting to several close-ups of him reading a book, even in the presence of the pretty young Barbara Griselle (Kim Parker), who acts as a spokesperson on the townspeople's behalf.

Cummings' manner rapidly changes as he discovers from Professor Walgate (Kynaston Reeves) that the killer is actually a creature, a mental vampire that survives by sucking the brains and spinal cords out of its victims. Galvanized into action by the need to save the village from imminent destruction, he ventures back into the nuclear power plant to blow up all the equipment, realizing that if he does so, he will deprive the creature of the nuclear energy that sustains it. Barbara admiringly observes of him: "I know that guy, and if anybody can get through, he can." Cummings' mission proves successful, and he returns to Barbara's willing embrace.

Thompson reprises the role of a dedicated member of the armed services as Carruthers in Edward L. Cahn's *It! The Terror Beyond Space* (also 1958). He begins the film by recounting his disastrous trip to Mars, where he was the only member of a nine-person crew to survive an assault by a monster (Ray Corrigan). For him, the planet was "alive with what came to be known as [...] death." Carruthers is now being escorted back from Mars by a group of service personnel to face a court-martial and possible death sentence for negligence. As they make their way home, the group makes jokes at Carruthers' expense; Carruthers himself remains tight-lipped, knowing that the monster is still at large on the spacecraft. No one actually believes him at first — they feel he has been both negligent *and* self-interested in choosing to save his own skin rather than protect his fellow officers on the original expedition. As the film unfolds, so Carruthers' reputation improves; once they become aware of the monster's presence, his comrades learn to trust in him. They admire him for doing "what he thought was right," and later admit that he "was right and we were all wrong." Nonetheless, Carruthers understands that even the best-laid plans might be doomed to fail; he initiates a final assault on the monster with the warning that "this [operation] is whether we die, or it dies."

The plot adumbrates Ridley Scott's *Alien* (1979), with the monster sucking the life-blood out of more victims in the bowels of the craft, while the remainder of the crew desperately tries to destroy it. In symbolic terms, the monster represents unbridled passion; Carruthers represents human reason, coordinating his fellow service personnel in a successful operation to kill the monster. At the end of the film, Carruthers reminds us that "Mars is death," peopled by an "alien and elemental life-force[s]." While *It! The Terror from Beyond Space* follows *Fiend Without a Face* in celebrating individual initiative, director Cahn offers a warning to those scientists charged with the responsibility of planning America's future space program. The safety of individual officers on any mission is as important (if not more so) than making scientific discoveries.

Thompson plays yet another member of the U.S. Armed Services in the British-made *First Man into Space* (1959), which like *It! The Terror from Beyond Space* focuses on the seamier side of the space race. As Commander Charles Ernest Prescott, he is responsible for an exploratory mission, with his brother Dan Milton Prescott (Bill Edwards) as the main pilot. Robert Day's film deliberately contrasts the upstanding, rule-bound Charles ("Chuck") with the maverick Dan. Despite Chuck's exhortations to return, Dan takes his craft further and further into space, proudly announcing that he has managed to achieve a journey of 250 miles. Like Icarus in ancient myth, however, Dan ignores his brother's instructions and eventually disappears, to return to Earth as a hideously disfigured monster, wreaking havoc amongst the local community. Chuck is both appalled and ashamed by what happens— his obsession with scientific and military procedures blinds him to his brother's faults, and contributes in no small way to Dan's mishap. Although the two brothers meet once more in a pressurized cabin, where Dan talks frankly about what happened, Dan eventually passes away due to lack of blood. Chuck looks down at the ground, valiantly trying to suppress his emotions as he mumbles, "There's nothing we can do." Although the film ends with Chuck's colleague Dr. Paul von Essen (Carl Jaffe) paying tribute to those "men who will accept the risks" of space travel, we cannot help feeling that this tragedy could have been avoided if Chuck had devoted more time to personal rather than professional commitments.

Kenneth Tobey

b. March 23, 1917, Oakland, California;
d. December 22, 2002, Rancho Mirage, California.

Jesse Kenneth Tobey was destined for the law until he began acting at the University of California Little Theater. He subsequently graduated to the New York Neighborhood Playhouse, where his contemporaries included Gregory Peck, Eli Wallach and Tony Randall. Tobey made his debut in a 1943 short *The Man on the Ferry* and subsequently played supporting roles in films such as *I Was a Male War Bride* (1949) and *Twelve o'Clock High* (also 1949).

Tobey made appearances in a series of science fiction classics throughout the 1950s, often playing figures of authority. In *The Thing from Another World* (1951), he plays Captain Patrick Hendry, the ever-dependable commander of a military unit supporting the work of scientist Dr. Arthur Carrington (ROBERT CORNTHWAITE) and his colleagues. Henry is suspicious of Carrington's research, which he considers unnecessary for the future of humankind; he prefers to uphold such qualities as loyalty and good fellowship amongst his troops. In the end, Hendry's skepticism is vindicated, as he discovers that the alien's (James Arness) true intention lies in taking over the Earth, despite Carrington's best attempts to tame it. Hendry organizes a sophisticated campaign to destroy it; we see several shots of him walking towards or away from the camera at the head of a group of troops, telling them all the while what they should be doing. In the film's climactic confrontation, Hendry stands at the head of his troops facing the alien, and initiates the process of destruction (which involves electrocution). Once his duties have been accomplished, Hendry can "settle down" to a life of marriage and domesticity with his girlfriend (and Carrington's erstwhile colleague) "Nikki" Nicholson (Margaret Sheridan).

In *The Beast from 20,000 Fathoms* (1953), he plays another army officer— Colonel Jack Evans, who masterminds the original Arctic atomic test (which inadvertently releases the monster), and subsequently leads the military

Kenneth Tobey in *The Thing from Another World* (1951). Granite-faced Tobey played many a reliable leading man in science fiction films of the 1950s, before moving into a long and profitable television career.

operation to destroy it. Immaculately dressed in army uniform, he comes across as a symbol of authority, whether sat in his office chair or talking more informally by leaning against his desk. Evans initially seems disinclined to believe in the monster's existence, but Tom Nesbitt (Paul Christian) and fellow-paleontologist Lee Hunter (Paula Raymond) convince him otherwise. Evans takes a deep breath and decides to investigate — much against his better judgment. As he observes in a throwaway line, his superiors will consider him "nuts."

Evans's decision ultimately proves correct, as he is shown standing behind a barricade, directing the military operation against the monster. As he peers through his binoculars and issues orders, he cuts a reassuring presence in the midst of chaos. However, Evans realizes that simply delegating responsibility is not enough; he has to involve himself in the task. In a classic David versus Goliath confrontation, he heroically confronts the master, with only a suit of fireproof clothing for protection and eventually lights the fire that destroys it. Tobey delivers banal lines such as, "It'd take a 3-inch shell to penetrate that skull," with intense conviction.

Tobey essays a similar role as Commander Pete Mathews in *It Came from Beneath the Sea* (1955). At the beginning of the film, it seems as if he is just an ordinary officer — part of a crew whose life seems particularly aimless aboard an atomic submarine that appears as easy to operate as "an automatic elevator." Aimlessness characterizes life on board, with nothing to pass the time but to "eat and sleep, and press a button if there's some work to be done." Technology has outpaced the ability of the ship's officers to understand it and they pilot in an abstract, switch-flipping mode, at considerable distance from their own labor. They sway not to the waves but to the lazy rhythms of Hawaiian beach music, piped through the ship's intercom. A giant octopus unexpectedly attacks the submarine: Mathews takes charge of the situation to ensure that the $55 million craft and its crew arrive safely back to port. Granite-faced, with an air of total professionalism, he seems just the kind of person to trust in a crisis. At the end of the film, he undertakes a daring mission to release the submarine from the octopus' tentacles and thereby enabling a torpedo to be fired into its brain. Although there is a considerable degree of danger involved, he insists on going in the belief that he would never ask his crew to do something that he could not do himself.

Pete Mathews is a career officer — someone who can be relied upon to cope with a crisis, but not particularly adept at handling personal relations. Although he is happy to fall in love with Professor Lesley Joyce (FAITH DOMERGUE), he cannot accept that she will not conform to prevailing stereotypes of femininity. As Joyce's colleague John Carter (Donald Curtis) observes, if Mathews wants to remain with her, he will have to acknowledge that she is "just as smart, just as courageous as men. And they [such women] are. They don't like to be over-protected or have their initiative taken away." Mathews half-hopes that Joyce might change and become an ideal mid–1950s mate — someone who will "get married [and] have families"— but by final reel he has at last begun to acknowledge that she is a good example of "a new breed of women."

In *The Vampire* (1957), Tobey plays a similar role as Sheriff Buck Donnelly, who spends much of his time investigating a series of brutal murders in his American small town. With his tall, ramrod-straight demeanor and common sense attitude to the events around him, he looks the epitome of a good law-enforcement officer. Director Paul Landres includes frequent close-ups of his impassive countenance, contrasting vividly with the fearful expressions of Dr. Paul Beecher (John Beal), as the doctor realizes to his horror that he has been transformed into the vampire. Donnelly uncovers the truth not through violence but by asking patient questions and carefully weighing up the evidence — as evidence by the way he continually walks round and round a room, his hands thrust deep into his pockets. He finally discovers the doctor's identity one night in a bar, as he throws darts at a board while talking to his subordinate George Ryan (Herb Vigran). While the sheriff's face remains passive, we understand the importance of his task by the way he turns away from the dart board, grabs his coat and hurries out, closely followed by George. Donnelly and Beecher have a fight to the death at the end: the sheriff is nearly strangled, but manages to break free and shoot the doctor dead. He walks away from the crime scene with his arm around Beecher's distraught girlfriend Carol (Coleen Gray). But his face remains impassive as he understands the importance of forgetting what had just happened and moving on to another case.

Regis Toomey

b. August 13, 1898, Pittsburgh, Pennsylvania;
d. October 12, 1991, Woodland Hills,
Los Angeles, California.

John Regis Toomey initially studied drama at the university of the same town. He considered a legal career, but eventually turned to acting, making his film debut in 1929. Although never a star, Toomey made his reputation as a character actor, often playing pillars of the community such as sheriffs, judges or police sergeants. In the early horror film *Murder by the Clock* (1931), he has a comic role as Officer Cassidy, an Irish cop obsessed with doing the right thing but lacking sufficient moral courage to trust in his judgments. He is far more interested in flirting with the attractive young maid Jane (Sally O'Neil), whom he eventually agrees to marry. Yet director Edward Sloman obviously has a soft spot for the officer — at one point he identifies the prime suspect in the murder case, but no one takes the trouble to listen to him. Cassidy retires to the kitchen, where he is shown meditatively eating chicken legs and commenting morosely on the pitfalls of being a police officer. In Robert Siodmak's horror noir *Phantom Lady* (1944), Toomey plays another detective who stands silently in the background chewing gum while Scott Henderson (Alan Curtis) is quizzed about his wife's murder. The detective does not speak much, but casts a threatening presence as he rhythmically chews

Regis Toomey publicity still (1932). Toomey's career as a character actor covered a variety of roles, from police officers to ingénues to villains.

gum while listening to Henderson's replies. Director Robert Siodmak zooms in to a close-up of the detective as he describes how the rope used to strangle Mrs. Henderson was "so tight that it had to be cut loose with a knife." The detective pauses, puts his hands in his pockets and moves out of the frame. His observation has the desired effect, as Henderson becomes more and more agitated and is eventually arrested for murder.

In Edgar G. Ulmer's horror noir *Strange Illusion* (1945), Toomey has a major supporting role as Dr. Vincent, consultant psychiatrist to Paul Cartwright (James Lydon), who suffers from a recurring dream, in which his mother Virginia (Sally Eilers) falls in love with a dangerous man Brett Curtis (Warren William), a dream which also contains Paul's father's death in mysterious circumstances. Vincent initially believes that Paul's dream is nothing more than a wild hallucination, "just a reaction from overwork at school," as he puts it. He takes the young man on a fishing trip and serves him breakfast, while listening sympathetically to the young man's outpourings. Vincent smokes a pipe, emphasizing the fact that he represents a source of stability for Paul. As the film unfolds, so Vincent's role changes, as he gradually comes to believe in the truth of Paul's dream. While maintaining a façade of respectability — as he willingly acquiesces to Professor Muhlbach's (Charles Arnt's) idea of committing Paul to an institution — Vincent realizes that Muhlbach is an accomplice of Curtis, and that both of them murdered Paul's father many years earlier. The psychiatrist assumes a far more active role within the drama, as he goes to the district attorney's office to verify Curtis's identity and leans insistently over the lawyer's desk until he discovers a satisfactory answer. With the police in tow, he dashes to the sanatorium, only to find that Paul has escaped. The film ends with a frantic car chase, with Vincent finding Paul in the nick of time as the police finally kill Curtis off. In the final sequence Vincent takes Virginia's hand, and the two of them walk with Paul towards the camera — an image that neatly sums expresses the psychiatrist's future as Paul's new father. Ulmer's film sums up the prevailing ideology of the period; that the father's role within the family was crucial as a way of ensuring that children grew up in a stable environment, and were not subject to the kind of influences — whether mental or otherwise — that might encourage them to depart from the moral straight and narrow.

Sometimes Toomey played leading roles — for example Tom Dean in *One Frightened Night* (1935). Initially, he comes across as a wastrel — although impeccably dressed in dinner-suit and wing collar, he has no aim in life other than to waste money. When Jasper Whyte (Charley Grapewin) promises him $1 million in his will, Dean's face lights up with the thought of being able to fritter it away as soon as possible. Dean covers up his shortcomings by telling jokes or describing himself as "a good-for-nothing scoundrel"; when he learns to his cost that he will not inherit the money after all, he observes wryly that "Santa Claus isn't coming after all." However, Dean undergoes something of a character change as the film progresses, as he realizes that Sheriff Jenks (Fred Kelsey) is making little or no progress in discovering the identity of the serial killer who seems bent on murdering every member of Jasper's family. Dean walks purposefully down the upstairs corridor, opening each door in turn to see whether anyone is hiding there; and makes a thorough investigation of one of the crime scenes (defying the sheriff's orders in the process). Dean also indulges in a little subterfuge, making everyone — including the audience — believe that he is actually the murderer. This little strategy works perfectly, as the real killer falls into Dean's trap and reveals himself. The film ends with Dean receiving his just rewards for his efforts, as he embraces Doris while the killer is led away at the back of the frame.

In *Mighty Joe Young* (1949), Toomey had a small supporting role as John Young, father of Jill Young (Terry Moore). Although heavily involved in hunting as a profession, he is very unwilling to countenance the idea of bringing up Joe Young the gorilla. Young Jill (Lora Lee Michel) finds an effective means of persuasion; she brings her musical-box to the living-room, where it plays the tune "Beautiful Dreamer."

The infant gorilla falls asleep in Jill's old cot, as happy as any baby might me. Confronted with such an idyllic scene, John cannot help but give his permission, even though he warns Jill that the infant will grow into a "huge, fierce, dangerous gorilla." The tune assumes an important function in the film; not only does it provides a means of pacifying Joe, whenever he loses his temper, but it also expresses Joe and Jill's worldview. Both are in a sense "beautiful dreamers," hoping for an idyllic life where they can be left alone in peace. They only discover this kind of existence at the film's end, when John Young has passed away.

Guy Usher

b. May 9, 1883, Mason City, Iowa;
d. June 16, 1944, San Diego, California.

Portly supporting actor in horror films of the late 1930s and early 1940s, usually playing industrialists or business people who seem powerless in the face of evil. This is certainly the case with Henry Morton in *The Devil Bat* (1940) — a typical executive type sitting behind an office desk issuing orders, who once employed Dr. Paul Carruthers (Bela Lugosi), but who later paid him off with a $5,000 check. Now Morton has become rich on Carruthers's research, but does not seem inclined to acknowledge his former employee's efforts, dismissing him as "a dreamer." Carruthers responds by calling Morton "feeble-brained" and plans to take revenge by creating the so-called "devil bats"—rodents that can attack and kill human beings. Morton himself reacts in fear; while earlier on in the film he had come across as a dominant personality, now he massages his neck with the shaving lotion given to him by Carruthers and glances uncertainly into the doctor's face. Although Morton understands that his life is in danger, he fails to understand that the shaving lotion is designed to attract the bats. He meets a predictably gory end, as the bat attacks his jugular vein in his own front doorway.

Usher takes a similar role in Monogram's *King of the Zombies* (1941) as Admiral Arthur Wainwright, a high-ranking officer in the U.S. Navy who is captured and interrogated by evil doctor Miklos Sangre (Henry Victor). As the doctor tries to force him to pass on vital military secrets, director Jean Yarbrough cuts to a close-up of the admiral's face — dripping with perspiration, his features screwed up as if unable to stand any more pain. Frustrated with his apparent lack of progress, the doctor springs up from his chair and forces the admiral to bend over, as if about to be beheaded. Fortunately nothing happens; this was nothing more than a strategy designed to persuade the admiral to talk. Eventually, the admiral is released from torture; at the film's end we see him once again in full dress uniform, thanking clean-cut hero Bill Summers (JOHN ARCHER) for his efforts, and thereby ensuring his country's future security in wartime.

In the Mr. Wong mystery *Doomed to Die* (1940), Usher plays Paul Fleming, a hotshot businessperson determined to gain control of his rival Cyrus P. Wentworth's (Melvin Lang) company. However, his aggressive façade soon

Guy Usher (left) in *Charlie Chan at the Opera* (1936) with Warner Oland and William Demarest (white hat). The stodgy Usher made his name playing figures of authority who were often unable to stand up to villains.

crumbles once Wentworth is murdered: Fleming becomes a worried man, perpetually clasping and unclasping his hands, or holding them across his chest as if protecting himself from being implicated in the crime. Alone in Wentworth's office, Fleming makes a desperate effort to recover the door key, which Fleming had previously thrown into a model ship for safekeeping. However, Wentworth's loyal employee Matthews (Wilbur Mack) catches him red-handed, and threatens Fleming with exposure. Fleming's suffering is painfully evident; his bottom jaw quivers, while his eyes look wildly around the room. However, he recovers sufficient composure to be able to return home and conceal his son Dick (William Stelling), who is suspected of having committed the murder. Fleming even admits to the crime, in a valiant attempt to exonerate Dick. Such nobility of spirit does the unfortunate man no good, as Matthews (the real murderer) kills him, and makes it look like suicide in a valiant attempt to divert Mr. Wong's (Boris Karloff) suspicions.

Usher had a slightly different role to play as Aldar, the ruler of the planet Saturn, in the science fiction serial *Buck Rogers* (1939). Sitting high on his throne, he announces that "Saturn wants no contact with outside planets!" Aldar continues: "In this age of science, we cannot hope to isolate ourselves from the rest of the universe, but we are dedicated to peace, and have no patience with rebels." However, the co-directors Ford Beebe and Saul A. Goodland suggest that this position cannot be sustained: Aldar has to commit himself to Buck Rogers' (Buster Crabbe) cause to ensure the safety of his people against the threat posed by Killer Kane (Anthony Warde), who lives up to the Biblical echoes of his surname.

Released a month before the outbreak of the Second World War in August 1939, and two years before America finally entered the conflict, *Buck Rogers* shows how Aldar rejects the ideology of absolute rule, in which his people carry out his orders without question, and turns instead to democracy and the rule of law, both of which are upheld by Buck Rogers and his intrepid crew — Wilma Deering (Constance Moore) and George "Buddy" Wade (Jackie Moran). Only then, as Aldar himself observes, will "the scientist of the free world" be able to create "the weapons and the craft that will make democracy invincible against any army. God bless America."

Such sentiments seemed equally pertinent in the early 1950s at the height of the so-called "Red Scare" that dominated the American political agenda. This perhaps helps to explain why *Buck Rogers* was re-released in 1953 as a 71-minute feature film *Planet Outlaws*, some fourteen years after its premiere as a serial. In this slimmed-down version of the serial, the contrast between Aldar and Buck is emphasized: Buck is a man of action, who regularly travels to and from Aldar's kingdom by spaceship. There are numerous sequences of Buck at the controls of his spaceship, or busily crossing the frame left to right, right to left, or diagonally. Even if he is faced with a difficult situation, his vigorous attitude to life ensures that he will be able to emerge triumphant. By contrast, Aldar is a completely passive figure; we only ever see him sitting on his throne, swathed in robes and pronouncing his lines in portentous tones, as befits someone in his elevated position. He has to rely on Buck to solve his political difficulties. Such passivity, it is suggested, renders Aldar vulnerable to corruption; bad guys such as Killer Kane (Anthony Warde) could exploit it for their own ends. The only way to resist Kane's malign influence, and hence guarantee national security is through direct action; to meet him head-on and destroy him.

Edward Van Sloan
b. November 1, 1882, Chaska, Minnesota;
d. March 6, 1964, San Francisco, California.

Born Edward van Sloun in Minnesota, Edward van Sloan made his name as a stage actor, playing Van Helsing in the 1927 Broadway production of *Dracula*. He repeated the role in Tod Browning's 1931 film version, casting an imposing presence over the action with his clipped tone of delivery ("We are dealing with the ... undead," with a long pause taken between the last two words) and fastidious gestures. While interviewing Renfield (DWIGHT FRYE), Van

Edward van Sloan (right) and Colin Clive in *Frankenstein* (1931). With his memorable, clipped delivery and rather sinister presence, van Sloan was an ideal choice for Universal's early horror films such as *Frankenstein* and *Dracula* (where he played van Helsing).

Helsing plays with a cap or his glasses in a deliberate attempt to suppress his emotions. The professor wields considerable power: Mina (Helen Chandler) allows him to place his hands round her throat, in full confidence that he will help her. Nor is he frightened of Dracula (Bela Lugosi); in a flash of inspiration he discovers the vampire's true nature when he sees that Dracula produces no reflection in the mirror of a small jewel box. Van Helsing picks the box up and shines the mirror directly in Dracula's face; the vampire can do nothing else but shy away.

Once Van Helsing is sure of his facts, nothing can stop him. Even when Dracula tries to intimidate him by staring directly into his eyes, Van Helsing stands resolute. His jaw quivers momentarily, but he soon recovers his self-possession as he reaches into his pocket and produces a cross to scare Dracula away. Van Helsing comes into his own during the final scene; in a long shot, we see him triumphantly driving a stake into Dracula's heart. Having resisted everything the vampire could throw at him, Van Helsing has mastered the situation. He shepherds Harker (DAVID MANNERS) and Mina away from Dracula's grave, and continues to clear up as the screen fades to black.

Van Sloan reprised the role in *Dracula's Daughter* (1936), directed by Lambert Hillyer. He appears once again as a practical, calm person, describing Dracula's power in emphatic tones—"The strength of the vampire is that he is unbelievable," with the stress placed on the final "is" for emphasis. Although no one is prepared to believe him, Van Helsing sticks to his guns—at one point he rises from his chair, looks Jeffrey Garth (Otto Kruger) straight in the eye and insists that Garth should believe him. He takes charge of the situation by laying a trap for Countess Marya Zaleska (aka Dracula's daughter) (Gloria Holden), insisting all the while that there should be "no mirrors hereabout," in case she should become suspicious. His voice acquires a strange intensity, as if believing that this is the only way forward. As it turns out, Van Helsing has little part to play in catching the vampire, other than to murmur in a low voice that even though she has had a wooden shaft cast through her heart, she "looks as beautiful as when she died ... a hundred years ago." This is the film's closing line; as he speaks, Van Helsing raises his eyes heavenwards, as if thanking the divinity for allowing Dracula's daughter to return from whence she came.

As Dr. Muller in *The Mummy* (1932), Van Sloan plays a similar role of an expert in his particular field, who knows how to resist the influence of evil. He relishes one climactic confrontation with Ardath Bey (Boris Karloff), as he hisses, "I'd break your dried flesh into pieces, but your power is too strong!" Muller holds a transcript of the Scroll of Thoth in front of Ardath's face, and pulls it away again when the mummy tries to grab it. In *Before I Hang* (1940) Van Sloan plays prison doctor Ralph Howard, who willingly helps condemned doctor John

Garth (Boris Karloff) in the search for a serum that can bring the dead back to life. Most of the time, Howard is content to play a supporting role, providing support and advice where necessary; but as time passes, he realizes that Garth is starting to behave very strangely — clasping the back of his neck and looking rather tired. Howard advises, with some justification, that "inoculation [of the serum] might kill Garth," but this has no effect whatsoever on Garth's desire to see the experiment through to its conclusion. In a climactic sequence, Howard is shown in close-up, his expression gradually changing from enthusiasm to terror, as he understands Garth's motives. By injecting himself with the serum, Garth used the blood of a recently deceased killer — as a result, he has inherited some of the killer's murderous tendencies. Director Nick Grinde intercuts close-ups of Howard's and Garth's expressions — one petrified, the other grimly determined — as Garth strangles his assistant. Garth eventually meets his just desserts, as he is hanged for his crimes, and the film ends with Dr. Paul Ames (Bruce Bennett) pronouncing sonorously that "in the war of science, people must die"— a pointed reference to the importance of continuing scientific research during wartime. However, we are left wondering why Howard had to perish during this "war of science"— after all, he was only trying to aid Garth's researches.

In *The Black Room* (1935), Van Sloan has an uncredited role as yet another doctor, replete with bushy beard and curly wig, announcing the birth of the Berghman twins. Their father, Baron Frederick de Berghman (Henry Kolker) announces dolefully that the family curse has struck once more: for several generations the family has spawned twins, and the younger sibling has invariably killed the older. The doctor shakes his head in disbelief and tells the Baron not to believe in such archaic superstitions. This proves a rash piece of advice: the twins eventually grow up into Barons Gregor and Anton (both played by Boris Karloff), while Gregor — the older sibling — ends up killing Anton (and hence flying in the face of tradition), Gregor meets a similar fate as a result of Anton's curse.

Sometimes, Van Sloan's experts are themselves guilty of going too far — as, for example, in James Whale's *Frankenstein* (1931). As Dr. Waldman, Van Sloan appears once again to be in control of the situation, as he gives a lecture on anatomy in a cool, detached tone and dismisses his students with a cheery wave. However, Waldman is also an ambitious man who relishes the chance to expand his scientific knowledge by reviving the monster (Boris Karloff). In one sequence, we see Waldman in full surgical regalia, bringing in a trolley full of medical instruments, while the monster lies apparently sleeping on a bed. The only snag is that the monster is actually awake; he rises from the bed and strangles the doctor to death. Despite his expertise, Waldman is just another vulnerable human being, to be cast aside like a rag doll. Van Sloan reprises the mad scientist in a small role in *Air Hawks* (1935). Speaking in a mid–European accent, he leads the villain Victor Arnold (DOUGLASS DUMBRILLE) into his workshop, claiming all that something "eenteresting" will be revealed within. It turns out to be a machine emitting forth an electric ray that will destroy aircraft instantly, "like touching something with a high-tech vire!" as Van Sloan claims. Eventually, the scientist is hoist with his own petard, as he is blown to pieces while trying to fire the weapon at a passing plane.

Van Sloan appears as himself in a prologue to *Frankenstein* (which was added after the film had been completed) in front of a stage curtain, warning the audience about what they are going to see. Hands clasped, his face wreathed in a bright smile, he warns us that the action "might even horrify you," with particular emphasis placed on the word "horrify." Should anyone wish to leave the theatre, he advises them that "now's your chance to ... ah ... well, we've warned you!" The last phrase is delivered with a sardonic laugh, as he quits the stage with an air of supreme self-confidence.

In *The Death Kiss* (1932), Van Sloan is cast against type as the film director Tom Avery, who turns out to be responsible for Myles Brent's (Edmund Burns) murder. Director Edwin L. Marin allows the actor full rein to indulge in a series of fastidious gestures, as he shepherds his cast about the set in a vain attempt to keep up with a tight production schedule. When his leading lady, Marcia Lane (Adrienne Ames), complains of exhaustion, Avery puts a paternal arm around her shoulder and murmurs: "I'll try and help you all I can." This turns out to be nothing more than a smokescreen, designed to cover up Avery's guilt. The director tries to escape the police, but is eventually shot dead.

Mel Welles
*b. February 17, 1924, New York City;
d. August 19, 2005, Norfolk, Virginia.*

Mel Welles (born Ira Meitcher) worked as a clinical psychologist, writer and disk jockey before turning to acting. He made his film debut in *Appointment in Honduras* (1953). Welles began his film career in small roles, such as the heavy Iban in *Abbott and Costello Meet the Mummy* (1955). Clad in a long gown with a small mustache and fez, he encapsulates most of the orientalist assumptions about Egypt past and present; that it is a dangerous place full of lowlife characters waiting to capture unfortunate American tourists—in this case, Peter Patterson (Bud Abbott) and Freddie Franklin (Lou Costello). Iban shows an unswerving devotion to his master Semu (Richard Deacon), even if it means placing himself in danger. In his view, however, it is much more important to rid Egypt of "infidels" (i.e., non–Muslims), as well as recovering a valuable medallion belonging to the mummy Klaris (Eddie Parker). Welles plays another heavy in *The 27th Day* (1957)— although he has no lines to speak, he cuts a threatening presence in the Kremlin as the Soviet general (Stefan Schnabel) interrogates Ivan Godofsky (Azemat Janti), as to the potential of the capsule that Godofsky has been given by an alien from space. The sequences suggest the fundamental cruelty of the Soviet regime in which individuals count for nothing.

Welles appeared in another horror spoof, the Bowery Brothers' *Hold That Hypnotist* (also 1957). As Blackbeard the pirate, Welles does not have much to do other than fill the screen with his imposing presence, while playing a game of chance with Horace Debussy ("Sach") Jones (Huntz Hall). Initially it appears as if Blackbeard will fleece Sach of all his money, but Sach eventually learns how to play the game and win. Blackbeard reacts predictably; he gets up with a start from the table, grabs Sach by the lapels and challenges him to a duel. The slapstick sword-fight ends with Blackbeard being thrown into a corner and hit with a wooden chair. *Hold That Hypnotist* recycles the plot of another Bowery Boys spoof, *Master Minds* (1949); as in the earlier film, where ALAN NAPIER took a similar role as the evil Dr. Druzik, in *Hold That Hypnotist* Welles is only required to play a pantomime villain. He does what he can with the role, laughing evilly on occasions and speaking with a pronounced English accent reminiscent of Laurence Olivier's Richard III.

Welles appeared in several low-budget horror and science fiction films of the late 1950s, mostly for Roger Corman. In *Attack of the Crab Monsters* (1957), he plays botanist Jules Deveroux with a heavy European accent. In his safari-suit and solar topee, he looks every inch the colonizer conducting experiments on an unin-

Mel Welles in *Outside the Law* (1956). A thickset leading actor whose career began with roles as villains and playing stooges (in Bowery Boys films), Welles later became a stalwart member of Roger Corman's acting troupe.

habited island in the interests of scientific research. He initially appears a confident personality, with a businesslike attitude to his work; once it has been completed, he will leave and return home to establish his reputation. However, his attitude soon changes as he admits his inability to understand the island's "small secret"—the presence of giant crabs. Deveroux's jaw starts to quiver, as he stammers at one point that he is nothing more than "a simple provincial botanist." All thoughts of scientific colonization have disappeared. He collapses to the ground and has his hand bitten off by a crab. Deveroux meets a violent end as he is eventually eaten alive.

Later that same year Welles had a bizarre role as the mad gravedigger Smolkin in *The Undead*. Describing himself proudly as "bewitched and robbed of all his senses," he has plenty of work to do, either burying corpses or opening a coffin to release Helene (Pamela Duncan) from a potentially grisly death. Smolkin is fond of singing popular nursery rhymes ("Humpty Dumpty," "Hickory Dickory Dock") in a dulcet faux–English accent, with alternative lyrics designed to express his melancholy state of mind, as someone so bewitched in an evil universe that he has been deprived of the power of rational thought. However, Smolkin undergoes something of a character change, as he cultivates a quasi-paternal desire to protect Helene from harm. This is no mean task, given that one of her major enemies is Livia the witch (Allison Hayes), who has the power to transform herself at will into a bat, and thereby elude capture. Inevitably, Smolkin fails in his self-appointed task, but he does have the chance to sum up the feelings of many people — living in the past and the present — who are all deprived of the power of self-determination, as he wistfully longs for the freedom to choose whether to live or die.

Welles' best and favorite part was that of the flower shop owner Gravis Mushnick — another mid–European with a heavy accent — in *Little Shop of Horrors* (1960). Tall, bearded, with a commanding presence, Mushnick resembles Deveroux with his air of confidence as he shouts at his staff or silences them with a sarcastic quip. However, once business has improved, due in no small part to Seymour Krelboin's (JONATHAN HAZE) exotic plant (christened Audrey 2), Mushnick's attitude changes. He becomes almost paternal in manner, rubbing his hands and referring to "my excellent Seymour," who will transform Mushnick into "Gravis Mushnick the bloom tycoon."

Mushnick experiences violent mood swings throughout the film; when he sees Seymour feeding human body parts to Audrey 2, he clasps his head in anguish, no doubt fearing that he will have trouble with the police. Detective Jos Fink (Wally Campo) duly enters; and Mushnick can hardly answer any questions due to nerves. There is little sign of the confident personality we encountered at the beginning. However, he remains at heart a decent man; as the police pursue Seymour in the belief that he is the prime suspect, Mushnick tries everything to impede their investigation, either by prevaricating or sticking a foot out in the hope of tripping them up. By the end of the film Mushnick has reassumed his role as a shop-owner; despite the fact that Audrey 2 is still devouring every human being in sight. Money talks, even if it means sacrificing a few lives in the process.

Welles portrays a protean figure who will do anything he can to increase profits. Unlike Seymour (who is transformed from a gawky shop-assistant into a serial killer taking a positive pleasure in finding new victims for Audrey), Mushnick never changes; for him life is a series of performances designed to make people part with their money.

Ian Wolfe

b. November 4, 1896, Canton, Illinois;
d. January 23, 1992, Los Angeles, California.

Versatile character actor born in Canton, Illinois, who served a long apprenticeship in the theatre before making his film debut in *The Barretts of Wimpole Street* (1934). In a long career spanning over five decades, Wolfe played just about everything from Shakespeare to *Dick Tracy* (1990), his last film.

Wolfe plays numerous memorable cameo roles in horror and science fiction films. In *The Raven* (1935), he plays Pinky, who offers some brief comic relief from the prevailing atmosphere of doom pervading Dr. Richard Vollin's (Bela Lugosi) house. Having announced—for no particular reason—that he likes horses, Pinky pours himself a glass of champagne and then starts suddenly, as he becomes aware of Edmond Bateman's (Boris Karloff) threatening presence behind him. With a nervous laugh, Pinky asks "the most unfortunate-looking fellow" Bateman to move away. Bateman obliges; but Pinky is clearly disturbed by what happens around him — particularly when Vollin tells him that the stuffed raven (which is placed on a mantelpiece) has traditionally been associated with death. As Louis Friedlander's (aka Lew Landers) film unfolds, Pinky's role becomes more and more peripheral; the script only allows him one laugh at the end, once Vollin and Bateman have perished. As everyone prepares to leave the house, Pinky observes, "We've forgotten the colonel"—a reference to Colonel Bertram Grant (Spencer Charters) who has slept peacefully throughout the entire evening and remains entirely unaware of what has happened. In *The Return of Dr. X* (1939), he has the briefest of roles as a cemetery caretaker who shows the grave of Dr. Maurice Xavier (Humphrey Bogart) to Dr. Mike Rhodes (Dennis Morgan) and campaigning journalist "Wichita" Garrett (Wayne Morris). The curator starts back in alarm; he exclaims, "I've been robbed," as he discovers that Xavier's corpse is no longer there. In the spoof horror film *Zombies on Broadway* (1945), Wolfe has another comic cameo as Professor Hopkins, a mad museum curator fond of carrying skeletons from place to place, and at one point enunciating the line "They [the zombies] are the LIVING DEAD!" in a deliberate attempt to frighten bungling press agents Jerry Miles (Wally Brown) and Mike Strager (Alan Carney).

In *Mad Love* (1935), Wolfe takes an uncredited role as Henry Orlac, the stepfather of Stephen Orlac (Colin Clive). Having spent a life in trade as a jeweler, Henry has little time for Stephen (who decided to pursue a career as a pianist, but whose career has been cut short by a horrific accident which results in the loss of his hands). Henry turns down Stephen's request

Ian Wolfe publicity still (1947). One of Hollywood's most versatile character actors, Ian Wolfe played everything from lawyers to gangsters to scientists and villains. He was truly like a chameleon: a man of many parts.

for money, and suggests in a sly, insinuating voice that his stepson should perhaps ask his wife Yvonne (Frances Drake) to "supplement her earnings" as an actress by turning to prostitution. Stephen responds by throwing a knife at him; Henry cowers in terror behind the counter. With his little goatee beard and intense, staring eyes, Henry is as much of an obsessive as Dr. Gogol (Peter Lorre) who admits that he has "conquered science" but can never conquer love.

In *The Invisible Man's Revenge* (1944), Wolfe has another cameo as the crooked lawyer Feeney, who strokes his coat and hat in a self-satisfied manner as he relishes the prospect of fighting a case of blackmail on Robert Griffin's (JON HALL) behalf. However, once he learns of Griffin's intentions, Feeney's attitude changes. He sidles out of the room, hoping against hope that no one will notice him leaving. As Lord Mayor Herman Brandon R. Clive in *The Brighton Strangler* (1945), Wolfe plays the innocent victim of crazed killer Reginald Parker (John Loder). Clive walks home one snowy night, and encounters the killer emerging from the bushes; although desperately trying to escape, the diminutive mayor is no match for Parker. Wolfe resembles a bird caught in a trap, his arms and legs flailing in all directions as Parker strangles him to death. In Mark Robson's *Bedlam* (1946), he assumes a more commanding role as mad lawyer Sidney Long, who has been consigned to Bedlam on the grounds of insanity yet proclaims all the while that he is the best advocate in the City of London. We might not believe his words, but we admire his resilience as he leads a card-school and stands up to Master Sims (Boris Karloff), the sadistic prison governor. When the oppressed inmates finally get their own back on Sims by binding him and putting him on a mock trial, Long acts as judge, taking little heed of Sims' insincere protestations that he was only sadistic because he was "frightened." Long eventually proclaims Sims' punishment with malicious glee; the ex-governor is to be permanently immured behind a dry stonewall in the remotest part of the prison.

Wolfe played numerous cameo roles in the Sherlock Holmes series for Universal. As the antique dealer in *Sherlock Holmes in Washington* (1943), he has to cope with Sherlock Holmes (Basil Rathbone) playing the part of a scatter-brained customer who accidentally drops a Ming vase on the ground, smashing it to smithereens. The dealer picks up the telephone in desperation and gasps: "The man's mad!" His boss, Henrich Hinkel (also known as Richard Stanley) (GEORGE ZUCCO) listens impassively, and requests Holmes's presence in his lair at the back of the shop. As the butler Drake in *The Scarlet Claw* (1944), Wolfe tries every possible means to escape from his employer Judge Brisson (MILES MANDER) in the belief that his life was in danger. Drake finally decamps to the nearest hostelry, where he proceeds to drown his sorrows in drink. The last we see of him is when he staggers out of the front door, vowing never to return to the village. In *The Pearl of Death* (1944), Wolfe plays a very different role — that of the jeweler Amos Hodder, a fastidious man prone to fits of absent-mindedness, whose glasses have the annoying habit of falling down from his forehead on to the bridge of his nose. Although full of good intentions, he proves no match for Holmes (Basil Rathbone). The same also applies to Wolfe's Commissioner of Scotland Yard in *Dressed to Kill* (1946), the final film in the series. While he may look important with his dark suit, horn-rimmed spectacles and balding pate shining in the artificial light of the police station, he has little or no clue about how to solve the case of the cheap musical boxes that people seem willing to kill for. All he can do is to sit back in his chair sipping tea, leaving Holmes to do the detective work.

Later on in his career, Wolfe took small parts in science fiction films such as *The Lost World* (1960), where he plays Burton White, the sole survivor of an expedition to the Lost World that ended in failure. For three years he has lived a half-life amongst the tribal natives, unable to see and cared for by an unnamed girl (Vitina Marcus). White encounters Professor George Edward Challenger (CLAUDE RAINS) and his fellow travelers; although pleased to see them, White realizes that he cannot be of much help, other than to tell them how they can successfully escape. He spread his arms in supplication and pleads with them to leave quickly in case the natives should catch them. With his long white hair and unkempt beard, Wolfe's character assumes a Christ-like appearance as he provides the way forward for the travelers lost in the wilderness of the Lost World.

George Zucco

b. January 11, 1896, Manchester, England;
d. May 29, 1960, Hollywood, California.

Born in Manchester, United Kingdom, George Zucco made his stage debut in Canada. After military service during World War I, he made his name on the London stage, leading to his film debut in 1931 in *Dreyfus* (1931) with CEDRIC HARDWICKE. Zucco never achieved major stardom in Hollywood, although he did have some juicy supporting roles — notably Professor Moriarty in *Sherlock Holmes in Washington* (1943) — a smooth-talking rogue speaking his lines in a rasping tone. It comes as no surprise to find that he is actually a Nazi in disguise, with an undisguised contempt for everything that Holmes stands for. He reprised the villain's role in *Midnight Manhunt* (1945), a low-budget thriller set in a wax museum (clearly referencing Michael Curtiz's 1933 film). As the jewel thief Jelke, Zucco goes through his repertoire of lip-curling gestures, taking a particular pleasure in being sadistic to over-inquisitive journalist Sue Gallagher (Ann Savage). Eventually, Jelke overreaches himself, and is brought to justice with the help of Sue's fellow reporter (and boyfriend) Pete Willis (William Gargan).

One of Zucco's nastiest roles was that of Andoheb in *The Mummy's Hand* (1940). Although superficially modeled on Boris Karloff's performance in the original *Mummy* (1932), Zucco comes across as a far more sinister figure in his long black gown, silver-rimmed spectacles and beetling eyebrows. On several occasions director Christy Cabanne cuts to close-ups of him staring directly to the camera, suggesting that Andoheb regards the audience as much of a threat to his way of life as the film's hero Steve Banning (DICK FORAN). Andoheb tries to scare people off through threats — in one sequence he is shown advising Marta Solvani (Peggy Moran) to leave the country: "I am so happy to hear that [you are going] [...] May I wish you a most pleasant journey back to your homeland." He places particular emphasis on the word "happy," and delivers the last sentence with pregnant pauses between each word ("a — most — pleasant — journey.") It becomes a pronouncement as well as a threat — should Marta not take the journey back home, she will inevitably be punished. Andoheb's prediction proves accurate — at the end of the film Marta is bound hand and foot to a stone slab, while Andoheb envisages a future in which "neither time nor death can touch us," eyeing her lasciviously as he does so. The idea of mummifying her clearly gives him considerable sexual thrills. Needless to say, Anhodeb never fulfills his wishes, as Babe Hanson (WALLACE FORD) shoots him dead, but we are nonetheless made well aware of the film's orientalist stance. While the Americans are portrayed as clean living and companionable, Egyptians like Andoheb indulge in perverted fantasies while claiming all the while that this is what the gods have ordained.

In *The Cat and the Canary* (1939), Zucco plays the family lawyer Crosby, who comes to a lonely house in the Bayou of Louisiana to read the will of rich eccentric Cyrus Norman for the rest of his family. He comes across as a practical, no-nonsense kind of personality, who will not be swayed by all the threats about the demon's presence within the house. However, he does realize that the legitimate heir to the fortune, Joyce Norman (Paulette Goddard) is in great danger; he is just about to explain why when a secret panel opens in the library, a hand shoots out and grabs him around the neck. His corpse is discovered later on in a cupboard adjacent to Joyce's bed.

Zucco played his fair share of mad scientists — as for example in Stuart Heisler's *The Monster and the Girl* (1941) for Paramount. As Dr. Parry, he informs Susan Webster (ELLEN DREW) in ringing tones that by transplanting the brain of her condemned brother Scot

George Zucco publicity still (1945). British-born Zucco rivaled Lionel Atwill as the most popular villain of Hollywood horror and science fiction films of the 1930s and 1940s.

(Philip Terry) into an ape, he can unlock the "treasure house" of the human brain. He does however not understand that the brain can turn towards evil as well as good: the ape decides to wreak violent revenge on those mobsters who have ruined Scot's and Susan's lives. In the Producers' Releasing Corporation (PRC's) *The Mad Monster* (1942), Zucco's Dr. Lorenzo Cameron transforms his dim-witted handyman Petro (GLENN STRANGE) into a werewolf, for the express purpose of taking revenge on his fellow scientists who laughed at Cameron's researches. Zucco gives a virtuoso performance, looking directly to the camera as he completes his researches, and then offering a mock-lecture about the potential of a wolf-man, who possesses "the animal lust to kill." He remains deliberate and businesslike in his movements, as if totally in control of the situation; when Petro tries to raise his voice, Cameron quells him with a stroke of his whip. As the film progresses, however, the doctor's attitude changes, as he becomes more and more power-crazed. His voice rises to a shrill shriek, and his eyes almost stand out on stalks as he administers the serum once again to Petro to transform the handyman into a werewolf. Inevitably Cameron meets a grisly end, as Petro turns on his master and throws him into the burning laboratory. In the same year, Zucco played another mad scientist, Dr. Robert Renault, in Twentieth Century–Fox's *Dr. Renault's Secret*, who transforms an ape into a human being, Noel (J. CARROL NAISH). The plot is virtually a rehash of *The Mad Monster*: the doctor mistreats his monster to such an extent that the monster eventually turns on him, only this time the doctor dies by strangulation rather than being thrown into a furnace.

In *Voodoo Man* (1944), Zucco has a bizarre role as Nicholas, sidekick to Dr. Richard Marlowe (Bela Lugosi). Nicholas initially comes across as a hard-working garage owner, dressed in sleeveless pullover and tie, offering help to any passing motorists—especially women. However, this is nothing more than an act, designed to entrap potential victims for the doctor's experiments in voodoo, designed to revive his wife Evelyn (Ellen Hall). Nicholas assumes the role of high voodoo priest, dressed in long cloak and headdress, delivering long speeches in a foreign tongue in slow, portentous tones. Zucco does what he can with the role, but he is clearly miscast.

In *The Mad Ghoul* (1943), Zucco has much more fun as Dr. Alfred Morris, a scientist acquainted with ancient Egyptian medicine (shades of Andoheb in *The Mummy's Hand*). He uses poison gas to reduce his unwitting research assistant Ted Allison (David Bruce) to a vegetable, answerable only to the doctor's orders. This gives Morris the chance to break up Ted's engagement to beautiful singer Isabel Lewis (EVELYN ANKERS) and use Ted as an assassin with specific instructions to kill Isabel's new boyfriend Eric Iverson (TURHAN BEY). Zucco has great fun with the role; his eyes dance with enthusiasm as he announces that good and evil no longer have any meaning for him. As a scientist, he is only interested in whether phenomena are true or false. He also reveals a considerable talent for role-play, as he pretends to be concerned for Ted's welfare, while administering further doses of the deadly poison gas to ensure the young man's continuing loyalty towards him. In *Scared to Death* (1947) Zucco once again cuts a sinister figure as Dr. Joseph van Ee in his white coat and heavy spectacles, declaiming in dulcet tones that "it was my belief, yes, even my hope, that that person was dead," with long pauses taken at each comma. His air of calm, quiet authority contrasts with that of Professor Leonide (Bela Lugosi), who paces around the room in a state of perpetual nervous tension. As the tale snakes its way through a maze of murders, hypnosis and a mysterious figure in a blue mask, Zucco remains perfectly calm; the only emotion he shows is to grab the lapels of his white coat in indignation when accused of medical malpractice. His presence stands out film notable for its abrupt tonal shifts between the macabre scenes involving Lugosi and the labored comic relief provided by "Bull" Raymond (Nat Pendleton).

In *The Black Raven* (1943) Zucco has a rare outing as a good guy Amos Bradford (aka The Raven), an innkeeper with a shady past who plays host to a variety of oddball characters ranging from a nervous guest trying to conceal a bag of stolen cash (Byron Foulger), to a jealous father (Robert Middlemass) trying to prevent his daughter (Wanda McKay) from eloping. Zucco again casts an imposing presence over the action through his deliberate method of delivery ("I protected ... myself") and his use of minimalist gestures. When a crisis looms, his sole reaction is to clasp his hands together; in this *Old Dark House*-like tale, where things go bump in the night and the guests' lives are at risk from an unidentified murderer, Zucco provides a rock of stability. Although he eventually dies in the end, the victim of the murderer's bullet, he not only solves the crime, but pays his debt to society. Now he can die as a free man. The last we see of him is when he looks directly into the camera and closes his "neon eyes" (as one critic described them).

One of Zucco's more interesting films is *Dead Men Walk* (1943) where he plays two roles — the kindly small-town physician Lloyd Clayton, and his twin brother Elwyn, who rises from the dead and assumes the role of a vampire out to seek revenge on his brother (who had a hand in Elwyn's premature death). The plot is a familiar one, of Lloyd gradually coming to accept the fact that his brother is a vampire, and making every effort to destroy him and thereby protect his niece Gayle (Mary Carlisle). However, the distinction between the two brothers is not as clear-cut as director Sam Newfield would like us to believe — on several occasions Lloyd is shown in close-up wondering whether he has become the victim of an insane hallucination, "too terrible to think about." Perhaps Elwyn doesn't really exist, but merely represents a satanic side of Lloyd's character that the doctor cannot acknowledge. On this view, the climactic fight between the two brothers can be seen as a struggle between good and evil for the right to control the doctor's soul. Both eventually perish in a fire, suggesting a kind of stalemate. The film ends with the minister (Sam Flint) praying that Lloyd will be free from pain and suffering in death; our experience of the film suggests that this will only be possible once the struggle between the two sides of his nature can be resolved.

Dead Men Walk gives Zucco the chance to incorporate the contradictory aspects of his screen image in a single film. His Lloyd Clayton recalls Amos Bradford in *The Black Raven*— a reassuring presence making every effort to protect Gayle from harm, while convincing her fiancé David Bently (Nedrick Young) that he is not actually the murderer. As the vampire Elwyn, Zucco's performance has all the malignant charm of his mad scientist in *The Mad Monster*, as he takes great pleasure in expressing a wish to subordinate Gayle to his will, as she lies asleep in front of him, his black shadow casting a threatening presence over her white face.

Filmography

Cast lists include stars as well as character actors when available.

Abbott and Costello Meet Dr. Jekyll and Mr. Hyde (1953). Prod.: Universal International Pictures. Dir.: Charles Lamont. Cast: Bud Abbott, Lou Costello.

Abbott and Costello Meet Frankenstein (1948). Prod.: Universal International Pictures. Dir.: Charles Barton. Cast: Bud Abbott, Lou Costello.

Abbott and Costello Meet the Invisible Man (1951). Prod.: Universal International Pictures. Dir.: Charles Lamont. Cast: Bud Abbott, Lou Costello.

Abbott and Costello Meet the Mummy (1955). Prod.: Universal International Pictures. Dir.: Charles Lamont. Cast: Bud Abbott, Lou Costello.

The Adventures of Sherlock Holmes (1939). Prod.: Twentieth Century–Fox Film Corporation. Dir.: Alfred L. Werker. Cast: Basil Rathbone, Nigel Bruce, George Zucco, Holmes Herbert.

A-Haunting We Will Go (1942). Prod.: Twentieth Century–Fox Film Corporation. Dir.: Alfred L. Werker. Cast: Stan Laurel, Oliver Hardy, Elisha Cook, Jr., Mantan Moreland.

Air Hawks (1935). Prod.: Columbia Pictures Corporation. Dir.: Albert S. Rogell. Cast: Ralph Bellamy, Douglass Dumbrille.

Ali Baba and the Forty Thieves (1942). Prod.: Universal Pictures. Dir.: Arthur Lubin. Cast: Maria Montez, Jon Hall, Turhan Bey, Harry Cording.

The Alligator People (1959). Prod.: Twentieth Century–Fox Film Corporation. Dir.: Roy del Ruth. Cast: Beverly Garland, Lon Chaney, Jr., Bruce Bennett.

The Amazing Colossal Man (1957). Prod.: American International Pictures. Dir.: Bert I. Gordon. Cast: Glenn Langan, William Hudson, Cathy Downs.

The Amazing Mr. X (1948). Prod.: Samba Pictures. Dir.: Bernard Vorhaus. Cast: Turhan Bey, Cathy O'Donnell, Richard Carlson.

Among the Living (1941). Prod.: Paramount Pictures. Dir.: Stuart Heisler. Cast: Albert Dekker, Susan Hayward.

Another Chance (1953). TV Film. Prod.: ABC Television. Dir.: Don Medford. Cast: Leslie Nielsen, Virginia Vincent.

The Ape (1940). Prod.: Monogram Studios. Dir.: William Nigh. Cast: Boris Karloff, Maris Wrixon, Henry Hall.

The Ape Man (1943). Prod.: Monogram Studios. Dir.: William Beaudine. Cast: Bela Lugosi, Wallace Ford, Henry Hall.

Appointment on Mars (1952). TV Film. Prod.: ABC Television. Dir.: Don Medford. Cast: Leslie Nielsen, Brian Keith.

Arabian Nights (1944). Prod.: Universal Pictures. Dir.: John Rawlins. Cast: Maria Montez, Jon Hall, Turhan Bey, Shemp Howard.

The Atomic Man (1955). Prod.: Merton Park Studios, United Kingdom. Dir.: Ken Hughes. Cast: Gene Nelson, Faith Domergue.

The Atomic Submarine (1960). Prod.: Allied Artists Pictures. Dir.: Spencer Gordon Bennet. Cast: Arthur Franz, Dick Foran, Tom Conway.

Attack of the Crab Monsters (1957). Prod.: Allied Artists Pictures. Dir.: Roger Corman. Cast: Richard Garland, Pamela Duncan, Mel Welles.

Attack of the 50-Foot Woman (1958). Prod.: Allied Artists Pictures. Dir.: Nathan Juran. Cast: Allison Hayes, William Hudson, Ken Terrell.

Attack of the Puppet People (1958). Prod.: Metro Goldwyn-Mayer. Dir.: Bert I. Gordon. Cast: John Agar, Scott Peters, John Hoyt.

Back from the Dead (aka *Bury Me Dead*) (1957) Prod.: Regal Films/Twentieth Century–Fox. Dir.: Charles Marquis Warren. Cast: Arthur Franz, Peggie Castle.

The Beast from 20,000 Fathoms (1953). Prod.: Jack Dietz Productions/Warner Bros. Pictures. Dir.: Eugene Lourié. Cast: Kenneth Tobey, Cecil Kellaway, Paula Raymond.

Beast of Yucca Flats (1961). Prod.: Not Known. Dir.: Coleman Francis. Cast: Tor Johnson, Douglas Mellor, Barbara Francis.

The Beast with a Million Eyes (1955). Prod.: San Mateo Productions/American Releasing Corporation. Dir.: David Kramarsky. Cast: Paul Birch, Chester Conklin.

The Beast with Five Fingers (1946). Prod.: Warner Bros. Pictures. Dir.: Robert Florey. Cast: Peter Lorre, Robert Alda, J. Carrol Naish.

Bedlam (1946). Prod.: RKO Radio Pictures. Dir.: Mark Robson. Cast: Boris Karloff, Elizabeth Russell, Ian Wolfe.

Before I Hang (1940). Prod.: Columbia Pictures Corporation. Dir.: Nick Grinde. Cast: Boris Karloff, Evelyn Keyes, Edward van Sloan.

The Beginning of the End (1957). Prod.: AB-PT Pictures Corporation. Dir.: Bert I. Gordon. Cast: Peter Graves, Peggie Castle, Morris Ankrum.

The Black Cat (1934). Prod.: Universal Pictures. Dir.: Edgar G. Ulmer. Cast: Boris Karloff, Bela Lugosi, David Manners, Harry Cording.

The Black Cat (1941). Prod.: Universal Pictures. Dir.: Albert S. Rogell. Cast: Basil Rathbone, Anne Gwynne, Gale Sondergaard.

Black Dragons (1942). Prod.: Monogram Studios. Dir.: William Nigh. Cast: Bela Lugosi, Clayton Moore.

Black Friday (1940). Prod.: Universal Pictures. Dir.: Arthur Lubin. Cast: Boris Karloff, Bela Lugosi, Anne Gwynne.

Black Magic (1944). Prod.: Monogram Pictures. Dir.: Phil Rosen. Cast: Sidney Toler, Mantan Moreland.

The Black Raven (1943). Prod.: Producers Releasing Corporation. Dir.: Sam Newfield. Cast: George Zucco, Wanda McKay, Glenn Strange.

The Black Room (1935). Prod.: Columbia Pictures Corporation. Dir.: Roy William Neill. Cast: Boris Karloff, Marian Marsh, George Burr Macannan.

The Black Scorpion (1957). Prod.: Jack Dietz Productions/Amex Productions. Dir.: Edward Ludwig. Cast: Richard Denning, Maria Corday.

The Blob (1958). Prod. Fairview Productions/Tonylyn Productions/Paramount. Dir.: Irving S. Yeaworth, Jr. Cast: Steve McQueen, Aneta Corsaut, Olin Howlin.

The Body Snatcher (1945). Prod.: RKO Radio Pictures. Dir.: Robert Wise. Cast: Boris Karloff, Bela Lugosi, Henry Daniell.

Bowery at Midnight (1942). Prod.: Banner Productions/Monogram Pictures. Dir.: Wallace Fox. Cast: Bela Lugosi, John Archer, Wanda McKay.

The Bowery Boys Meet the Monsters (1954). Prod.: Allied Artists Pictures. Dir.: Edward Bernds. Cast: Leo Gorcey, Huntz Hall, Lloyd Corrigan.

The Bride of Frankenstein (1935). Prod.: Universal Pictures. Dir.: James Whale. Cast: Boris Karloff, Elsa Lanchester, Ernest Thesiger, E. E. Clive, Dwight Frye.

Bride of the Gorilla (1951). Prod.: Jack Broder Productions, Inc. Dir.: Curt Siodmak. Cast: Raymond Burr, Tom Conway, Paul Cavanagh.

Bride of the Monster (1955). Prod.: Rolling M. Productions. Dir.: Edward D. Wood, Jr. Cast: Bela Lugosi, Tor Johnson.

The Brighton Strangler (1945). Prod.: RKO Radio Pictures. Dir.: Max Nosseck. Cast: John Loder, Miles Mander, Rose Hobart, Ian Wolfe.

Brute Force (1947). Prod.: Mark Hellinger Productions/Universal International Pictures. Dir.: Jules Dassin. Cast: Burt Lancaster, Whit Bissell, Sir Lancelot.

The Brute Man (1946). Prod.: Universal Pictures. Dir.: Jean Yarbrough. Cast: Rondo Hatton.

Buck Rogers (1939). Prod.: Universal Pictures. Dir.: Ford Beebe, Saul A. Goodkind. Cast: Buster Crabbe, Constance Moore, Guy Usher.

A Bucket of Blood (1959). Prod.: Alta Vista Productions/American International Pictures. Dir.: Roger Corman. Cast: Dick Miller, Antony Carbone, Barboura Morris.

Calling Dr. Death (1943). Prod.: Universal Pictures. Dir.: Reginald LeBorg. Cast: Lon Chaney, Jr., J. Carrol Naish, Holmes Herbert.

The Cape Canaveral Monsters (1960). Prod.: Compagnia Cinematografica Montoro (CCM). Dir.: Phil Tucker. Cast: Scott Peters, Linda Connell.

Captain America (1944). Prod.: Republic Pictures. Dir.: Elmer Clifton, John English. Cast: Dick Purcell, Lionel Atwill.

Captive Wild Woman (1943). Prod.: Universal Pictures. Dir.: Edward Dmytryk. Cast: Acquanetta, John Carradine, Evelyn Ankers, Lloyd Corrigan.

The Cat and the Canary (1939). Prod.: Paramount Pictures. Dir.: Elliott Nugent. Cast: Bob Hope, Paulette Goddard, Gale Sondergaard, George Zucco.

The Cat Creeps (1946). Prod.: Universal Pictures. Dir.: Erle C. Kenton. Cast: Noah Beery, Jr., Douglass Dumbrille, Rose Hobart.

Cat People (1942). Prod.: RKO Radio Pictures. Dir.: Jacques Tourneur. Cast: Simone Simon, Kent Smith, Tom Conway, Elizabeth Russell, Alan Napier.

Catman of Paris (1946). Prod.: Republic Pictures. Dir.: Lesley Selander. Cast: Carl Esmond, Douglass Dumbrille.

Charlie Chan at Treasure Island (1939). Prod.: Twentieth Century–Fox Film Corporation. Dir.: Norman Foster. Cast: Sidney Toler, Cesar Romero, Douglass Dumbrille.

The Climax (1944). Prod.: Universal Pictures. Dir.: George Waggner. Cast: Boris Karloff, Turhan Bey, Gale Sondergaard.

The Clutching Hand (aka *The Amazing Exploits of the Clutching Hand*) (1936). Prod.: Weiss Productions. Dir.: Albert Herman. Cast: Jack Mulhall, Jon Hall (as Charles Locher).

Cobra Woman (1944). Prod.: Universal Pictures. Dir.: Robert Siodmak. Cast: Maria Montez, Jon Hall, Lon Chaney, Jr.

Condemned to Live (1935). Prod.: Invincible Pictures Corporation. Dir.: Frank R. Strayer. Cast: Ralph Morgan, Pedro de Cordoba, Mischa Auer.

The Corpse Vanishes (1942). Prod.: Banner Productions/Monogram Pictures. Dir.: Wallace Fox. Cast: Bela Lugosi, Angelo Rossitto, Elizabeth Russell.

Creature from the Black Lagoon (1954). Prod.: Universal International Pictures. Dir.: Jack Arnold. Cast: Richard Carlson, Richard Denning, Whit Bissell.

The Creature from the Haunted Sea (1961). Prod.: Roger Corman Productions. Dir.: Roger Corman. Cast: Antony Carbone, Betsy Jones-Moreland.

The Creature Walks Among Us (1956). Prod.: Universal International Pictures. Dir.: John Sherwood. Cast: Jeff Morrow, Rex Reason.

Creature with the Atom Brain (1955). Prod.: Clover Productions/Columbia Pictures. Dir.: Edward L. Cahn. Cast: Richard Denning, Angela Stevens.

The Crime of Dr. Crespi (1935). Prod.: Liberty Pictures/Republic Pictures. Dir.: John H. Auer. Cast: Erich von Stroheim, Dwight Frye, Jean Brooks (as Jeanne Kelly).

The Crimson Ghost (1946). Prod.: Republic Pictures. Dir.: Fred C. Brannon, William Witney. Cast: Charles Quigley, Clayton Moore, Ken Terrell.

Cult of the Cobra (1955). Prod.: Universal International Pictures. Dir.: Francis D. Lyon. Cast: Faith Domergue, Marshall Thompson.

Curse of the Cat People (1944). Prod.: RKO Radio Pictures. Dir.: Gunther von Frisch, Robert Wise. Cast: Simone Simon, Kent Smith, Elizabeth Russell, Sir Lancelot.

Curucu, Beast of the Amazon (1956). Prod.: Jewel Productions/Universal Pictures. Dir.: Curt Siodmak. Cast: John Bromfield, Beverly Garland.

The Cyclops (1956). Prod.: B&H Productions/Allied Artists. Dir.: Bert I. Gordon. Cast: James Craig, Gloria Talbott, Lon Chaney, Jr.

Danger Woman (1946). Prod.: Universal Pictures. Dir.: Lewis D. Collins. Cast: Don Porter, Brenda Joyce, Patricia Morison.

Dark Waters (1944). Prod.: Benedict Bogeaus Productions/United Artists. Dir.: André de Toth. Cast: Franchot Tone, Merle Oberon, Elisha Cook, Jr., Alan Napier.

Daughter of Dr. Jekyll (1957). Prod.: Film Venturers/Allied Artists Pictures. Dir.: Edgar G. Ulmer. Cast: John Agar, Gloria Talbott, Ken Terrell.

Daughter of the Dragon (1931). Prod.: Paramount Pictures. Dir.: Lloyd Corrigan. Cast: Werner Oland, Bramwell Fletcher, Holmes Herbert, Anna May Wong.

The Day the Earth Stood Still (1951). Prod.: Twentieth Century–Fox Film Corporation. Dir.: Robert Wise. Cast: Michael Rennie, Patricia Neal.

The Day the World Ended (1955). Prod.: Golden State Productions/American Releasing Corporation (ARC). Dir.: Roger Corman. Cast: Richard Denning, Paul Birch, Jonathan Haze.

Dead Men Walk (1943). Prod.: Producers' Releasing Corporation. Dir.: Sam Newfield. Cast: George Zucco, Dwight Frye.

The Death Kiss (1932). Prod.: K. B. S. Productions, Inc./Worldwide Pictures Inc. Dir.: Edwin L. Marin. Cast: Bela Lugosi, David Manners.

Dementia (aka *Daughter of Horror*) (1955). Prod.: H. K. F. Productions, Inc./J. J. Parker Productions. Dir.: John Parker. Cast: Adrienne Barrett, Jonathan Haze.

Destination Moon (1950). Prod.: George Pal Productions/Eagle Lion Productions. Dir.: Irving Pichel. Cast: John Archer, Tom Powers.

The Devil and Daniel Webster (aka *All That Money Can Buy*) (1941). Prod.: William Dieterle Productions/RKO Radio Pictures. Cast: Simone Simon, Edward Arnold.

The Devil Bat (1940). Prod.: Producers' Releasing Corporation. Dir.: Jean Yarbrough. Cast: Bela Lugosi, Guy Usher.

Devil Bat's Daughter (1946). Prod.: Producers' Releasing Corporation. Dir.: Frank Wisbar. Cast: Rosemary La Planche, Michael Hale.

Dr. Cyclops (1939). Prod.: Paramount Pictures. Dir.: Ernest B. Schoedsack. Cast: Albert Dekker, Paul Fix.

Dr. Jekyll and Mr. Hyde (1931). Prod.: Paramount Pictures. Dir.: Rouben Mamoulian. Cast: Fredric March, Rose Hobart, Holmes Herbert.

Dr. Jekyll and Mr. Hyde (1941). Prod.: Metro Goldwyn-Mayer. Dir.: Victor Fleming. Cast: Spencer Tracy, Donald Crisp, Ingrid Bergman.

Dr. Renault's Secret (1942). Prod.: Twentieth Century–Fox Film Corporation. Cast: Harry Lachman. Cast: J. Carrol Naish, George Zucco.

Dr. X (1932). Prod.: First National Pictures. Dir.: Michael Curtiz. Cast: Lionel Atwill, Fay Wray.

Doomed to Die (1940). Prod.: Monogram Pictures. Dir.: William Night. Cast: Boris Karloff, Guy Usher, Angelo Rossitto.

Dracula (1931). Prod.: Universal Pictures. Dir.: Tod Browning. Cast: Bela Lugosi, David Manners, Dwight Frye, Edward van Sloan.

Dracula's Daughter (1936). Prod.: Universal Pictures. Dir.: Lambert Hillyer. Cast: Otto Kruger, Edward van Sloan, Irving Pichel, E. E. Clive.

Dragonwyck (1946). Prod.: Twentieth Century–Fox Film Corporation. Dir.: Joseph L. Mankiewicz. Cast: Gene Tierney, Vincent Price, Glenn Langan.

Dressed to Kill (1946). Prod.: Universal Pictures. Dir.: Roy William Neill. Cast: Basil Rathbone, Nigel Bruce, Holmes Herbert, Harry Cording, Ian Wolfe.

Drums of Jeopardy (1931). Prod.: Tiffany Productions. Dir.: George B. Seitz. Cast: Warner Oland, Mischa Auer.

Fallen Angel (1945). Prod.: Twentieth Century–Fox Film Corporation. Dir.: Otto Preminger. Cast: Alice Faye, Dana Andrews, John Carradine, Olin Howlin (as Olin Howland).

The Feathered Serpent (1949). Prod.: Monogram Pictures. Dir.: William Beaudine. Cast: Roland Winters, Mantan Moreland.

Fiend Without a Face (1958). Prod.: Producers' Associates/Amalgamated Productions (GB). Dir.: Arthur Crabtree. Cast: Marshall Thompson, Kynaston Reeves.

First Man into Space (1959). Prod.: Amalgamated Productions (GB). Dir.: Robert Day. Cast: Marshall Thompson, Marla Landi.

Flash Gordon Conquers the Universe (1940). Prod.: Universal Pictures. Dir.: Ford Beebe, Ray Taylor. Cast: Buster Crabbe, Anne Gwynne.

Flight to Mars (1951). Prod.: Monogram Pictures. Dir.: Lesley Selander. Cast: Cameron Mitchell, Arthur Franz.

Fog Island (1945). Prod.: Producers' Releasing Corporation. Dir.: Terry O. Morse. Cast: George Zucco, Lionel Atwill.

Forbidden Planet (1956). Prod.: Metro Goldwyn-Mayer. Dir.: Fred M. Wilcox. Cast: Walter Pidgeon, Anne Francis, Leslie Nielsen.

The Four Skulls of Jonathan Drake (1959). Prod.: Vogue Pictures/United Artists. Dir.: Edward L. Cahn. Cast: Henry Daniell, Paul Cavanagh, Valerie French.

Francis in the Haunted House (1956). Prod.: Universal International Pictures. Dir.: Charles Lamont. Cast: Mickey Rooney, Paul Cavanagh.

Frankenstein (1931). Prod.: Universal Pictures. Dir.: James Whale. Cast: Boris Karloff, Edward van Sloan, Dwight Frye, Colin Clive.

Frankenstein Meets the Wolf Man (1943). Prod.: Universal Pictures. Dir.: Roy William Neill. Cast: Patric Knowles, Lionel Atwill, Maria Ouspenskaya, Dwight Frye.

Freaks (1932). Prod.: Metro Goldwyn-Mayer. Dir.: Tod Browning. Cast: Wallace Ford, Angelo Rossitto.

Fright Night (1947). Prod.: Columbia Pictures Corporation. Dir.: Edward Bernds. Cast: Shemp Howard, Larry Fine, Moe Howard.

From the Earth to the Moon (1958). Prod.: Waverly Productions/RKO Radio Pictures. Dir.: Byron Haskin. Cast: Joseph Cotton, George Sanders, Henry Daniell, Patric Knowles.

The Frozen Ghost (1945). Prod.: Universal Pictures. Dir.: Harold Young. Cast: Lon Chaney, Jr., Evelyn Ankers, Douglass Dumbrille.

The Ghost Breakers (1940). Prod.: Paramount Pictures. Dir.: George Marshall. Cast: Bob Hope, Paulette Goddard, Richard Carlson, Noble Johnson, Lloyd Corrigan.

The Ghost Chasers (1951). Prod.: Monogram Pictures. Dir.: William Beaudine. Cast: Leo Gorcey, Huntz Hall, Lloyd Corrigan.

The Ghost Goes Wild (1947). Prod.: Republic Pictures. Dir.: George Blair. Cast: James Ellison, Anne Gwynne, Lloyd Corrigan.

The Ghost of Frankenstein (1942). Prod.: Universal Pictures. Dir.: Erle C. Kenton. Cast: Cedric Hardwicke, Lionel Atwill, Evelyn Ankers, Holmes Herbert, Harry Cording.

Ghost Ship (1943). Prod.: RKO Radio Pictures. Dir.: Mark Robson. Cast: Richard Dix, Sir Lancelot.

The Ghost Talks (1949). Prod.: Columbia Pictures Corporation. Dir.: Jules White. Cast: Shemp Howard, Larry Fine, Moe Howard.

Ghost Writer (1953). TV Movie. Prod.: American Broadcasting Corporation. Dir.: Don Medford. Cast: Leslie Nielsen, Gaby Rodgers.

The Ghoul (1933). Prod.: Gaumont British Picture Corporation (GB). Dir.: T. Hayes Hunter. Cast: Boris Karloff, Cedric Hardwicke, Ernest Thesiger.

The Giant Claw (1957). Prod.: Clover Productions/Columbia Pictures. Dir.: Fred F. Sears. Cast: Jeff Morrow, Mara Corday.

Glen or Glenda (1953). Prod.: Screen Classics. Dir.: Edward D. Wood, Jr. Cast: Edward D. Wood, Jr., Bela Lugosi, Lyle Talbot.

Godzilla, King of the Monsters (1956) (orig. release 1954). Prod.: Toho Enterprises, Jewell Enterprises, Inc. Dir.: Ishirō Honda, Terry O. Morse. Cast: Raymond Burr.

Gorilla at Large (1954). Prod.: Panoramic Productions/Twentieth Century–Fox Film Corporation. Dir.: Harmon Jones. Cast: Cameron Mitchell, Raymond Burr.

Half Human (aka *Half Human: The Story of the Abominable Snowman*) (1958). Prod.: Toho Company. Dir.: Ishirō Honda, Kenneth G. Crane. Cast: John Carradine.

Hangover Square (1945). Prod.: Twentieth Century–Fox Film Corporation. Dir.: John Brahm. Cast: Laird Cregar, George Sanders, Glenn Langan, Alan Napier.

Hokus Pokus (1949). Prod.: Columbia Pictures Corporation. Dir.: Jules White. Cast: Shemp Howard, Larry Fine, Moe Howard.

Hold That Ghost (1941). Prod.: Universal Pictures. Dir.: Arthur Lubin. Cast: Bud Abbott, Lou Costello, Mischa Auer, Richard Carlson, Evelyn Ankers, Shemp Howard.

Hold that Hypnotist (1957). Prod.: Allied Artists Pictures. Dir.: Austen Jewell. Cast: Huntz Hall, Stanley Clements, Mel Welles.

Horror Island (1941). Prod.: Universal Pictures. Dir.: George Waggner. Cast: Dick Foran, Peggy Moran.

Hound of the Baskervilles (1939). Prod.: Twentieth Century–Fox Film Corporation. Dir.: Sidney Lanfield. Cast: Basil Rathbone, Nigel Bruce, John Carradine, Lionel Atwill, E. E. Clive.

House of Dracula (1945). Prod.: Universal Pictures. Dir.: Erle C. Kenton. Cast: Lon Chaney, Jr., John Carradine, Lionel Atwill, Glenn Strange.

House of Fear (1945). Prod.: Universal Pictures. Dir.: Roy William Neill. Cast: Basil Rathbone, Nigel Bruce, Paul Cavanagh, Harry Cording, Holmes Herbert.

House of Frankenstein (1944). Prod.: Universal Pictures. Dir.: Erle C. Kenton. Cast: Boris Karloff, J. Carrol Naish, John Carradine, Anne Gwynne, Lionel Atwill, George Zucco.

House of Horrors (1946). Prod.: Universal Pictures. Dir.: Jean Yarbrough. Cast: Rondo Hatton, Alan Napier, Martin Kosleck.

The House of the Seven Gables (1940). Prod.: Universal Pictures. Dir.: Joe May. Cast: George Sanders, Nan Grey, Dick Foran, Cecil Kellaway, Miles Mander, Alan Napier.

House of Wax (1953). Prod.: Bryan Foy Productions/Warner Bros. Pictures. Dir.: André de Toth. Cast: Vincent Price, Paul Cavanagh.

The House on Haunted Hill (1959). Prod.: William Castle Productions/Legend Films. Dir.: William Castle. Cast: Vincent Price, Elisha Cook, Jr.

I Married a Monster from Outer Space (1958). Prod.: Paramount Pictures. Dir.: Gene Fowler, Jr. Cast: Tom Tryon, Gloria Talbott.

I Married a Witch (1942). Prod.: René Clair Productions/United Artists. Dir.: René Clair. Cast: Fredric March, Veronica Lake, Cecil Kellaway.

I Walked with a Zombie (1943). Prod.: RKO Radio Pictures. Dir.: Jacques Tourneur. Cast: Frances Dee, Tom Conway, Sir Lancelot.

I Was a Teenage Frankenstein (1957). Prod.: Santa Rosa Productions/American International Pictures. Dir.: Herbert L. Strock. Cast: Whit Bissell, Phyllis Coates, Gary Conway.

I Was a Teenage Werewolf (1957). Prod.: Sunset Productions/American International Pictures. Dir.: Gene Fowler, Jr. Cast: Michael Landon, Whit Bissell.

I'll Never Forget You (aka *The House in the Square*) (1951). Prod.: Twentieth Century–Fox Film Corporation. Dir.: Roy Baker. Cast: Tyrone Power, Ann Blyth, Michael Rennie.

The Incredible Petrified World (1957). Prod.: GBM Productions/Governor Films. Dir.: Jerry Warren. Cast: John Carradine, Phyllis Coates.

The Indestructible Man (1956). Prod.: C. G. K. Productions/Allied Artists Pictures. Dir.: Jack Pollexfen. Cast: Lon Chaney, Jr., Ken Terrell.

Invaders from Mars (1953). Prod.: National Pictures Corporation/Twentieth Century–Fox Film Corporation. Dir.: William Cameron Menzies. Cast: Arthur Franz, Helena Carter.

Invasion of the Body Snatchers (1956). Prod.: Allied Artists Productions/Walter Wanger Productions. Dir.: Don Siegel. Cast: Kevin McCarthy, Carolyn Jones, Whit Bissell.

Invasion of the Saucer Men (1957). Prod.: Malibu Productions/American International Pictures. Dir.: Edward L. Cahn. Cast: Steven Terrell, Gloria Castillo, Scott Peters.

The Invisible Agent (1942). Prod.: Frank Lloyd Productions/Universal Pictures. Dir.: Edwin L. Marin. Cast: Ilona Massey, Jon Hall, Cedric Hardwicke, Holmes Herbert.

Invisible Invaders (1959). Prod.: Robert E. Kent Productions/United Artists. Dir.: Edward L. Cahn. Cast: John Agar, John Carradine, Robert Hutton.

The Invisible Man (1933). Prod.: Universal Pictures. Dir.: James Whale. Cast: Claude Rains, Holmes Herbert, E. E. Clive, Dwight Frye.

The Invisible Man Returns (1940). Prod.: Universal Pictures. Dir.: Joe May. Cast: Cedric Hardwicke, Dick Foran, Nan Grey, Cecil Kellaway, Alan Napier, Harry Cording.

The Invisible Man's Revenge (1944). Prod.: Universal Pictures. Dir.: Ford Beebe. Cast: Jon Hall, John Carradine, Gale Sondergaard, Ian Wolfe.

The Invisible Woman (1940). Prod.: Universal Pictures. Dir.: A. Edward Sutherland. Cast: John Barrymore, Virginia Bruce, Shemp Howard.

Island of Lost Souls (1932). Prod.: Paramount Pictures. Dir.: Erle C. Kenton. Cast: Charles Laughton, Richard Arlen, Bela Lugosi.

Isle of the Dead (1945). Prod.: RKO Radio Pictures. Dir.: Mark Robson. Cast: Boris Karloff, Ellen Drew, Alan Napier.

It Came from Beneath the Sea (1955). Prod.: Clover Productions/Columbia Pictures. Dir.: Robert Gordon. Cast: Kenneth Tobey, Faith Domergue.

It Came from Outer Space (1953). Prod.: Universal International Pictures. Dir.: Jack Arnold. Cast: Richard Carlson, Barbara Rush.

It Conquered the World (1956). Prod.: Sunset Productions/American International Pictures. Dir.: Roger Corman. Cast: Peter Graves, Beverly Garland, Jonathan Haze, Dick Miller.

It! The Terror from Beyond Space (1958). Prod.: Robert E. Kent Productions/United Artists. Dir.: Edward L. Cahn. Cast: Marshall Thompson, Shirley Patterson.

The Jade Mask (1945). Prod.: Monogram Pictures. Dir.: Phil Rosen. Cast: Sidney Toler, Mantan Moreland, Henry Hall.

Journey to the Center of the Earth (1958). Prod.: Twentieth Century–Fox Film Corporation/Cooga Mooga/Joseph M. Schenck Enterprises. Dir.: Henry Levin. Cast: James Mason, Pat Boone, Alan Napier.

Jungle Captive (1945). Prod.: Universal Pictures. Dir.: Harold Young. Cast: Otto Kruger, Rondo Hatton.

Jungle Woman (1944). Prod.: Universal Pictures. Dir.: Reginald LeBorg. Cast: Acquanetta, Evelyn Ankers, J. Carrol Naish, Douglass Dumbrille.

Just Imagine (1930). Prod.: Fox Film Corporation. Dir.: David Butler. Cast: Maureen O'Sullivan, Mischa Auer.

Killers from Space (1954). Prod.: Planet Filmplays/RKO Radio Pictures. Dir.: W. Lee Wilder. Cast: Peter Graves, James Seay.

King Kong (1933). Prod.: RKO Radio Pictures. Dir.: Ernest B. Schoedsack and Merriam C. Cooper. Cast: Fay Wray, Robert Armstrong, Noble Johnson.

King of the Wild (1931). Prod.: Mascot Pictures. Dir.: B. Reeves Easton, Richard Thorpe. Cast: Walter Miller, Mischa Auer.

King of the Zombies (1941). Prod.: Monogram Pictures. Dir.: Jean Yarbrough. Cast: Dick Purcell, Mantan Moreland, John Archer, Guy Usher.

Kronos (1957) Prod.: Regal Films/Twentieth Century–Fox Film Corporation. Dir.: Kurt Neumann. Dir.: Jeff Morrow, Barbara Lawrence.

The Last Woman on Earth (1960). Prod.: Roger Corman Productions. Dir.: Roger Corman. Cast: Antony Carbone, Betsy Jones-Moreland.

The Leech Woman (1960). Prod.: Universal International Pictures. Dir.: Edward Dein. Cast: Coleen Gray, Gloria Talbott.

The Leopard Man (1943). Prod.: RKO Radio Pictures. Dir.: Jacques Tourneur. Cast: Dennis O'Keefe, Jean Brooks, Isabel Jewell.

Little Shop of Horrors (1960). Prod.: Santa Clara Productions/The Filmgroup. Dir.: Roger Corman. Cast: Mel Welles, Jonathan Haze, Dick Miller, Jack Nicholson.

The Lodger (1944). Prod.: Twentieth Century–Fox Film Corporation. Dir.: John Brahm. Cast: George Sanders, Merle Oberon, Cedric Hardwicke, Laird Cregar.

The Lost City (1935). Prod.: Super Serial Productions, Inc. Dir.: Harry Revier. Cast: William "Stage" Boyd, Kane Richmond, Henry Hall.

The Lost Jungle (1934). Prod.: Mascot Pictures. Dir.: Armand Schaefer, David Howard. Cast: Clyde Beatty, Henry Hall.

The Lost Moment (1947). Prod.: Walter Wanger Productions/Universal Pictures. Dir.: Martin Gabel. Cast: Robert Cummings, Susan Hayward, John Archer.

The Lost World (1960). Prod.: Irwin Allen Productions/Twentieth Century–Fox Film Corporation. Dir.: Irwin Allen. Cast: Michael Rennie, Claude Rains, David Hedison.

The Mad Doctor (1941). Prod.: Paramount Pictures. Dir.: Tim Whelan. Cast: Basil Rathbone, Ellen Drew.

The Mad Doctor of Market Street (1942). Prod.: Universal Pictures. Dir.: Joseph H. Lewis. Cast: Una Merkel, Lionel Atwill, Noble Johnson.

The Mad Ghoul (1943). Prod.: Universal Pictures. Dir.: James P. Hogan. Cast: Evelyn Ankers,

George Zucco, Robert Armstrong, Turhan Bey, Rose Hobart.

Mad Love (1935). Prod.: Metro Goldwyn-Mayer. Dir.: Karl Freund. Cast: Peter Lorre, Ian Wolfe, Isabel Jewell (deleted scenes).

The Mad Monster (1942). Prod.: Producers' Releasing Corporation. Dir.: Sam Newfield. Cast: George Zucco, Glenn Strange, Henry Hall.

Man in the Attic (1953). Prod.: Panoramic Productions/Twentieth Century–Fox Film Corporation. Dir.: Hugo Fregonese. Cast: Jack Palance, Isabel Jewell, Harry Cording.

Man Made Monster (1941). Prod.: Universal Pictures. Dir.: George Waggner. Cast: Lionel Atwill, Lon Chaney, Jr.

The Man Who Turned to Stone (1957). Prod.: Clover Productions/Columbia Pictures. Dir.: László Kardos. Cast: William Hudson, Paul Cavanagh, Victor Jory.

Mark of the Vampire (1935). Prod.: Metro Goldwyn-Mayer. Dir.: Tod Browning. Cast: Bela Lugosi, Holmes Herbert, Lionel Atwill.

Master Minds (1949). Prod.: Monogram Pictures. Dir.: Jean Yarbrough. Cast: Leo Gorcey, Huntz Hall, Alan Napier, Glenn Strange.

Mesa of Lost Women (1953). Prod.: Ron Ormond Productions/Howco Productions Inc. Dir.: Ron Ormond, Herbert Tevos. Cast: Lyle Talbot, Jackie Coogan, Angelo Rossitto.

Midnight Manhunt (1945). Prod.: Pine-Thomas Productions/Paramount Pictures. Dir.: William C. Thomas. Cast: George Zucco, William Gargan.

Mighty Joe Young (1949). Prod.: Argosy Pictures/RKO Radio Pictures. Dir.: Ernest B. Schoedsack. Cast: Terry Moore, Robert Armstrong, Regis Toomey.

The Mole People (1956). Prod.: Universal International Pictures. Dir.: Virgil W. Vogel. Cast: John Agar. Hugh Beaumont, Alan Napier.

Monkey Business (1952). Prod.: Twentieth Century–Fox Film Corporation. Dir.: Howard Hawks. Cast: Cary Grant, Ginger Rogers, Marilyn Monroe, Robert Cornthwaite.

The Monster and the Girl (1941). Prod.: Paramount Pictures. Dir.: Stuart Heisler. Cast: Ellen Drew, George Zucco, Paul Lukas.

Monster from the Ocean Floor (1954). Prod.: Palo Alto Productions/Lippert Pictures. Dir.: Wyatt Ordung. Cast: Anne Kimbell, Jonathan Haze.

The Monster Maker (1944). Prod.: Producers' Releasing Corporation. Dir.: Sam Newfield. Cast: J. Carrol Naish, Glenn Strange, Ralph Morgan.

Monster on the Campus (1958). Prod.: Universal International Pictures. Dir.: Jack Arnold. Cast: Arthur Franz, Joanna Moore, Judson Pratt.

The Monster Walks (1932). Prod.: Ralph M. Like Productions. Dir.: Frank R. Strayer. Cast: Rex Lease, Mischa Auer.

Moonrise (1948). Prod.: Republic Pictures/Chas. K. Feldman Group Productions Inc., Marshall Grant. Dir.: Frank Borzage. Cast: Dane Clark, Ethel Barrymore, Lloyd Bridges.

The Most Dangerous Game (1932). Prod.: RKO Radio Pictures. Dir.: Irving Pichel, Ernest B. Schoedsack. Cast: Joel McCrea, Fay Wray, Robert Armstrong, Noble Johnson.

The Mummy (1932). Prod.: Universal Pictures. Dir.: Karl Freund. Cast: Boris Karloff, Edward van Sloan, David Manners, Bramwell Fletcher, Noble Johnson.

The Mummy's Curse (1944). Prod.: Universal Pictures. Dir.: Leslie Goodwins. Cast: Lon Chaney, Jr., Holmes Herbert.

Mummy's Dummies (1948). Prod.: Columbia Pictures Corporation. Dir.: Edward Bernds. Cast: Shemp Howard, Larry Fine, Moe Howard.

The Mummy's Ghost (1944). Prod.: Universal Pictures. Dir.: Reginald LeBorg. Cast: John Carradine, George Zucco, Lon Chaney, Jr.

The Mummy's Hand (1940). Prod.: Universal Pictures. Dir.: Christy Cabanne. Cast: Dick Foran, Wallace Ford, George Zucco, Cecil Kellaway, Ken Terrell.

The Mummy's Tomb (1942). Prod.: Universal Pictures. Dir.: Harold Young. Cast: Dick Foran, Wallace Ford, George Zucco, Turhan Bey, Lon Chaney, Jr., Harry Cording.

Murder at Dawn (1932). Prod.: Big 4 Film. Dir.: Richard Thorpe. Cast: Jack Mulhall, Mischa Auer.

Murder by the Clock (1931). Prod.: Paramount Pictures. Dir.: Edward Sloman. Cast: William "Stage" Boyd, Regis Toomey, Irving Pichel.

The Murder of Marie Roget (1942). Prod.: Universal Pictures. Dir.: Phil Rosen. Cast: Patric Knowles, Lloyd Corrigan, Maria Montez, Maria Ouspenskaya.

Murders in the Rue Morgue (1932). Prod.: Universal Pictures. Dir.: Robert Florey. Cast: Bela Lugosi, Sidney Fox, Noble Johnson.

Murders in the Zoo (1933). Prod.: Paramount Pictures. Dir.: A. Edward Sutherland. Cast: Charles Ruggles, Lionel Atwill, Randolph Scott.

The Mystery of Edwin Drood (1935). Prod.: Universal Pictures. Dir.: Stuart Walker. Cast: Claude Rains, David Manners, E. E. Clive, Harry Cording.

The Mystery of the Wax Museum (1933). Prod.: Warner Brothers Pictures. Dir.: Michael Curtiz. Cast: Lionel Atwill, Fay Wray, Holmes Herbert.

The Neanderthal Man (1953). Prod.: Global Productions/United Artists. Dir.: Ewald André Dupont. Cast: Robert Shayne, Beverly Garland.

Night Monster (1942). Prod.: Universal Pictures. Dir.: Ford Beebe. Cast: Bela Lugosi, Lionel Atwill, Don Porter.

Night of Terror (1933). Prod.: Bryan Foy Productions/Columbia Pictures. Cast: Wallace Ford, Bela Lugosi.

Night of the Ghouls (1959). Prod.: Not Known. Dir.: Edward D. Wood, Jr. Cast: Tor Johnson, Kenne Duncan.

Not of this Earth (1957). Prod.: Los Altos Productions/Allied Artists Pictures. Dir.: Roger Corman. Cast: Paul Birch, Beverly Garland, Jonathan Haze, Dick Miller.

The Old Dark House (1932). Prod.: Universal Pictures. Dir.: James Whale. Cast: Boris Karloff, Melvyn Douglas, Ernest Thesiger.

One Body too Many (1944). Prod.: Pine-Thomas Productions/Paramount Pictures. Dir.: Frank McDonald. Cast: Jack Haley, Bela Lugosi, Lyle Talbot.

One Frightened Night (1935). Prod.: Mascot Pictures. Dir.: Christy Cabanne. Cast: Regis Toomey, Wallace Ford, Charley Grapewin.

One Thrilling Night (1942). Prod.: Monogram Pictures. Dir.: William Beaudine. Cast: John Beal, Wanda McKay.

The Pearl of Death (1944). Prod.: Universal Pictures. Dir.: Roy William Neill. Cast: Basil Rathbone, Nigel Bruce, Evelyn Ankers, Miles Mander, Ian Wolfe, Holmes Herbert, Rondo Hatton.

Perils of Nyoka (aka *Nyoka and the Lost Secrets of Hippocrates*) (1942). Prod.: Republic Pictures. Dir.: William Witney. Cast: Kay Aldridge, Clayton Moore, Ken Terrell.

The Phantom Empire (1935). Prod.: Mascot Pictures. Dir.: Otto Brower, B. Reeves Eason. Cast: Gene Autry, Dorothy Christy, Henry Hall.

The Phantom Killer (1942). Prod.: Monogram Pictures. Dir.: William Beaudine. Cast: Dick Purcell, Mantan Moreland, Joan Woodbury.

Phantom Lady (1944). Prod.: Universal Pictures. Dir.: Robert Siodmak. Cast: Franchot Tone, Ella Raines, Elisha Cook, Jr., Regis Toomey.

The Phantom of the Opera (1943). Prod.: Universal Pictures. Dir.: Arthur Lubin. Cast: Nelson Eddy, Claude Rains, Miles Mander.

The Phantom Speaks (1943). Prod.: Republic Pictures. Dir.: John English. Cast: Richard Arlen, Stanley Ridges.

The Picture of Dorian Gray (1945). Prod.: Metro Goldwyn-Mayer. Dir.: Albert Lewin. Cast: Hurd Hatfield, George Sanders, Miles Mander, Cedric Hardwicke (narrator).

Plan Nine from Outer Space (1959). Prod.: Reynolds Pictures/Distributors' Corporation of America. Dir.: Edward D. Wood, Jr. Cast: Bela Lugosi, Regis Toomey, Tor Johnson.

Planet Outlaws (1953). Prod.: Universal Pictures. Dir.: Ford Beebe, Saul A. Goodkind. Cast: Buster Crabbe, Henry Hall.

Port Sinister (1953). Prod.: American Pictures Company/RKO Radio Pictures. Dir.: Harold Daniels. Cast: James Warren, Paul Cavanagh.

Queen of Outer Space (1958). Prod.: Allied Artists Pictures. Dir.: Edward Bernds. Cast: Zsa Zsa Gabor, Eric Fleming, Paul Birch.

The Racket (1951). Prod.: RKO Radio Pictures. Dir.: John Cromwell. Cast: Robert Mitchum, Robert Ryan, Don Porter.

Radar Men from the Moon (1952). Prod.: Republic Pictures. Dir.: Fred C. Brannon. Cast: George Wallace, Aline Towne, Clayton Moore.

The Raven (1935). Prod.: Universal Pictures. Dir.: Lew Landers. Cast: Boris Karloff, Bela Lugosi, Ian Wolfe.

Red Planet Mars (1952). Prod.: Melaby Pictures Corporation/United Artists. Dir.: Harry Horner. Cast: Peter Graves, Andrea King.

Return of Dr. X (1939). Prod.: Warner Brothers Pictures. Dir.: Vincent Sherman. Cast: Humphrey Bogart, Wayne Morris, Olin Howlin (as Olin Howland).

Return of the Vampire (1944). Prod.: Columbia Pictures Corporation. Dir.: Lew Landers. Cast: Bela Lugosi, Nina Foch, Miles Mander.

Revenge of the Creature (1955). Prod.: Universal International Pictures. Dir.: Jack Arnold. Cast: John Agar, Lori Nelson.

Revenge of the Zombies (1943). Prod.: Monogram Pictures. Dir.: Steve Sekely. Cast: John Carradine, Mantan Moreland.

Riders to the Stars (1954). Prod.: Ivan Tors Productions/United Artists. Dir.: Richard Carlson. Cast: Richard Carlson, Herbert Marshall.

Rocketship X-M (1950). Prod.: Lippert Pictures. Dir.: Kurt Neumann. Cast: Lloyd Bridges, Osa Massen.

The Rogues' Tavern (1936). Prod.: Mercury Pictures Corporation. Dir.: Robert F. Hill. Cast: Wallace Ford, Joan Woodbury.

Satan Met a Lady (1936). Prod.: Warner Brothers Pictures. Dir.: William Dieterle. Cast: Bette Davis, Warren William, Olin Howlin (as Olin Howland).

Scared to Death (1947). Prod.: Golden Gate Pictures. Dir.: Christy Cabanne. Cast: Bela Lugosi, George Zucco, Angelo Rossitto.

The Scarlet Claw (1944). Prod.: Universal Pictures. Dir.: Roy William Neill. Cast: Basil Rathbone, Nigel Bruce, Paul Cavanagh, Miles Mander, Ian Wolfe.

Secret Agent X-9 (1945). Prod.: Universal Pictures. Dir.: Lewis D. Collins, Ray Taylor. Cast: Lloyd Bridges, Keye Luke.

Secret Beyond the Door (1947). Prod.: Diana Production Company/Universal Pictures. Dir.: Fritz Lang. Cast: Joan Bennett, Michael Redgrave, Paul Cavanagh.

The Seventh Victim (1943). Prod.: RKO Radio Pictures. Dir.: Mark Robson. Cast: Tom Conway, Jean Brooks, Isabel Jewell.

The She-Creature (1956). Prod.: Golden State Productions/American International Pictures. Dir.: Edward L. Cahn. Cast: Chester Morris, Tom Conway, William Hudson.

She-Devil (1957). Prod.: Regal Films/Twentieth Century–Fox Film Corporation. Dir.: Kurt Neumann. Cast: Mari Blanchard, Albert Dekker, John Archer, Paul Cavanagh.

Sherlock Holmes and the Secret Weapon (1943). Prod.: Universal Pictures. Dir.: Roy William Neill. Cast: Basil Rathbone, Nigel Bruce, Lionel Atwill, Holmes Herbert, Harry Cording, George Burr Macannan.

Sherlock Holmes and the Spider Woman (1944). Prod.: Universal Pictures. Dir.: Roy William Neill. Cast: Basil Rathbone, Nigel Bruce, Gale Sondergaard, Harry Cording, Angelo Rossitto.

Sherlock Holmes and the Voice of Terror (1942). Prod.: Universal Pictures. Dir.: John Rawlins. Cast: Basil Rathbone, Nigel Bruce, Evelyn Ankers, Henry Daniell, Harry Cording.

Sherlock Holmes in Washington (1943). Prod.: Universal Pictures. Dir.: Roy William Neill. Cast: Basil Rathbone, Nigel Bruce, Henry Daniell, George Zucco, John Archer, Holmes Herbert.

She-Wolf of London (1946). Prod.: Universal Pictures. Dir.: Jean Yarbrough. Cast: Don Porter, June Lockhart, Lloyd Corrigan.

Shivering Sherlocks (1948). Prod.: Columbia Pictures Corporation. Dir.: Del Lord. Cast: Shemp Howard, Larry Fine, Moe Howard.

A Shriek in the Night (1933). Prod.: Allied Pictures Corporation. Dir.: Albert Ray. Cast: Ginger Rogers, Lyle Talbot.

Sirens of Atlantis (1949). Prod.: Seymour Nebenzal Productions/United Artists. Dir.: Gregg C. Tallas. Cast: Maria Montez, Jean-Pierre Aumont, Henry Daniell.

Son of Dracula (1943). Prod.: Universal Pictures. Dir.: Robert Siodmak. Cast: Lon Chaney, Jr., Evelyn Ankers.

Son of Dr. Jekyll (1951). Prod.: Columbia Pictures Corporation. Dir.: Seymour Friedman. Cast: Louis Hayward, Alexander Knox, Paul Cavanagh.

Son of Kong (1933). Prod.: RKO Radio Pictures. Dir.: Ernest B. Schoedsack. Cast: Robert Armstrong, Helen Mack.

Sorry, Wrong Number (1948). Prod.: Paramount Pictures. Dir.: Anatole Litvak. Cast: Barbara Stanwyck, Burt Lancaster, Holmes Herbert.

The Spider Woman Strikes Back (1946). Prod.: Universal Pictures. Dir.: Arthur Lubin. Cast: Gale Sondergaard, Rondo Hatton, Brenda Joyce.

The Spiral Staircase (1945). Prod.: RKO Radio Pictures. Dir.: Robert Siodmak. Cast: Dorothy McGuire, Kent Smith, Elsa Lanchester.

Spooks Run Wild (1941). Prod.: Monogram Pictures. Dir.: Phil Rosen. Cast: Bela Lugosi, Leo Gorcey, Huntz Hall, Angelo Rossitto.

Strange Confession (1945). Prod.: Universal Pictures. Dir.: John Hoffman. Cast: Lon Chaney, Jr., J. Carrol Naish, Lloyd Bridges.

The Strange Case of Dr. RX (1942). Prod.: Universal Pictures. Dir.: William Nigh. Cast: Patric Knowles, Lionel Atwill, Anne Gwynne, Shemp Howard, Mantan Moreland.

Strange Door (1951). Prod.: Universal International Pictures. Dir.: Joseph Pevney. Cast: Boris Karloff, Charles Laughton, Alan Napier, Paul Cavanagh.

Strange Illusion (1945). Prod.: Producers' Releasing Corporation. Dir.: Edgar G. Ulmer. Cast: Warren William, Jimmy Lydon, Regis Toomey.

Strangler of the Swamp (1946). Prod.: Producers' Releasing Corporation. Dir.: Frank Wisbar. Cast: Rosemary La Planche, Blake Edwards.

Supernatural (1933). Prod.: Paramount Pictures. Dir.: Victor Halperin. Cast: Carole Lombard, Randolph Scott, George Burr Macannan.

Svengali (1931). Prod.: Warner Brothers Pictures. Dir.: Archie Mayo. Cast: John Barrymore, Donald Crisp, Bramwell Fletcher.

Swamp Women (1956). Prod.: Bernard Woolner Productions/American International Pictures. Dir.: Roger Corman. Cast: Beverly Garland, Marie Windsor, Jonathan Haze.

Tangled Destinies (1932). Prod.: Mayfair Pictures Corporation. Dir.: Frank R. Strayer. Cast: Gene Morgan, Doris Hill, Henry Hall.

Tarantula (1955). Prod.: Universal International Pictures. Dir.: Jack Arnold. Cast: John Agar, Leo G. Carroll, Mara Corday.

Tarzan and the She-Devil (1953). Prod.: Sol Lesser Productions/RKO Radio Pictures. Dir.: Kurt Neumann. Cast: Lex Barker, Joyce Mackenzie, Raymond Burr, Tom Conway.

Teenage Monster (1957). Prod.: Marquette Productions Ltd. Dir.: Jacques R. Marquette. Cast: Anne Gwynne, Stuart Wade, Charles Courtney.

Them! (1954). Prod.: Warner Brothers Pictures. Dir.: Gordon Douglas. Cast: Edmund Gwenn, James Arness, Olin Howlin.

The Thing from Another World (1951). Prod.: Winchester Pictures Corporation/RKO Radio Pictures. Dir.: Christian Nyby, Howard Hawks. Cast: Robert Cornthwaite, Kenneth Tobey, Margaret Sheridan.

This Island Earth (1955). Prod.: Universal International Pictures. Dir.: Joseph M. Newman. Cast: Jeff Morrow, Faith Domergue, Rex Reason.

Three Live Ghosts (1936). Prod.: Metro Goldwyn-Mayer. Dir.: H. Bruce Humberstone. Cast: Richard Arlen, Beryl Mercer.

Tobor the Great (1954). Prod.: Dudley Pictures Corporation/Republic Pictures. Dir.: Lee Sholem. Cast: Charles Drake, Karin Booth, Lyle Talbot.

Tormented (1960). Prod.: Cheviot Productions/Allied Artists Productions. Dir.: Bert I. Gordon. Cast: Richard Carlson, Susan Gordon.

Torture Ship (1939). Prod.: Producers' Pictures Corporation/Producers' Distributing Corporation (later Producers' Releasing Corporation). Dir.: Victor Halperin. Cast: Lyle Talbot, Irving Pichel.

Tower of London (1939). Prod.: Universal Pictures. Dir.: Rowland V. Lee. Cast: Boris Karloff, Basil Rathbone, Nan Grey, Miles Mander, Rose Hobart, Harry Cording.

12 to the Moon (1960). Prod.: Luna Productions, Inc./Columbia Pictures Corporation. Dir.: David Bradley. Cast: Tom Conway, Muzaffer Tema, Francis X. Bushman.

The 27th Day (1957). Prod.: Romson Productions/Columbia Pictures. Dir.: William Asher. Cast: Gene Barry, George Voskovec, Paul Birch.

The Undead (1957). Prod.: American International Pictures/Balboa Productions. Dir.: Roger Corman, Cast: Richard Garland, Mel Welles, Allison Hayes, Dick Miller.

The Undying Monster (1942). Prod.: Twentieth Century–Fox Film Corporation. Dir.: John Brahm. Cast: James Ellison, Bramwell Fletcher, Heather Angel.

The Unearthly (1957). Prod.: AB-PT Pictures Corp. Dir.: Boris Petroff. Cast: John Carradine, Tor Johnson, Myron Healey.

The Uninvited (1944). Prod.: Paramount Pictures. Dir.: Lewis Allen. Cast: Ray Milland, Donald Crisp, Alan Napier.

The Unknown Terror (1957). Prod.: Emirau Productions, Regal Films, Twentieth Century–Fox Film Corporation. Dir.: Charles Marquis Warren. Cast: John Howard, Sir Lancelot.

The Valley of Gwangi (1969). Prod.: Warner Brothers/Seven Arts/Morningside Productions. Dir.: Jim O'Connolly. Cast: Richard Carlson, James Franciscus, Laurence Naismith.

The Vampire (1957). Prod.: Gramercy Pictures/United Artists. Dir.: Paul Landres. Cast: Coleen Gray, Kenneth Tobey.

The Vampire Bat (1932). Prod.: Majestic Pictures. Dir.: Frank R. Strayer. Cast: Lionel Atwill, Fay Wray, Melvyn Douglas, Dwight Frye.

Village of the Damned (1960). Prod.: Metro Goldwyn-Mayer. Dir.: Wolf Rilla. Cast: George Sanders, Barbara Shelley.

Voodoo Island (1957). Prod.: Aubrey Schenck Productions/Bel-Air Productions/United Artists. Dir.: Reginald LeBorg. Cast: Boris Karloff, Elisha Cook, Jr.

Voodoo Man (1944). Prod.: Banner Productions/Monogram Pictures. Dir.: William Beaudine. Cast: Bela Lugosi, John Carradine, George Zucco, Wanda McKay, Henry Hall.

Voodoo Woman (1957). Prod.: American International Pictures/Carmel Productions. Dir.: Edward L. Cahn. Cast: Tom Conway, Maria English.

The War of the Colossal Beast (1958). Prod.: Carmel Productions/American International Pictures. Dir.: Bert I. Gordon. Cast: Duncan "Dean" Parkin, Sally Fraser, Glenn Langan.

The War of the Worlds (1953). Prod.: Paramount Pictures. Dir.: Byron Haskin. Cast: Gene Barry, Robert Cornthwaite, Cedric Hardwicke (narrator).

War of the Satellites (1958). Prod.: Allied Artists Pictures/Santa Cruz Productions. Dir.: Roger

Corman. Cast: Dick Miller, Susan Cabot, Richard Devon.

The Wasp Woman (1960). Prod.: Film Group Feature/Santa Cruz Productions, Inc./The Filmgroup. Dir.: Roger Corman. Cast: Susan Cabot, Barboura Morris.

Weird Woman (1944). Prod.: Universal Pictures. Dir.: Reginald LeBorg. Cast: Lon Chaney, Jr., Evelyn Ankers, Anne Gwynne, Elizabeth Russell.

The Whip Hand (1951). Prod.: RKO Radio Pictures. Dir.: William Cameron Menzies. Cast: Raymond Burr, Elliott Reid.

White Zombie (1932). Prod.: Edward Halperin Productions/Victor Halperin Productions/United Artists. Dir.: Victor Halperin. Cast: Bela Lugosi, Madge Bellamy, George Burr Macannan.

The Wolf Man (1941). Prod.: Universal Pictures. Dir.: George Waggner. Cast: Claude Rains, Lon Chaney, Jr., Patric Knowles, Maria Ouspenskaya, Evelyn Ankers, Harry Cording.

The Woman in Green (1945). Prod.: Universal Pictures. Dir.: Roy William Neill. Cast: Basil Rathbone, Nigel Bruce, Henry Daniell, Paul Cavanagh.

The World Gone Mad (1933). Prod. Majestic Pictures. Dir.: Christy Cabanne. Cast: Pat O'Brien, J. Carrol Naish, Edward van Sloan.

Zombies on Broadway (1945). Prod.: RKO Radio Pictures. Dir.: Gordon Douglas. Cast: Wally Brown, Alan Carney, Bela Lugosi, Ian Wolfe, Sir Lancelot.

Bibliography

There are innumerable books and articles available on the history of Hollywood films, but few that focus directly on actors' performances. Hence this bibliography is selective rather than inclusive.

General Books

Atkins, Rick (1997). *Let's Scare 'Em: Grand Interviews and a Filmography of Horrific Proportions, 1930–1961*. Jefferson, NC: McFarland.

Auerbach, Nina (1997). *Our Vampires, Ourselves*. Chicago: University of Chicago Press.

Balio, Tino (1996). *Grand Design: Hollywood as a Business Enterprise, 1930–1939*. Los Angeles: University of California Press.

Barrios, Richard (2005). *Screened Out: Playing Gay in Hollywood from Edison to Stonewall*. London and New York: Routledge.

Basinger, Jeanine (2009). *The Star Machine*. New York: Vintage.

Beck, Calvin Thomas (1975). *Heroes of the Horrors*. New York: Collier.

_____ (1979). *Screen Queens*. New York: Collier.

Berenstein, Rhoda J. (1996). *Attack of the Leading Ladies: Gender, Sexuality, and Spectatorship in Classic Horror Cinema*. New York: Columbia University Press.

Berkwitz, Jeff (2001). "Aside from Good Acting and Snappy Special Effects..." *Outré* 26: 12–13.

Billington, Michael (2002). *Stage and Screen Lives*. Oxford: Oxford University Press.

Bishop, Nancy (2009). *Secrets from the Casting Couch: On-Camera Strategies for Actors from a Casting Director*. London: Methuen Drama.

Bradley, Doug (1996). *Monsters: Behind the Mask of the Horror Actor*. London: Titan.

Christensen, Jerome (2008). "Studio Authorship, Corporate Art" (2006), in Barry Keith Grant (ed.), *Auteurs and Authorship: A Reader*, 167–180. Malden, MA: Blackwell.

Clarens, Carlos (1997). *An Illustrated History of Horror and Science-Fiction Films: The Classic Era, 1895–1967*. New York: Da Capo Press.

Clark, Mark (2004). *Smirk, Sneer and Scream: Great Acting in Horror Cinema*. Jefferson, NC: McFarland.

De Cordova, Richard (1991). "Genre and Performance: An Overview," in Jeremy G. Butler (ed.), *Star Texts: Image and Performance in Film and Television*. 115–125. Detroit: Wayne State University Press.

Denning, Michael (1987). *Mechanic Accents: Dime Novels and Working-Class Culture in America*. London: Verso.

Dick, Bernard F. (1997). *The City of Dreams: The Making and Remaking of Universal Pictures*. Lexington: University Press of Kentucky.

Dyer, Richard (2003). *Heavenly Bodies: Film Stars and Society*. London and New York: Routledge.

Fischer, Dennis (2000). *Science Fiction Film Directors, 1895–1998*. Jefferson, NC: McFarland.

Freud, Sigmund (1956). *Beyond the Pleasure Principle* (1920), in *The Complete Psychological Works of Sigmund Freud*, trans. James Strachey and Anna Freud. Vol. XVIII: 7–64. London: The Hogarth Press.

Giddins, Gary (2010). *Warning Shadows: Home Alone with Classic Cinema*. New York: W.W. Norton.

Heffernan, Kevin (2002). "The Hypnosis Horror Films of the 1950s: Genre Texts and Industrial Context." *Journal of Film and Video* 54, no. 2: 56–70.

Hendershot, Heather (2006). "Ghouls, Gimmicks, and Gold." *Film Quarterly* 60, no. 2: 73–74.

Hills, Matt (2004). "Doing Things with Theory: From Freud's Worst Nightmare to (Disciplinary) Dreams of Horror's Cultural Value," in Steven Jay Schneider (ed.), *Horror Film and Psychoanalysis: Freud's Worst Nightmare*. 205–222. Cambridge: Cambridge University Press.

Hutchings, Peter (2004). *The Horror Film*. London: Longman.

Jess-Cooke, Carolyn (2009). *Film Sequels*. Edinburgh: Edinburgh University Press.

Joslin, Lyndon W. (1999). *Count Dracula Goes to the Movies: Stoker's Novel Adapted, 1922–1995*. Jefferson, NC: McFarland.

Kael, Pauline (1987). *State of the Art: Film Writings, 1983–1985*. London: Marion Boyars.

Kane, Paul (2010). *Voices in the Dark: Interviews*

with Horror Movie Writers, Directors and Actors. Jefferson, NC: McFarland.

King, Claire Sisco (2007). "Acting Out and Sounding Off: Sacrifice and Performativity in *Alice, Sweet Alice*." *Text and Performance Quarterly* 27, no. 2: 123–142.

Kubie, Lawrence S. (1947). "Psychiatry and the Films." *Hollywood Quarterly* 2, no. 2: 113–117.

Mank, Gregory William (1999). *Women in Horror Films: 1930s*. Jefferson, NC: McFarland.

_____ (1999). *Women in Horror Films: 1940s*. Jefferson, NC: McFarland.

Mathijs, Ernest (2011). "Referential Acting and the Ensemble Cast." *Screen* 52, no. 1: 89–96.

Matthews, Melvin E. (2007). *Hostile Aliens, Hollywood and Today's News: 1950s Science Fiction Films and 9/11*. New York: Algora.

Morin, Edgar (1960). *The Stars*. Trans. Richard Howard. New York: Grove Press.

Nowell, Richard (2011). "'Now Some Movies Start Trends...' Towards an Industrial Model of Film Analysis." *Repetition/repetition*. Paper delivered April 7, 2011, at the University of Kent Film Centre. http://www.kent.ac.uk/arts/film/filmcentre/repetitionpapers.html (accessed August 18, 2011).

O'Neill, Rosary (1992). *The Actor's Checklist: Creating the Complete Character*. Fort Worth: Harcourt College.

Paul, Louis (2007). *Tales from the Cult Trenches: Interviews with 36 Actors from Horror, Science Fiction and Exploitation Cinema*. Jefferson, NC: McFarland.

Peary, Danny (1991). "Introduction." *Cult Movie Stars*. New York: Simon and Schuster/Fireside.

Pitts, Michael R. (2002). *Horror Film Stars*. Jefferson, NC: McFarland.

Quinlan, David (1985). "Foreword." *Quinlan's Illustrated Dictionary of Film Character Actors*. London: B. T. Batsford Ltd.

Rose, Lew (1980). *Movie Kings: Hollywood's Famous Tough Guys and Monsters*. New York: Xerox Education.

Rosenbaum, Jonathan, and J. Hoberman (1991). *Midnight Movies*. New York: Da Capo Press.

Sante, Luc, and Melissa Holbrook Pierson (1999). "Preface." *OK You Mugs: Writers on Movie Actors*. New York: Pantheon.

Schaefer, Eric (1999). *Bold! Daring! Shocking! True! A History of Exploitation Films, 1919–1959*. Durham: Duke University Press.

Sher, Ben (2007). "How do you Cast a Horror Film?" *Back Stage West* 14, no. 31.

Skal, David J. (1990). *Hollywood Gothic: The Tangled Web of Dracula from Novel to Stage to Screen*. New York: W.W. Norton.

Smith, Don G. (1999). *The Poe Cinema: A Critical Filmography of Theatrical Releases Based on the Works of Edgar Allan Poe*. Jefferson, NC: McFarland.

Smith, J. (1985). "The Movie's the Thing (Good Acting in Horror Films)." *Films in Review* 36, no. 12: 597–601.

Snelson, Tim, and Mark Jancovich (2011). "No Hits, No Runs, Just Terrors," in Richard Maltby, Daniel Biltereyst and Philippe Meers (eds.), *Explorations in New Cinema History: Approaches and Case Studies*. 199–212. Malden, MA: Blackwell.

Sobchack, Vivian (1987). *Screening Space: The American Science Fiction Film*. New York: Frederick Ungar & Co.

Stanfield, Peter (2002). *Horse Opera: The Strange History of the 1930s Singing Cowboy*. Urbana and Chicago: University of Illinois Press.

Telotte, J. P. (1995). *Replications: A Robotic History of the Science Fiction Film*. Urbana: University of Illinois Press.

Thorp, Margaret Farrand (1946). *America at the Movies* (1939). London: Faber and Faber.

Torry, Robert (1991). "Apocalypse Then: The Benefits of the Bomb in Fifties Science Fiction Films." *Cinema Journal* 31, no. 1: 7–21.

Twomey, Alfred E., and Arthur F. McClure (1969), "Preface," *The Versatiles: Supporting Character Players in the Cinema 1930–1955*. South Brunswick: A.S. Barnes.

Tyler, Parker (1949). "Documentary Technique in Film Fiction." *American Quarterly* 1, no. 2: 99–115.

Valley, Richard (2005). "Smirk, Sneer, and Scream." *Scarlet Street* 53.

Warren, Bill (2010). *Keep Watching the Skies! American Science Fiction Movies of the Fifties. The 21st Century Edition*. Jefferson, NC: McFarland.

Weaver, Tom (1994). *Attack of the Monster Movie Makers: Interviews with 20 Genre Giants*. Jefferson, NC: McFarland.

_____ (2003). *Eye on Science Fiction: 20 Interviews with Classic SF and Horror Filmmakers*. Jefferson, NC: McFarland.

_____ (2006). *Interviews with "B" Science Fiction and Horror Movie Makers: Writers, Producers, Directors, Actors, Moguls, and Makeup*. Jefferson, NC: McFarland.

_____ (2009). *I Talked with a Zombie: Interviews with 23 Veterans of Horror and Sci-fi Films and Television*. Jefferson, NC: McFarland.

_____ (2004). *It Came from Horrorwood: Interviews with Moviemakers in the SF and Horror Tradition*. Jefferson, NC: McFarland.

_____ (1998). *Science Fiction and Fantasy Film Flashbacks: Conversations with 24 Writers, Producers and Directors from the Golden Age*. Jefferson, NC: McFarland.

_____ (2002). *Science Fiction Confidential: Interviews with Monster Stars and Filmmakers*. Jefferson, NC: McFarland.

_____ (2006). *Science Fiction Stars and Horror Heroes: Interviews with Actors, Directors, Producers and Writers of the 1940s Through the 1960s*. Jefferson, NC: McFarland.

_____ (2010). *A Sci-Fi Swarm and Horror Horde: Interviews with 62 Filmmakers*. Jefferson, NC: McFarland.

_____ (1995). *They Fought in the Creature Features: Interviews with 21 Classic Horror, Science Fiction and Serial Stars*. Jefferson, NC: McFarland.

White, Dennis L. (1971). "The Poetics of Horror: More than Meets the Eye." *Cinema Journal* 10, no. 2: 1–18.

Wood, Bret, and Feaster, Felicia (1999). *Forbidden Fruit: The Golden Age of the Exploitation Film*. New York: Midnight Marquee Press.

Žižek, Slavoj (1992). *Looking Awry: An Introduction to Jacques Lacan Through Popular Culture*. Cambridge, MA: MIT Press.

Specialized Studies of Individual Actors

Agar, John (2007). *On the Good Ship Hollywood*. New York: BearManor Media.

Bansak, Edmund G. (2003). *Fearing the Dark: The Val Lewton Career*. Jefferson, NC: McFarland.

Béghin, Cyril (2007). "Acteur: George Sanders, Malgré lui." *Cahiers du Cinéma* 67.

Corman, Roger (1998). *How I Made a Hundred Movies in Hollywood and Never Lost a Dime*. New York: Da Capo Press.

Field, Amanda J. (2009). *England's Secret Weapon: The Wartime Films of Sherlock Holmes*. Hendon, UK: Middlesex University Press.

Fleming, Michael (2000). *The Three Stooges: From Amalgamated Morons to American Icons*. New York: Bantam Doubleday.

Fujiwara, Chris (2001). *Jacques Tourneur: The Cinema of Nightfall*. Baltimore: Johns Hopkins University Press.

Hanke, Ken (2004). *Charlie Chan at the Movies: History, Filmography and Criticism*. Jefferson, NC: McFarland.

Kerr, Paul (2008). "My Name is Joseph H. Lewis" (1983), in Barry Keith Grant (ed.), *Auteurs and Authorship: A Reader*. 234–249. Malden, MA: Blackwell.

Lanchester, Elsa (1983). *Elsa Lanchester: Herself*. New York: St. Martin's Press.

Mank, Gregory William (1998). *Dwight Frye's Last Laugh*. New York: Midnight Marquee Press.

_____ (1999). *Hollywood's Maddest Doctors: Lionel Atwill, Colin Clive, George Zucco*. New York: Midnight Marquee Press.

Moir, Patricia (1998). "Gods and Monsters: James Whale." *Cinefantastique* 30, no. 11: 45–48.

Nielsen, Leslie, and David Fisher (1993). *The Naked Truth*. New York: Simon & Schuster.

Parla, Paul, and Charles P. Mitchell (2000). "Faith Domergue: *This Island Earth*," in *Screen Sirens Scream: Interviews with Twenty Actresses from Science Fiction, Horror, Film Noir and Mystery Movies, 1930s to 1960s*. 57–77. Jefferson, NC: McFarland.

Rhodes, Gary D. (2006). "Lugosi vs. Karloff: Eternally!" *Midnight Marquee* 75: 16–22.

Skal, David J., and Jessica Rains (2010). *Claude Rains: An Actor's Voice*. Lexington: University Press of Kentucky.

Smith, Don G. (1996). *Lon Chaney Jr.: Horror Film Star, 1906–1973*. Jefferson, NC: McFarland.

Soister, John T. (1999). *Claude Rains: A Comprehensive Illustrated Reference to his Work in Film, Stage, Radio, Television, and Recordings*. Jefferson: McFarland.

Sondergaard, Gale (1950). *On the Eve of Prison: Two Addresses*. New York: The Arts, Science and Professions Council.

Stanley, John (2007). *I Was a TV Horror Host: Memories of a Creature Features Man*. San Francisco: Creatures at Large.

Starr, Michael Seth (2009). *Hiding in Plain Sight: The Secret Life of Raymond Burr*. New York: Applause.

Upchurch, Adam (1993). "The Dark Queen." *Film Comment* 29, no. 1: 1–11.

Van der Beets, Richard (1993). *George Sanders: An Exhausted Life*. New York: Madison Books.

Weaver, Tom (1996). "Anne Gwynne," in *It Came from Weaver Five: Interviews with Movie Makers in the Science Fiction and Horror Traditions*. 147–160. Jefferson, NC: McFarland.

_____ (2008). *John Carradine: The Films*. Jefferson, NC: McFarland.

Wood, Edward D., Jr. (1998). *Hollywood Rat Race*. New York: Da Capo Press.

Wood, Gary L. (2002). "Boris Karloff." *Cinefantastique* 34, no. 6.

Index

Names and page numbers in **bold** indicate primary entries.

A-Haunting We Will Go 56, 140
Abbott, Bud 12, 25, 41, 58, 82, 109, 136, 195
Abbott and Costello in the Foreign Legion 117
Abbott and Costello Meet Dr. Jekyll and Mr. Hyde 58, 182
Abbott and Costello Meet Frankenstein 177
Abbott and Costello Meet the Invisible Man 82
Abbott and Costello Meet the Mummy 195
Acquanetta 12, 44, 75, 145
Adams, Jane 102, 147
Adams, Julia 31, 43
Addams, Dawn 42
The Adventures of Robin Hood 121, 139
The Adventures of Sherlock Holmes 51
Agar, John 9–11, 148, 152, 153, 181
Air Hawks 75, 194
Airplane! 148
Albert, Eddie 60
Albertson, Frank 23
Alderson, Erville 172
Aldridge, Kay 139
Alexis, Dmitri 154
Ali Baba and the Forty Thieves 3, 26, 163
Alien 186
Allan, Elizabeth 106
Allbritton, Louise 12
Allen, Lewis 64
Allgood, Sara 99
Allied Artists 29
The Alligator People 88–89
Allister, Claude 16
The Amazing Colossal Man 10, 112–113, 127, 152–153
Amazing Mr. X 25, 27, 41–42
American International Pictures (AIP) 4–5, 31
Ames, Adrienne 195
Ames, Ramsay 45
Among the Living 67–68
Anderson, Richard 150
André, Nicki 160
Andrews, Dana 2, 111
Angel, Heather 134, 160
Ankers, Evelyn 5, **11–14**, 26, 41, 44, 68, 93, 112, 121, 166, 200
Ankrum, Morris 46
"Another Chance" (TV show) 149–150
The Ape 95–96

The Ape Man 19, 82, 96
Appointment in Honduras 195
"Appointment on Mars" (TV show) 149
Arabian Nights 26, 97–98, 109
Archer, John 6, **14–16**, 68, 136, 157, 191
Arlen, Richard 16–17
Armstrong, Robert 18–20, 44, 107, 116
Arne, Peter 72
Arness, James 58, 111, 187
Arnold, Edward 170
Arnold, Jack 9, 31, 43, 69, 84
Arnt, Charles 190
Arrest Bulldog Drummond 50
The Aspern Papers (novel) 15
Asther, Nils 22
The Atomic Man (aka Timeslip) 71–72
Atomic Submarine 79–80, 83–84
Attack of the Crab Monsters 195–196
Attack of the 50 Foot Woman 6, 113, 183
Attack of the Puppet People 10, 152, 153
Atwater, Edith 65
Atwill, Lionel 4, **20–22**, 58, 99, 116, 130, 158, 177, 199
Auer, Mischa 23–25
Aumont, Jean-Pierre 66
Autry, Gene 95

Back from the Dead 84
Baclanova, Olga 80, 163
Baker, Fay 15, 68
Baldwin, Peter 181
Ball, Frank 24
Bamber, Judy 40, 137
Bancroft, Anne 36
Banks, Leslie 18, 116
Barclay, Jerry 38
Barclay, Joan 138
Bari, Lynn 25, 27, 41
Barker, Lex 37, 53
Barnett, Vince 134
Barrat, Robert 83, 128
Barrett, Adrienne 102
The Barretts of Wimpole Street 196
Barrier, Edgar 26
Barry, Gene 60
Barrymore, Ethel 171, 172
Barrymore, John 62, 77, 108, 129, 163
Barrymore, Lionel 22, 106
Barton, Charles 110
Batanides, Arthur 117, 118

Batchelor, Stephanie 94
Batman (TV series) 3, 146, 147
Beal, John 135, 189
Beast from 20,000 Fathoms 6, 120–121, 187–188
Beast of Yucca Flats 118–119
Beast with a Million Eyes 28
Beast with Five Fingers 146
Beatty, Clyde 94
Beaudine, William 96, 135, 136, 141
Beaumont, Hugh 14, 52
Bedlam 165–166, 198
Beebe, Ford 175, 192
Beecher, Ruth 94
Beery, Noah, Jr. 76, 108
Before I Hang 193
The Beginning of the End 90–91
Begley, Ed 104
Bell, James 35, 114
Bellamy, Ralph 11, 58, 75
Bells of St. Mary's 11
Belmore, Lionel 85
Bender, Russ 103
Bennett, Bruce 194
Bennett, Joan 47
Bennett, Linda 70
Berghof, Herbert 89–90
Best, Willie 116
Bey, Turhan 13, **25–27**, 41, 44, 79, 82, 175, 200
The Bill of Rights 126
Birch, Paul 27–30, 69, 88, 102, 103, 137
Birell, Tala 75, 144, 176
Bissell, Whit 30–32
The Black Cat (1934) 44, 56, 134
The Black Cat (1941) 174
Black Dragons 138–139
Black Friday 17, 92–93
Black Magic 141
The Black Raven 136, 176, 200–201
The Black Room 3, 130, 194
The Black Scorpion 70
Blanchard, Mari 15, 49, 68
Blane, Sally 80
Blithe Spirit 62
The Blob 111–112
The Body Snatcher 65
Bogart, Humphrey 40, 54, 197
Bohn, John 34, 86
Bond, David 109
Bonner, Paul 57
Borg, Veda Ann 45
Borzage, Frank 33
Bosworth, Hobart 23
Bowery at Midnight 14, 135–136
Bowery Boys 61, 147, 177, 195

217

Index

The Bowery Boys Meet the Monsters 62
Boyer, Charles 151
Bradley, David 54
Bradley, Leslie 115
Brahm, John 77, 147, 168
Brannon, Fred C. 139
Brent, George 126, 173
The Bride Goes Wild 95
Bride of Frankenstein 51, 86, 124–125, 184–185
Bride of the Gorilla 36, 47, 52–53
Bride of the Monster 4, 117–118
Bridge, Alan 141
Bridges, Lloyd 3, 32–33
The Brighton Strangler 107–108, 131, 132, 197–198
Bringing Up Baby 41
Brocco, Peter 139
Bromfield, John 87
Bromley, Sheila 155, 178
Brooke, Hillary 47
Brooks, Jean **34–35**, 52, 114, 115
Brown, Phil 13
Brown, Wally 123, 197
Browning, Ricou 31, 43, 68
Browning, Tod 22, 80, 133, 163, 192
Bruce, David 13, 19, 200
Bruce, Nigel 46, 58, 60, 65, 122, 130
Bruce, Virginia 108
Brute Force 30, 124
The Brute Man 101–102
Buck Benny Rides Again 72
Buck Rogers 192
A Bucket of Blood 39–40, 137–138
Buckland, Vera 50
Bulldog Drummond at Bay 105
Burke, Kathleen 16, 22
Burns, Edmund 194
Burr, Raymond 3, **35–37**, 47, 53
Burton, Julian 40, 137
Burton, Robert 31
Butler, David 23

Cabanne, Christy 78, 81, 120, 164, 199
Cabot, Susan 5, **37–39**, 137
Cahn, Edward L. 11, 54, 66, 70, 186, 187
Calling Dr. Death 104, 145–146
Camille 64
Campo, Wally 196
Cape Canaveral Monsters 153
Captain America 158
Captive Wild Woman 12, 27, 44–45, 61, 62, 75, 101
Carbone, Antony **39–41**, 137
Cardoza, Anthony 118
Carlisle, Mary 81, 201
Carlson, Richard 12, 31, **41–44**, 68, 109
Carlyle, Rita 85
Carney, Alan 123, 197
Carnival Rock 38
Carradine, John 1, 12, 22, **44–47**, 93, 97, 110, 118, 136, 140
Carrillo, Leo 79
Carroll, Leo G. 9
Carroll, Lewis 40

Carson, Rene 161
Carter, Ann 123, 165, 172
Carter, Helena 83
Castillo, Gloria 94, 152
Castle, Peggie 84, 91
Castle, William 56
The Cat and the Canary (1939) 3, 173–174, 175, 199
The Cat Creeps 76, 108
Cat People (1942) 5, 51–52, 54, 165, 168, 169, 170–171
Catman of Paris 75–76
Cavanagh, Paul 36, **47–50**, 53, 66, 68, 147, 182
Chandler, Helen 133, 193
Chaney, Lon, Jr. 5, 11, 13, 22, 25, 33, 45, 53, 58, 79, 82, 89, 93, 98, 99, 104, 105, 109, 121, 122, 144, 145, 151, 163, 166, 177, 180, 183
Channel Four (UK TV station) 1
Chapman, Ben 31, 43, 68
Chapman, Marguerite 83
Charge of the Light Brigade (1936) 121
Charlie Chan at the Opera 191
Charlie Chan at Treasure Island 75
Charlie Chan in Shanghai 96
Charters, Spencer 197
Chase, Alden ("Stephen") 111
Cherokee Strip 79
China Corsair 97
Christian, Paul 120, 188
Christine, Virginia 105
Christy, Dorothy 95
Circus Boy (TV series) 111
Clair, René 3, 120
Clark, Cliff 26
Clark, Dane 33
Clark, Ken 54
Claydon Treasure Mysteries 11
Clifton, Elmer 158
The Climax 26–27, 173, 175
Clive, Colin 85, 86, 122, 184, 193, 197
Clive, E.E. 50–51, 159
The Clutching Hand 95, 96–97
The Clyde Mystery 177
Coates, Phyllis 31
Cobra Woman 3, 98
Coburn, Charles 59–60
Coe, Peter 93
Cohan, George M. 62
Cole, Dona 28
Collier, Lois 13
Collins, Lewis D. 32, 156
Collins, Ray 157
Colman, Ronald 168
Colmar, Eric 87
Columbia Pictures 30, 32, 71, 80, 110, 132, 181
Condemned to Life 24
Conlan, Frank 128
Connell, Linda 153
Connors, Touch 29, 69, 88, 102
The Conqueror 183
Convy, Bert 137
Conway, Gary 31
Conway, Tom 5, 35, 37, **51–54**, 167, 168, 170

Coogan, Jackie 164
Cook, Elisha, Jr. **54–56**
Cooper, Gary 16
Cooper, Gladys 174
Cooper, Merian C. 18, 19, 66, 116
Corday, Mara 70, 143
Cording, Harry 1–2, **56–58**, 134
Corman, Roger 1, 3, 5, 28–29, 38–41, 87, 88, 90, 102, 136, 137, 138, 195
Cornell, Katharine 20, 171
Cornthwaite, Robert 6, **58–60**, 169, 187
The Corpse Vanishes 164, 165
Corrigan, Lloyd **60–62**, 76, 122, 151
Corrigan, Ray 12, 44, 186
Corsaut, Aneta 111
Costello, Lou 12, 25, 41, 58, 82, 109, 136, 195
Cotten, Joseph 65, 122, 168
Cottrell, William 48, 57
Coward, Noël 183
Crabbe, Buster 192
Crabtree, Arthur 186
Craig, James 170, 180
Cramer, Marc 74
Crane, Kenneth G. 47
Crane, Richard 89
Crawford, Broderick 174
Crawford, Joan 80
Creature from the Black Lagoon (1954) 9, 31, 43, 68–69, 142
Creature from the Haunted Sea 40–41
The Creature Walks Among Us 142–143
Creature with the Atom Brain 70
Cregar, Laird 100, 126, 147, 168
The Crime of Dr. Crespi 34, 86
Criminal Court 53
The Crimson Ghost 139, 182
Crisp, Donald 3, **62–64**, 77, 106
Criswell 118
Cromwell, John 3, 157
Cronyn, Hume 30, 124
Crowley, Kathleen 69
Cult of the Cobra 72, 185–186
Cummings, Robert 15
Currie, Louise 82
Currier, Betty 136
Curse of the Cat People 123, 169, 170, 171
Curtis, Alan 55, 189
Curtis, Donald 27, 188
Curtis, Tony 38
Curtiz, Michael 20, 199
Curucu, Beast of the Amazon 87–88
The Cyclops 180

Dade, Frances 76
Daheim, John 82
Daktari 185
Damerel, Myrtle 137
Danger Woman 156–157
Daniell, Henry 47, 49, **64–66**
Daniels, Harold 9
Dark Waters 147
Darnell, Linda 126, 147, 168
Dassin, Jules 30, 37

Daughter of Dr. Jekyll 10, 180–181, 183
Daughter of the Dragon 76
David Copperfield (1935) 51, 103, 131
Davis, Bette 110
Davis, John 12
Day, Robert 187
The Day the Earth Stood Still (1951) 6, 161–162
The Day the World Ended 3, 28–29, 69, 102
Deacon, Richard 195
Dead Men Walk 86, 201
Dean, Julia 165
The Death Kiss 134, 194
The Declaration of Independence 74
De Cordova, Leander 154
Dee, Frances 52, 123
Dehner, John 62
Dekker, Albert 66–68
Del Ruth, Roy 89
Demarest, William 72
Dementia 102
Denning, Michael 5
Denning, Richard 28–29, 31, 43, **68–70**, 102
Dent, Vernon 109
Destination Moon 6, 14, 155
Destination Tokyo 112
De Toth, André 147
The Devil and Daniel Webster 169–170
Devil Bat 191
Devil Bat's Daughter 128–129
Devon, Richard 38, 137
Dick Tracy (1990) 196
Dickens, Charles 51, 57, 103, 160
Dieterle, William 110, 169
Dinehart, Allan 130
Dix, Richard 123
Dmytryk, Edward 12, 44, 61
Dr. Cyclops 66–67
Dr. Jekyll and Mr. Hyde (1931) 63, 104–105, 107, 183
Dr. Jekyll and Mr. Hyde (1941) 63
Dr. Renault's Secret 145, 200
Dr. X 20
Dodsworth 151
Domergue, Faith 6, **70–72**, 142, 186, 188
Donnelly, Ruth 62
Donovan, King 42
Donovan's Brain (novel) 17
Doomed to Die 164, 191–192
Douglas, George 183
Douglas, Melvyn 20, 85–86, 183
Downs, Cathy 112, 113, 127
Dracula (1931) 3, 84–85, 133, 192–193
Dracula's Daughter 51, 91, 154, 155, 193
Dragonwyck 126–127
Drake, Charles 42, 179
Drake, Frances 197
Drake, Tom 180
Dressed to Kill (1946) 58, 106, 198
Drew, Ellen 72–74, 135, 199
Dreyfus (1931) 198
Drums Across the River 182

Drums of Jeopardy 24
Duel at Silver Creek 71
Dufour, Val 137
Dumbrille, Douglass 74–76, 194
Duncan, Isadora 124
Duncan, Pamela 196
Dunn, Josephine 24
Dunne, Irene 151
Dupont, Ewald André 87
Duprez, June 108
Durbin, Deanna 91, 127

Earles, Harry 80, 163
East Side Kids 163
Edwards, Bill 187
Edwards, Blake 128
Eilers, Sally 190
Eldredge, George 42
Eldredge, John 181
Ellison, James 52, 62, 77–78, 94
Elmer Gantry 183
Emery, John 143
The Enchanted Valley 93
English, John 17, 158
English, Marla 112
Erickson, Hal 121
Erickson, Leif 155
Ersley, Fred 39
Esmond, Carl 75
Evans, Maurice 142
Evans, Rex 151
Everybody's Hobby 126

The Falcon 53
Fallen Angel 46, 110–111
Fanny with the Cheeks of Tan 87
Farmer, Frances 67
Farrell, Timothy 179
Father Knows Best (TV series) 112
Fawcett, William 87
Faye, Alice 46
The Feathered Serpent 141–142
The Feminine Mystique (book) 68
Fiend Without a Face 186, 187
Find the Lady 166
Fire Over England 11
The First Born 130
First Man Into Space 187
First National Pictures 20
Flash Gordon (1946) 175
Flash Gordon Conquers the Universe 93
Fleming, Rhonda 126
Fleming, Victor 63
Fletcher, Bramwell 63, **76–78**
Flight to Mars 83, 84
Flint, Sam 201
Flynn, Errol 121
Fog Island 21
Foran, Dick 25, **78–80**, 81, 84, 92, 120, 199
Ford, Wallace 25, 78, **80–82**, 120, 199
Forrest, Sally 48
Foster, Norman 75
Foster, Susanna 26, 161, 175
Foulger, Byron 201
The Four Skulls of Jonathan Drake 49, 64, 66

Fowler, Gene D., Jr. 32, 181
Francis, Alan 119
Francis, Anne 150
Francis, Ronald 119
Francis in the Haunted House 48
Franciscus, James 44
Frankenstein (1931) 3, 18, 20, 51, 85, 116, 117, 122, 193, 194
Frankenstein Meets the Wolf Man 86, 122, 151
Franz, Arthur 31, 80, **82–84**
Franz, Edouard 66
Fraser, Sally 90
Frawley, William 82
Frazer, Robert 20
Freaks 80, 163
Fregonese, Hugo 115
French, Valerie 64, 66
French Without Tears 72
Freund, Karl 77, 133
Friderici, Blanche 154
Friedan, Betty 68
Fright Night 109
From Here to Eternity 40, 71
From the Earth to the Moon 65, 122–123, 168
Frost, Terry 136
The Frozen Ghost 13, 109–110
Frye, Dwight 1, 3, 4, **84–86**, 192

Gabel, Martin 15
Gabor, Zsa Zsa 29
Galli, Rosina 116
The Garden Murder Case 171
Gardner, Ava 27
Gargan, William 199
Garland, Beverly 29, **86–89**
Garrick, John 23
Gay, Gregory 70
Genius at Work 22
George Carlin: Playin' with Your Head 177
The Ghost Breakers 41, 61, 116
The Ghost Chasers 61–62
The Ghost Goes Wild 62, 94
The Ghost of Frankenstein 11, 58, 99, 105
Ghost Ship 123
The Ghost Talks 109
"Ghost Writer" (TV show) 150
The Ghoul 185
The Giant Claw 143
Gidget 156
Gilbert, Billy 109
Gillmore, Lowell 167
The Girl in the Crowd 121
Gish, Lillian 171
Gleason, James 19
Glen or Glenda 179
Goddard, Paulette 41, 61, 199
Godzilla, King of the Monsters 36–37
Gone with the Wind 110, 114
Goodland, Saul A. 192
Gorcey, David 163
Gorcey, Leo 62
Gordon, Bert I. [Robert] 10, 43, 71, 90, 113, 127, 180
Gordon, Bruce 95
Gordon, Christine 52

Index

Gordon, Gavin 124
Gordon, Susan 43, 152
Gorilla at Large 36–37
Graham, Frank 17
Granger, Michael 70
Grant, Cary 41, 59
Grant, Lawrence 76
Grapewin, Charley 81, 190
Graves, Peter 89–91, 103
Gray, Coleen 181, 189
Gray, Lorna 182
Greene, Billy 153
Grey, Nan 78, **91–92**, 98, 154
Grey, Virginia 69, 100, 147
Griffith, Chuck (Charles H.) 41
Griffith, D.W. 62
Grinde, Nick 194
Gwenn, Edmund 111
Gwynne, Anne 4, 5–6, 62, **92–94**, 122, 166

Haden, Sara 156
Hale, Michael 128
Haley, Jack 178
Half Human 46–47
Hall, Ellen 46, 200
Hall, Henry 3, **94–96**
Hall, Huntz 61, 62, 147, 177, 195
Hall, Jon (aka Charles Locher) 4, 13, 26, 96–98, 99, 175, 197
Hall, Porter 110
Halperin, Victor 130, 154
Halsey, Brett 84
Halton, Charles 67
Hamilton, Hale 24
Hamilton, John 140, 157
Hamilton, Neil 144
Hamilton, Patrick 168
Hampden, Walter 23
Hangover Square 126, 147, 168
Hardwicke, Sir Cedric 2, 6, 11, 58, 60, 92, 97, **98–100**, 106, 119, 198
Hardy, Oliver 56, 140
Hare, Lumsden 62, 77
Harrigan, William 160
Haskin, Byron 28, 60, 65, 123
Hatfield, Hurd 167
Hathaway, Henry 37
Hatton, Rondo 3, 4, **100–102**, 117, 133, 147, 174
Hawks, Howard 58, 59
Hawthorne, Nathaniel 78, 92, 119, 131, 166
Hayakawa, Sessue 76
Hayes, Allison 6, 113, 118, 183, 196
Hayes, Helen 20, 133
Hays Office 27, 57, 132
Hayward, Louis 48
Hayward, Susan 67
Hayworth, Vinton 82
Haze, Jonathan 3, 29, **102–104**, 136, 138, 196
He Married his Wife 55
Healy, Myron 118
Hedison, David 161, 163
Heisler, Stuart 67, 73
Hell Harbor 100
Helm, Fay 44
Hepburn, Katharine 142

Herbert, Holmes 1, 22, 76, **104–106**
Herbert, Hugh 174
Hervey, Irene 155
Heydt, Louis Jean 75
Hill, Mary 164
Hillyer, Lambert 51, 91, 154, 193
Hinds, Samuel S. 47, 122
His Woman 74
Hitchcock, Alfred 57, 63
Hitler, Adolf 159
Hobart, Rose 104, **106–108**
Hobbes, Halliwell 63, 107
Hobson, Valerie 185
Hoey, Dennis 51, 58, 61, 130
Hokus Pokus 109
Hold That Ghost 12, 25, 41, 109
Hold That Hypnotist 195
Holden, Gloria 91, 154, 155, 193
Holliman, Earl 150
Holmes, Taylor 179
Homans, Robert 156
Homolka, Oscar 108
Honda, Ishirō 47
Hope, Bob 2, 41, 61, 116, 173
Hopkins, Miriam 104
Horne, Victoria 33
Horror Island 79
Horton, Edward Everett 62
The Hound of the Baskervilles (1939) 46, 51
House, Billy 166
House of Dracula 22, 44–45, 177
The House of Fear 58, 106
House of Frankenstein 22, 93–94, 176, 177
House of Horrors 3, 100–101, 147
The House of the Seven Gables 3, 5, 78, 92, 119–120, 131, 166–167
House of Wax (1953) 48, 118, 147
The House on Haunted Hill 55–56
Howard, David 94
Howard, John 50, 73, 78
Howard, Shemp 108–110
Howland, Olin 110–112
Hoyt, John 10, 153
Hubbard, John 26, 79, 82
Hudson, William 6, 49, **112–113**, 183
Hughes, Howard 70
Hughes, Kathleen 72, 186
Hughes, Ken 72
Humberstone, H. Bruce 16
Hunt, Jimmy 83
Hunt, Marsha 84
Hunter, Kim 35, 52, 115
The Hurricane 97
Hurst, Brandon 129
Hussey, Ruth 64
Huston, John 54
Huston, Virginia 83
Huston, Walter 127, 170
Hutton, Robert 11
Hyams, Leila 80
Hymer, Warren 157

I Married a Monster from Outer Space 181
I Married a Witch 3, 120
I Walked with a Zombie 52–53, 123
I Was a Male War Bride 187

I Was a Teenage Frankenstein 30–31
I Was a Teenage Werewolf 31–32
I'll Be Your Sweetheart 161
I'll Never Forget You (aka *The House on the Square*) 162
Incredible Petrified World 46
The Indestructible Man 179, 182–183
Inescort, Frieda 89, 132
Invaders from Mars 83, 84
Invasion of the Body Snatchers (1956) 83, 181
Invasion of the Saucer Men 152
The Invisible Agent 97, 98–99
Invisible Invaders 11
The Invisible Man (1933) 4, 50, 105, 159–160
The Invisible Man Returns 57, 91–92, 98, 99, 119, 120, 175
The Invisible Man's Revenge 4, 13, 97, 197
The Invisible Woman 108–109
Ironside (TV series) 35–36
Irving, George 12
Island of Dr. Moreau (novel) 16
Island of Lost Souls 16
Isle of the Dead 74, 148
It Came from Beneath the Sea 3, 71, 188–189
It Came from Outer Space 42
It Conquered the World 88, 90, 103, 136–137
It! The Terror Beyond Space 186–187
Ivers, Robert 181

The Jade Mask 96, 141
James, John 129
Janti, Azemat 195
Jarmyn, Jil 88
Jess-Cooke, Carolyn 3
Jewell, Isabel 35, **113–115**
Johann, Zita 133
Johnson, Noble 5, **115–117**
Johnson, Tor 4, **117–119**
Jones, Morgan 88
Jones-Moreland, Betsy 39–41
Jory, Victor 49, 113
Joseph, Jackie 104
Journey to the Center of the Earth (1958) 148
Journey's End 133
Joyce, Brenda 33, 101, 144, 156, 174
Jungle Captive 101
Jungle Woman 12, 75, 101, 145
Jurgens, Adele 29
Just Imagine 23

Karloff, Boris 22, 26, 44, 48, 51, 55, 56, 65, 74, 77, 85, 92, 96, 107, 125, 130, 133, 134, 148, 159, 166, 175, 177, 184, 185, 192, 193, 194, 197, 199
Karnes, Robert 42, 46
Katch, Kurt 26, 98
Kay, Mary Ellen 53
Keene, Tom 179
Keith, Brian 149
Kellaway, Cecil 3, 6, 57, 78, 81, 92, **119–121**
Kellogg, John G. 37
Kelly, Jack 15, 68

Kelly, Nancy 55
Kelsey, Fred 81, 190
Kendall, Cy 32
Kenney, June 10, 152, 153
Kenton, Erle C. 16, 105, 177
Kerr, Paul 5
Killer Leopard 87
Killers from Space 90
King, Andrea 89
King, Henry 100
King, Loretta 117
King Kong (1933) 18, 43, 44, 47, 68, 116, 127, 145, 154, 180
King of the Wild 25
King of the Zombies 14, 140, 157, 191
Kipling, Rudyard 33
Kiss of Death 37
Knowles, Patric 47, 60, **121–123**, 151
Knox, Alexander 48
Knox, Elyse 26
Kolker, Henry 194
Kosleck, Martin 100, 147
Kramarsky, David 28
Kronos 143
Kruger, Otto 101, 154, 193

Ladies' Lake 169
Lady and the Monster 17
The Lady Vanishes (1938) 63
La Gallienne, Eva 23, 133
Lake, Florence 24
Lake, Veronica 120
Lamont, Charles 82, 182
Lamont, Molly 129
Lancaster, Burt 104, 124
Lancelot, Sir 123–124
Lanchester, Elsa 124–126, 185
Landers, Lew (aka Louis Friedlander) 197
Landon, Michael 32
Landres, Paul 189
Landry, Margaret 34
Lane, Vicky 101
Lang, Fritz 47
Lang, Melvin 191
Langan, Glenn 113, **126–127**, 152
Langtry, Lily 20
Lansbury, Angela 167
La Planche, Rosemary **127–129**
Lassie Come Home 62
The Last Woman on Earth 40
La Torre, Charles 145
Laughton, Charles 16, 48, 57, 124, 147
Launer, S. John 70
Laurel, Stan 56, 140
Lawrence, Barbara 143
Lawrence of Arabia 97
Lazarus Laughed 154
Lean, David 62
Leary, Nolan 128
Le Borg, Reginald 13, 145–146
Ledebur, Frederick 49
Lee, Anna 166
Lee, Rowland V. 57
Leech Woman 181–182
Leonard, Sheldon 82
The Leopard Man 5, 34–35, 114–115
Lewin, Albert 167

Lewis, Joseph H. 116
Lewis, Sheldon 24
Lewton, Val 5, 34, 123, 165, 170, 171
The Life of Paul Muni 173
Liliom 106
Lincoln Motion Picture Company 117
Lindsay, Margaret 78, 92
Lippert Pictures 33
Litel, John 110, 151
Little Shop of Horrors (1960) 3, 103–104, 138, 196
Little Women (1949) 111
Litvak, Anatole 104
Livingston, Robert 141
Lloyds of London 166
Lockhart, June 156
Loder, John 108, 132, 197
The Lodger (1928) 57
The Lodger (1944) 99–100, 168
Loftus, Cecilia 174
Lombard, Carole 130
Lord, Marjorie 14
Lorre, Peter 97, 99, 146, 197
The Lost City 95
Lost Horizon (1937) 113
The Lost Jungle 94–95
The Lost Moment 15
The Lost World 161, 162–163, 198
Lourié, Eugene 120–121
Love Affair 151
Lowery, Robert 45, 140
Lowndes, Marie Belloc 168
Loy, Myrna 21
Lubin, Arthur 3, 26, 101, 131, 160, 175
Lucan, Arthur (aka Old Mother Riley) 112
Ludwig, Edward 70
Lugosi, Bela 14, 22, 46, 56, 82, 85, 92, 96, 112, 116, 117, 122, 129, 132, 133, 134, 135, 136, 138, 151, 163, 164, 177, 191, 193, 197, 200
Luke, Edwin 141
Luke, Keye 141
Lydon, James 190
Lyon, Francis D. 72, 186
Lys, Lya 110

Macannan, George Burr 3, **129–130**
MacBride, Donald 108
Mack, Helen 18
Mack, Michael 39
Mack, Wilbur 192
MacKenzie, Joyce 37
Mad About Music 127
The Mad Doctor 72–73, 74, 135
The Mad Doctor of Market Street 116
The Mad Ghoul 12–13, 19, 26, 107, 200
Mad Love 114, 146, 197
The Mad Monster 175–176, 177, 200
Madreguera, Enrico 34
The Maltese Falcon (1941) 54, 110
Malvern, Judy 14
Malyon, Eily 46
Mamoulian, Rouben 104–105, 107
The Man I Love 16
Man in the Attic 57, 115

Man Made Monster 22
The Man on the Ferry 187
The Man Who Turned to Stone 48–49, 112–113
Mander, Miles 13, 100, 108, **130–133**, 160, 198
Mankiewicz, Joseph L. 126
Manners, David 5, 51, 56, **133–134**, 160, 193
March, Fredric 104, 120
Marco, Paul 118
Marcus, Vitina 198
Margo 34, 114
Marin, Edwin L. 97, 99, 134, 194
Mark of the Vampire 22, 106
Marlowe, Faye 147, 168
Marquette, Jacques (Jack) 40
Mars, Monica 129
Marsh, Marian 63, 77, 130
Marshal, Alan 56
Marshall, Herbert 42
Martin, Lewis 35
Martin, Richard 35
Mason, James 148
Massen, Osa 33
Massey, Ilona 97, 122
Massey, Raymond 183
Master Minds 147, 195
Mather, Aubrey 58, 106
Matheson, Murray 150
Matthews, Lester 13
Mattox, Martha 23, 154
Maurer, Norman 110
Maxwell, Edwin 21
May, Joe 3, 166
Mayer, Arthur 5
Mayo, Archie 77
Maytime 180
Mazurki, Mike 145
McClory, Sean 115
McClure, Arthur F. 2–3, 4
McCrea, Joel 117
McGrail, Walter 154
McGuire, Dorothy 125, 172
McHugh, Frank 21
McHugh, Matt 80
McKay, Wanda 46, **134–136**, 144, 201
McKenzie, Robert 81
McKinnon, Mona 118
McNaughton, Charles 16
McQueen, Steve 111
Medford, Don 149
Meeker, George 80
Mengele, Josef 67, 144
Menzies, William Cameron 83
Mercer, Beryl 17
Mesa of Lost Women 164, 179
Metro Goldwyn-Mayer Pictures 22, 51, 113, 114, 124, 168, 185
Michel, Lora Lee 190
Middlemass, Robert 136, 201
Middleton, Robert 149
Midnight Manhunt 199
Mighty Joe Young 19, 47, 95, 190–191
Milland, Ray 64, 106, 146
Miller, Dick 38, 40, 103, **136–138**
Miller, Ken 152
Miller, Walter 25

Index

Les Misérables (1935) 98
Mission, Impossible (TV series) 89
Mitchell, Cameron 83
Mitchell, Laurie 29, 152
Mitchum, Robert 157
Moffett, Sharon 65
Mohr, Gerald 73
The Mole People 10, 11, 148
Monkey Business 59–60
The Monkey's Paw (1933) 77
Monogram Studios 4, 14, 45, 61, 135, 140, 157, 164, 191
Monroe, Marilyn 59
The Monster and the Girl 73–74, 199–200
Monster from the Ocean Floor 102
The Monster Maker 136, 144, 176
Monster on the Campus 31, 84
The Monster Walks 23–24
Montez, Maria 3, 26, 65–66, 97, 98, 151
Montgomery, Douglass 51, 134, 160, 174
Moonrise 33
Moore, Clayton 138–140
Moore, Constance 192
Moore, Dennis 164
Moore, Eva 183
Moore, Terry 19, 190
Moorehead, Agnes 15
Moran, Jackie 192
Moran, Peggy 78, 79, 120, 199
Moreland, Mantan 3–4, 108, **140–142**, 157
Morgan, Dennis 110, 126, 197
Morgan, Ralph 22, 24, 136, 144, 155, 166, 176
Morison, Patricia 58, 146, 156
Morris, Barboura 138
Morris, Chester 54, 112
Morris, Wayne 110, 197
Morrow, Jeff 142–143
Morse, Terry O. 21, 37
The Most Dangerous Game 18, 116–117
Motion Picture Production Code 6, 102
Mulhall, Jack 81, 97
The Mummy (1932) 77, 109, 133, 193, 199
The Mummy's Curse 105
Mummy's Dummies 109
The Mummy's Ghost 45–46
The Mummy's Hand 25, 78, 81, 82, 120, 199, 200
The Mummy's Tomb 25, 78–79, 82
Murder Among Friends 74, 178
Murder at Dawn 24
Murder by the Clock 154, 189
The Murder of Marie Roget 60, 122, 151–152
Murders in the Rue Morgue 5, 116
Murders in the Zoo 22
Murphy, Audie 38, 182
Mystery of Edwin Drood 50–51, 57, 134, 160
Mystery of the Wax Museum 20–21

Nagel, Anne 22

Naish, J. Carrol 33, 75, 136, **143–146**, 176, 177, 200
The Naked City 37
The Naked Gun 149
Napier, Alan 3, 4, 10, 57, 101, **146–148**, 177, 195
Nash, Mary 98
Navarro, Mario 70
Neal, Patricia 162
Neal, Tom 102, 135
The Neanderthal Man 87
Neill, Roy William 65, 174
Nelson, Gene 71
Nelson, Lori 9, 69
Neumann, Kurt 143
Newfield, Sam 86, 144, 176, 201
Newton, Mary 115
Nicholson, Jack 104
Nielsen, Leslie 3, 148–150
Nigh, William 96, 122, 139, 164
Night Monster 22, 155–156
Night of Terror 80–81
Night of the Ghouls 118
Nixon, Allan 164
Norris, Edward 122
Nosseck, Max 132
Not of This Earth 3, 28–29, 88, 103, 137
Nowell, Richard 6–7
Nyby, Christian 58

Oberon, Merle 27, 100, 147, 168
O'Connolly, James 44
O'Connor, Una 159
O'Day, Neil 151
O'Donnell, Cathy 27
O'Driscoll, Martha 45, 53
Oh, Yeah? 19
Ohmart, Carol 56
O'Keefe, Dennis 34, 114
Oland, Werner 24, 76
The Old Dark House 183–184, 201
Oliver, Gordon 172–173
Olivier, Laurence 195
O'Moore, Patrick 124
On with the Dance 183
One Body Too Many 178–179
One Frightened Night 81, 190
One Hundred Men and a Girl 127
One Thrilling Night 135
O'Neil, Barbara 91
O'Neil, Sally 189
O'Neill, Eugene 154
O'Neill, Rosary 4
Ormond, Ron 164
Osborne, Vivienne 130
O'Sullivan, Maureen 23
O'Toole, Peter 97
Ouspenskaya, Maria 61, **150–152**
Out West 109
Outside the Law 195

Paine, Robert 73
Paiva, Nestor 9–10
Palmer, Byron 57
"Paramount Case" (1942) 4
Paramount Pictures 16, 22, 41, 72, 73, 134–135, 173
Parker, Cecilia 16

Parker, Eddie 195
Parker, John 102
Parker, Kim 186
Parkin, Duncan 180
Parma, Tina 114
Parma, Tula 34
Patrick, Cynthia 10
Pawley, Edward 21–22
Payton, Barbara 36, 47, 53
The Pearl of Death 13, 100, 101, 106, 198
Peary, Danny 2, 4
Peck, Gregory 187
Pendleton, Nat 200
Pepper, Barbara 81
Perils of Nyoka (aka *Nyoka and the Lost Secrets of Hippocrates*) 139, 182
Perkins, Gil 94
Perry, Vic 72
Perry Mason (TV series) 35–36
Peters, Scott 152–153
Petroff, Boris 118
Phantom Empire 3, 95
Phantom Killer 140, 157–158
Phantom Lady 54–55, 189–190
Phantom of the Opera (1943) 131, 160
The Phantom Speaks 17
Philco Television Playhouse 76
Pichel, Irving 14, 91, 116–117, **154–155**, 178
The Picture of Dorian Gray 167–168
Pidgeon, Walter 150
Pierson, Melissa Holbrook 2
Plan Nine from Outer Space 4, 118, 179
Planet Earth 69
Planet Outlaws 192
Poe, Edgar Allan 86, 122, 174
Port Sinister 49–50, 182
Porter, Don 155–157
Possessed 80
Powell, Michael 121
Power, Tyrone 162
Powers, Mala 124
Price, Stanley 139
Price, Vincent 48, 55, 57, 91, 92, 98, 107, 118, 119, 126, 127, 131, 166–167
The Primrose Path 94
The Private Life of Henry VIII 130
The Private Lives of Elizabeth and Essex 62, 64
Producers' Releasing Corporation 128, 200
Purcell, Dick 14, 140, **157–158**

Qualen, John 109
Queen of Outer Space 29–30
Quigley, Charles 139, 182
Quigley, Juanita 17
Quinlan, David 2

The Racket 3, 157
Radar Men from the Moon 139–140
Radford, Basil 63
Raines, Ella 30, 55
Rainier, Luise 142
Rains, Claude 2, 50, 51, 82, 97, 105, 131, 134, 151, **159–161**, 163, 198

Ralston, Vera Hruba 17
Rand, Edwin 10
Randall, Bob 136
Randall, Tony 187
Randolph, Jane 123, 165, 170–171, 172
Rathbone, Basil 13, 22, 51, 58, 65, 73, 91, 107, 122, 130, 131, 132, 174, 197, 198
The Raven 196–197
Rawlins, John 97
Raymond, Paula 188
Reason, Rex 71, 142
Reason, Rhodes 55
Reckless Age 185
Red Planet Mars 89–90
Redfield, William 149
Reding, Juli 43
Redwing, Rodd 10, 148
Reed, Donna 167
Reeves, Kynaston 186
Reeves, Richard 69
Reicher, Frank 18, 116
Reichow, Otto 84
Reid, Elliott 35
Rembrandt 49
Renault, Lynne 145
Rennie, Michael 6, **161–163**
Republic Studios 4, 17, 75, 92, 110, 139, 157, 158, 182
Return of Dr. X 110, 126, 197
Return of the Vampire 132
Return to the Forbidden Planet 149, 150
Revenge of the Creature 9, 142
Revenge of the Zombies 45, 140
Revere, Anne 46
Revier, Harry 95
Reynolds, Vera 24
Richards, Grant 66
Riders to the Stars 42–43
Ridges, Stanley 17, 92–93
Rilla, Wolf 168
RKO Radio Pictures 5, 34, 35, 169
Road to Rio 117
Roark, Robert 69
The Robe 142
Roberts, Lynne 17
Robertson, Willard 20
Robson, Mark 52, 74, 166
Rocketship X-M 33
Rocky Jones: Space Ranger (TV series) 112
Rodgers, Gaby 150
Roerick, William 38
Rogell, Albert S. 75
Rogers, Ginger 59–60, 178
The Rogues' Tavern 81
Romero, Cesar 75
Rooney, Mickey 48
Rose, Sherman A. 69
Rosen, Phil 60, 122, 151–152
Rosener, George 20
Rossitto, Angelo 163–165
Roy Rogers Show 112
The Runaway Bride 62
Russell, Elizabeth 13, 93, 123, 164, **165–166**

Russell, Gail 64, 106, 146
Russell, Jane 70
Ryan, Robert 157

Sabu 98
Saint Joan 183
Samson and Delilah 164
Sanders, George 3, 51, 53, 78, 92, 100, 119, 123, 131, **166–169**
Sanders, Lugene 43
Sands of Iwo Jima 112
Sante, Luc 2
Satan Met a Lady 110
Savage, Ann 199
Scared to Death 164, 200
The Scarlet Claw 198
Schaefer, Armand 94
Schallert, William 49, 182
Schnabel, Stefan 195
Schoedsack, Ernest B. 18, 19, 66, 116
Schwarzwald, Arnold 139
Scott, Randolph 22, 130
Scott, Ridley 186
Sea Hunt 33
Sears, Fred F. 143
Sebastian, Dorothy 67
Secret Agent X-9 32
Secret Beyond the Door 47
Seitz, George B. 24
Sekely, Steve 140
Selander, Lesley 76, 83
Selznick, David O. 9
Sergeant, Richard 28
The Seventh Victim 35, 52–53, 115
Shadow of Chinatown 3
Shakespeare, William 57, 130
Shaner, John 104
Shaw, George Bernard 183
Shayne, Robert 87, 183
The She-Creature 54, 112
She-Devil 15, 49, 68
She-Wolf of London 61, 156
Sheffield, Johnny 87
Shelley, Barbara 168–169
Sheridan, Margaret 187
Sherlock Holmes and the Secret Weapon 22, 58
Sherlock Holmes and the Spider Woman 3
Sherlock Holmes in Washington 14, 65, 198–199
Shields, Arthur 10, 180
Shirley, Anne 170
Shivering Sherlocks 109
A Shriek in the Night 177–178
Simon, Simone 51, 54, 123, 165, **169–171**
Sinclair, Ronald 57
Sing Your Sinners 72
Siodmak, Curt 17, 87
Siodmak, Robert 54, 98, 172, 189, 190
Sirens of Atlantis 66
Skaff, George 46
Skelton, Red 110
Skinner, Cornelia Otis 64, 106
The Sky Dragon 141
Sloman, Edward 154, 189
Smith, Janet 171

Smith, Kent 123, 125, 165, 170, **171–173**
Snow White and the Seven Dwarfs 173
Snowden, Leigh 143
Son of Dr. Jekyll 48
Son of Dracula 12
Son of Kong 18, 47
Sondergaard, Gale 3, 101, **173–175**
Sorry, Wrong Number 104
Space, Arthur 31
Spencer, Douglas 59
The Spider Woman (aka *Sherlock Holmes and the Spider Woman*) 3, 174
The Spider Woman Strikes Back 101, 174–175
The Spiral Staircase (1945) 125–126, 172
Spooks Run Wild 163–164
Stamboul Quest 21
Stanley and Livingstone 98
Stanwyck, Barbara 104
Steele, Bob 45
Stelling, William 192
Stephens, Martin 169
Stevens, Angela 70
Stevens, Craig 58
Stevens, Onslow 45, 73, 177
Stevenson, Robert Louis 47, 65
Stirling, Linda 139
Stone, Lewis 51
Stone, Milburn 13, 26, 44, 61, 107, 145, 156
Strange, Glenn 147, **175–177**, 200
Strange Cargo 66
Strange Case of Dr. RX 47, 108, 121–122
Strange Confession 33, 109, 144–145
Strange Door 47–48, 57, 147–148
Strange Illusion 190
Strangler of the Swamp 128
Strayer, Frank R. 20, 23, 24, 85
Stuart, Gloria 159, 183
Studio One 76
Supernatural 130
Suspicion 98
Sutherland, A. Edward 109
Sutton, John 91, 119
Svengali (1931) 62–63, 77, 109, 129
Swamp Women 88, 102–103

Talbot, Lyle 155, **177–180**
Talbott, Gloria 10, **180–182**
A Tale of Two Cities (1935) 113
Tales of Tomorrow (TV series) 149
Talman, William 157
Tangled Destinies 95
Tarantula 10
Target Earth 30–31
Tarver, Leonard 28
Tarzan and the She-Devil 37, 53
Tashman, Lilyan 154
Taylor, Elizabeth 111
Taylor, Ray 32
Teenage Monster 94
Tema, Muzaffer (aka Tema Bey) 54
Temple, Shirley 9
The Ten Commandments 98, 183

Terrell, Ken **182–183**
Terrell, Steve 152
Terry, Philip 181, 199
Tevos, Herbert 164
That Hamilton Woman (aka *Lady Hamilton*) 131
Thatcher, Heather 78
Thayer, Lorna 28
Them! 111
Thesiger, Ernest 86, 125, **183–185**
The Thin Man 122
The Thing from Another World (1951) 3, 6, 58–59, 169, 187, 188
This Island Earth 6, 71, 142
Thompson, Marshall 72, **185–187**
Thor, Larry 112
Thorp, Margaret Farrand 5
Thorson, Russell 46
Three Live Ghosts 16
Three Smart Girls 91
Three Smart Girls Grow Up 91
The Three Stooges 108–109, 110
Tierney, Gene 126
Tilbury, Zeffie 50, 160
The Time Tunnel 30
To Be or Not to Be (1942) 131
Tobey, Kenneth 3, 58, 71, **187–189**
Tobor the Great 179
Todd, Sally 118
Toler, Sidney 75, 96, 141
Tone, Franchot 55
Tonge, Philip 11
Toomey, Regis 81, **189–191**
Tormented 43
Torture Ship 154–155, 178
Tourneur, Jacques 34, 51–52, 165, 172
Tower of London 57, 91, 107, 131
Towne, Aline 139
Tracy, Spencer 63–64
Traxler, Virginia 77
Treasure Island (1950) 49
Treat 'Em Rough 60
Tree, Beerbohm 159
A Tree Grows in Brooklyn 180
Trowbridge, Charles 166
Tryon, Tom 181
Tucker, Phil 153
Turner, Lana 63
Twelve O'Clock High 187
12 to the Moon 54
Twentieth Century–Fox 51, 58, 126, 127, 145, 148, 161, 168, 200
The 27th Day 30, 195
Twomey, Alfred E. 2–3, 4

Ulmer, Edgar G. 10, 134, 180, 183, 190
The Undead 137, 196
The Undying Monster 77–78
The Unearthly 117, 118
The Uninvited 64, 106, 146
Universal Pictures 1, 4, 11, 12, 17, 22, 38, 50, 51, 57, 58, 60, 61, 71, 76, 78, 84, 91, 92, 100, 121, 131, 142, 155, 156, 157, 159, 174, 177, 185
Unknown Singer 169
The Unknown Terror 124
Usher, Guy 191–192

Vail, Myrtle 104
Valley of Gwangi 43–44
The Vampire 189
The Vampire and the Robot (aka *Old Mother Riley Meets the Vampire*) 112
The Vampire Bat 20, 85–86
Van Cleef, Lee 88, 90, 103
Van Sloan, Edward 5, 18, 85, 133, **192–195**
Van Vooren, Monique 37
Varga, Carol 36
Vendetta 71
Verne, Jules 168
Viana, Wilson 87
Vickers, Martha 44
Vickers, Yvette 113, 183
Victor, Henry 14, 80, 157, 191
Vigran, Herb 189
Village of the Damned 168–169
Vincent, June 26, 175
Vincent, Virginia 149
The Virginian 16
The Voice of Terror (aka *Sherlock Holmes and the Voice of Terror*) 13, 65, 130
Von Fritsch, Gunther 165
Von Stroheim, Erich 17, 34, 86
Voodoo Island 55
Voodoo Man 46, 96, 136, 200
Voodoo Woman 53–54
Vorhaus, Bernard 27
Voskovec, George 30

Wade, Stuart 94
Waggner, George 11, 22, 26, 79
Wain, Edward (aka Robert Towne) 40
Waldis, Otto 35
Walker, Robert 95
Walker, Stuart 160
Wallace, George 139
Wallach, Eli 187
Walters, Luana 164
Walton, Douglas 124
War of the Colossal Beast 127
War of the Satellites 38–39, 137
The War of the Worlds (1953) 6, 27–28, 60, 100
Ward, Amelita 101
Warde, Anthony 192
Warner, H.B. 130
Warner Brothers Pictures 62, 68, 70, 78, 110
Warren, Charles Marquis 84, 124
Warren, James 49
Warren, Jerry 46
Warwick, Robert 20
The Wasp Woman 5, 39
Wayne, Naunton 63
Webster, Philip 73
Weird Woman 5, 13, 93, 109, 112, 166
Welles, Mel 103, 138, **195–196**
Welles, Merri 104
Wells, H.G. 16, 159
Wells, Jacqueline (aka Julie Bishop) 56, 134, 155, 178
Werbisek, Gisela 36
Wessel, Dick 109

Westcott, Helen 58, 182
Wexler, Paul 49, 62
Whale, James 18, 20, 51, 82, 122, 124, 133, 159–160, 177, 183, 184, 185, 194
Whelan, Tim 73
The Whip Hand 35–36
White, Marjorie 23
White Zombie 3, 129–130
Whitman, Ernest 67
Whitman, Gayne 140
Whitmore, James 111
Wilcox, Fred M. 150
Wilde, Oscar 167
Wilder, W. Lee 90
Wiley, Jan 102
Wilkins, Martin 54
William, Warren 110, 190
Williams, Grant 181
Williams, Rhys 125
Willis, Marlene 153
Willis, Matt 132
Wills, Brember 184
Wilson, Charles 110
Windsor, Marie 88
Wings 16
Winters, Roland 141
Wisbar, Frank 128
Wise, Robert 162, 165
Witney, William 139
Wizard of Oz 173
The Wolf Man 11, 109, 121, 151
Wolfe, Ian 108, **196–198**
The Woman in Green (aka *Sherlock Holmes and the Woman in Green*) 47, 65
Wong, Anna May 76
Wood, Edward D., Jr. 4, 117, 118, 178, 179
Woodbury, Joan 157
Woody Woodpecker 14
The World Gone Mad 144
Worlock, Frederick 61
Wray, Fay 18, 20, 21, 116, 117, 180
Wuthering Heights (1939) 119, 131
Wyndham, John 168

Yarbrough, Barton 99
Yarbrough, Jean 100, 101–2, 156, 157, 177, 191
Yeaworth, Irvin S., Jr. 112
York, Duke 109
Young, Clara Kimball 81
Young, Harold 26, 79
Young, Nedrick 201
Young, Roland 51
The Young in Heart 41
Yung, Victor Sen 75, 141

Zanuck, Darryl F. 169
Zombies on Broadway 123–124, 197
Zucco, George 4, 13, 14, 19, 22, 25, 26, 46, 73–74, 78, 81, 86, 107, 120, 136, 145, 164, 173, 175, 176, **198–201**

www.ingramcontent.com/pod-product-compliance
Lightning Source LLC
Chambersburg PA
CBHW081553300426
44116CB00015B/2868